A Normative Approach to War

A NORMATIVE APPROACH TO WAR

Peace, War, and Justice in Hugo Grotius

EDITED BY

ONUMA YASUAKI

CLARENDON PRESS · OXFORD

1993

This book has been printed digitally and produced in a standard design in order to ensure its continuing availability

OXFORD
UNIVERSITY PRESS

Great Clarendon Street, Oxford OX2 6DP

Oxford University Press is a department of the University of Oxford. It furthers the University's objective of excellence in research, scholarship, and education by publishing worldwide in

Oxford New York

Athens Auckland Bangkok Bogotá Buenos Aires Cape Town Chennai Dar es Salaam Delhi Florence Hong Kong Istanbul Karachi Kolkata Kuala Lumpur Madrid Melbourne Mexico City Mumbai Nairobi Paris São Paulo Shanghai Singapore Taipei Tokyo Toronto Warsaw

with associated companies in Berlin Ibadan

Oxford is a registered trade mark of Oxford University Press in the UK and in certain other countries

Published in the United States by Oxford University Press Inc., New York

Reprinted 2001

ISBN 0-19-825709-0

Preface

This book is the product of a joint research project on *De Jure Belli ac Pacis libri tres* (hereafter referred to as *JBP*) carried out by the Research Group on the Fundamental Theory of International Law, headed by the editor. It was written by six contributors, all members of the Group. A keen awareness among a group of young international law scholars in Japan of the need to reconsider the methodology and fundamental problems of international law led to the formation of the Group in September 1976. Its purpose is to carry out basic research on the theory of international law, including its validity as law, the normativity and rationalizing function of international law, and the relations between international law and, in particular, international politics, justice, war, structural violence, and colonialism. Through these researches the Group seeks to clarify its own views, to understand current issues of international law within their philosophical, political, historical, and multi-cultural context, and ultimately to develop an approach which can overcome the defects of the so-called 'positivistic' approach without reducing the science of international law to an ideology whose actual role is to justify the values, power position, and interests of dominant states.

Though it may seem a roundabout way of achieving these objectives, we believe that it is essential to understand the classical writings that have influenced the development of modern international law against the historical background in which they were written. We started with Grotius's *JBP*, long regarded as (at least one of) the most important work(s) in the development of international law, and engaged in a process of collective reading and study of the work over more than a decade. In conjunction with it we studied *The Future of International Law* (edited by Richard Falk and Cyril Black), and also Pufendorf's *De Jure Gentium et Naturae libri octo*. Our further study plans involve Vitoria, Vattel, and other important writers. Our intermediate aim is to attempt to reconstruct, or reconstrue, the history of modern international law. The issues to be investigated include positivism and international law, imperialism and international law, socialism and international law, the various regional 'world orders' of the seventeenth, eighteenth, and nineteenth centuries, and the globalization of European international law.

In our study of *JBP*, we adopted the following procedure:

1. *De Jure Belli ac Pacis libri tres*, translated by Francis W. Kelsey et al. (Oxford, 1925), an English translation of the Amsterdam edition published in 1646, was used as our text. This is not necessarily the best translation. However, published as one of the volumes of 'The Classics of International Law' (ed. by James B. Scott, Publications of the Carnegie Endowment for International Peace), it has been most frequently used and referred to by modern international lawyers, and is widely accessible.
2. A check was made of the Latin text (Amsterdam, 1646 edition) to discover possible errors in the Kelsey translation, and to give as much uniformity to our interpretations as possible. The following translations were also used: *Le Droit de la guerre et da la paix*, nouvelle traduction, Jean Barbeyrac, I, II (Amsterdam, 1724); *Le Droit de la guerre et de la paix*, nouvelle traduction, M. P. Pradier-Fodéré, I–III (Paris, 1867); and *De Jure Belli et Pacis libri tres*, accompanied by an abridged translation by William Whewell, I–III (Cambridge, n.d. [1853]). Barbeyrac's translation is strongly coloured by his own bold interpretations. It is not always reliable as a translation of *JBP*. The contributors also referred individually to the Amsterdam editions of 1650, 1680, and 1720, the Latin text of the 1751–2 Lausanne edition, and Gronovius's annotations to these editions (except the 1650 edition). Reference was also made to the Japanese translation (translated by Ichimata Masao, *Senso to heiwa no ho*, I–III (Tokyo, 1950–1)) and to the German translation (*Drei Bücher von Recht des Krieges und des Friednes, Paris 1625, Neuer deutscher Text und Einleitung von Walter Schätzel* (Tübingen, 1950)). These translations were only referred to as subsidiary sources, because both (especially the Japanese translation) are sometimes unreliable.
3. A bibliography of basic readings was prepared in order to assure a minimum level of common understanding of the text by all the members of the Research Group. The bibliography contained not only scholarly works on international law, but

also those on the history of legal and political theory (principally Hobbes, Locke, and Rousseau) with which we contrasted Grotius's work.

4. The series of joint-study meetings of the Research Group were concluded in October 1978. From October 1981 to August 1982, the contributors to this book held periodic study meetings to prepare their papers. These were published in the *Horitsu Jiho*, 54/11–56/12, under the title 'Senso to heiwa no ho no kenkyu (Studies on *De Jure Belli ac Pacis*)' (1)–(24), from November 1982 to December 1984. After the revision and elaboration of these papers, the Japanese edition of the book, entitled *Senso to heiwa no ho* (*The Law of War and Peace*), edited by Onuma was published (Toshindo Ltd., February 1987).

The English edition is based on this Japanese work. However, each contributor has made revisions to the original manuscript to reflect subsequent research and to make the Japanese draft easier to translate. The first chapter of the Japanese edition 'Historical Background' has been omitted. The revised drafts were then translated into English by Sakamoto Mikio, a lecturer at Meisei University. The draft translations were checked and revised by each of the contributors and by Professor Tajima Horoshi, Professor of Anglo-American Law at Osaka City University. They were further revised by the editor in conjunction with Professor James Crawford, Whewell Professor of International Law at the University of Cambridge, formerly Challis Professor of International Law at the University of Sydney. The editing has been substantial, reducing the size of original papers by approximately one-third.

Acknowledgements

We are greatly indebted to many people for the publication of this book, especially to Takano Yuichi, Professor Emeritus at the University of Tokyo, Tabata Shigejiro, Professor Emeritus at Kyoto University, Ito Fujio, formerly Professor Emeritus at Kyushu University, now deceased, Fukuda Kan-ichi, Professor Emeritus at the University of Tokyo, and Professor Richard A. Falk of Princeton University.

All the contributors to this book studied, directly or indirectly, under Professor Takano, one of the most respected international lawyers in Japan. The liberality of his teaching prepared the academic ground on which the Research Group of the Fundamental Theory of International Law was established. Professor Tabata initiated the study of history of ideas in international law in Japan. How to follow, and if possible to add to, the Tabata school of the history of ideas in international law has remained an important question for the contributors. The late Professor Ito built a firm foundation of study of Vitoria, Suárez, Grotius, and other thinkers from which we could advance. Professor Fukuda is also a major figure in the study of the history of ideas in Japan. We are grateful to Professor Fukuda for pointing out the significance of Hobbes, Locke, and Rousseau in the history of European thought, as contrasted with the continental natural-law school. Professor Falk has given students of international law, who are today apt to be tormented by a sense of powerlessness, both courage and valuable suggestions, emanating from his unrelenting vitality and outstanding scholarship. He has also given us encouragement and advice in our plan to publish our joint work in English.

We are particularly grateful to Mr Sakamoto Mikio for his English translation of the Japanese version of this book, and to Professor Tajima Hiroshi for his valuable and time-consuming work, commenting on and revising Mr Sakamoto's translation. Although the final manuscript underwent a very substantial editing by this editor and Professor Crawford, Mr Sakamoto's translation provided a firm basis for our editorial work. We are also grateful to Professor Yanagihara Masaharu of Kyushu University for checking the accuracy of Latin expressions used throughout this book and to Associate Professor Nakagawa Junji of Tokyo Institute of Technology for his preparation of the bibliography and the final checking of the notes and bibliography. We are further grateful to Ms Yoshino Hiromi, Mr Mori Tadashi, Mr Hayashida Kazuhiko, Mr Arthur Wang, and Mr Jeff Sacknowitz for their technical assistance.

We also wish to thank Professor Peter Haggenmacher of the Graduate Institute of International Studies, Dr C. G. Roelofsen of the University of Utrecht, Professor Neil MacCormick of the University of Edinburgh, Dr Peter Sack of Australian National University, Professor Michael Reisman of Yale University, Professor Ian Brownlie of Oxford University, Professor Kinoshita Tsuyoshi of Rikkyo University, and Professor Kato Setsu of Seikei University, for their valuable comments. Professor Marius Jansen of Princeton University greatly encouraged us when we had difficulties with the English publication. This book would not have been possible without the encouragement and severe but warm criticisms of all these scholars, as well as from our fellow researchers in international law, political thought, philosophy of law, history, and history of ideas.

Finally our greatest debt is owed to Professor James Crawford for his indispensable assistance in completing the English version. Translating from Japanese into English is a particularly difficult task because the two languages are based on entirely different logical structures. Professor Crawford offered valuable suggestions and advice not only as to English expressions but also as to content. However, the contributors assume ultimate responsibility for the contents.

The publication of this book was made possible by grants from the Japan Foundation, the Takahashi Sangyo Keizai Kenkyu Foundation, the Suenobe Foundation, Yoshida Shigeru Memorial Foundation, and SDC Inc. The University of Sydney Law School and the Research School of Social Sciences of the Australian National University provided hospitality and facilities for the editor during the lengthy process of revising the manuscripts. The secretaries of the editor at the University of Tokyo, especially Ms Otaki Naoko, worked heroically in the preparation of the manuscript.

On behalf of the contributors, I would like to express my

deepest gratitude to all these people and institutions. This book is dedicated to Professor Takano Yuichi and Professor Tabata Shigejiro.

One of the contributors, Professor Tanaka Tadashi, passed away on 18 September 1992. We regret that he was unable to see the publication of this book. He played an important role in the joint research which formed the basis of this work.

ONUMA Yasuaki
December 1992

Contents

Editorial Policy

1. This is the English version of a joint research project on Hugo Grotius's *De Jure Belli ac Pacis libri tres* (*JBP*). The Japanese version was published by Toshindo Ltd. in 1987 under the title *Senso to heiwa no ho: Hugo Grotius ni okeru senso, heiwa, seigi.* Although the two versions have the same method, analyses, and conclusions, they are different in several respects. First, due to the time-lag in the publication of the two versions, the contributors have included in the English version references to recent studies of their own and by other scholars. This has also had some effect on the argumentation and analysis.

Secondly, the editorial work on individual chapters has been far more substantial in the English version than in the Japanese original. Although the editor has made every effort to respect each contributor's original intention, there remain inescapable differences, or at least nuances, in terms of content, style, and emphasis between the original Japanese and the final English chapters.

2. As to *JBP* itself, the Latin text and translation by F. W. Kelsey *et al.* (Oxford, 1925) was used as the basic text. In some cases, however, we adopted our own English translation because we found the Kelsey translation inaccurate, or at least misleading. Book (*liber*), chapter, and section numbers were provided in the first edition (1625), and followed by later editions; they will be cited here as, for example, I. i. 1. Subsection numbers, including the divisions used in the Prolegomena, were first included in the 1667 Amsterdam edition: they are cited as, for example, I. i. 1(1); Prol. 28. References to a particular page appear as follows: II. i. 5(1) (Lat. 103); II. i. 5(1) (Eng. 174).

3. The 'Classics of International Law' series, which we use as a primary text of both the original-language and English translation of the major classical works (including *JBP*), has unique citation characteristics: (1) it has a series number, starting with Zouche (*JBP* is no. 3); and (2) it publishes works in their original language in one or two volumes, followed by the English translation in the succeeding volume(s). To avoid confusion, for all citations from

the 'Classics of International Law' series, we omit both the serial release number and the original and translation volume numbers.

4. For a number of Latin terms in *JBP* we adopted our own terminology (or used the Latin original) rather than the Kelsey translation. The reasons for deviating from the Kelsey translation vary, and are referred to in the relevant chapters. But one common reason was to avoid projecting modern concepts uncritically on to the past, and thus 'understanding' particular ideas or institutions out of their historical context. We hope that readers will thus be reminded of the different meanings or nuances between terms in *JBP* and their translations (e.g. *civitas*/state, *jus gentium*/law of nations). Major terms for which the Kelsey translation is not followed are shown in the table. For similar reasons we have found it necessary to adopt, in some cases, analytical concepts or translations of Grotius's terms which sound rather odd in English: for example, 'supreme governing power' (rather than 'sovereign(ty)'), 'author of war' (rather than 'belligerent' or 'aggressor'), 'Grotius's utility-oriented approach' (rather than 'utilitarian' or 'pragmatic').

TABLE. Translations of terms used in *De Jure Belli ac Pacis*

Latin original	Kelsey translation	This book
bellum justum	lawful/just war	just war
bellum publicum	public war	public war
bellum solenne	public/formal war	formal war
fides	vow/(good) faith	(good) faith
imperium	sovereign power	governing power/governing power and authority, right to rule
magistratus	subordinate official	subordinate ruler
occupatio	occupation/possession	occupation
possessio	possession	possession
proprietas	proprietary (right)	ownership
restitutio	recovery	restitution/recovery
summa potestas	sovereign power	supreme power
summum imperium	sovereignty/sovereign power	supreme governing power
utilitas	expediency	utility

Again the risk of confusion with rather different modern meanings outweighed the demands of euphony.

5. The references cited in the notes generally indicate the name of the author, date of publication, and page number(s); further details, such as the title of the book or article and the place of publication, are indicated in the Bibliography. If the particular author has more than one publication in the same year, they are cited as 1975*a*, 1975*b*, etc.

6. As far as possible, reference is made to the original-language texts of any work. When it is necessary to use a translation, the footnotes give the name of the author, the date of publication of the translation, and the page(s), with fuller details listed in the Bibliography.

7. Reprinted editions are cited as, for example, Gentilis 1933 ⟨1612⟩. This citation indicates that the contributor used the 1933 reprint of the 1612 edition. Divisions, such as I. i. 1 (Eng./Lat. 1), indicated after the year of publication ⟨1612⟩, follow the same divisions as in *JBP*.

8. Japanese names are given in their proper order, i.e. the family name precedes the given name.

List of Figures

Contributors and Collaborators

Editor

Onuma Yasuaki, Professor of International Law, University of Tokyo

Consulting Editor

James Crawford, Whewell Professor of International Law, University of Cambridge; formerly Challis Professor of International Law, University of Sydney

Contributors

Furukawa Terumi, Professor of International Law, Hosei University

Kasai (Okuwaki) Naoya, Professor of International Law, Rikkyo University

Kimura Makoto, Professor of Law, Saitama University

Onuma Yasuaki, Professor of International Law, University of Tokyo

Tanaka Tadashi, Professor of International Law, Daito Bunka University

Yanagihara Masaharu, Professor of International Law, Kyushu University

Collaborators

Kato Setsu, Professor of Political Thought, Seikei University

Tajima Yutaka, Professor of Anglo-American Law, Osaka City University

Translator

Sakamoto Mikio, bilingual professional translator, Visiting Lecturer, Meisei University

Introduction

Over four centuries have passed since Hugo Grotius (Huig de Groot) was born. Almost throughout this period his main work, *De Jure Belli ac Pacis libri tres* (hereafter referred to as *JBP*) has been considered the greatest classic in the history of international law, and Grotius has been called the 'father of international law' (as well as the 'father of modern natural law'). On the other hand, criticisms have been directed since the nineteenth century at Grotius's asserted paternity of both disciplines. A number of significant studies of Grotius were published in and around 1983, the quadricentennial of his birth, many of which were reluctant to concede these glorious titles.[1]

The fundamental problem is not whether Grotius is the 'father' of international law. Such expressions are misleading and inappropriate.[2] The significance of inquiring into the work of a certain figure lies not only in understanding the fruitfulness, depth, and universality of his (or her) thought, but also in clarifying its limitations in terms of the period, region, and culture in which it was framed, and assessing its enduring value as well as its influence in its own time. To accomplish these objectives, it is necessary to inquire not only into the thinker, but also into the historical context and the spirit of his time. This book looks at *JBP* as a whole from such a perspective. Specifically, we are interested in: (1) the reconsideration of the history of international legal studies from a methodological point of view, in particular having regard to the pervasive problem of Eurocentric ways of thinking about international law; (2) the reappraisal of the importance of Grotius's practical approach in *JBP*; and (3) his quest for peace and its relation to his study.

[1] The best of these studies is Haggenmacher 1983, although it tends to exaggerate the continuity between *De Jure Praedae Commentarius* and *JBP*; see Tuck 1986: 87–92, for an assessment of Haggenmacher's excellent work.

[2] e.g. James Brown Scott's attempt at deifying Vitoria can hardly be considered a scholarly achievement: for a criticism of Scott's arguments, see Nussbaum 1954: 296–306.

(1) *Reconsidering the History (and the History of Ideas) of International Law*

To reconsider traditional views of the history (and the historiography) of international law is a central aim of this book. Scholars of the history of international law have traditionally focused on writers such as Vitoria, Suárez, Gentilis, Zouche, Grotius, Pufendorf, Wolff, Vattel, Bynkershoek, and Martens. But it is far from clear what position international law occupied in the theoretical framework of each of these writers. For example, Grotius is an important thinker not only in the field of international law, but also of natural law, private law, the Enlightenment, political philosophy, and humanism. International law scholars have not taken these aspects sufficiently into account. Although Vitoria and Suárez were often cited as precursors or even as rival candidates for the 'paternity' of international law, and Pufendorf and Vattel as disciples or again as candidates for paternity, much less consideration has been given to Hobbes or Locke. Other prominent figures in Western thought, such as Rousseau, Montesquieu, Bentham, Austin, Kant, and Hegel, who occupy an important position in any discussion of the theory of law and state, are often virtually ignored in studies of international law. Non-Western thought has also been almost totally ignored.

It is true that some of these thinkers may have devoted only a passing chapter or section to international law. But if this explains the tendency of studies of international law to pass over them, it does not justify such neglect. The real problem lies in the question: how should international lawyers respond to this *negative awareness* of international law, according to which international law has been discussed only in a limited or subsidiary manner by most of the major theorists of law and state.

It is no doubt important to understand Grotius in the perspective of the traditional history of international law, alongside such writers as Vitoria, Suárez, Gentilis, Pufendorf, Wolff, and Vattel. But it is equally important to explore him in relation to social-contract theorists such as Hobbes, Locke, and Rousseau. By comparing him with these writers, one can see how he posits a political society (*civitas*) made up of the traditional elements (i.e. the *paterfamilias*, the head of the household, as a political and social being (*zoon politikon*)). Since Grotius's concepts of 'international society' (which, in its modern meaning, did not exist in his theory) and of *jus gentium* are characterized by these notions of *paterfamilias* and of *civitas*, it is necessary to discuss them with reference to the social-contract theorists.[3]

A second methodological question involves the problem of how later generations can, and should, understand and evaluate major figures and works in their proper perspective. Some scholars have claimed that they found in Grotius (and other great thinkers of the past) the same or similar terms as refer to their own ideas or contemporary institutions, and have insisted that it is possible to detect in those thinkers the 'origin' of these terms, ideas, or institutions. For such claims to be established, it is necessary to determine what those terms and expressions meant for the thinkers concerned and for the societies in which they lived, and to examine carefully the difference between the way they were used by those thinkers and the way they are used today. This is not always done.

Other scholars in their criticisms of earlier thinkers have assumed their own standpoint as self-evident. For example, a legal positivist, who draws a sharp line between law and morality, may criticize Grotius's concept of law as naïve or unsophisticated on the ground that it confuses law and morality. A strict Thomist may argue that his concept of law amounts to a form of moral or religious apostasy, in which God's providence and man's reason are severed. Had Grotius written *JBP* from either standpoint he might have achieved greater internal coherence, but at the expense of most of what he sought to gain. In his age, it would have been impossible both to describe the realities and to influence the behaviour of states while maintaining *such* internal coherence. As will be shown in the following chapters, it was precisely through his adoption of a complex, sometimes contradictory combination of norms, and by a superadded appeal to love and utility, that Grotius sought to achieve his paramount aim of regulating and restraining war.

There is a huge difference of historical context between Grotius and later scholars. Take for example the problem of power. The situation in the era of Grotius was clearly different from that of today where power and authority are virtually monopolized by the state and the naked individual is pitted against it. *Paterfamilias* possessed the right to rule over the members of his household and

[3] Although some of the contributors' views of Hobbes and Rousseau may be too schematic and modernistic, the need for, and *raison d'être* of, this reference is clear.

the power to give effect to that right. Although a private person's right to resort to war to vindicate his rights had been severely restricted by the time of Grotius, the state did not yet—either in theory or in practice—monopolize public power. Between 'states' and 'private persons' were a variety of intermediate corporate bodies (*corps intermédiaires*) possessing various forms and degrees of governing power and authority. No sharp distinction was made between public and private law, between criminal and civil law, or even between law, morality, and ethics. Although Europe was in the midst of violent religious wars, they were still struggles between Catholics and Protestants within the framework of Christianity. To repudiate Christianity itself, or to go beyond the framework of Christianity, was a purely theoretical exercise. And it is clear that Grotius did *not* live in such a purely theoretical world. Nor was *JBP* written as a purely theoretical exercise.

In describing the ideas prevailing at the time, we should exercise the utmost caution in using such terms as 'state', 'sovereignty', 'individual', 'public law', 'private law', 'religion', 'morality', 'cause', 'politics', 'society', 'nation', 'people', 'international law', and the like. Uncritically to apply these terms to *JBP* would involve reading it on very different assumptions. A researcher in a later age must be careful not to project onto the past the dominant concepts and images of the age he or she happens to live in.[4]

The third methodological problem involves Eurocentrism. The once dominant view of Grotius as undisputedly the 'father of international law' is now rejected among experts. And yet Grotius is still generally so accepted. This coincides with the dominant view in the study of international politics that regards the Westphalia system as the starting-point of modern international relations. Underlying this persistently held view is the undeniable fact that the Eurocentric way of thinking about international law and relations remains dominant today.

In truth the Westphalia system, generally regarded today as the prototype of modern international relations, was nothing but a system of and for the emerging European (even Western European) nations. Grotius too assumed the normative relationships between Western European bodies politic as *universal* relationships between nations in general. This again is nothing but the egocentric illusion

[4] See e.g. Oudendijk's strictures (1980) of van Vollenhoven for his arbitrary interpretation of Grotius and Vattel.

of universalism prevalent in the West. When we refer to international law, we usually refer to the period from the seventeenth century to the present.[5] During most of this period, societies to which a great majority of human beings on earth belonged (and which were responsible for most of the world's production of goods and services)[6] were practically excluded from the scope of 'international law', either because they were under colonial rule or because they were not regarded as subjects of international law for lack of a common civilization. In fact, rival regional systems existed, composed of bodies politic with their own normative relations centred on politically, economically, and culturally superior powers—for example the 'world order' centred on China, with Confucian norms, accepted, at least to a certain extent, by East Asian nations as common regulatory norms.

Nevertheless, it is taken for granted that when one refers to international law the reference is to European international law and not to Chinese or Islamic international law. This is largely due to the fact that, from the fifteenth century, European nations came to dominate peoples belonging to other regional orders, and that their domination was not only political, military, and economic, but intellectual as well.

International law played an important role in this European domination of the world. Some rules were explicitly used to justify the colonization of the world by European nations: for example the justification of colonial rule based on the doctrine of effective occupation and on agreements with various bodies politic in Asia, the Americas, and Africa. In addition, international law was established as a closed system which excluded most non-Western nations as subjects of law. By remaining such a closed system, international law played, however passively and implicitly, the role of justifying the domination of the world by the West.[7] It is true that treaty practice between European nations and Afro-Asian nations had

[5] Among experts in the history of international law, this view is now being criticized and corrected from various angles: e.g. Grewe 1984*a*; Preiser 1984.

[6] Kennedy 1987: 149.

[7] After gaining its independence, the United States, originally a European colony, became an heir to European civilization and served as an important base for the latter's system of world domination. Japan, an Asian nation, was for a long time alienated from the Euro-American culture dominating the culture of the modern world, but in the latter half of the 19th century adopted the policy of 'Extricating from Asia and Entering Europe' and brought Taiwan and Korea under its colonial rule.

some bearing upon the formation of modern international law. In this process, Western nations adopted certain notions or ideas from the East. Yet, basic premisses, frameworks, ideas, and ways of thinking or argumentation in modern international law are all distinctly Western. To distinguish truly universal and valuable aspects of this European-oriented international law from its parochial aspects, and to revitalize it, are important tasks for contemporary international legal studies.

From this viewpoint, *JBP* as a subject of study is significant for two reasons: according to dominant Eurocentric thinking, *JBP* has been considered the foremost classic in the history of international law, and on any view it is one of the classics in the history of international law. Grotius claimed that his legal theory has universal validity, is applicable to all rational beings and corporate bodies, including states. He seemed to be successful in achieving this universality by dissociating, in principle, law from God, i.e. the Christian God. Nevertheless, the universality asserted in *JBP* was, in truth, nothing other than commonness within the framework of the Christian world. This is evidenced not only by the *hypothetical* nature of the 'secularization of natural law', but also by the basic assumption, maintained throughout *JBP*, that equates the concept of general law with the laws commonly applied throughout Christendom.[8] Grotius's universality was only plausible because European nations were shortly to achieve universal domination through a global colonial system under which—for a time at least—European civilization came to be equated with world civilization.

Recognizing this should lead us to re-examine the dominant view that early seventeenth-century Europe was the starting-point for the modern international system, the birth of international law (via Grotius) and of the state system (via the Westphalia system). For if the superiority of power was decisive in making European international law into global international law, the prototype of the combination of theory and power was already to be seen in the early sixteenth century in the work of Vitoria and the Spanish colonization of the Americas. Thus, reflection on Eurocentrism requires a study of the history of international law as a whole. In carrying out this task, however, one should not ignore the positive aspects of Grotius, or of other thinkers in the Western tradition. It

[8] See Onuma 1987: 438–43.

was not by naked power alone, but by its combination of power, technology, and thought that European civilization was able to penetrate and, at least to a certain degree, to be positively accepted by peoples of other regions.

(2) *Reappraising Grotius's Practical or Utility-Oriented Approach*

Grotius was part—even an important part—of this overall process: however critical one may be of his particular arguments, one cannot deny that he was a great speculative thinker. As a politician and diplomat, however, his credentials and achievements are less impressive: one might even argue that it was his failure as politician and diplomat that gave him time to devote to scholarship and speculation. Later scholars have thus tended to pay attention only to Grotius as a speculative, idealistic thinker.[9] Most have ignored, or at least undervalued, Grotius as a pragmatist who made full use of arguments based on practicality and utility to persuade his readers. Grotius himself seems to reject the argument from utility (Prol. 57), but his words should not be taken at face value. As will be shown in the following chapters, Grotius consistently appeals to utility when he encounters difficult issues of critical importance. *JBP* cannot be read as a coherent work if one ignores the central role played by arguments from utility and practicality.

Although his declared aim was to establish a general theory of law (*jurisprudentia*) applicable to nations in general (Prol. 1, 3, 30), he knew well that a mere theory of law was not sufficient to restrain the behaviour of states. He therefore incorporated into his normative theory moral, ethical, and religious norms, in an appeal to the sentiments of love and sympathy of contemporary Europeans. But even these might not prevail against motives of profit or expediency, the greed for power or the sense of honour which urged rulers and people to war. Thus Grotius ultimately appealed to utility, which he had ostensibly repudiated (Prol. 57), in order to achieve his paramount aim of minimizing bloodshed.

(3) *Grotius's Quest for Peace*

To regulate and restrain the use of violence is a difficult task in any age and in any culture. What law can do in this regard is limited. There is even less room for law in restricting the use of

[9] Roelofsen rightly criticized this approach (1983*a*: 20; 1990: 97–8, 122–3, 130–1).

force between states with enormous organized means of violence at their disposal. Today's international law appears virtually powerless to suppress war. Partly as a result, international lawyers today tend to avoid direct confrontation with the fundamental problems of war and peace, and to engage in technical issues more easily dealt with according to the 'positive' rules of international law.

But this does not mean that international law cannot play any normative role in the domain of war and peace. The very 'powerlessness' noted above is partly due to the prevalent formalistic concept according to which international law is confined to an unreasonably narrow sphere. Even if 'positive' rules stipulated in treaties are considered formally binding, they will be dead rules if they deviate from the general normative consciousness prevailing not only among those in authority but also among ordinary people. Conversely, if the notion of international law is liberated from the formalistic restraints of 'positive' law, and is redefined in terms of its societal functions and a substantive binding force based on the normative consciousness of ordinary people, it has potential for a more dynamic normative power, including regulating the use of force, or even minimizing violence in general, including structural violence. Although we must avoid overestimating the normative function of international law and thus spreading illusions of its effectiveness, we must not belittle the significance of international law by ignoring certain roles it is capable of playing.

If we turn our attention to Grotius, we can gain valuable insights into how the science of international law confronts the demands of each era. Grotius lived during the Thirty Years War, when pillaging and massacres were rampant. It was a period when the medieval European world (in its own terms, the 'universal' world) was being dismantled. The stable normative consciousness of law, morality, and religion, as well as the authority of the church and the pope that effectively sanctioned them, were being shaken to their foundations. Under these circumstances, Grotius dared to confront the difficult task of regulating the behaviour of the states and other bodies politic, behaviour otherwise based only on the 'principle' of naked interest and greed. In order to overcome the tragedies caused by endless religious wars, he sought by all available means to bring within the domain of justice the relations of those independent powers, including states, which were capable of employing force.

In doing so Grotius in principle liberated legal norms from religion, a valuable step in view of the fact that the latter was often used as an excuse for resorting to war. On the other hand, he incorporated religion and morality into his normative system because they were still important societal norms which had a great influence upon the behaviour of contemporary European peoples. Grotius has been called 'the father of modern natural law' because of this 'secularization of natural law'.[10] He carried out this revolutionary task in intellectual history in an attempt to achieve his practical aim of regulating and restraining war. Here emerges the figure of a true jurist, who not only makes full use of legal technicalities but is deeply committed to tackling the critical issues of his time.

This assessment does not require us to sanctify Grotius as the 'sage of Delft'. Living during the turbulent period of the Thirty Years War, and determined to minimize actual bloodshed, he ignored the problems of 'war which is contained in peace', i.e. structural violence, in order to secure a state of no war, or 'negative peace'.[11] Not only this practical aim but also his theoretical premiss contributed to this recognition of the *status quo*. Unlike Hobbes, Locke, and Rousseau, Grotius constructed his theory of law without seeking to dismantle the household and the various intermediate corporate bodies. He adhered to the traditional view of man (as *zoon politikon*) that had prevailed in Europe since Aristotle, assuming the existence of multi-layered independent powers. His concept of natural law tended to justify existing political institutions rather than criticize them from the viewpoint of justice. Later developments reveal, however, that war and peace are not so much opposing phenomena as on the same continuum. States that repress human rights, persecute ethnic minorities, or rely on military and police power at home, have tended to provoke international conflicts, intentionally or otherwise, as well.[12]

In the following chapters, we seek to clarify not only the signifi-

[10] While there have been many criticisms of this view, to treat *JBP* as 'liberating law from religion' is, in principle, not inaccurate. See 3.1.4.

[11] One might say that in locating the notion of *justice* at the centre of his system, Grotius sought to overcome structural violence. But when he was forced to make the ultimate decision between 'justice' and '(negative) peace', he did not hesitate to choose the latter. Yet, it might be said that for Grotius the very act of choosing peace *constituted* justice.

[12] In stressing the idea of structural violence, one must not overlook the tragedy, brutality, and human cost of war. It is true that Grotius frequently lapsed into a normative justification of the existing order. But in the actual circumstances of the time, even if it means only the absence of war, the value of negative peace was—and still is—undeniably important.

cance but also the limitations of Grotius's theory, with all its contradictions: the abundance of his ideas and their tendency to justify the *status quo*, his methodological innovation and substantive reliance on tradition, his sincere desire for peace and his acquiescence in the existing structural violence. Whatever these inconsistencies in argumentation, however, Grotius's will to tackle the problem of war and peace still moves us centuries later. This is the decisive significance of Grotius for the twentieth century—and for future generations. This is why *JBP* can be regarded as the greatest classic in the history of international law. For the problem of war and peace, whether in Europe or elsewhere, and however differently it may be presented from one period to another, is a pervasive problem in the history of mankind, and continues to present its greatest challenge.

1

Grotius's Method: With Special Reference to Prolegomena

1.1. Introduction

Grotius lived through the Netherlands' War of Independence. He experienced imprisonment as a result of political struggle—and made a bold escape. He lived in exile during most of the Thirty Years War and died before the Peace of Westphalia.[1] In short, he constantly witnessed disturbances and wars. This was the main reason he wrote his masterpiece, *JBP*. He belonged to the Arminian school of Calvinism, and sought to overcome denominational differences and to unite the church from the standpoint of an advocate of religious tolerance.[2] Again this is evident throughout *JBP*. His appointment as ambassador from Sweden to France enabled him to deepen his awareness of what causes disputes between bodies politic. But he also occupied a status close to that of the burghers, who were accumulating great wealth through commercial activities at a time when the Netherlands was emerging as a major power. However, we risk distorting our understanding of Grotius's method or approach in *JBP* if we overestimate these external elements. This chapter seeks to outline an approach to Grotius by examining the characteristic features of his methodology in *JBP*.

The first thing that comes to mind when one talks about 'Grotius's method', is the mathematical method that had such an impact on his age. It is clear that Grotius was interested in this method, especially from *De Jure Praedae Commentarius*.[3] But

[1] For standard biographies of Grotius, see Vreeland 1917; Someren 1965.

[2] Edwards 1981: 2–4.

[3] Dufour 1980: 41–4. Dufour rejects the claim that Grotius's method was influenced by Descartes, and characterizes it as geometrical. While Dufour leaves the direct source of Grotius's method in doubt, Vermeulen seeks it in Simon Stevin (Vermeulen 1983: 63–6). Considering Grotius's familiarity with and leanings

despite the breadth of his knowledge, he made virtually no statements on mathematics or natural science in *JBP*.[4] Descartes's mathematical method exerted what can only be called a devastating influence, but Descartes had not yet been published when Grotius wrote *JBP*.[5] Wieacker looks instead to Pufendorf to carry the so-called mathematical method to its logical conclusion.[6] Pufendorf's works, including the *De Jure Naturae et Gentium*, take the rigorous form of asserting propositions as axioms and deducing detailed conclusions from them. Such a 'deductive' method is maintained neither in *De Jure Praedae Commentarius* nor in *JBP*.

Moreover, Grotius's interest in methodology recedes to the background in *JBP*. He wrote *JBP* in an attempt to regulate and restrain war by rules based on reason,[7] as from the following passage:

> Fully convinced . . . that there is a common law among nations, which is valid alike for war and in war, I have had many and weighty reasons for undertaking to write upon this subject. Throughout the Christian world I observed a lack of restraint in relation to war, such as even barbarous nations should be ashamed of; I observed that men rush to arms for slight causes, or no cause at all, and that when arms have once been taken up there is no longer any respect for law, divine or human; it is as if . . . frenzy had openly been let loose for the committing of all crimes.[8]

The rules Grotius is relying upon for the regulation of wars are more extensive, but centred on natural law. He formulates his basic task in the following terms:

> That body of law . . . which is concerned with the mutual relations among states or rulers of states (*inter populos plures aut populorum rectores*), whether derived from nature, or established by divine ordinances, or having its origin in custom and tacit agreement, few have touched upon . . . yet the welfare of mankind demands that this task be accomplished.[9]

towards the classics, it is unreasonable to seek the source of his method in a single contemporary scholar.

[4] According to Ter Meulen and Diermanse 1950: 145–9, apart from a small article on physics that Grotius wrote in his days at Leiden Univ., the only other research in mathematics or natural science was a Latin trans. of Simon Stevin's article on the method of measuring triangles.

[5] Takashima *et al.* 1962: 60–1.

[6] Wieacker 1967: 307–8.

[7] Grotius was in no way an absolute pacifist, nor was he a realist who uncritically abided by empirical facts. While sympathizing with the motive behind the absolute pacifism of Ferus and Erasmus, Grotius rejects its consequences (Prol. 29).

[8] Prol. 28.

[9] Prol. 1.

To regulate war by means of law, it is necessary first to clarify what constitutes law. Grotius must construct a jurisprudence (*jurisprudentia*).[10] But the study of law and the construction of a jurisprudence ultimately serve the goal of regulating war by means of law. The problem of method is not an end in itself.[11]

Grotius to some extent presents his method in the Prolegomena. For example, he explains his reason for leaving aside contemporary controversies by comparing law to mathematics.[12] In writing *JBP* he claims to have taken special care (1) to express clearly the reasons for his conclusions, (2) to present the items to be treated in the right order,[13] and (3) to distinguish clearly between things that at first glance look similar but are actually different.[14] His prolific references to a wide range of sources are characteristic of his method. But since he does not seek for methodology in itself, it is wrong to conclude, from selective quotations, that he adopted a mathematical method. What he did was to adopt a method congenial to the intellectual climate of his time.[15]

Our task here is to examine Grotius's methodological approach, with special reference to the Prolegomena. This raises the question of how the Prolegomena is to be read. When researchers refer to Grotius, they often treat the Prolegomena as a self-contained whole and ignore how the ideas introduced in it are developed in the text. Such a partial reading is misleading. The explanations of 'law' and other key concepts in the Prolegomena have to be analysed in the context of the entire volume. In particular, the proof of the existence of laws which regulate war is both the starting-point

[10] Prol. 30.

[11] Prol. 32. Grotius himself declares that 'what method (*via*) we think should be followed we have shown by deed rather than by words in this work' (Prol. 32).

[12] Prol. 58. For discussion on the distinction between those things which are obvious under natural law and those which are not, see II. xx. 43(1).

[13] As Haggenmacher and Vermeulen point out, in *De Jure Praedae Commentarius* Grotius regards the two concepts *methodus* and *ordo* as his methodological criteria. The former is a method of discovering rules a priori through consideration of autonomous reason. The latter is a method of demonstration involving deduction of corollaries and conclusions from basic rules (*regula*) and laws (*lex*) (Grotius 1950 ⟨1604⟩ (Eng. 6–7); Haggenmacher 1983: 57–60; Vermeulen 1983: 64). Thus the term *ordo* can be construed as the suggestion of method by Grotius. See Haggenmacher 1983: 453.

[14] Prol. 56. Haggenmacher regards these as Grotius's methodological maxim in *JBP*, and says that the 3rd maxim plays the decisive role in distinguishing the law of nature from the law of nations (1983: 452–6).

[15] Strömholm 1985: 154–5.

and the ultimate goal of *JBP*. Thus the Prolegomena should not be regarded as a self-contained discourse. While keeping these limitations in mind, we must ask how his approach can best be characterized—perhaps by analogy with Troeltsch's description of Grotius's humanitarian theology as a direct generalization of the Renaissance and the Reformation.[16]

1.2. Dialectic of Law

1.2.1. Human Nature, Justice, Utility: Critique of Carneades

Grotius asserts the existence of laws applicable between nations or rulers of nations by first resorting to the technique of refutation. He refutes such fallacious, and therefore unacceptable, arguments as that power is justice, that a state cannot avoid committing injustice, or that war is incompatible with law. He singles out the Sceptic Carneades,[17] for criticism.[18] The crux of Carneades's argument was: (1) that men impose laws upon themselves from the viewpoint of expediency or utility (*utilitas*); and (2) that there is no such thing as unchangeable natural law or justice because men, like all other animals, are impelled by nature to seek their own advantage. Grotius refutes these assertions on four counts: by arguing from human nature, utility, the existence of the law of nations, and the concept of justice.

[16] Troeltsch 1959: 18.

[17] Carneades is introduced briefly in B. Russell 1969: 236–8; Iwasaki 1982: 66, 308, 374. A philosopher of the 2nd cent. BC, he was a founder of the New Academy. Succeeding to the Epicurean school, he criticized the Stoics from the standpoint of the so-called Sceptics. Carneades is discussed in Cicero's *De Republica*, 3. 5–20 (see Sabine 1963: 133, n. 9). However, according to the editor of Cicero's *De Republica*, a considerable part of chs. 5–20 is lost. Therefore it is difficult to get a clear picture of Carneades. Cicero 1928: 190–209). According to Keyes, even 'Carneades' piece of board'—often cited as an example of the state of necessity (*Notstand*)—is inferred from Lactantius. See also Rommen 1956: 17.

[18] Tuck maintains that Grotius's criticism of Carneades was directed at scepticism—especially that of Charron—which had a strong influence in the 16th and early 17th cents. Instead of rejecting scepticism outright, Grotius, like Hobbes, incorporated key assertions such as self-preservation into his theory. That made it possible for Grotius's theory to become the starting-point for political science which followed scepticism (Tuck 1983: 43–62).

(1) *Human Nature and Law*

Grotius rejects the view that man, like all other animals, merely seeks his own advantage, a view which involves the denial of natural law and justice. Although man is an animal, man belongs to the highest species. The fundamental human characteristic is *appetitus societatis*; the desire for a peaceful and organized social life which corresponds to his intelligence. To satisfy this desire, man is endowed with the capacity to know and act in accordance with general principles (*praecepta*). The maintenance of social order which is consonant with human intelligence is the source of law, in particular of natural law.[19]

The significance of this 'law' leads to a 'law' with an even wider meaning. Man possesses not only a strong bent towards sociability or social life,[20] but the power of estimating advantages and disadvantages of his acts. It is the nature of man to follow the directives of a sound judgement within the limitations of his intelligence. To be clearly at variance with such judgement is to be contrary to natural law, i.e. against human nature.[21] In other words, law is that which is presented by the sound judgement of man's intelligence backed by his sociability.

It is in this context that Grotius makes his famous statement: 'What we have been saying would have a degree of validity even if we should concede that which cannot be conceded without the utmost wickedness, that there is no God, or that the affairs of men are of no concern to Him (. . . *etiamsi daremus . . . non esse Deum, aut non curari ab eo negotia humana*) (Prol. 11). This is a hypothetical proposition.[22] Grotius himself declares that the assumption is contrary to reason and that man is, without exception, obligated to obey God. After confirming God's supremacy, he cites God's free will, in addition to nature, as a source of law, thereby accepting the

[19] Prol. 6–8.

[20] As another basis for sociability (*affectus socialis*), Grotius argues that all men are born of the same first parents (Adam and Eve) (Prol. 14).

[21] Prol. 9.

[22] Grotius specifies four conditions which all religions must satisfy to be considered true religion; two of which he regards as universal principles which are absolutely necessary for all religion. The first is the notion that God exists (whether he is the only god or not), the second that God has a care for human affairs (II. xx. 45–6). This shows the hypothetical character of the *etiamsi daremus* passages, since Grotius believes that it is self-evident that these two conditions do exist. Grotius sought to present religion as a relative concept, and thus to moderate religious wars.

existence of divine volitional law. Natural law also arises from the inherent nature (*principia*) of man, and since God desires man to possess such an inherent nature, natural law can be said 'ultimately' to originate in God.[23]

We examine the significance of this hypothetical proposition in I.4. But it is necessary to attend to its context, which emphasizes the existence of laws based on the inherent nature of man in opposition to the Sceptics' view. Therefore, the evaluation of this proposition leads to that of Grotius's entire understanding of human nature. Second, Grotius distinguishes between human nature and the will of God as a source of law. This assumed considerable significance in the classification of laws, in particular in the differentiation of natural law from divine volitional law. But whenever possible Grotius plays down the effect of his hypothetical proposition: to discuss that proposition out of context is to risk misunderstanding his true intention.[24]

(2) *Utility or Expediency*

Grotius rejects the Sceptics' argument that whatever is advantageous for kings and states cannot be unjust,[25] an argument that implies that utility or expediency is, as it were, the mother of law. Natural law springs from the inherent social nature of man.[26] Municipal law relies on the obligation that arises from mutual consent, and since the binding force of this obligation is based on natural law, natural law is, to extend the metaphor, the grandmother, and the inherent nature of man is the great-grandmother of municipal law.[27] Thus Grotius's refutation is based on the premiss that all law is ultimately attributed to the inherent social nature of man.

At the same time, he admits that, in the world of law, utility or expediency does have a certain role. It reinforces natural law. In addition, the source of municipal law is the rule of natural law

[23] Prol. 11–13.

[24] S. Strömholm 1985: 154.

[25] Prol. 3. 'Imperial city' is the trans. of the *civitas* in this section. Kelsey *et al.* usually trans. *civitas* as 'state', but in some cases they trans. *re(s)publica* and *populus* as 'state'. The Kelsey trans. is inconsistent, but it is clear that *civitas* is not 'a city', although Hobbes a generation later often used the term 'city' in the sense of state. The section concerned is probably based on Cicero's expression 'utilitatis specie in republica saepissime peccantur' (Cicero 1913: III. xi. p. 314).

[26] Schiedermair points out that Grotius sought a secular basis for society in order to realize religious peace (1983: 406–7).

[27] Prol. 16.

which requires man to abide by pacts (*pacta*). Grotius says that those who had associated themselves with a ruler or rulers had either expressly promised, or the nature of the transaction implied they had promised, that they would conform to the decisions of the majority or of the ruler. This association and subjection are rooted in utility.[28] In particular, in presenting the concept of the law of nations, Grotius emphasizes the importance of a utility-oriented approach.

(3) *Existence of the Law of Nations*

Grotius criticizes Carneades for ignoring the law of nations in his discussion of war. According to Grotius, just as municipal laws take into consideration the advantage of their respective states (*civitates*), so by mutual consent it has become possible for certain laws to exist between all or a great many states, to the advantage of the world or the whole of mankind.[29] This law is called the law of nations. Its origin is sought in consent between states, and its *raison d'être* is the common interest of nations. The law of nations is distinguished from the law of nature in that, while the latter can be deduced from self-evident principles, the former cannot.[30] Grotius, in distinguishing these two laws, assumes the existence of the law of nations. He says:

> when many at different times, and in different places, affirm the same thing as certain, that ought to be referred to as a universal cause; in the lines of inquiry which we are following, it must be either a correct conclusion drawn from the principles of nature, or common consent. The former points to the law of nature; the latter to the law of nations.[31]

Thus he presupposes the existence of the law of nations and attempts to distinguish it from the law of nature. The criterion for this distinction is whether a rule can be deduced from a self-evident principle. But the judgement of self-evidence cannot avoid being

[28] Prol. 15–16.

[29] Prol. 17. The Latin original is '(utilitas) magnae illius universitatis'. But Grotius did not have any independent notion of 'international society', as is shown by the fact that he does not use such concepts as Wolff's *civitas maxima*, by his assertion that the binding force of natural law is felt in all places, and by the decision to commence his argument with private war. Grotius merely had a vague notion of mankind in general (e.g. 'the bond of human society' in II. viii. 26), or of a union of many states.

[30] Prol. 40.

[31] See also II. xviii. 4(2).

subjective. And Grotius's argument for the existence of the law of nations is not particularly convincing.

(4) *Justice*

Finally Grotius asserts that Carneades, who ridiculed justice as folly, contradicted himself, since he himself admitted that a national who obeys the laws of his own country is not foolish, even though he may lose some immediate advantage as a result. Thus for a nation to seek advantage for its own people to the point of disregarding the laws common to nations, i.e. the laws of nature and of nations, is to break down with its own hands the bulwarks which safeguard that nation's own future peace. Even if there were no such advantages, to act in conformity with the higher nature of man (that is to say, in conformity with justice) is a mark of wisdom, not of folly.[32]

1.2.2. Other Issues Concerning Law and War

In *JBP* Grotius characteristically proceeds by taking up an erroneous assertion, refuting it, and offering his own view in its place.[33]

(1) *Laws and Sanctions*

Some observers believe that laws were created from fear of injustice and of suffering evil, and that men can be compelled by force to promote justice.[34] Grotius disagrees. This thought is valid only for institutions and laws (*leges*) devised to facilitate the enforcement of justice or right. True, a law will not have any external effect if it is not backed up by the fear of some sanction. But this does not mean that such a law is invalid. While justice brings about peace of mind, is approved by all good men, and is protected by God; injustice is accompanied by pangs of conscience, is criticized by all good men, and is inimical to God.[35]

Grotius here seems to treat justice and law as synonymous. However, while the 'law of love' and 'internal justice' are virtually

[32] Prol. 18.

[33] Grotius rejected the view that *summum imperium* always resides in the people (I. iii. 8–24).

[34] Here, as indicated in the marginal note, Grotius has in mind *Graukon*'s remark and others in Plato's *Politica*, 2.2 (Plato 1976: 108).

[35] Prol. 19–20.

equivalent to the contents of natural law, they are different from natural law itself, since they lack any legal means of realization through just cause for waging war.[36] Grotius's assertion that a law which lacks sanctions is still valid is to be understood in a limited sense, as a refutation of the argument that denies the existence of natural law.

(2) *The Necessity of Law Common to All Nations*

Some observers believe that since states, unlike individuals, can exist in isolation, the standard of justice, as a virtue that aims to promote amicable relationship with others, cannot be applied to relations between nations or their rulers. According to Grotius, this view is flawed because it considers law only from the viewpoint of the advantages it generates. Even the most powerful peoples and kings seek alliances, but alliances would lose their significance if laws existed only within state boundaries. If we grant that human society (*communitas*) cannot be maintained without law, the society which binds the human race (*genus humanum*), or many nations (*populi*), together has need of law.[37]

(3) *War and Law*

Grotius also criticizes the idea that in war all laws are in abeyance. On the contrary, war should not be undertaken except for the enforcement of *jus*, and even when it has commenced, it should be waged only within the bounds of law and faith. War should be waged as scrupulously as judicial proceedings. Thus, while conceding that municipal laws, which are adapted to times of peace, may remain silent in the midst of arms, Grotius insists that laws with perpetual validity and accommodated to all times, such as natural law and the law of nations, cannot do so.[38]

According to Grotius, history reveals how great in war the influence of the belief that one has justice on one's side can be,[39] and expresses the naïve expectation that 'justice will win'. It is obvious that this cannot be demonstrated by argument. Nevertheless Grotius relied on this faith to reinforce the proposition that war can and should be regulated by law.

[36] See 2.2. [37] Prol. 21–3. [38] Prol. 25–6. [39] Prol. 27.

1.3. The Construction of a Jurisprudence: Grotius's Attempt to Systematize Law

In order to construct a system of jurisprudence,[40] it is necessary to distinguish between those elements of law which are instituted from those which are natural. The latter are unchangeable and easily systematized; the former have a strong positive character, and are difficult to treat systematically because they vary in place and time. Grotius explains that a system of jurisprudence is constructed by examining and synthesizing this unchangeable law which stems from nature,[41] and by showing the relations of this law to positive laws.

Criticism of Past Research

Grotius asserts that past research on the subjects taken up in *JBP* was woefully inadequate. He hardly finds any argument worth referring to in the writings of the Greek philosophers (even Aristotle), of the early Christians, or of the ancient Romans on *jus feciale*.[42] The laws of war were treated by Vitoria and other theologians, and by Legnano and other jurists, but they are virtually worthless because they do not treat their subjects systematically and because they confuse natural law, divine law, the law of nations, and canon law. The works of Ayala and Gentilis, which seek to compensate for the deficiencies of the earlier works, are useful to a degree, but they too have many shortcomings, such as insufficient and inappropriate reasoning and bias towards one of the belligerent parties in contemporary conflicts.[43]

Grotius was undoubtedly influenced by these earlier theories. However, his criticisms cannot be ignored when considering his relationship to earlier writers.[44] In particular, while he dissociates

[40] In the Kelsey trans. *jurisprudentia* is rendered 'the philosophy of the law'. Properly speaking, *jurisprudentia* in the Roman classical age was a casuistic, practical learning (Shibata 1976: 32–41; Tsuneto 1977: 131–4). But *jurisprudentia* in Grotius's age seems to have been looked upon as a part of learning not limited to the practical study of law but related to various cultural pursuits (see Prol. 30). Thus jurisprudence was considered one of the liberal arts (Huizinga 1968: 111).

[41] Prol. 30–1.

[42] On *jus feciale* or *fetiale*, see Nussbaum 1947: 16–17 and Cicero 1928: 395–6, 412–13.

[43] Prol. 36–8.

[44] Most of those who consider Grotius simply as a successor to the late Scholastics overlook his criticism. For a discussion which recognizes both the 'novelty' of Grotius and the influence of the Scholastics, see Grewe 1984*a*: 228–30.

himself from religious sects,[45] claiming to follow the liberty of the early Christians from the authority of any school or sect, he adds comments on philosophy, history, poetry,[46] oratory, the Bible, canon law, the words and deeds of the early Christians, the Scholastics, and Roman law. Of these, some at least have an important bearing on Grotius's position.

(1) Criticism and Evaluation of Aristotle Opinions are divided on whether Grotius is to be considered an Aristotelian.[47] This issue provides an important frame of reference in examining Grotius's 'modernity'. He appears at first to regard Aristotle as holding the highest position among philosophers. But he then criticizes the medieval Scholastics for according Aristotle a tyrannical position, with harmful results for scholarship.[48] He also criticizes Aristotle's doctrine of 'virtue' (*arete*), stating that the most serious difficulty in Aristotle's thinking is the idea that the very nature of virtue is a 'mean' in passions and actions.[49] No doubt 'right reason', which virtue everywhere follows, at times dictates that a middle course be followed, but at other times the highest degree of affection should be aimed at, as in expressing one's love of God.[50] Most important, however, is his critical account in I. i of Aristotle's doctrine of justice as it relates to the concept of law, particularly the concepts of *jus* in the sense of right.[51] Grotius maintains that power or right in the true sense (*facultas*) is concerned with *justitia expletrix*, or justice properly so-called, while expectation (*aptitudo*) is concerned with attributive justice (*justitia attributrix*), and he criticizes Aristotle for identifying the former with contractual justice. A person in possession of something I own is under obligation to return it to me. Although this does not result from a 'contract', it is a typical example of *justitia expletrix*. Grotius claims that it is more appropriate to describe this as restorative or corrective justice, which Aristotle regards as synonymous with contractual justice. On the

[45] Prol. 42.

[46] Rousseau sneered at Grotius for relying on the words of poets (1969: 836). Grotius says that they are used merely as embellishment (Prol. 47).

[47] e.g. Wolf 1982: 33. Tuck concludes that, although Grotius considered himself an Aristotelian, he was far from being so (1979: 63; 1983: 50).

[48] Prol. 42.

[49] The description in the Kelsey trans. (Eng. 25) is misleading because it can be read as 'to assign to truth extremes between . . .'. In Aristotle 1934, 'truth', one of the virtues, is the mean between 'ostentation' and 'modesty'. For a concise summary of Aristotle's doctrine of 'virtue', see Yamamoto 1977: 135–58.

[50] Prol. 43–5.

[51] I. i. viii.

other hand, Grotius equates *justitia attributrix* with Aristotle's distributive justice.

Grotius's understanding of Aristotle was early criticized by Barbeyrac as inaccurate.[52] There are indeed doubts as to Grotius's interpretation of Aristotle's theory of justice. First, both Aristotle's distributive justice and his corrective justice are subcategories of partial justice,[53] and Grotius overlooks Aristotle's concept of universal justice, i.e. the whole of virtue, together with the equation of universal justice with what is lawful in the broadest sense.[54]

Secondly, Aristotle refers to contractual justice independently from corrective justice and distributive justice,[55] both of which are subcategories of partial justice. Judging from Aristotle's argument, contractual justice seems to be distinguished from corrective justice; it may be also possible to interpret contractual justice as a part of corrective justice. In any case, Grotius's understanding is incorrect because he simply equates corrective with contractual justice.[56]

Thirdly, Grotius claims that aptitude is concerned with attributive justice as equated with Aristotle's distributive justice since it relates to virtues that aim to do good to others, for example, showing tolerance or sympathy. Grotius apparently does not accept that justice of this kind belongs to the field of *jus* in the strict sense. But what Aristotle calls distributive justice is a concept that assumes a *polis*; to distribute things proportionately in accordance with status or responsibility within a *polis* is still a legal problem for Aristotle.[57]

Grotius's views, particularly on the concept of virtue, are not Aristotelian. Grotius tries to strike a compromise with tradition, praising Aristotle while distancing himself from the Aristotelianism of the Scholastics.[58] He is far from being a mere extension of the late Scholastics.

[52] Grotius = Barbeyrac 1724: I. 43–6 n. viii(1)–(11).

[53] Aristotle 1926: 267.

[54] Ibid. 257–61.

[55] Ibid. 279–83.

[56] Adam Smith also equated the two (1963 ⟨1811–12⟩, I. 478).

[57] Aristotle 1934: 291–7. Grotius does not seem to regard this as a question of law properly so-called (Prol. 10).

[58] Fukuda says that Grotius depends on Aristotle most for determining the modes of justice (1971: 27). But while Grotius often quotes Aristotle on individual questions, he distances himself from him when it comes to major issues such as justice.

(2) The Bible Grotius objects to the idea that natural law is set forth in the Old Testament, since most of those rules stem from God's free will. But those rules do not contradict natural law, and as long as care is taken to distinguish between the law of God and that of men, the Old Testament can be used as a source of natural law. By contrast, the New Testament[59] is primarily used as an authority to explain what is permissible for Christians, and is distinguished from natural law. In the lofty laws of the New Testament, a greater degree of moral perfection is enjoined than natural law would require. But since it is noble of human beings to strive towards the highest degree of moral perfection, man should not ignore even 'those things that are recommended rather than enjoined'.[60]

Overall, then, Grotius distinguishes the contents of the Bible from natural law, a tendency which again separates him from medieval theology and the Scholastic tradition. He does not assert this separation in such clear terms in the development of his argument. He rejects the notion that natural law originates in God's will, and gives divine law a place of its own. But he does not always distinguish the contents of natural law from those of divine law. While assuming this separation, he relies heavily on the Bible to support his normative argument for regulating war and moderating its harmful consequences.

(3) Other Sources Grotius quotes a multitude of cases from Rome and Greece, on the basis that the shared judgement of many historians tends to show the existence of natural law to a certain extent, as well as being the only way to prove the existence of the law of nations. By contrast, he does not show much appreciation of the Scholastics, although he avoids open criticism of them. As for the Scholars of Roman law,[61] he divides them into three groups: (1) the authors of works cited in the Pandects (*Digesta*), the Codes of Theodosius and Justinian, and the Imperial Constitutions (*Novellae*); (2) the glossators such as Accursius; and (3) the

[59] For a discussion of Grotius's interpretation of the New Testament, see Jonge 1983: 59–66.

[60] Prol. 48, 50. In this regard, authentic synodical canons and customs of the early Christians are also regarded as authority for divine law and biblical interpretations (Prol. 51).

[61] On this point, see Shibata 1976 and Sasaki 1976.

humanistic school of jurisprudence. He attributes greatest value to those in the first category, and hardly any to those in the third (Covarruvias, Vazquez,[62] Bodin, and Hotman are exceptions).[63] Thus he attaches most importance to the classics, while tending to criticize or ignore more recent writers, an approach consistent with the humanistic trend of his age.

1.4. The Prolegomena and the Design of *JBP*

Although the Prolegomena is not a self-contained section, and we should not draw hasty conclusions about Grotius's method from it alone, it is not merely an introduction to *JBP* but is also a kind of generalization.[64] To that extent it provides important clues to understanding the text.

1.4.1. What Underlies *JBP*

The substantive assertions Grotius makes in the Prolegomena may be reduced to the notion that laws do indeed exist which regulate both the resort to war and the conduct of war once it is initiated. He claims to construct a complete system of those laws.[65] The rest is merely enunciation of policy or presentation of materials. One has to wait until Book I for a development of the substantive and specific contents of the law of war and peace. The Prolegomena is thus the introduction to a treatise in which general remarks are contained in the first Book—particularly the first and second chapters—and item-by-item discussions are contained in the other two Books.[66]

Rather than dealing with substantive issues, in the Prolegomena Grotius outlines a three-pronged approach: (1) to discuss the important elements in an all-inclusive manner; (2) to cite extensively from classical sources, adopting in the process the 'freedom enjoyed by the early Christians', and (3) to avoid in his discussion all current topics. But it is doubtful whether this approach could

[62] On the influence of Vazquez on *De Jure Praedae Commentarius* in particular, see Tuck 1979: 59–60; Ito 1984: 15–21.

[63] On the influence of Hotman, see Meyjes 1981: 3–29.

[64] Haggenmacher assumes that the *Prolegomena* was written after the 3 vols. were completed (1983: 449). That Grotius made only slight changes in the Prolegomena in the 2nd edn. of *JBP* reveals that he himself believed that he had more or less maintained the course outlined in the Prolegomena. See Sasaki *et al.* 1985.

[65] Cassirer 1962: 6, 293.

[66] Haggenmacher 1983: 449–50.

be carried out without contradiction. There is a tension between a systematic approach and the extensive citation of diverse authorities,[67] and he often sacrifices the former.[68] It is possible to avoid mentioning current controversies, but these must have been in his mind when he grappled with such questions as *dominium* and *imperium* over the sea[69] or the disputes about succession.[70] Moreover, although he seems to rely on various sources, Grotius is undoubtedly concerned to avoid supporting either side in current religious disputes.[71] But it would be harsh to fault him for such contradictions. His main goal was to subject war and the actions of kings and nations to rational rules, and to achieve this goal by appealing as much as possible to man's autonomy. He is persistent, even dogged, in seeking to achieve this end, asserting what needs to be asserted without fear of theoretical difficulties. This awareness of the issues is expressed fully in the Prolegomena: in that sense, it is a condensation of the entire text of *JBP*.

Grotius's abhorrence of bloodshed is clearly expressed in the Prolegomena and underlies *JBP* as a whole. He devotes three chapters near the end of Book II to urging avoidance of war not only when it is unjust or when its justness is in doubt, but even when it is obviously just.[72] The same appeal is made in the second half of Book III where *temperamenta*, peace, and faith are discussed.[73] The theological just-war doctrine was originally advanced to mitigate the absolute nature of 'love' espoused in the New Testament, and to justify certain types of war.[74] By contrast, in Grotius's just-war doctrine, the rejection of absolute pacifism and the encouragement of the renunciation of war are two sides of the same coin, and his abhorrence of bloodshed is its most outstanding characteristic.[75]

[67] Pufendorf sought to construct a logical theory of natural law by means of a mathematical method far more systematic than anything Grotius attempted. In doing so he pushed custom and practice into the world of history, removing them from his theory of law (Pufendorf 1934 ⟨1688⟩, II. iii. 23).

[68] See 3.3.4.

[69] II. ii. 3. for a discussion of the difference from *De Jure Praedae Commentarius*, see Ito 1984: 161–89.

[70] II. vii. 3–37. See also 5.5.2.

[71] Schiedermair emphasizes Grotius's commitment to religious peace, and stresses the fact that *JBP* was dedicated to Henry III. See the reference in n. 26.

[72] II. xxii–xxiv. [73] III. xi–xxiv. [74] Ito 1957*b*: 66–7 n. 1.

[75] To this extent, Meinecke is correct in pointing out that 'Grotius should occupy a much wider place in the history of the idea of pacifism than in the history of the idea of *raison d'état*' (1924: 247).

1.4.2. Sociability as Inherent Human Nature

Grotius endeavours to construct a system of jurisprudence through a deductive method starting with axioms whose validity he believes to be beyond doubt. In particular, inherent human nature includes an unquenchable sociability.[76] This is not induced from actual observations of behaviour but asserted a priori. As compared with Hobbes and Rousseau, who based their theories on an enquiry into man's nature, Grotius accepts human sociability as given.[77] This is reminiscent of Aristotle's proposition that man is a political being, a proposition which, though interpreted in various ways, was widely accepted from ancient times. Thus people in Grotius's time could well regard man's innate sociability as self-evident.[78] Despite the frequent occurrence of wars which 'even savages would be ashamed of', Grotius took an optimistic view of the human capacity for reason, and thus tended to follow tradition rather uncritically, for example, in adopting the view of the state as a 'complete association'.[79] The desire for society may lead to an association of men but not necessarily to the specific form of association known as a state. This uncritical acceptance of tradition is one of the factors responsible for Grotius's tendency to affirm the *status quo*, despite the innovation of placing natural law on a secular basis. It also explains why *JBP* did not have the impact one might have expected, considering its great and continuing reputation.

1.4.3. 'Even if we concede there is no God': The Autonomy of Reason and the Independence of Law

Any assessment of Grotius must be influenced by the interpretation of the proposition in the Prolegomena that a law deduced from man's inherent nature would have a degree of validity, 'even if we should concede that . . . there is no God, or that the affairs of men are of no concern to Him'. Obviously, this statement is not to be accepted at face value. Grotius himself declares that his hypothetical proposition might be as serious a sin as blasphemy. The question is rather what this proposition reveals about this ideological position. Cassirer,[80] Brimo,[81] and others interpret it as the divorce of natural-law doctrine from theology, allowing the construction of a system of jurisprudence based solely on reason. Conversely, for

[76] Welzel 1980: 126. [77] Strömholm 1985: 158. [78] Mitteis 1971: 36.
[79] I. i. 14. [80] Cassirer 1919: 98–100. [81] Brimo 1978: 99–101.

Rommen[82] and Sauter,[83] the hypothetical proposition is a manifestation of the fact that, against the background of the late medieval controversy between rationalists and voluntarists, Grotius assumes an eclectic position, while ultimately supporting the rationalists.[84] Daring Scholastics before Grotius had advanced similar hypothetical propositions.[85]

We cannot accept Sauter's and Rommen's neo-Thomist interpretation that locates Grotius's hypothesis solely within the framework of medieval theological controversy. Grotius must have been familiar with the controversy between Luther, the advocate of 'enslaved will', and Erasmus, the advocate of 'free will',[86] and have been fully aware that the controversies over intellect and will, or grace and freedom, extended well beyond the domain of theology and focused on the autonomy of reason. The voluntarists asserted that divine will is omnipotent and that what God wills is just and therefore law. The rationalists contended that that which is judged to be just through the use of right reason, which (though clouded by the fall of man) is inherent in human nature and common to God's nature, is immutable and therefore enjoined by God. The rationalist–voluntarist opposition is an opposition over primary causes; the two proceed on the shared assumption that divine law and natural law are in agreement. But in Grotius, divine volitional law and natural law are distinguished in terms of their origin.[87] Grotius used the hypothetical proposition precisely to make this distinction, which is why he is often credited with the 'secularization of natural law'.[88] His refusal to admit the contradistinction

[82] Rommen 1956: 56–9, 71–2.

[83] Sauter 1932: 91–3.

[84] While stating that Grotius clearly takes the standpoint of the rationalists, Welzel admits that there is something new in his method and in the content of his natural law (1980: 127–9).

[85] Since Pufendorf (Pufendorf 1934 ⟨1688⟩, II. iii. 19), it has been possible to see the source of this hypothetical proposition in Marcus Aurelius (1952: 278). But while the hypothetical propositions themselves may be expressed in a similar way, their contexts are entirely different. For studies that examine the precursors of the hypothetical proposition and recognize its novelty while seeing its direct predecessors in Gregorius of Rimini and the late Spanish Scholastics, see Hervada 1983: 3–20; Haggenmacher 1983: 496–507.

[86] Against Erasmus's *Diatribe de Libero Arbitrio*, publ. in 1524, Luther wrote *De Servo Arbitrio*, which the former refuted in *Hyperaspistes*. For concise general views, see Huizinga 1965: 169–77; Kikumori 1977: 186–207.

[87] See Hervada 1983: 19.

[88] With regard to 'secularization', see the articles included in Dilcher and Staff 1984.

between natural law and divine volitional law can be explained as an attempt to bridge them on the basis of an initial acceptance of their difference.[89]

But we should not conclude that Grotius is a modernist simply from the hypothetical statement. To be sure, he distinguishes natural law from divine volitional law in terms of its origin, but he also gives the latter a place of its own, and uses it as a secondary standard, after natural law, for judging whether war, punishment, and the like, are just or unjust. There is a clear distinction between this method and that adopted by Hobbes and Pufendorf, who banished divine law from their theory of jurisprudence.

Nevertheless, something novel is to be found in this hypothetical proposition. According to Grotius's methodological position, his initial axioms had to be self-evident, unsupported by arguments from divine will. Had they been based on divine law, they would have lost their a priori character. Moreover, most of the wars Grotius sought to regulate by means of law were religious wars in which both sides were striving to achieve their respective aims in the name of God. Appeals to divine law were particularly useless in dealing with religious wars: thus there was no choice but to embark on the task of giving reason a status independent of divine will, removing natural law from theology.[90] To emphasize this aspect of his argument would have antagonized at least some Christian sects: hence the decision to present it as a hypothetical proposition.

In fact, the hypothetical proposition in *JBP* was accepted as something new both by his contemporaries and by those who followed.[91] While describing Grotius as the teacher of all modern scholars in the field of 'le droit politique', Rousseau placed Grotius and Hobbes in the same category, asserting that they differed only in their terminology.[92] Rousseau did not see Grotius as within the Scholastic tradition. Montesquieu's expression 'We should love justice even if there is no God',[93] is modelled on Grotius, even though it is not a mere hypothetical phrase since it asserts that

[89] Hazard 1973: 334.

[90] For a study stressing Grotius's notion of 'love' from the same perspective, see Johnson 1983: 21–34.

[91] Finnis (1980: 36–48) points out that Clark took this position.

[92] Rousseau 1969: 836. Also Rousseau 1964: 132.

[93] Montesquieu 1949: 256.

justice is of supreme value to both the pagan and the atheist. Montesquieu perhaps detected in Grotius's hypothetical proposition a desire, or at least a tendency, to turn divinity into a relative concept.

Borkenau was right to claim that the nuances of Grotius's hypothetical proposition are decidedly non-Catholic.[94] Cassirer emphasizes that Grotius stressed the transcendence of the *idea of law*, according to which law is not based on any existence, empirical or absolute.[95] In short, despite retaining some traces of Scholasticism in his content, Grotius's hypothetical proposition should be understood as an attempt to open up a new horizon by establishing a new, secular foundation for law. It is an affirmation that it is possible, in this world, to separate man's reason from God on a basis of autonomy, enabling natural law to be independent and self-sufficient.[96] In his methodological posture, Grotius clearly breaks with the Scholastics.

1.4.4. Utility

Grotius excludes utility from his discussion on the ground that it is extraneous to law and belongs to the realm of politics. He remarks that Aristotle rightly treated politics by itself, and criticizes Bodin for mixing politics with law. When he does mention expediency or utility, he does so in order to distinguish it from what is lawful.[97] The central point of Grotius's criticism of Carneades lies in his refutation of the latter's notion that law is based solely on utility. However, as we have seen, there is a definite role for utility in natural as well as volitional law. In particular the law of nations is based on agreements between nations which are advantageous to all or most nations.[98] In calling for restraint of war, ends and means are weighed in the balance in terms of utility.[99] The acceptance of slavery, which Rousseau criticized,[100] was for Grotius based on the utilitarian comparison of death in liberty with life under subjection.[101] In this sense, utility plays an important role in *JBP* as an actual standard of judgement.

[94] Borkenau 1934: 145. [95] Cassirer 1962: 297–9.
[96] Haggenmacher 1983: 468; Wolf 1927: 52–4.
[97] Prol. 57.
[98] Tsuneto also regards this as an explanation that takes utilitarianism into account (1977: 260).
[99] II. xxiv. 5. [100] Rousseau 1964: 353, 355–8. [101] II. xxiv. 6.

1.4.5. *JBP* AND 'INTERNATIONAL LAW'

Grotius asserts the existence of laws that regulate both the decision to resort to war and the conduct of war. Unlike municipal law, these laws are applied to relationships between nations and between rulers of nations. But we should not conclude that they are directly linked to international law as it emerged in later ages. Not only are natural law, divine volitional law, and the law of nations standards for judging whether a war is just or not, but also a large part of these laws, such as the rules as to ownership, agreement, punishment, and the like, discussed in Book II, should be applied to the relations between private persons as well as between nations. In other words, their content corresponds to municipal law.[102] The purpose of *JBP* is, given such an array of laws, to expound the rules which kings and nations ought to observe in their relations with each other. It is thus too simple to say that, 'the theory of natural law aside, Grotius achieved great results in laying the foundation for the theory of international law',[103] or conversely that 'Grotius is merely a link in the chain of the history of ideas in international law that begins with Vitoria and Suarez.'[104]

As long as Grotius's 'law of war and peace', consisting of natural law and the law of nations, is valid for the mutual relations between kings and nations, it has in common with modern international law both the subject-matter and actors to be regulated. But the former is not limited to these mutual relationships, nor does it have the same content as later international law. Rather, the law of nature is valid *even* for the relations between kings and nations because of its universality and self-evidence, while the law of nations is valid for these relations because of its wide acceptance. It is natural for Grotius that these laws should have much in common both with laws enforced within a state and with divine law. He does not have any conception of international law as a law that regulates *solely* relations between nations, and as such as independent of laws

[102] To seek among the assertions in the Prolegomena only elements of modern private and criminal law is to overlook the structure of *JBP* where Grotius treats individual municipal laws as outside its scope, but analyses such general concepts as ownership, succession, and punishment, which have a universal character beyond the reach of individual municipal laws, and which can be causes of war. In this sense, Wieacker's assessment (1967: 287–301) is questionable.

[103] Sauter 1932: 97.

[104] Verdross 1958: 85. See also Scott 1934.

enforced within a state, laws expounded in the Bible, or natural law. The question whether Grotius is the father of international law can only be answered if these points are taken into account. If (as is often the case) they are not, any answer is virtually meaningless.

2

Grotius's Concept of Law

2.1. Introduction

In Prolegomena, Grotius asserts the fundamental principles of the autonomy of reason and the independence of natural law from God.[1] On that basis, he reveals his intention[2] to bring war under the control of law, expressing his conviction 'that there is a common law among nations, which is valid alike for war and in war'.[3] His first problem is the just-war doctrine, with a tradition dating back to the European Middle Ages or even to Ancient Greece and Rome. He asks whether there can ever be a just war, and if so, what kind of war is just. However, he does not rely on the just-war doctrine of the European medieval theologians, but re-examines the just-war doctrine from the viewpoint of natural law based solely on reason.[4] He thus begins with two questions: what is war and what is law? In this chapter, we attempt to understand Grotius's concept of law, focusing in particular on I. i.

2.2. *Jus*

2.2.1. Threefold Meaning of *Jus*

In defining war and law, Grotius first points out that the word *jus* has a threefold meaning.

(1) Jus *as the Rightful Attribute of Acts, or Justness*

First, *jus* is defined as a particular attribute of acts (*attributum actionis*), i.e. the justness of an act. Grotius uses the word 'just' in the broadest sense: he explains that what is not unjust is 'just',

[1] See 1.4.3. Also see Friedrich 1963: 64–6.

[2] As can be deduced from its content and style, Prolegomena was written after Books I–III were completed. See Haggenmacher 1983: 449.

[3] Prol. 28. [4] I. i. 2(3).

and that what is contrary to the social nature of man as a being endowed with reason is unjust.[5] By adopting a negative definition—that which is not 'unjust' is 'just'—Grotius distances himself from the theological just-war doctrine, which had regarded as 'just' only acts of which God would positively approve. While Grotius's understanding of what is 'just' and 'unjust' allows him to brand as unlawful those acts which are clearly contrary to the social nature of man, it is also likely to function as a rationale for approving much of the existing order.

(2) Jus *as a Moral Quality*

Secondly, *jus* is considered as the moral quality of a person (*qualitas moralis personae*) that enables him to do or to have something justly. In other words, when 'a person is judged to be just in doing or having something', he has *jus* in the second sense.[6] *Jus* in this sense may be called a subjective *jus* because it is defined from the viewpoint of its subject.[7] It is closest to what we would today call 'right', but it also includes freedom and latent power (*potentia*). *Jus* in this sense applies only to human beings; that something is just or not is a judgement about human beings, whether it involves rights over things (*jus in rem*) or over persons (*jus in personas*).

Grotius divides *jus* in this sense into what is perfect and what is imperfect in its moral quality. He uses the term *facultas* for a perfect *jus*, aptitude (*aptitudo*) for an imperfect.[8] Faculty is further divided into power (*potestas*), ownership (*dominium*), and contractual rights (*credita*).[9] Power over oneself is called freedom (*libertas*); power over others includes that of the head of a household (*potestas patria*) or of a master over his slaves (*potestas dominica*). The right

[5] I. i. 3. *Jus* in the broadest sense is said to be divided into justice or law between equals (*jus aequatorium*), which is applicable to those with equal status, and rectorial law (*jus rectorium*), which is applicable to those who rule and those who are ruled. This distinction is not fully developed, but see II. xxiv. 7, where the obligation of a superior to protect his subordinates, which corresponds to the obedience of the latter to the former, is regarded as rectorial justice. See Haggenmacher 1983: 463, esp. n. 98.

[6] This differs from the first meaning of *jus*, but according to Grotius derives from it.

[7] Haggenmacher notes that the subjective and objective aspects of *jus* are not distinguished in *De Jure Praedae Commentarius* (1983: 462).

[8] I. i. 4. For a discussion that stresses the distinction between faculty and aptitude, see Eikema Hommes 1979: 90–2.

[9] I. i. 5.

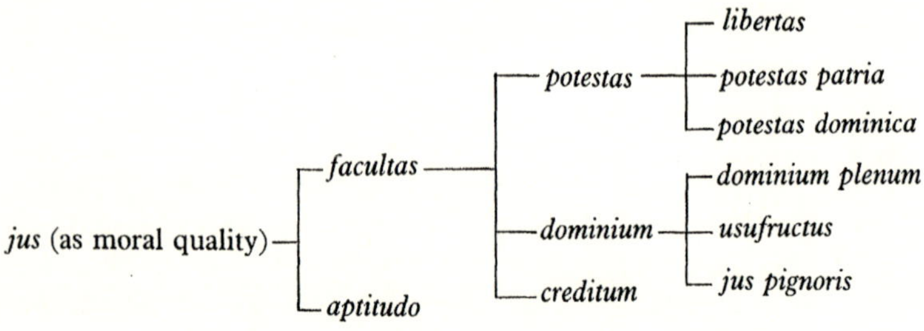

FIG. 2.1. Grotius's classification of *jus*

of ownership includes usufruct and the right of pledge (*jus pignoris*), in addition to full ownership (*dominium plenum*). Where there is a contractual right, there is a corresponding contractual obligation (*debitum*). Thus Grotius's classification is as shown in Fig. 2.1.

On the basis of another criterion, *facultas* is divided into common (*vulgaris*) and superior (*eminens*). A power is superior if it is exercised by the community over its members and their property for the common good. Accordingly, with regard to people, the king has at the same time the power of the father and that of a master over his slaves, and with regard to things, the king has a right of eminent domain (*dominium eminens*) over the possessions of his subjects, which is superior to private ownership (*dominium privatum*). Moreover, a subject owes a greater obligation to the state than to a private creditor.[10] These are the contents of *facultas*, conceived by Grotius as a perfect legal right which is the concern of expletive justice.[11]

On the other hand, aptitude means 'worthiness or that which is worth something'. It is said to be the concern of distributive justice.[12] So it is quite incorrect to call aptitude a right. The mere fact that something is suitable or appropriate for a person does not

[10] I. i. 6. In the Kelsey trans., this can be read to mean that, since public rights are superior to private rights, subjects are under a greater pecuniary obligation to the state than to a private creditor. The Latin original is better interpreted as explaining power, the right of ownership, and contractual right, respectively, in relation to royal power. Haggenmacher suggests that Grotius may have been influenced by Covarruvias and other Spanish scholars, as evidenced by the inclusion of public faculty in his notion of faculty, where *JBP* is different from *De Jure Praedae Commentarius* (1983: 464–5).

[11] Grotius says that a legal right is called by the jurists 'the right to one's own (*suum*)' (I. i. 5). Eikema Hommes (1979: 93–4) attaches importance to this concept as used by Grotius.

[12] I. i. 7–8(I).

mean that he can claim ownership over it for that reason. It is thus necessary to distinguish between aptitude and a right when both coexist in relation to one and the same matter.[13] Whereas the violation of a right may constitute a just cause of war, the violation of an aptitude cannot.

(3) Jus *as 'Law'*

There is also a third meaning of *jus*, to which we can apply the word 'law' without serious misunderstanding. Here *jus* is defined as a rule (*regula*), synonymous with law (*lex*) in its broadest sense, a body of rules which obligate man to what is right (*rectus*). In other words, it is a body of objective norms indicative of justness.[14] *Jus* in this sense connotes obligation (*obligatio*). It does not include requirements which are only recommendations. Permission (*permissio*) is in principle not a function of law but its negation.[15] *Jus* in this sense will be discussed in 2.3.

2.2.2. Connection between the Three Meanings of *Jus*

As the Roman jurists stressed, *jus* refers not only to objective laws but also to the subjective rights conferred on each person by those laws.[16] The idea that these two aspects of *jus* were subsumed in the concept of justice was also accepted by the Scholastics.[17] There is nothing new in Grotius's three-part definition of *jus*; however, his arrangement is suggestive in placing the concept of *jus* within the wider tradition of legal thought.

(1) *The Inseparability of Natural Right from Natural Law*

Grotius argues that *jus* has two aspects—objective law and subjective right—which share the same basis, i.e. justice. This suggests that, while recognizing the difference in the three meanings of *jus*, Grotius does not draw a sharp distinction between them,[18] but regards them as forming an inseparable whole.

[13] II. xvii. 2(2)–3.

[14] See n. 7 above, but *jus* in the meaning of law is not always regarded as equivalent to *lex*. See Nerseshantz 1986: 73–4.

[15] I. i. 9.

[16] See Kaser 1977: 22; Mishima 1980: 108–11.

[17] Cicero 1928: 312–53. For Ulpian's discussion of Cicero's view of justice, see Tsuneto 1977: 163–4. See also Kern 1956: part i.

[18] Thus the term '*De jure belli*' as used in the opening passages of I. i. 2(1) and I. i. 3(1) has three related meanings: the justness of war, the right of war, and the law of war.

It was Hobbes who clearly distinguished law from right, particularly in terms of the distinction between natural law and natural right.[19] On the one hand, Hobbes placed the laws of nature outside the scope of law properly so-called, stating that these are 'laws' only when a commonwealth is established and only so far as they are incorporated in the positive law of the commonwealth, defined as the command of the sovereign. On the other hand, he claimed that, though most of the liberty men enjoyed in the state of nature is given up, the natural right to defend one's body continues to exist even after the establishment of the commonwealth.[20] For Hobbes, the state or commonwealth is established on the basis of a social contract to secure self-preservation, which lies at the core of natural right.[21] D'Entrèves points out that this shift in the centre of gravity from natural law to natural right is the key to explaining the process by which modern natural-law theories developed into the revolutionary dogmas that transformed the world.[22] It is dangerous to generalize, because thinkers such as Rousseau[23] do not fit into such categories, but D'Entrèves's statement is none the less apt, in that the natural-rights theories provided the intellectual impetus for the Age of Revolution.[24] In the present context, it is revealing that Grotius himself completely fails to consider the possibility of right becoming separated from law. In Grotius's system, municipal law which is contrary to natural law cannot have any binding force; conversely, in the domains where municipal law is competent to restrict the freedom that individual people possessed before states were formed, it is impossible to approve of resistance or revolution to attain natural rights. To that extent, Grotius's position is remote from later ideas of natural right. If his arrangement of the three meanings of *jus* prepared the way for the coming semantic change, that development went beyond, and was contrary to, Grotius's intentions.

On the other hand, it was the inherent connection between

[19] Hobbes 1966 ⟨1839⟩, 116–17, 146–7, 253–4. See also Fukuda 1971: 43–69.

[20] Hobbes 1966 ⟨1839⟩, 157–8, 204–6.

[21] However, according to Tuck, the content of natural right and the significance of natural law and natural right differ from one work of Hobbes to the next (1979: 119–42).

[22] D'Entrèves 1970: 60–2.

[23] Ogasawara 1979: 109–15, 147–52; Tsuneto 1968: 129–36. For a discussion of Rousseau's view of natural law, see Derathé 1970: ch. 3.

[24] For a similar view, see Hobsbawm 1962: 1–5.

justice and law that made possible the revival of natural law and the development of neo-naturalism.[25] That connection presupposes that anyone endowed with reason can agree on what is just, whatever the issue. If this assumption does not hold, the identification of justice with law turns out to be nothing but ideology.[26] This is why legal positivism, including Austin's analytical jurisprudence, separated justice from law.[27] But because legal positivism centres its concern upon the positive law alone, it cannot embody any higher standard by which positive law can be judged. Therefore, it readily serves as an ideology to justify the existing legal order. The rise and defeat of Fascism in Italy, Nazism in Germany, and Militarism in Japan, produced a strong trend in favour of the renaissance of natural law.[28]

(2) *The Substance of Justness*

Grotius's explanation of what is just is not always clear. He says that *jus* in the third sense, i.e. as a body of law, is equivalent to *lex* in the broadest sense, which imposes an obligation with respect to what is right (*rectus*). Law relates not only to justice (*justitia*) strictly speaking but also to other virtues, and that '[n]evertheless that which, in accordance with this law, is right, in a broader sense is called just'.[29] In relation to the second meaning of *jus*, i.e. right, *facultas* is 'the concern of expletive justice (*justitia expletrix*), which is entitled to the name of justice properly or strictly so-called'. As to the first meaning of *jus*, what is not unjust, i.e. not contrary to the social nature of man, is called just. Thus we can infer that Grotius conceives of justness[30] at three different levels: *justitia expletrix*, legality or what is in accord with law,[31] and what is not unjust.

This view of justness permits two interpretations of the concept of just war. One is that, in order for a war to be just, it should meet

[25] Le Fur 1927: 263–4; Mitteis 1948: 3–4.

[26] See Kelsen 1928: 36–41; Kelsen 1957: 1–24, 137–73.

[27] e.g. Austin 1885: 87, 154–5; Hart 1961: 181–207.

[28] McCoubrey 1987: 169–70.

[29] I. i. 9(1).

[30] The law of love and other higher virtues are on a different level from the 'justness' discussed here, although these virtues are also appealed to in *JBP* to regulate war.

[31] In I. ii. 1(1), and elsewhere, Kelsey usually renders *justus* as 'lawful'. This tends to ignore the multi-faceted meaning of the term.

the requirements of *justitia expletrix*; it is not enough for it to be just at the second or third level. This interpretation tends to restrict war more rigorously. The other is that, if a war does not meet the requirements of *justitia expletrix*, it may nevertheless be just if it is legal in the formal sense, or even more extreme, that a war is just as far as it is clearly not unjust. On the latter interpretation, Grotius's intention to subject war to law to the greatest extent possible will be denied.

2.3. Natural Law and Volitional Law

Grotius, after the manner of Aristotle,[32] divides law, *jus* in the third sense, into natural law and volitional law.

2.3.1. Natural Law

(1) *Definition and Immutability of Natural Law*

The law of nature (*jus naturae/jus naturale*) is, above all, a dictate of right reason (*recta ratio*), which indicates whether a certain act is consistent with rational nature. An act which is contrary to rational nature has a quality of moral baseness (*turpitudo*), and consequently is forbidden by God, the author of nature. An act which is in conformity with rational nature has a quality of moral necessity, and consequently is enjoined by God. Where there is a dictate of right reason in regard to a certain act, that act is either obligatory or unlawful, and is therefore either enjoined or forbidden by God.[33] In this regard, the law of nature is sharply distinguished from volitional law, human as well as divine.[34]

[32] Among Roman jurists Gaius adopted a dichotomy of law, and Ulpian a trichotomy. Grotius's concept, strictly speaking, agrees with neither. Kelsey's marginal note to I. i. 9(2) (Eng. 38) indicates that the relevant passage is quoted from Aristotle's *Nichomachean Ethics*, V. x. It should be V. vii.

[33] Edwards insists that Grotius agrees with Suárez in recognizing the double obligation by natural law itself and by the command of God (1981: 63–4). In *JBP*, Grotius considers that the primary cause of the obligation under natural law is the inherent justness of the thing itself.

[34] I. i. 10(1)–(2). In *De Jure Praedae Commentarius*, Grotius adopted a form of voluntarism which based the primary natural law (*jus naturae primarium*), and ultimately all laws, on God's will (Grotius 1950 ⟨1604⟩ (Eng. 8–29); Ito 1963: 184–96). Most commentators regard the 'shift' in *JBP* as significant, but Haggenmacher is less categorical, doubting whether Grotius consciously modified the voluntarist stance of *De Jure Praedae Commentarius*. Haggenmacher argues that

Since rules of natural law are derived from conformity or contradiction with rational nature, they are immutable and cannot be changed, even by God. 'Just as even God, then, cannot cause two times two not to make four, so He cannot cause that which is intrinsically evil not to be evil.'[35] Natural law is immutable because it is derived directly from man's social and rational nature. But this applies only to the law of nature properly so-called, in other words, to mandatory natural law.

(2) *Flexibility of Natural Law*

Despite the rigid definition of natural law, Grotius gives it greater flexibility in four ways.

First, in addition to things enjoined or forbidden by natural law, there are certain things which are permitted by natural law. Grotius says that such things are part of natural law 'by reduction', i.e. they are not in conflict with natural law.[36] No strict obligation is imposed under natural law about things which are merely permitted under it. Strictly speaking, this permissive domain of natural law is outside the sphere of natural law,[37] and therefore subject to regulation by volitional law.[38]

Grotius divides the permission accorded by law into perfect and less perfect permission: the former gives the right to do anything at all, while the latter only grants freedom from human punishment, i.e. the right to non-interference by others. As to the former, what volitional law stipulates is not contrary to the law of nature, while for the latter it may be.[39] A more detailed examination of Grotius's argument shows that there are at least four kinds of permissibility:

(*a*) that which is permissible because it is morally just in itself, although there may be something more praiseworthy;[40]

(*b*) that which is morally neutral, i.e. neither just nor evil in itself;[41]

(*c*) that which is not morally approved, although it may be done

Grotius did not break entirely from voluntarism: in other words, the shift involved a revision of more minor character, made to maintain his basic assertion as to the validity and stability of natural law (1983: 466–523).

[35] I. i. 10(5). [36] I. i. 10(3). [37] I. i. 9(1); I. ii. 5(1).

[38] I, ii. 5(1); II. i. 10(1); II. iii. 5. See also 2.5.2(1).

[39] I. i. 17(2). See also III. iv. 2.

[40] III. iv. 2(1).

[41] II. i. 10(1). An example is the possession of movable things (II. iii. 5).

with impunity among men, to which a limited right of non-interference by others is accorded;[42]

(*d*) that which is morally evil and not accorded and right, to which only the effect of impunity is granted.[43]

Thus it is desirable to establish volitional law to require (*a*). Category (*b*) is open to regulation by volitional law. It is admissible to establish volitional law to grant (*c*) impunity and the right of non-interference for practical purposes. Category (*d*) is contrary to the law of nature, but the effect of impunity accorded thereto is considered a necessary evil. Grotius declines to call it *jus*.[44]

This categorization serves as a framework for judging the rules of human volitional law from the moral point of view.[45] Thus it is highly undesirable to lay down rules of volitional law to forbid category (*a*) or to enjoin category (*d*). But such a possibility is not excluded by Grotius's argument. Categories (*c*) and (*d*) may function to justify existing institutions which are contrary to the requirements of justice. On the other hand, the reference to what may be more praiseworthy in category (*a*) may lead to confusion between the law of nature and higher virtues, a misunderstanding which according to Grotius leads to the misuse of the term 'natural law'.[46]

A second level of flexibility is introduced by the concept of 'the nature of the institution'. Grotius says that:

> the law of nature deals not only with things which are outside the domain of the human will, but with many things also which result from an act of the human will. Thus ownership, such as now obtains, was introduced by the will of man; but once introduced, the law of nature points out that it is wrong for me, against your will, to take away that which is subject to your ownership.[47]

Thus Grotius speaks of 'the nature of *summum imperium*',[48] 'the nature of war',[49] and 'the nature of contract'.[50] As long as rules

[42] An example is the marriage of a man to his sister, which is not prohibited by natural law but by divine volitional law (II. v. 12–13).

[43] e.g. interest that exceeds fair compensation (II. xii. 22).

[44] e.g. the impunity of a master who killed his slave (II. i. 1(2)).

[45] The same argument also applies to divine volitional law (I. ii. 5(1)), but since God cannot be unjust, it is virtually impossible to doubt the justness of divine volitional law (I. i. 17(2)).

[46] I. i. 10(3).

[47] I. i. 10(4).

[48] II. iv. 13.

[49] III. iv. 1.

[50] II. xii. 9.

deduced from the institutions introduced by the human will are judged to be inherent in the institution, these rules are accorded the status of natural law. In fact, the expression 'naturally (*naturaliter*)' is often used for rules deriving from such institutions.[51] It should be noted that this argument risks obscuring the enquiry into the rightness or wrongness of the very institution in question, and thus, by reinforcing institutions, tends to justify the *status quo*.[52]

A third level of flexibility involves the manipulation of the immutability of natural law. Grotius says that when there appears to be a change in what natural law ordains, it is not the law of nature but the thing subject to the law of nature that has changed. For example, if God should command that someone be slain, it does not mean that homicide will become permissible, but that it will not be a case of homicide because the deed is done by authority of the Supreme Lord of life and property.[53] This argument also may serve as a conservative principle to justify capital punishment or killing enemies in war.

A fourth level of flexibility is introduced by the concept of 'natural law in relation to a certain state of things (*pro certo rerum statu*)'. Before the right of ownership was established, the primitive community of things was the natural usage, and before the introduction of the positive law, there was the right to defend one's own by force.[54] This conception is used to advocate the freedom of the seas as well as the right of private defensive war in case of imminent danger.

By these and other devices, including the 'interpretation'[55] of rules and institutions, Grotius makes natural law flexible enough to accommodate almost any situation. But this runs the risk of turning natural law centred on 'justness' into a mere name.

(3) *The Proof of Natural Law*

There are two ways to prove that something is in accordance with natural law, by proof a priori or a posteriori. Proof a priori consists

[51] e.g. II. v. 24(2); II. xi. 6; II. xii. 8.

[52] For a similar view, see Kelsen 1977: esp. 138–42; Fukuda 1971: 28.

[53] I. i. 10(6).

[54] I. i. 10(7). There are similar expressions in II. viii. 26, with regard to acquisition of things, and in II. xiv. 6(2), with regard to self-help.

[55] Laun 1950: 190–1.

in demonstrating the inevitable concordance of a rule with the rational and social nature of man; proof a posteriori in concluding that it is in accordance with natural law as understood by all nations, or by all nations advanced in civilization. The latter is less exact and certain than the former, but has sufficient probability, because a universal effect demands a universal cause, and the cause of such universal opinion can only be the common sense of man (*sensus communis*).[56] The great number of quotations in *JBP* suggests that Grotius relies mainly on this method of proof. This makes it possible for Grotius to develop his theory of natural law in a specific and detailed manner.[57] But the question arises how to distinguish between proof a posteriori of natural law and proof of the law of nations based on the common testimony of many writers.[58]

One answer is provided in the comment that, outside the sphere of natural law, there is hardly any law that is common to all nations.[59] But this sounds tautological. Properly speaking, the universality of a given rule is proved inductively, i.e. through examination of rules actually observed by many nations. Such an inductive approach is contrary to the deductive method on which Grotius purports to rely. The comment cited is rather concerned to emphasize that, whereas natural law is an immutable and universal law emanates from the inherent nature of man, the law of nations can claim neither immutability nor universality in the true sense because it is derived from changeable human will. Though a clear distinction may be drawn between natural law and the law of nations in terms of their origins, no clear standard—other than self-evidence and universality—is provided for distinguishing them in terms of their legal content. There is no methodological difference between proof a posteriori of natural law and proof of the law of nations. Only self-evidence can serve as the standard for distinguishing between them. Grotius seems to have given the name 'natural law' to what he considered highly self-

[56] I. i. 12(1). See also Prol. 8, 16, 39, 40.

[57] For a similar view, see Welzel 1980: 129.

[58] Sauter criticizes this confusion (1932: 97). Faucci claims that Vico, while influenced by Grotius, set up a category called 'natural law of nations' in addition to natural law pure and simple. This is a possible interpretation of the confusion (1980: 126–7).

[59] I. i. 14(1).

evident, or 'natural', in the light of his own sense of justice and reason.[60] No doubt he strove to avoid intruding his own prejudices, confident that his argument would coincide with the views of others based on shared human reason, and would therefore have strong persuasive power. But he could not rid himself of his European background, as is evidenced by the expression 'nations more advanced in civilization', which refers only to European Christian nations.[61]

This methodological weakness is left unresolved throughout *JBP*. Pufendorf later banished to the domain of history those elements of the so-called law of nations that could not be subsumed under natural law, and thereby constructed a systematic theory of natural law, in which only rules alleged to be of universal validity are included. At the same time, he saw God as 'the Almighty Creator', who 'had decreed to create [*man a*] rational and social animal', and declared that it was impossible for the natural law not to agree with His constitution.[62] This construction paradoxically enabled Pufendorf to treat specific legal rules and institutions as natural law itself. This does not free him from his European bias. Nevertheless, his methodology is based on a critical succession to Grotius, one which is fully cognizant of the latter's methodological weakness.

2.3.2. Volitional Law

Rooted directly in the will of God or man, volitional law has a different origin from natural law.[63]

(1) *Human Volitional Law*

Human volitional law has three categories: municipal law (*jus civile*), law narrower in scope than municipal law, and law broader in scope than municipal law, i.e. the law of nations (*jus gentium*). Municipal law emanates from state power (*potestas civilis*).[64] The law which is narrower in scope than municipal law includes the command of a father over his children, of a master over his slaves,

[60] Within the field of natural law, however, Grotius distinguishes between general principles, other principles which are similarly self-evident, and inferences which cannot be regarded as self-evident (II. xx. 43(1)). Thus even self-evidence is not necessarily a workable criterion.

[61] I. i. 12(2) and n. 1.

[62] Pufendorf 1934 ⟨1688⟩, II. iii. 5–12, 20.

[63] I. i. 13. See also II. xx. 41–3.

[64] For a discussion of Grotius's concept of the state, see 4.2.4.

and similar commands: these are ranked below municipal law.[65] The law broader in scope than municipal law is the law of nations, which derives from the will of all nations or at least many nations. The law of nations, like unwritten municipal law, is proved through customs that have lasted for generations or through the testimony of those skilled in it, such as Roman jurists and historians.[66]

In *De Jure Praedae Commentarius*, Grotius distinguishes primary natural law (*jus naturae primarium*) from secondary natural law (*jus naturae secundarium*), the former being natural law common to all living creatures, and equates secondary natural law (which is common only to human beings as rational creatures) to the primary law of nations (*jus gentium primarium*).[67] He then contrasts the latter with the secondary law of nations (*jus gentium secundarium*), which is based on the consent of nations.[68] In line with his change of view on natural law, i.e. the denial of the concept of natural law common to all living creatures,[69] Grotius abandons the concept of the primary law of nations in *JBP* and treats the law of nations as pure human volitional law.[70] At the same time, as the *raison d'être* of the law of nations, Grotius emphasizes the interests of the great society of nations,[71] or the bond of human society.[72] The prevailing view is that Grotius was influenced by Suarez to regard the law of nations as pure human volitional law, in contrast to natural law which is based on the rational and social nature of man.[73] But in *JBP* Grotius refers to Suarez in only four places, far less frequently than to either Vazquez or Vitoria. Moreover, he admitted in a letter he wrote in 1618 that he had read virtually none of the works of Spanish scholars other than Vazquez, and asked for a loan of some of their works.[74] It is doubtful then that Grotius had been influenced by Suarez. Instead, the categorical distinction between natural law and the law of nations, when compared with *De Jure*

[65] Grotius does not indicate why these commands are included in the concept of law, but this is probably to be inferred by analogy from the classification of the rights of a father, a slave owner, or the state as *potestas* (I. i. 5). Such a line of argument leads to the justification of slavery, the baseness of which Grotius himself acknowledges (II. v. 27(1)).

[66] I. i. 14.

[67] Grotius 1950 ⟨1604⟩ (Eng. 12, 26).

[68] Ibid. 26. See Ito 1963: 185–91; Haggenmacher 1983: 361–82.

[69] I. i. 11(1).

[70] For a similar view, see Haggenmacher 1983: 523–5.

[71] Prol. 17; III. xxv. i.

[72] II. viii. 26.

[73] See e.g. Ito 1963: 210–7.

[74] Tuck 1979: 58–9.

Praedae Commentarius, probably resulted from his desire to distance himself from any particular sect of Christianity, after his bitter involvement in political struggle and imprisonment.

It is true that, by placing the law of nations within the domain of pure volitional law, Grotius was able to confirm the basic character of natural law as a self-sufficient system deduced from self-evident principles. But the distinction between natural law and the law of nations, with the latter subordinated to the former, raised difficulties about the justifiability of the law of nations, especially the law of war. Thus Grotius had to distinguish between two types of the law of nations: that which is true law in every respect, and that which only provides some kinds of act with external effect.[75] The former includes the right of legation, the right of burial, prescription, and the right of intestate succession.[76] The law of war typically belongs to the latter. In a formal war, the external effects of impunity and ownership are conceded equally to both parties. Properly speaking, it would be inconsistent with natural law for the party waging an unjust war to kill those belonging to the opposing party (those who are engaged in a just war). How could this prohibition, of killing those waging a just war, under natural law be lifted by the law of nations? This is the essential significance to the notion of external effects. It enables Grotius, by differentiating between the level of the law of nations and that of natural law, to reserve judgement on the justice or injustice of acts committed in a formal war and to re-examine them from the viewpoint of internal justice. Though he could not overcome the logical difficulty, he at least avoided the literal contradiction between natural law and the law of nations.

(2) *Divine Volitional Law*

Divine volitional law originates in God's will: it is not because certain things are just that God wills them, but certain things become just and obligatory because they are willed by God.[77] Grotius goes on to distinguish between volitional law directed to mankind as a whole and that directed only to a particular nation. The former was given to mankind three times: when God created

[75] See 8.5.2. See also Kasai 1984: 40–2.

[76] II. xviii–xix, esp. II. xix. 6.

[77] I. i. 10(2); I. i. 15(1); II. xx. 42. Le Fur 1927: 299–306, attaches little importance to this difference in argumentation.

man, immediately after the Flood, and when Christ appeared. It binds all people so far as it is sufficiently revealed to them.[78]

As an example of divine volitional law directed to a particular nation, Grotius focuses on Hebrew law. In general, laws bind only those to whom they have been given.[79] As a matter of principle, Grotius defines Hebrew law as binding only Hebrews and denies its universality. He thus set a limit on the scope and validity of special divine volitional law, distinguishing it from general divine volitional law, and both from natural law.[80]

He avoids making these distinctions too clear or rigid, and attempts to link divine volitional law and natural law in two ways. First, with the promulgation of the Gospel, which, together with the collapse of the Hebraic state,[81] led to the abandonment of Hebraic law, it became possible for non-Hebrews to unite with Hebrews in the same church.[82] The advent of Christ revealed that the grace of God extended to all peoples through the covenant (*foedus*) with God. Although Grotius distinguishes between the special character of Hebraic law and the universality of the teachings of Christ, he asserts the universal normative validity of the latter as applied to various nations, transcending religious and doctrinal differences.

Secondly, the specific rules of Hebraic law whose universality Grotius denies are limited to the customs and rituals peculiar to the Jews, such as the prohibition against eating the flesh of a creature which died a natural death, and the offering of sacrifices. He attributes great value to the law of Moses:[83] what the law of Moses enjoins is not contrary to natural law; those who possess *imperium* among Christians may enact the same laws as the law of Moses; and the virtues enjoined by the law of Moses and required of the Apostles by Christ should be observed by Christians in general.[84]

[78] I. i. 15(2). [79] I. i. 16(1)–(7).

[80] Grotius brings into relief the character of divine volitional law as positive law by using the term *lex* (I. i. 16–17, except for the title and the opening sentence of I. i. 16), contrasting it with *jus naturae*.

[81] I. i. 16(7). [82] I. i. 16(7)–(8).

[83] For a discussion on the relationship with the law of the Twelve Tables and similar positive laws, see II. i. 12.

[84] I. i. 17(2)–(4). As an example of the virtues enjoined by the law of Moses and to be observed by Christians, Grotius mentions tithes. This also reveals his tendency to support the *status quo*. For a discussion of 'divine law' as conceived by Grotius and other natural-law theorists, see Link 1982: 77–80.

Thus, after distinguishing divine volitional law from natural law, Grotius fails to pursue the separation, and indeed strives to construct a bridge between them. The same can be said with respect to the relation between general and specific volitional law.[85] It is too harsh to criticize Grotius for this inconsistency. Considering the purpose for which he wrote *JBP*, passive tolerance—his stance not to take sides with one or other religious denomination—must have been a good first step in overcoming the confessionalism of an age ravaged by religious wars.[86] Moreover, he was reluctant to attach too much importance to theoretical consistency, if that meant neglecting an area of law which could significantly contribute to the restraint of war. But, whatever his intention, later thinkers consistently pursued the independence of reason in an advance towards deism, which treats God as a mere object of rational recognition, or towards a purely secular theory of natural law and natural right. For these developments we must wait for Hobbes and Pufendorf,[87] and in the field of religion, for Voltaire's theory of tolerance.[88]

2.4. Basic Legal Concepts

2.4.1. The First Principles of Nature

Grotius defines natural law as the dictate of right reason, but in another context, drawing upon Cicero, he introduces the concept of the first principles of nature (*prima naturae*), i.e. self-preservation, as man's first duty.[89] Both Cicero[90] and Ulpian[91] embraced the concept of a natural law common to animals and man, and the first principles of nature are related to this. In *JBP* Grotius denies the existence of a natural law common to animals and man,[92] yet quotes, without qualification, Cicero's explanation that the first principles of nature are common to animals and man. He avoids

[85] See Hazard 1973: 334.
[86] For a similar view, see e.g. Borkenau 1934: 142–7.
[87] See Fukuda 1971: 33–41. [88] Voltaire 1970: 7–139.
[89] I. ii. 1(1), (4). [90] Cicero 1913: I. 4. 11.
[91] Digest, I. i. 1(2)–(3).
[92] I. i. 11. In *De Jure Praedae Commentarius*, the law common to all living creatures is regarded as the first natural law (*jus naturae primarium*). See n. 34 and 2.3.2 (1) above. On this point, there is also a shift in *JBP*, which Midgley seems to overlook (1975: 157).

contradiction by contrasting the notion of the conformity of things with reason and the first principles of nature: although of later origin, the former is superior to and prevails over the latter.[93] Thus the first principles of nature are not, as such, included in natural law. However, the content of the two may coincide: for example, Grotius says that everyone by nature has the right to resist in order to ward off injury.[94]

If there is some danger that self-preservation as the first principles of nature may collide with the concept of society or of law, we cannot detect any awareness of this tension in Grotius. He seems to exude a naïve optimism that the first principles of nature are in harmony with man's reason and desire for society.[95] He thus affirms, nearly unconditionally, the proposition that it is more worthy to prefer to be killed than to kill a ruler, on whose shoulders rests the welfare of many.[96]

2.4.2. The Law of Love

Grotius often refers to love (*caritas*, *delectio*), the law of love (*lex caritatis*, *lex dilectionis*), or the rules of love (*caritatis regulae*),[97] as rules[98] broader than those of law.[99] But he does not provide a general explanation of their sources or contents. We find two contexts in which Grotius relies on the law of love. The first is when he argues that one should refrain from resort to war, even if permissible by law in the strict sense, following the law of love, which should be observed even towards one's enemy.[100] The second is when he says that human laws may enjoin what the law of love only urges,[101] or that the law of the Gospel obliges man to do what love itself does not require.[102] Judging from these expressions, we can say that the law of love is basically a virtue of a higher order, one that transcends law in the strict sense. It is distinguished

[93] I. ii. 1(2). [94] I. iv. 2.

[95] Dilthey 1957: 450–1. Cf. Cassirer 1962: 293–4.

[96] II. i. 8. In the section where he discusses resistance, Grotius seems more hesitant (I. iv. 7(4)–(7)).

[97] We also find the expression *norma caritatis* (II. xii. 16). The title of this section includes the term *lex diligendi*, which may be translated as the law of love.

[98] II. i. 11. [99] III. xiii. 4.

[100] II. xxiv. 2–3. Such a method of argument is also found in *temperamenta*, e.g. III. xi. 2; III. xiii. 4. See also 9.4.2 (2).

[101] I. iv. 7(2). Some rules are incorporated into Hebraic or Roman law (II. i. 12(4)).

[102] II. i. 10(1).

also from internal justice, which corresponds to natural law in terms of content, but is devoid of any means of being realized in this world, once external effects are recognized according to the law of nations.[103]

In the Prolegomena Grotius says that, although the teachings of the New Testament are divine volitional law, they include things which are recommended rather than enjoined, so that men may strive to reach the highest degree of moral excellence.[104] Since he relates the law of love to the New Testament,[105] there is some correspondence between the law of love and this recommendation. But what is actually expounded under the name of natural law is neither a mere recommendation,[106] nor directed to Christians alone: it should be understood as an appeal to humanity, so that all men may realize virtue of a higher order.[107]

Grotius also uses such terms as the rules of humanity (*regulae humanitatis*),[108] natural equity (*aequitas naturalis*),[109] internal justice (*interna justitia*),[110] rules dictated by prudence (*regulae prudentiae*),[111] the duty of Christians (*officium Christiani hominis*),[112] virtue (*virtus*),[113] and humanity (*humanitas*),[114] in some cases interchangeably with the law of love.[115] None of these norms can be invoked as a just cause of war, but nevertheless it is advisable that they be obeyed. Moreover, if they are followed in the usage or practice of various nations and are sufficiently connected to the inherent nature of human institutions, then they may be identified with the law of nations or natural law. Thus these concepts in part overlap with law, but they are more extensive; by appealing to them, Grotius extends the scope of law to vast peripheral domains.

[103] III. x. 3; III. xi. 2. See also 9.4.3 (2).

[104] Prol. 50.

[105] II. i. 4(1), where the law of love constitutes the content of the law of the Gospel. Also see I. ii. 8(10); II. xxiv. 2(3). An example where the law of love and the law of the Gospel are differentiated is II. i. 10(1).

[106] Sometimes the law of love 'enjoins' something (II. i. 9(3)).

[107] Cassirer 1919: 132; Johnson 1983: 33.

[108] III. xiii. 4(3). [109] II. iv. 12(1); II. xi. 1(4).

[110] The title of III. xi. 2; III. xiv. 1(1); the title of III. xiv. 2; III. xiv. 6(4); etc.

[111] The title of II. xxiv. 5.

[112] III. xi. 19.

[113] I. ii. 6(5); III. xxiv. 1; III. xii. 8(1); etc.

[114] III. xiii. 4(2); III. xiv. 6(4), 9(1); III. xv. 1.

[115] For a similar use of internal justice and the law of love, see III. xi. 2. For humanity and the law of love, see III. xiii. 4. The use of the term virtue in III. x. 1(1) resembles the way Grotius refers to the law of love.

2.4.3. Obligation, Duty, and their relation to Right

(1) *Obligation and Duty*

There are three main concepts relating to obligation in *JBP*: *obligatio*, *debitum*, and *officium*. Grotius refers to obligation (*obligatio*) as an essential element of law when he explains the third meaning of *jus*. But he uses the terms *debitus* and *debeo*, adjectival and verbal forms of *debitum*, almost interchangeably with the concept of being under an obligation.[116] According to the second meaning of *jus*, *debitum* is said to correspond to *creditum*.[117] In another context, he divides duty (*debitum*) into obligation in the strict sense imposed by *justitia expletrix* and into what cannot be neglected with honour, although not imposed by *justitia expletrix*.[118] Here *debitum* clearly has a wider meaning than *obligatio*. Thus, *debitum* is used in three ways, whereas *obligatio* has a more confined meaning.

Duty (*officium*) properly refers to what is weaker in effect than *obligatio*. For example, when something is contrary to rules of *officium* but is given an effect of impunity, *officium* refers to that which is required by justice but which cannot be enforced once external effects are established by the law of nations.[119] *Officium* also includes what is required as virtue of a higher order. Examples are: *officium*, the failure to fulfil which is not unjust but contrary to the law of love,[120] and the *officium* of Christians to pardon the wrongs done to them.[121] However, when Grotius says that it is man's first duty (*officium*) to preserve himself in the same condition as that given by nature,[122] this does not necessarily mean what is required by a virtue of a higher order. And when he speaks of the *officium* of subordinates to their superiors,[123] it also includes the *obligatio* not to resist. Thus *obligatio*, *debitum*, and *officium* form a continuum, though they originally had a distinct scope or coverage.

(2) *The Relation between Right and Duty*

Right in the strict sense, which is the concern of *justitia expletrix*, corresponds to obligation.[124] In defining the concept of *jus*, Grotius

[116] I. i. 9–10. [117] I. i. 9(1), 10(2)–(3), 15(1).
[118] II. vii. 4(1). [119] III. iv. 2(2). [120] II. xii. 9(2).
[121] II. xxiv. 3(1); III. xi. 19. Also see I. ii. 7(9), (11).
[122] I. ii. 1(1). [123] Prol. 33. [124] II. xvii. 2(2), 3; II. xx. 2.

classifies right as the second aspect of *jus*, while including obligation as an inherent element in the third aspect. This suggests that he does not regard right and obligation as corresponding concepts. He declares that it is not unusual for an obligation to arise on one side without the other side acquiring a corresponding right, citing a form of unilateral promise (*pollicitatio*) as an example.[125] Even less does obligation correspond to the right of action (*actio*) under municipal law.[126] Similarly, in a formal war, external effects are conferred with respect to the right to kill and wound enemies and the right to acquire enemy property, which are permissible under the law of nations, but it does not follow that there are obligations which correspond to these rights.

It appears that Grotius formulates laws, especially natural law, mainly from the viewpoint of obligation or duty, acknowledging the existence of corresponding rights in cases which he judges are of concern as a matter of expletive justice. This is illustrated by the obligation, arising from the right of ownership (*dominium*),[127] or the duty of self-preservation.[128] Grotius has not yet reached the stage of development where laws are treated from the point of view of rights.[129] And his concepts of *obligatio*, *debitum*, and *officium* have a wider range than that of rights. The notion of natural right espoused by Hobbes and Locke never occurred to Grotius: again he was far from developing a theory that would have a truly revolutionary impact.[130]

2.5. The Relation between Various Laws

2.5.1. The Hierarchy of Laws

It is beyond doubt that for Grotius natural law, which cannot be changed even by God, has the highest rank among laws. He refers to divine volitional law, next to natural law, as the standard for judging the justness of things. While it is impossible for God to be

125 II. xi. 3; II. xiv. 6(1). 126 II. x. 9(1); II. xi. 1(4).

127 II. x; II. xvii. 2(2). 128 I. ii. 1(1).

129 In this respect, Hobbes's theory is the turning point. See Mizuta 1963: 7–8, 144–59; Berki 1977: 132–42. Although strongly influenced by Hobbes, Pufendorf constructed his system of natural law as a system of duties (*officia*).

130 D'Entrèves 1970: 58–63.

unjust,[131] human volitional law is not necessarily free from unjustness, since human weakness (*imbecillitas*)[132] must be taken into account.[133] Moreover, if a ruler orders what is contrary to natural law or God's will, one should not obey such orders.[134] Thus we can conclude that Grotius ranks divine volitional law higher than human volitional law.[135]

Regarding the municipal law and the law of nations, Grotius does not take up the problem of which is ranked higher, in accordance with his basic policy of not discussing municipal law. But laws narrower in scope than municipal law—e.g. the commands of a father to his children or of a master to his slaves, are ranked lower than either municipal law or the law of nations.

Though human volitional law is inferior to natural law, some rules which have their origin in human volitional law (e.g. the obligation of restoration deriving from the right of ownership)[136] may be incorporated into natural law through the concept of the nature of an institution.[137] Such rules thereby become superior to the volitional law, human as well as divine.

2.5.2. The Correlation of Laws

(1) *Natural Law and Volitional Law*

Grotius asserts that natural law cannot be changed by volitional law.[138] How then is volitional law related to natural law within this mandatory domain? First, volitional law may affirm or reiterate natural law.[139] Secondly, volitional law may reinforce obligations imposed by natural law by, for example, granting the right of action under municipal law.[140]

131 I. i. 17(2).

132 This is the key concept in the social-contract theory of Pufendorf (1934 ⟨1688⟩, II. i. 8; II. iii. 14).

133 I. iv. 7(2). 134 I. iv. 1(3).

135 See also II. xii. 22. 136 II. viii. 1(2); II. x. 1(5).

137 I. i. 10(4). See Fukuda 1971: 28–9. 138 I. i. 10(5), 17(2); I. ii. 5(1).

139 e.g. 'Thou shalt not kill' (Exod. 20: 13) is affirmed by every system of municipal law. See I. ii. 5(2). Also see II. x. 12.

140 This effect of reinforcement may also be brought about by the right of ownership or by contracts. See II. vi. 14(1); II. xvii. 2(1). However, the proposition, which has been so highly praised (e.g. Wieacker 1967: 293–4), that a bare agreement (*nudum pactum*), which under Roman law gives no right of action, has effect under natural law so long as the promisor's true intention is made known by some external act (II. xi. 4), the relation between natural law and municipal law is not sufficiently examined.

However, the proper role of volitional law is to regulate human conduct in the permissive domain of natural law. Grotius makes a distinction between matters in which moral goodness (*honestas*) is, as it were, a point that does not permit the slightest deviation, and those in which moral goodness has a wider range. It is with the latter class that both divine and human volitional law are wont to concern themselves.[141] But, given the diversity of the permissive domain of natural law, it is logically possible for rules of human volitional law, which only provide actions with external effects, to be contrary to natural law.[142]

This is necessarily a preliminary and general account: the relationship between natural law and volitional law cannot be understood schematically, since they often overlap and penetrate each other. The way in which this occurs will be discussed in detail in subsequent chapters.

(2) *Divine and Human Volitional Laws*

Grotius insists on the existence of the permissive domain also in divine volitional law.[143] He relativizes divine volitional law through this concept, as well as through the concept of specific divine volitional law and through the interpretation of the Bible. The purpose of this is to secure room for human volitional law concerning things whose justness is dubious in the light of the literal meaning of the teachings in the Bible. The argument in favour of the permissibility of just war is a typical example.[144]

(3) *Municipal Law and the Law of Nations*

As already noted, in principle, the relation between these two kinds of law should not present any difficulty for Grotius. But one specific context in which problems arise involves the use of concepts defined by municipal (especially Roman) law, but which

[141] I. ii. 1(3). See also I. ii. 5(1); II. i. 10(1).

[142] See 2.2.1. It would be totally inconsistent to accept at face value Grotius's statement: 'the law of nations . . . permits many things which are forbidden by natural law' (III. iv. 15(1)). Here permissibility just means impunity. See also 8.4.1.

[143] I. ii. 7(8). In both natural law and volitional law, those domains which are still without binding rules are domains in which everyone is allowed to act freely. But this does not mean that Grotius, like Hobbes, accepted that there was a sharp opposition between natural freedom and the state, or between the freedom of subjects and the law.

[144] I. ii. 5–9.

also concern the law of nations. Examples include ownership, inheritance, and agreement. According to Grotius, the law of nations in the strict sense concerns the mutual society among nations (*mutua gentium inter se societas*). He distinguishes it from the coincidence of various municipal laws, and also from common customs which emerge at different times and in different places, which are mistakenly called the law of nations.[145] But the law of nations by definition does not exclude customs prevalent in particular geographical regions, i.e. in Europe.[146] No clear standard is given to judge whether 'the custom accepted by many nations', which Grotius says should be distinguished from natural law,[147] means the law of nations in the strict sense or mere common custom. Thus there is room for an arbitrary interpretation of rules and institutions, some being approved in the name of the law of nations and others discarded as the mere coincidence of municipal laws or mere common custom.

(4) *Law in the Strict Sense and the Law of Love*

The law of love, partially overlapping with law in the strict sense, forms a vast peripheral domain which cannot be incorporated as law without some intermediary because, although it possesses a higher moral quality, human law should be laid down taking into account human frailty. But it is likewise difficult to ignore the law of love, as long as it overlaps for a large part with the law of the Gospel, and its precepts are sometimes incorporated into municipal law. The law of love and similar virtues are found mainly in the Bible. Thus the law of love not only provides an inexhaustible fountainhead of laws, but also secures the flexibility to interpret the Bible to reach Grotius's desired result.

(5) *The 'System' of Law*

Divine volitional law cannot be contrary to natural law. Human volitional law has its basis in the obligation to abide by agreements under natural law. Thus the various kinds of law discussed so

[145] II. iii. 5; II. viii. I.

[146] I. i. 14(1).

[147] II. xx. 41. When Grotius says that private acts of kings are subject to common rules of law (*communes legum regulae*), that law, as contrasted to natural law, embraces both municipal law and the law of nations (II. xiv. 2(2), 5).

far consist of a grand 'system' which, though not free from inconsistency, ultimately converges on natural law.[148]

2.6. Conclusion

As the discussion so far shows, Grotius's 'system' of law is strongly coloured by features that support the *status quo* and affirm the existing order. His 'system' is also fraught with contradictions and inconsistencies, some of a fundamental character.[149] On the other hand, those who read *JBP* seeking practical norms for regulating war will hesitate to say whether Grotius would have approved or disapproved of a war. In some sections of *JBP* Grotius affirms war, in others he calls for restraint. This ambivalence is inherent in the structure of *JBP*, which aims to regulate and restrain war at a number of different levels. Grotius avoids absolute pacifism and approves just wars. He seeks to restrain war by first eliminating unjust wars. He then calls for self-restraint even with respect to just wars. While recognizing, at the level of external effects, the equal lawfulness to both belligerents of killing and wounding enemies in a formal war, Grotius again calls for self-restraint in the exercise of this right. Grotius's distinction between rights properly so-called and aptitude led him to reject the justness of wars based only on the latter. By avoiding a direct correspondence between rights and obligations, he was able to insist that, even if one side has an obligation, the other side does not necessarily have a just cause for war against it. Rather, it may be possible to prevent war in advance by demanding that the obligation be carried out. The law of love, which we located within a peripheral domain to law, may also contribute to mitigating the ravages of war by being 'mistaken' for law. In this sense, whether the law of love is to be included in the domain of law properly so-called has only a secondary significance for Grotius. What is important is that this device for regulating war at various levels may indeed work to deter wars.

This lack of theoretical concern had consequences which Grotius could not have foreseen. Under this vulnerable 'system', through the diversity and ambiguity of its arguments, everything came to be ultimately based on natural law, and hence on human nature.

148 Dilthey 1957: 278.

149 Borkenau 1934: 148–51.

If man's social and rational nature were to be denied, Grotius's 'system' would fall apart. Indeed, within a few decades of the publication of *JBP*, this axiom faced a fundamental challenge from Hobbes's critical study of human nature. What remained was a motley collection of specific legal rules and regulations, natural as well as positive, secularized, and rooted in man-made institutions. Later still, from this motley assemblage emerged, among other things, a secular theory of private ownership, of contract, and of punishment.[150] Most of all, the later science of international law drew from it the idea of rules and principles regarded as valid among nations on essentially empirical grounds. If it was his methodological stance that gained for Grotius the reputation of being 'the father of modern natural law', what brought him the title of 'the father of international law' was that which survived the collapse of his 'system'—a development which he certainly would have been most reluctant to accept.

[150] Wieacker 1967: 290–9.

3

War

3.1. Definition and Lawfulness of War

3.1.1. Definition of War

(1) *All-Inclusiveness of the Concept of War*

How to regulate and restrain war was Grotius's primary aim in writing *JBP*. This is not only his own expressed view.[1] The whole structure of *JBP* is designed to achieve that practical aim. Grotius sought to construct a general theory of law for regulating and restraining wars in general. The war he actually assumed, however, was defined by the realities of war in his time. He conceived of war as armed conflict, including armed conflict between private persons (*privati*), i.e. private war (*bellum privatum*),[2] or more precisely, between independent powers at various levels, as well as armed conflict between states or nations, i.e. public war (*bellum publicum*). At the same time he understood war as having essentially the same function and structure as a lawsuit: as a remedy for violation of rights.

In the opening passage of I. i, Grotius recognizes the possibility that controversies may develop into war when they involve those who are not private persons belonging to different nations, kings, and those who have the same rights that kings have, such as nobles and free peoples.[3] Since war is 'undertaken in order to secure

[1] See Prol. 28 and letter from Hugo Grotius to Johann Crellius, 10 May 1631, in Meulenbrock 1964: 392–3 (English trans. in *Biblioteca Visseriana*, 7 (1928), 208).

[2] A struggle involving the use of force between private persons was generally called *bellum privatum*, and Grotius adopted this terminology (I. i. 2(1)). However, in those days a state did not have a monopoly over the use of force. Therefore, the term *bellum privatum* as used by Grotius is fundamentally different from what is today considered a struggle between private persons. See 3.3.4.

[3] '[F]ree peoples (*populi liberi*) in I. i. 1 (Lat. 1) refer to peoples constituting political bodies with supreme governing power. Instead of the expression 'conflicts between states', Grotius uses various expressions such as *reges ipsi, quique par regibus jus obtinent*, including *optimates* and *populi liberi*, when he refers to authors of public

peace', it is expected that the very act of dealing with war 'will finally conduct us to peace as its ultimate goal'.[4] As this statement demonstrates, *JBP* was, for Grotius, an attempt passively to realize the value of peace by controlling war as a negation of value. Such positive values as justice or goodness he considered only in terms of the realization of this passive value of 'peace'. This is shown in the expression 'x is not repugnant to (*non repugnare*) A', which appears consistently in *JBP*. Here x stands for the various institutions in the secular world, while A refers to standards of judgement such as nature, reason, justice, the law of nature, the law of nations, divine law, and the law of the Gospel. For Grotius what is important is 'not to be repugnant to' these standards of judgement. The positive realization of A is not at issue.[5]

The definition of war presented in I. i. 2 clearly indicates the all-inclusive nature of Grotius's concept of war. He defines war as 'the status of those contending by force (*status per vim certantium*)' and adds that this definition includes all categories of war, including private war. He maintains this theoretical framework throughout *JBP*. In the chapters following I. ii, Grotius first discusses wars in general and the substantive rights on which they are based, in terms of private wars and the laws that regulate the relations between private persons. He then proceeds to explain public wars between supreme rulers as possessing certain characteristics and effects, as well as discussing the laws that regulate the relations between such rulers.

The all-inclusiveness of Grotius's concept of war must be understood against the background of (1) its relation to preceding theories, (2) his concept of those with the authority to use force, and (3) the historical situation. As to the first, war had been treated in the history of European thought principally as involving the problem of whether it was permissible for Christians to take up arms, that is, how war could be justified in conformity with Christian teachings.[6] This was a central issue of the just-war doctrine developed by the Scholastics. In this doctrine, war is

wars (I. i. 1 (Lat. 1)). Such terminology indicates that the concept of 'state' had not yet developed fully as a concept independent of any specific person or political entity (whether a king or of an entire nation or people). See Bull 1977: 29.

[4] I. i. 1 (Lat. 1).

[5] See also Villey 1975: 620.

[6] Capital punishment was also discussed within the same context because its interpretation had to be in harmony with the precept 'Thou shalt not kill'.

considered basically from the viewpoint of one of the belligerent parties. Is a person, whether a king who decides to wage a war or a soldier who actually fights, allowed to kill or to wound others? Under what conditions are such acts allowed? These were major questions for the Scholastics.

In the case of the Scholastic just-war doctrine, the permissibility of self-defence involving the use of force was regarded as virtually self-evident. The discussion was focused on the permissibility of non-defensive war (offensive war or war of restitution). Moreover, since public authority was generally required to wage war, the question of private war was seldom discussed. Thus in the opening passage of his *De Bello*, Francisco Suárez (1548–1617) referred to wars between states as war properly so-called (*proprie dictum bellum*) and distinguished them from rebellions (*seditiones*), armed conflicts (*rixe*) between private persons, and duels (*duella*).[7] This does not mean that his concept of war completely excluded private war. It was difficult, if not impossible, to limit the concept of war to public war from within the strict Scholastic just-war tradition, since its major concern was whether and when an individual Christian could rightly kill his enemies.

By contrast, Balthazar Ayala (1548–84) and Albericus Gentilis (1552–1608) considered war as a phenomenon which should be subject to laws of war, and concluded that only wars between states or nations should be properly regarded as war. In particular, Gentilis not only limited war to public war but also paved the way for regarding as just any war between states or nations that met the formal requirements of legality.

Advocates of the traditional Scholastic just-war doctrine discussed four prerequisites for the lawfulness of war—its substantive causes (*causae materiales*), its authors (*causae efficientes*), its methods (*causae formales*), and its objectives or intentions (*causae finales*)—and insisted that all four be just. By contrast, in his definition of war as 'a just struggle between public armed forces (*publicorum armorum justa contentio*)',[8] Gentilis understood the term 'just' not necessarily in the sense of having a substantively just cause for initiating a war, but in the sense of being formally just in carrying out a war according to law. Thus Gentilis cleared the way for

[7] Suárez 1944 ⟨1621⟩ (Lat. 797).
[8] Gentilis 1933 ⟨1612⟩, I. ii (Lat. 17).

calling any war, whether just or unjust in its substantive cause, 'just' as long as it satisfied the formal requirements of legality.[9]

Gentilis's limitation of war to public war and his new interpretation of just war had great significance for Grotius, as is shown in the way he advances his argument concerning the application of the laws of war to formal war (*bellum solenne*). According to Grotius, a war formally declared by a supreme ruler is called formal war under the law of nations, and the term 'formal (*solenne*)' is used synonymously with 'just (*justum*)'. Moreover, regardless of the substantive just cause claimed by either belligerent party, a war may be just from the viewpoint of either side in the sense that the right to kill or wound the enemy, or to acquire property, is conferred upon both sides as a legal effect of a formal war.[10]

Yet Gentilis's concept of war was apparently insufficient for Grotius, who in an age of religious wars was determined to help restore peace to Europe. Grotius certainly lamented the fact that 'when arms have once been taken up there is no longer any respect for law'. He took great care to establish rules aimed at regulating the conduct of wars already started. But he regarded as no less crucial the task of restraining the propensity of men to 'rush to arms for slight causes, or no causes at all'.[11] This dual operation—regulating and restraining *both* the outbreak of war and the carrying out of war once started—is developed throughout *JBP*. Although he fails at times to maintain some of the lofty principles expressed in the Prolegomena in some parts of the body of *JBP*, Grotius never changes his attitude as far as this dual operation is concerned. The lengthy argument in Book II would have been unnecessary had his purpose been merely to restrain violence in the conduct of war between states or nations. In this sense, it is wrong to consider Grotius's concept of war merely from the viewpoint of the formalization of the concept of war and the regulation of its conduct.[12]

Secondly, in his attempt to construct a general theory of law with the aim of regulating and restraining war, Grotius assumed that a basic constituent unit of society was the household, with its head (*paterfamilias*) having governing power over his wife, children, and slaves. This reflects his admiration of European antiquity, a view shared by many of his contemporary thinkers. Grotius defined the

[9] Gentilis 1933 ⟨1612⟩, (Lat. 17–22).
[10] I. iii. 4(1); II. xxiii. 13(1) and (5); III. iv. 1–5.
[11] Prol. 28.
[12] e.g. Schmitt 1950: 131–4.

power of the head of a household as essentially similar to the power of the state, except that (1) whereas the former was supposed to assume a 'public' character, the latter assumed a 'private' character; (2) as a matter of fact, the latter was much less powerful than the former. However, these distinctions were of limited significance because the distinction between 'public' and 'private' was not well established, and the state itself was largely dependent upon the decentralized power structure. Consequently, in Grotius's system those who initiate and wage war on their own account range widely from states (*civitates*), kings (*reges*), or peoples (*populi*) to individual heads of households (*paterfamilias*).

Although this created difficulties about the relevance of certain issues to the realities of seventeenth-century Europe,[13] it can none the less be argued that an all-inclusive concept of war was appropriate to the conditions of his time. The European political structure in the early seventeenth century was not characterized by the coexistence of a limited number of sovereign states monopolizing the right and authority to use violence. Although absolutist states were steadily absorbing subordinate political entities, overlapping independent powers existed at various levels, all claiming the right to use force in achieving their legitimate aims. There was thus an extremely complicated political structure, a network of feudal relations, involving lords and vassals and a series of religious and political relations of alliance and hostility.[14] Because his concept of war was all-inclusive, Grotius was able to ensure the possibility of its universal application to the armed conflicts in Europe while avoiding, for example, the opposition that Ayala's theory may well have generated. According to Ayala, the armed conflict between Spain and the Netherlands was not a 'war'. Spain could have sought to 'suppress' the 'insurgents' without applying the laws of war. Such an attitude would have invited even more stubborn resistance from the Netherlands. Some later scholars argued that Gentilis's definition of war was superior to Grotius's because, in the former, war was limited to public war.[15] This argument ignores the basic difference between Grotius's age and that of scholars writing

[13] e.g. Grotius gives a detailed account of war slaves, but admits that enslaving prisoners of war was no longer usual practice in Europe (III. vii. 9). As to his dependence on the authorities of European antiquity, see also Sandifer 1940: 461.

[14] See 3.3.4.

[15] e.g. Nys 1894: 94; Phillipson 1933: 32*a* and 33*a*. For a more careful and persuasive comparison between Gentilis and Grotius, see Haggenmacher 1990: 133–76, esp. 156–72.

when the legitimate use of violence came to be virtually monopolized by states.

(2) *Criticism of the War-as-Status Theory*

As noted earlier, Grotius adopts the definition of war as 'the status of those contending by force', saying that it is more common to apply the term war to a specific status (*status*) than to a specific action (*actio*). As a consequence, Grotius is regarded by many as an originator of the doctrine of war as a status.[16] But it is difficult to identify Grotius's concept of war with the war-as-status theory, typically found in the non-discriminatory view of war which prevailed in the nineteenth and early twentieth century.

This war-as-status theory constituted the core element of the dualistic structure of the international law of war and of peace. Here war and peace were clearly distinguished by the metajuridical fact of the outbreak of war. For the international law of war, a system completely distinct from the international law of peace, to be applied, war had to be defined as a status independent of specific acts of belligerency. Historically, this dualistic concept of international law developed as a result of the rejection of the substantive concept of just war and of the monistic structure advanced by Grotius and other advocates of the just-war doctrine.

By contrast, the 'laws of war' in the just-war doctrine amounted to nothing more than a set of positive laws incorporated into the framework of a monistic system. According to Grotius, war is to be conceived as the same in principle as a lawsuit. Although the freedom to resort to war, granted to everyone under the law of nature, is severely restricted with the establishment of a state, it continues to be permitted if judicial procedure ceases to be available.[17] Consequently, there are as many causes of war as there are causes of lawsuits, and injury received (*injuria facta*) is the only just cause for undertaking war (*causa justa belli*). The fundamental character of a lawsuit as a measure for remedying the violation of rights is common to war.[18] To Grotius, peacetime and wartime are legally on the same continuum, being incorporated into a single framework.[19]

[16] McNair 1925: 31–3; Ishimoto 1958*b*: 291–3, 295 n. 5; Wright 1965: 9; Kelsen 1966: 23.

[17] I. iii. 2.

[18] II. i. 1(4) and 2(1).

[19] The view that Book II of *JBP* embodies the international law of peace, and Book III the international law of war (Vollenhoven 1931: 100–29; Vollenhoven 1934: 420) fails to account for this fundamental feature.

It is true that in *JBP* Grotius abandoned the definition of war as a specific action (*armata in armatum exsecutio*, the term *exsecutio* being synonymous with *actio*), which he had adopted in *De Jure Praedae Commentarius*,[20] and replaced it with the definition of war as a specific status. He did this for two reasons: to establish his all-inclusive concept of war; and to adopt the viewpoint of a third party independent of either party engaged in a war.[21] Grotius's definition of war certainly constitutes a revision of the Scholastic tradition that considered war from the viewpoint of one of the belligerent parties, a viewpoint which naturally tends to the definition of one war as a specific action. However, his concept of war is not so different from that of the Scholastics as his definition might suggest.

Rather, as Haggenmacher points out, Grotius adheres to the war-as-action theory as an important basis of his theory.[22] One can say that the definition of war as a status is a device to correct the narrowness of the war-as-action theory. For example, Grotius cites the argument advanced by Philo and Servius to the effect that the concept of war should include its preparatory stages.[23] Grotius adopted this definition to emphasize that war is not limited to purely hostile acts but includes a wider range of actions.

Were we to identify the definition of war as a status with the war-as-status theory, we would have to conclude that it is hardly realized in the entire presentation of *JBP*. The general definition of war as a status given in I. i has virtually no significance in *JBP* so far as specific arguments about war are concerned. This is only natural because Grotius wrote *JBP* within the framework of monistic just-war doctrine. Thus his definition of war as a status is by no means identical with the definition of war linked to the dualistic theory of international law prevailing in the nineteenth and early twentieth century.[24] His definition should be regarded as a general, non-technical one, with the war-as-action theory at its

[20] Grotius 1950 ⟨1604⟩, II (Lat. 14).

[21] For a similar view, see Haggenmacher 1983: 461.

[22] Ibid. 458–60.

[23] I. i. 2(1).

[24] It can be argued that the dualistic doctrine of international law became dominant as European capitalism reached a certain stage and demanded guarantees of private property and commerce even in time of war, as a private domain distinct from the public relations of states. In the 17th cent., Europe had not yet experienced such a development of industrial capitalism. See Ishimoto 1958*a*: 75–99; Ishimoto 1958*b*: 304–5 n. 22.

foundation.[25] To treat him as the 'father' of the war-as-status theory is to ignore the structure of *JBP* as a whole.

3.1.2. Lawfulness of War

In I. i, Grotius limits his discussion to a simple definition of war, as already indicated. He then gives a detailed discourse on the lawfulness of war in I. ii; iii. 1–5; and iv.

(1) *Lawfulness under Natural Law*

In I. ii, where Grotius demonstrates the lawfulness of war itself, the permissibility of war under natural law is proved a priori in I. ii. 1 and a posteriori in I. ii. 2, 3. The a priori argument is made up of two viewpoints: (1) what Cicero called the 'first principles of nature (*prima naturae*)', i.e. self-preservation; and (2) 'right reason (*recta ratio*) and the inherent nature of society (*natura societatis*)'. There are relatively few difficulties in justifying wars from the second viewpoint. Judging from the definitions given by Grotius—law is that which is not unjust; unjust is that which is repugnant to the inherent nature of society composed of rational beings; the law of nature is that which is dictated by right reason—it is natural that right reason and the inherent nature of society should serve as the standard for judging the permissibility of war under the law of nature. Neither of these forbid all forms of the use of force; they forbid only the use of force against society, i.e. a use of force that violates the rights of others. This conclusion follows from the given definitions and is theoretically coherent.

By contrast, there are many difficulties in introducing the principle of self-preservation. It is of course possible to base the concepts of self-defence and self-help on the principle of self-preservation. In *JBP*, however, the position of self-preservation according to natural law is not defined. Grotius leaves unclear the relationship between self-preservation (which he says should be taken into account first) and right reason, which should then be taken into account and which is regarded as the essence of the law of nature.

After commenting on the permissibility of war in the light of the first principles of nature, Grotius states:

[25] Haggenmacher also doubts whether Grotius took sufficient care to define accurately the term *status* (Haggenmacher 1983: 458). See also Kingsbury and Roberts 1990: 25.

> After these things have received due consideration, there follows a notion of the conformity of things with reason, which is superior to the body. Now this conformity, in which moral goodness becomes the paramount object, ought to be considered more precious than the things to which alone instinct first directed itself, because the first principles of nature commend us to right reason, and right reason ought to be more dear to us than those things through whose instrumentality we have been brought to it. Since this is true and without other demonstration would easily receive the assent of all who are endowed with sound judgment, it follows that in investigating the law of nature it is necessary first to see what is consistent with those fundamental principles of nature, and then to come to that which, though of later origin, is nevertheless more worthy—that which ought not only to be grasped, if it appears, but to be sought out by every effort.[26]

This passage is based on an abridgement of Cicero's *Teologia*.[27] However, because its argument is not fully developed it is not clear *why* and *how* the principle of self-preservation commends people to right reason. The ambiguity of Grotius may be contrasted with the clarity of Hobbes. While also starting from man's instinct for self-preservation, Hobbes claims that everyone must abandon his freedom and strive toward the establishment of a state, for otherwise the freedom granted to him for the sake of self-preservation will result in a condition of 'war of all against all (*bellum omnium contra omnes*)' and deny him the very right of self-preservation.

In justifying war from the viewpoint of self-preservation, Grotius says that 'since nature has given all animals sufficient strength to defend and preserve themselves . . . [in] the first principles of nature there is nothing which is opposed to war; rather, all points are in its favour'.[28] But this is hardly consistent with his position defining the law of nature as the dictate of right reason and rejecting the notion that it is common to both man and animal.[29] It can be argued that there would be no formal contradiction between the reference to animals and the permissibility of war under the law of nature if the 'first principles of nature' were not included in the law of nature. They are certainly not included in the *formal* definition of the law of nature as the dictate of right reason. However, the permissibility of war in the first principles of nature is discussed within the framework of the permissibility of war under the law of

[26] I. ii. I(2) (Lat. 15). [27] III. v and vi (ss. 17 ff.).
[28] I. ii. I(4). [29] I. i. II.

nature.[30] Furthermore, the justification of war from the viewpoint of self-preservation and self-defence, which allows counter-attacks by force against attacks by force, constitutes the most important ground for demonstrating the permissibility of war under the law of nature, the law of nations, and the law of the Gospel.[31] This indicates that Grotius regards the use of force for self-preservation and self-defence as the most natural and self-evidently justifiable use of force. The very use of the term *prima naturae* supports this. Thus 'the first principles of nature' can be characterized as falling within the framework of natural law, and their relationship with 'reason' should have been explained.

The relations between the law of nature as the dictate of right reason and the first principles of nature as embodying the principle of self-preservation are thus highly problematic. On the one hand, Grotius, like Hobbes, introduced the notion of self-preservation in justifying war. On the other hand, he constructed his entire theory on the assumption of the social nature of man, without dismantling the traditional view of man as *zoon politikon* (social and political being) which had prevailed since Aristotle. One of the main reasons why he failed to develop a clear argument locating the concept of self-preservation within natural law as the dictate of right reason lies in this traditional and unquestioning assumption of the social nature of human beings.

The permissibility of war under the law of nature is also proved a posteriori. Here the examples in the Old Testament and the opinions of writers in European antiquity are used as authority, proving that war has been unanimously recognized as permissible by various nations. In *JBP* the Old Testament is used in three ways: (1) as proof of the existence of natural law; (2) as proof of the existence of general divine law;[32] and (3) as a basis of a special divine law applied only to the Hebrew people. It is obvious that the use of the Old Testament here comes under the first of these categories. Two instances are cited as the basis of permissibility of war under the law of nature: (*a*) when wars were carried on without the special mandate of God; and (*b*) when God prescribed for his people general and perpetual laws concerning the method of

[30] See heading and text of I. ii. I. [31] I. ii. 1–4, 6–8.

[32] The law of the Gospel, which is provided in the New Testament, also belongs to general divine law—'general' as a concept prevalent in 17th-cent. Europe in the sense that it was valid for all Christians. But Grotius discussed the law of the Gospel under a separate heading. See below 3.1.2(4) and n. 43.

carrying on war.[33] Here one notices an implicit assumption that wars must have been permitted since they were carried out even without the special mandate of God and were recorded in the Old Testament. Such use of the Old Testament as the basis for inferring a general law may be problematic, since Grotius employs the Old Testament not only as a basis for general laws but also as a basis for a special divine law applied only to the Hebrew people.

The materials Grotius uses in his proof a posteriori based on the opinion of writers in European antiquity are virtually identical with those he uses in his proof a priori. The opinions of the Stoic school beginning with Cicero are first cited, followed by the jurists of ancient Rome. Despite the statements in Prol. 30, 58, and I. i. 12, Grotius rather relies on proof a posteriori, using the staggering volume of materials available, even in an area where he avowedly adopts proof a priori.[34]

(2) *Lawfulness under the Law of Nations*

Only a single sentence is devoted to the question of the permissibility of war under the law of nations: Grotius simply argues that there is sufficient evidence for its permissibility in the histories, laws, and customs of all nations (*historiae, & omnium populorum leges ac mores*).[35] He emphasizes that it is a mistake to say that wars were introduced by the law of nations. Only the definite form of and rules for initiating and waging war and certain legal effects accompanying such a war were introduced by the law of nations. These legal effects are only external ones recognized by those who wage formal war regardless of whether or not they had a substantive just cause for initiating the war.[36] This 'formal war accompanied by external effects' is one of the key concepts in Book III.

(3) *Lawfulness under Divine Law*

The permissibility of war under divine law is demonstrated by various references to the Old Testament. In principle, the argument goes as follows. According to nature it is not unfair for man

[33] I. ii. 2(1); I. ii. 2(2).

[34] See also Huizinga's critical remarks: 'Grotius's genius lies in his use of inexhaustible wealth of knowledge to explain and verify his theory through logical proofs, not in exploring and discovering the unknown. Thus antiquity and the biblical age still towered as an extremely solemn authority for Grotius' (1941: 477).

[35] I. ii. 4 (Lat. 18).

[36] Ibid.

to suffer to the full extent for whatever evil he may have committed, and that it is therefore permissible to avenge a death by killing the murderer.[37] This conceded, it will then be possible to justify the right to kill or wound (i.e. the right to make war against) anyone guilty of violating those values which are rated equal to life (e.g. honour and chastity), as well as those without which life cannot be safe (e.g. respect for political authority (*imperium*)),[38] on the ground that such a violator is no better than a murderer.

The function of divine law is to regulate human behaviour within a permissive domain where natural law neither dictates nor prohibits. To this extent, divine law has its own *raison d'être*. However, even as a basis for permitting war under divine law, judgement based on *natura* constitutes the starting-point: 'According to nature it is not unfair that each suffer to the full extent of the evil he has committed'.[39] Divine law is led by natural law, with God as the author of divine law confirming the proposition already prescribed by the law of nature: 'He who slew a homicide should be blameless.'[40] In other words, for Grotius, the nature of things or natural inclination exists even within the permissive domain of natural law, although there may be differences of intensity. Since this state of nature is based on reason that is common to God, the role of divine law is to confirm and make explicit the natural inclination of things existing in a dormant form.[41] Even though natural law and divine law are mutually independent in form, they are located on the same continuum in substance.

This logic is maintained throughout Grotius's demonstration of the permissibility of war under divine law, based on examples drawn from the Old Testament. To strengthen it, Grotius also uses the technique of turning some precepts of Hebrew law into general law. He states:

> [Because] it is absurd to think that on the one hand the Hebrew people were allowed to protect their moral code and safety . . . by means of capital punishment and to defend themselves by war, and that, on the other, the same course of action was not permissible to other kings and nations . . . [T]he law which was given through Moses justifies the inflicting of capital punishment by reasons which carry no less weight among other peoples than with the Hebrew people.[42]

[37] I. ii. 5(3) and (5). [38] I. ii. 5(7).
[39] I. ii. 5(3). [40] I. ii. 5(5).
[41] See also Johnson 1983: 32–3. [42] I. ii. 5(9).

But Grotius fails to indicate the basis for distinguishing the case where the Old Testament is interpreted as a special law applied only to the Hebrews. We can only say that Grotius 'solves' this problem by applying what we may term the principle of common sense in terms of societal norms. This will be discussed in 3.1.3.

(4) *Lawfulness under the Law of the Gospel*[43]

In his effort to demonstrate the lawfulness of war under various types of law, Grotius strove meticulously to demonstrate the lawfulness of war under the law of the Gospel. While he uses a total of only six pages (in the Latin text) in discussing the lawfulness of war under natural law, the law of nations, and divine law, he spends as many as fifteen pages on the lawfulness of war under the law of the Gospel. On the one hand, the Gospel provided the materials necessary for Grotius to regulate and restrain both the outbreak of war itself and acts of hostility during the war. But on the other hand, the Gospel presented a serious difficulty for Grotius. This is because it contains numerous passages on which the Christian doctrine of absolute renunciation of war (absolute pacifism) can be based. Grotius was in no way an advocate of such a doctrine, and thus he had to exercise extreme caution in dealing with the Gospel.

Grotius's basic attitude in demonstrating the lawfulness of war under the law of the Gospel consists of refusing to identify the law of nature with the law of the Gospel, and limiting the obligatory nature of the precepts contained in the Gospel. According to Grotius, acts which are forbidden by the Gospel are not always evil in themselves, but are treated as evil only after they are thus characterized by divine law. To observe the precepts of the Gospel is certainly preferable in terms of morality, but failure to comply does not necessarily constitute a breach of obligation. The precepts in the Gospel which forbid counter-attacks are more in the nature

[43] Here the law of the Gospel (*jus evangelicum*) can be found in the entire New Testament, in the teachings of patristic theology, in the interpretations of the New Testament by later popes, etc. Moreover, according to Grotius the law of the Gospel is considered 'the more perfect divine volitional law' (I. iii. 3). Therefore, in terms of the sources of law, the law of the Gospel is included in divine law. Logically speaking it is thus inappropriate to classify the subdivisions of law as the law of nature, the law of nations, the divine law, and the law of the Gospel. Grotius adopted this classification because he realized that the New Testament includes not only laws, but also what should be called lofty virtue, and because it was of great practical importance. This reveals his deep commitment to the practical viewpoint even at the cost of systematic consistency.

of advice to virtuous followers of Christ than obligations.[44] In terms of formal logic, this argument could invalidate the entire doctrine of the renunciation of war based on the Gospel. However, Grotius did not rely solely on such formalistic arguments to demonstrate the validity of his position. In particular he used two techniques which together constitute his main method of proof, and hold the key to understanding the framework of his thought.

The first involves sanctioning various existing secular institutions related to war, thereby indirectly justifying war itself. Grotius argues that Christians have always been involved in these institutions, and that neither Christ, the disciples, nor the church have ever repudiated them. The institutions cited by him range from military service and capital punishment to taxes and political authority in general. Grotius claims that if killing a person for just causes is permitted, then wars should also be permitted provided they have just causes. It is undeniable that political authority (including the institutions of capital punishment and the armed forces) has been generally acknowledged and accepted. This means nothing less than the approval of war.[45] According to this argument, existing institutions such as taxes and military service are taken for granted: on this very basis Grotius seeks to resolve the fundamental theoretical question of the lawfulness of war.

On this methodological issue, Grotius again differs significantly from Hobbes. The latter advanced an analysis of the most fundamental theoretical question concerning the establishment of a body politic by abstracting human beings from all existing social institutions and putting them, as it were, in a morally neutral and indifferent position.[46] This is why Grotius has been criticized as seeking

[44] I. ii. 6(1) and (2), 9(2) and (4).

[45] I. ii. 7.

[46] Hobbes (as well as Locke) is often said to have dismantled intermediate corporate bodies and begun his theoretical discourse with an analysis of the morally indifferent individual. However, it is difficult to say that even he was able to conceive of an 'individual' *completely* stripped of his traditional status as the head of the household (e.g. in *Leviathan*, xvii, Hobbes sometimes uses the concept of men and that of families synonymously; in xxii, he affirms the governing power of the head of the family). Similarly, in *Two Treatises of Government*, *Second Treatise*, v. 28, Locke assumes that the labour of a servant can be regarded as 'my labour', in vii. 85, he endorses the existence of slaves who 'cannot be considered as any part of Civil Society'. Also see Murakami 1979: 82–4, 119–29, 152–63, 224–39; Naruse 1984: 103–7, 123–5. But as Fukuda 1971 stresses, it is certainly true that there is a difference over this critical issue between *JBP* and *Leviathan*, taken in their entirety.

'to arrange . . . the existing social order as the substance of the law of nature'.[47]

Another often-used technique is to deny the general implications of the anti-war precepts in the Gospel. The passage in the Sermon on the Mount, 'whosoever shall smite thee on the right cheek, turn to him the other also' is not construed as meaning that no injury should be resisted, but is restricted to such minor injuries as a slap on the cheek. The precept 'Love thy enemy' (Matthew 5: 44) is incorporated into a hierarchy of discriminatory love based on the 'law of properly ordered love'. 'Recompense no man evil for evil' (Romans 12: 17) is interpreted as a prohibition of vengeance based on some private motive, not as a ban on revenge inflicted upon by a public power.[48] In short, the unconventional and 'dangerous' teachings of Christ—idealistic in theory, but perhaps too unrealistic in practice—are transformed into commonsensical precepts and rendered harmless.

3.1.3. Grotius's Framework of 'Common Sense'

The foregoing discussion bears on Grotius's basic posture, a posture that ultimately defines not only his attitude in interpreting the law of the Gospel, but all his argument. As noted earlier, Grotius's demonstration of the lawfulness of war under the law of the Gospel is based on (1) distinguishing between natural law and the law of the Gospel, and (2) restricting the obligatory nature of the precepts contained in the Gospel. However, Grotius provides hardly any justification for making the distinction mentioned in (1). The only substantive—and decisive—argument he offers is the rhetorical question 'who would say that we are bound by the law of nature to do what the law of Christ enjoins, that we expose ourselves to the danger of death for others?[49] Underlying this question is Grotius's conviction that no one with common sense could say anything so absurd. Presumably this conviction was shared by the overwhelming majority of his intended audience, so there was no need for further demonstration (proof a priori!).

The significance of this presumed common sense is also observed in (2). Since the Gospel is regarded as the most important support for absolute pacifism, Grotius presents a detailed argument demonstrating the lawfulness of war and rebutting the arguments of the

[47] Fukuda 1971: 28. [48] I. ii. 8(3), (9), and (12). [49] I. ii. 6(2).

absolute pacifists. Underlying his argument is the tacit assumption that the precepts contained in the Gospel cannot possibly be taken at their face value so long as they are aimed at human beings and not at angels. This assumption appears not only in Grotius's transformation of extraordinary precepts such as the principle 'Love thy enemy' into harmless, commonsensical precepts, but also in his adoption of a practical and utility-oriented approach.

While it may not be possible to ignore the significance of practicality and utility (*utilitas*) in *JBP*,[50] it cannot occupy such a prominent position in theory, considering Grotius's firm belief in justice.[51] And Grotius certainly did try to demonstrate the lawfulness of war from the viewpoint of justice. Nevertheless, he actually tended to adopt the practical and utility-oriented approach in *JBP*. This constitutes its basic feature, one which appears at all the critical points in its argument. It is evidenced, for example, by the line of argument Grotius adopts for (1) the ultimate basis for the binding force of agreements; (2) urging nations to refrain from waging punitive wars after having approved them as lawful; and (3) calling for moderation (*temperamenta*) in war after having allowed belligerents in a formal war to exercise their right to inflict injury under the laws of war. These examples will be discussed later.

Grotius's practical 'common sense' approach even makes it possible for him to justify the use of force by a private person under the law of the Gospel. When Grotius claims that private wars are allowed even after judicial tribunals have been established, he does not justify the use of force in general, but only for the purpose of defence. This is already suggested in I. iii. 1, where Grotius uses the expression 'the use of force to ward off injury is not in conflict with the law of nature'.[52] It is more directly shown in his interpretation of the precepts 'Recompense no man evil for evil' (Romans 12: 17) and 'Avenge not yourself, but leave your injuries to God's wrath' (Romans 12: 19). According to Grotius, these passages prohibit only revenge, not defence. The same is true of what was said to Peter, 'He that smiteth with the sword shall perish with the sword' (Matthew 26: 52). This certainly prohibits the use of arms, but it does *not* prohibit the use of arms on the grounds of self-defence.[53]

[50] Prol. 17–19.
[51] See Prol. 5–6, 16, and 57.
[52] I. iii. 1(2).
[53] I. iii. 3(6) and (7).

No other proof is given of the lawfulness of private war for self-defence, which can be established only by the hidden assumption of 'common sense' that it would be absurd to think that God prohibits a man to defend himself. While conceding that God has the right to order man to be killed rather than to kill, Grotius asks, 'But did God purpose to bind us in so extreme a fashion?'[54] The question contains its own answer, as evidenced by the statement: 'no such degree of forbearance is required'.[55]

Grotius's approach, assuming men of common sense, plays a decisive role in his interpretation of natural law as well. The law of nature is the basic frame of reference throughout *JBP*, and the most important specific standard for judging the lawfulness of war. It is also the most fundamental in the sense that it forms the basis of other specific standards of judgement, such as the law of nations and divine law, and more or less bears on every aspect of human social life.[56] Despite the importance attached to the law of nature as the standard in judging human affairs, it is supposed to be self-evident, as in the statement 'if only you pay strict heed to them, [the principles of natural law] are in themselves manifest and clear'. To verify his argument, Grotius uses a highly abstract test: 'whether anything is necessarily in agreement or disagreement with the rational and social nature of man'.[57] No conceptual framework is provided to ensure objectivity, or to prevent the contents of natural law based on such an abstract standard of judgement from being determined arbitrarily.

Grotius's overwhelming knowledge of Stoic philosophy, Aristotelianism, Roman law, canon law, and European history undoubtedly plays an important role in buttressing the objectivity of his argument. However, this vast knowledge merely provides the materials upon which he constructs his argument. He uses them not only when he claims that something is proved a posteriori but also a priori. It is the framework of common sense that constitutes the standard by which Grotius can *select* from his vast range of materials those necessary for him to support his general propositions.[58] Grotius has been highly valued for the 'transcendental'

[54] I. iii. 3(1). [55] I. iii. 3(3). [56] See 3.1.2(3). Also see I. i. 10(4).

[57] Prol. 39; I. i. 12(1).

[58] It cannot be denied that Grotius's theory, as a whole, tends to justify the existing order, which had traditional features, by means of the modern concept of law (see Borkenau 1934: 143–5; Fukuda 1971: 28–32). On the other hand, the

nature of his legal doctrine, in which justice is considered to possess the highest value and its significance is independent of other values.[59] Equally important, however, is the role of the standard or framework of common sense, including the practical or utility-oriented approach, without which one cannot grasp Grotius's theory in its entirety.[60]

3.1.4. Significance of the 'Secularization of Natural Law': The Theoretical Independence of Law from Religion and its Substantial Dependence

A key to the overwhelming success of *JBP* is the fact that the role of common sense is ingeniously linked to the revolutionary feature of Grotius's theory, the 'secularization of natural law'. It has been repeatedly pointed out that Grotius was not the first scholar to conceive the idea contained in Prol. 11: 'What we have been saying would have a degree of validity even if we should concede that which cannot be conceded without the utmost wickedness, that there is no God, or that the affairs of men are of no concern to Him.'[61] One can find similar expressions in earlier theories, especially those of the realists, who stood in opposition to the nominalists.[62] Still, *JBP* was epoch-making. As a matter of principle, Grotius consistently built his entire theory of the law of nature independent of God, thereby freeing Western legal thought from its long dependence on Christianity.[63]

existing order so justified is not merely an order of traditional social status but one which Grotius arranges to fit his own views. In this sense, it should be remembered that Grotius's natural law fulfilled the important function of *selecting* a certain number of institutions from those in existence. See also Bourquin 1926: 95; Villey 1975: 613, 617.

[59] Cassirer 1932: 323.

[60] The role of common sense can be seen not only in Grotius's practical and utility-oriented approach but also in his eclecticism. See Prol. 29.

[61] See also I. i. 10(5): 'The law of nature . . . is unchangeable—even in the sense that it cannot be changed by God. Measureless as is the power of God, nevertheless it can be said that there are certain things over which that power does not extend . . . Just as even God, then, cannot cause that two times two should not make four, so He cannot cause that which is intrinsically evil be not evil'.

[62] Sauter 1932: 87, 91–2; Rommen 1947: 71–2, 74; Gierke 1981: 73–5 nn. 44, 45; Haggenmacher 1983: 470–96 (but it is necessary to pay attention to the point the author makes at p. 501 n. 308). As to the detailed history on this point, see St. Leger 1962.

[63] On this point, Cassirer's *Aufklärung* (1932: 316–25), especially its philosophical and ideo-historical evaluation of Grotius goes to the heart of the issue. See also Link 1983: 13.

However, the independence of law from religion espoused by Grotius signifies neither the severance of law from religion nor the removal of religious elements from legal thinking. When Grotius published *JBP*, Europe was still Christian, although divided into Catholics and Protestants. While both sides were involved in protracted religious wars, the overwhelming majority of people in Europe remained pious Christians. As a matter of realistic political consideration, a monarch had to avoid the stigma of being seen as an impious Christian. Otherwise he would encounter great difficulty in winning the support and co-operation of feudal lords, noblemen, and knights willing to become allies or to fight under his command.

The seventeenth century is known in European history as the period of absolutism. However, none of the European monarchs of this period actually had absolute power. Anxious to gain the support of great feudal lords, church authorities, and the local independent powers, European monarchs advanced their rule only by paying careful attention to the delicate balance of multi-layered political powers. The monarchs and their ideologues, while insisting on absolute monarchical authority, admitted that monarchs obeyed the law of God and emphasized that they were pious Christians. Even Louis XIV, generally regarded as the model of an absolute monarch, was obligated to obey God because he regarded himself as an agent of God.[64]

JBP was written against this historical background and with full awareness of its significance. In this sense, the statement that the law of nature would be valid even if there were no God is a purely hypothetical proposition,[65] as Ernst Cassirer stressed.[66] True, Grotius made law independent of religion in an attempt to overcome the antagonism between Catholics and Protestants. But he continued to expound the normative *contents* of the law unfettered by religious sects but still defined by Christianity, taking in the full weight of Christianity's spiritual domination in Europe over the previous millenium.

In this most difficult task, Grotius had to be careful not to

[64] See Hartung 1949: 15–17, 20.

[65] Haggenmacher shares this view (1983: 496–503). But since Haggenmacher emphasizes—perhaps over-emphasizes—the continuity of *JBP* and *De Jure Praedae Commentarius*, he tends to overestimate the significance of voluntarism in *JBP*. See also Grotius's final claim to piety in Prol. 61.

[66] Cassirer 1932: 322. See also Sandifer 1940: 463.

incorporate any Christian precepts that were sharply in conflict with contemporary social and political realities. What he needed were precepts shared by his European contemporaries and capable of regulating human behaviour in the secular context of his time. In other words, only precepts that could function as societal norms were useful. These precepts were naturally based on ideas commonly accepted and shared by his European contemporaries, i.e. on their common sense.

In the case of proof a posteriori of natural law, this is explicitly recognized in the statement that 'an effect that is universal demands a universal cause; and the cause of such an opinion [that it be recognized among all nations, or at least the majority of civilized nations] can hardly be anything else than the feeling which is called the common sense (*sensus communis*) of humankind'.[67] It also constitutes the implicit assumption of the proof a priori of natural law, as noted earlier. The commonly accepted ideas referred to here were naturally those of the social class to which readers of *JBP* supposedly belonged, not necessarily the ideas generally shared by the masses. This is because *JBP* was addressed to those with direct or indirect control over the problem of war and peace.

Despite the declaration in the Prolegomena to the contrary (Prol. 11), modern readers are left with the impression that everywhere in *JBP* Grotius confuses law with morality, law with religion, and law with ethics. Despite this confusion, Grotius's claims are ultimately not *based on* Christian precepts, although they may *agree with* them. While achieving in principle the independence of law from religion, in reality Grotius uses Christian precepts as societal norms throughout *JBP*, thereby strengthening the persuasiveness of his argument to the maximum extent.[68] This seems to have been crucial in the widespread acceptance of *JBP* by his contemporaries.

Despite Grotius's genius, it is not surprising, considering the enormously difficult aim of restraining war, that *JBP* exerted only limited influence on the course of history.[69] Nevertheless, had it

[67] I. i. 12(1).

[68] Haggenmacher is quite right in criticizing the tendency of scholars to overestimate the significance of 'secularization' in Grotius (1983: 519–23). On the other hand, for the reason given in n. 65, Haggenmacher is prone to underestimate the theoretical independence of law from religion.

[69] Conversely, since *JBP* allows its readers wide scope for interpretation, it can be said that *JBP* served to reinforce in one way or another the claims of different types of monarchs, from pacifist to jingoist. Grotius is said to have uttered these

been even slightly biased in either of the two directions between which Grotius consistently balanced his argument, it could not have exerted even the influence it actually had.[70] In this sense, the criticism of 'confusing law with morality' made by positivists is rather a tribute to him, as is the criticism of 'corrupting the law of nature' made by rigorous Thomists.[71]

3.2. Just Causes of War

3.2.1. Causes of War in General

In this section we examine the problem of causes of war (discussed in II. i, xxii–xxiii), and present an outline of II. xvii–xix. The causes of war as discussed in *JBP* may be summarized as follows:

A. Just causes of war
  1. Defence (*defensio*) against imminent attacks on life, body, property, or other legal rights and entitlements: II. i. 3–18
  2. Restitution of Things (*Recuperatio rerum*): II. ii–xix
     (*a*) That which belongs to us: ii–x
     (*b*) That which is owed to us: xi–xix
        (i) That which is based on agreement (*pactio*): xi–xvi
        (ii) That which is based on wrongful act (*maleficium*): xvii
        (iii) That which is based on law (*lex*): xviii, xix

final words: 'By undertaking many things I have accomplished nothing' (Knight 1925: 289). No doubt these reflect Grotius's bitterness about his disappointing political and diplomatic life. However, his words also suggest the grave gap between the great ideals he sought to realize (regulating and restraining war, and perhaps even more importantly, reunifying the church) and his achievements.

[70] Falk rightly points out that 'what Grotius proposed seemed like the only way to acknowledge sovereign prerogatives without endorsing their most nihilistic implications. By drawing on rationality and natural law, Grotius encouraged the European rulers of his day to reconcile their practical pursuits as statesmen with their spiritual and intellectual heritage and thereby to fill, in an acceptable form, the moral vacuum created by the weakening, if not the total collapse of the Roman Church as a source of international unity and authority' (Falk 1983: 27).

[71] Such critics simply treat their own premisses as self-evident, reproaching other thinkers while ignoring their historical context. They also fail to understand a complex, multi-layered normative structure in *JBP* (see below 11.4), and simply label this complexity as Grotius's failure of distinction between law and morality (see e.g. Draper 1990: 193).

3. Punishment (*punitio*): II. xx, xxi

B. Unjust causes of war: II. xxii

C. Doubtful causes of war: II. xxiii

In II. ii–xix, Grotius discusses the substantive rights that, when violated, constitute the causes of just war, the interpretation of such violations, and related matters. His arguments in II. ii–xix deal with the specific content of the substantive rights which are to be protected not only by wars of restitution, but also by defensive and punitive wars. For it would be impossible even to discuss war unless the specific content of the rights to be protected (whether by a war of restitution, defence, or punishment) were established.

According to Grotius (II. i. 2 and xvii. 1), II. xviii–xix are supposed to deal with rights based on law (*ex lege*) as the third source of that which is owed to us (*id quod nobis detur*). However, he says in II. xviii. 1 that the various rights under the law of nature have already been analysed in II. ii–xvii, and proceeds to take up only rights under the law of nations in II. xviii–xix. Therefore one can also divide A(2) on 'restitution of things' into II. ii–xvii, which deals with rights under the law of nature, and II. xviii–xix, which deals with rights under the law of nations.

The problem of just causes of war is the most important issue about war in the history of European thought. As a theoretical question, however, it is treated only briefly in II. i. According to Grotius, the causes of war can be categorized as just or justifiable causes (*causae justificae*),[72] which should be considered from the viewpoint of justice, or persuasive causes (*causae suasoria*), considered from the viewpoint of utility or expediency. While virtually all those who wage war have persuasive causes, they do not always have just causes. There is no other just cause for waging war than 'injury received'. Wars lacking this are either wars of robbery, motivated by the desire for material profit, or wars of barbarity, waged for the sake of slaughtering the enemy.[73]

'Injury received' must involve the violation of rights in the strict sense. One should seek judicial redress when one's right is violated. But if judicial procedure is not available, it is permissible to resort to war as an alternative.[74] This does not mean that there is always

[72] Grotius uses the terms *causa justa* and *causa justifica* interchangeably. Both terms will be trans. as 'just cause'.

[73] II. i. 1(4); II. xxii. 2 and 3.

[74] I. iii. 2(1); II. i. 2(1).

an obligation to file a lawsuit before initiating a war. While private persons may have access to a court, there is no court with jurisdiction over supreme rulers. It is only natural that they should not be obligated to file lawsuits. Nor are they generally obligated to appeal to diplomatic negotiation or mediation prior to initiating war, although a higher morality always requires self-restraint.

Specifically, there are three just causes of war: defence, restitution, and punishment.[75] Defence (II. i. 3–18) basically consists of counter-attacks against imminent attacks on one's life, body, or property. Recovery of property is also included in the concept of defence, as long as the violation in question is presently being committed. The other two causes are involved when an act of violation has already been committed. Of these, restitution is an extremely comprehensive cause. It is not limited to wars against violation of property rights. Other rights guaranteed by war include the right to rule, or governing power (*imperium*), over others, rights held by supreme rulers provided in treaties, and rights under the law of nations concerning diplomatic missions and burying of the dead. Punishment is an 'evil of pains which is inflicted because of an evil of action'. Because of their evil-doing, those committing such acts place themselves in a position inferior to other human beings. Consequently, according to the law of nature, anyone other than those in the same inferior position is entitled to inflict punishment on the evil-doer.[76]

In this respect Grotius differs from the traditional doctrines of the Scholastics. A typical example of the latter may be seen in the doctrine of punitive war espoused by Francisco Suárez,[77] who formulated the doctrine of the late Scholastics in its most refined form. In order to characterize a war between equals as punitive war, the Scholastics limited the capacity to wage such a war to public authority, and placed that authority above its adversary by characterizing it as a minister or agent of God (*minister Dei*). Grotius was aware of his break with the Scholastic tradition on this point. This is evident in his *De Jure Praedae Commentarius*, where he states: 'The overwhelming majority of people insist that the right of punishment has been vested only in the state . . . However . . . every right [vested in the state] originates in each private

[75] II. i. 2(1) and (2).

[76] II. xx. 1, 2 and 3.

[77] Suárez 1944 ⟨1621⟩, sec. IIII. 6 (Lat. 805). See also Ito 1957*b*: 74–80, 180–1.

person . . . Thus it is evident that the right of punishment was held by private persons even before it was held by the state.'[78]

Having clarified this scheme of the just causes of war, Grotius indicates precisely and exhaustively what rights are capable of functioning as just causes. This is necessary in order to be able to pass judgement on whether a war that has broken out is just. At the same time, according to Grotius's way of thinking, as long as man is a rational being, he is expected to regard the catalogue of just causes as the only standard of judgement and to refrain from resorting to war by invoking causes that do not conform to those standards. Conversely, if one makes a demand that conforms to the catalogue of just causes, the person on whom the demand is made is also expected to recognize the reasonableness of the demand and to abide by it, for he too *should* act rationally.[79] To resort to war on an unjust demand, or to fail to comply with a just demand, is not only morally blameworthy but may actually cause a person to suffer various disadvantages. The outbreak of war itself will thus be restrained. In this way, to indicate specifically and exhaustively the substantive rights capable of functioning as just causes not only indicates the specific standards for determining what is just for and in war, but also constitutes the basic scheme for achieving Grotius's fundamental aim of minimizing the outbreak of war itself.[80] Thus he devotes all the chapters after II. ii to cataloguing comprehensively the substantive rights on the basis of which just wars may be waged.

[78] Grotius 1964 ⟨1604⟩, VIII (Eng. 89, 92). Tuck cites this as a basis for speaking of Grotius's commitment to individualism and for placing him in the genealogy of natural-right theorists (1979: 62–3). However, considering Grotius's traditional view of man stated in 3.1, Tuck's interpretation is doubtful. See also Onuma 1989: 135–6.

[79] See e.g. Prol. 16, 18, 20, 25, 27, 28, 29 and 39. This way of thinking, characteristic of the Enlightenment, is maintained throughout *JBP*. Considering Grotius's assumption of pre-established normative harmony (that man should behave rationally), we cannot help but recognize some truth in Meinecke's evaluation of Grotius: 'Great ethical ideals are rarely born without illusions' (1924: 262, trans. by Onuma). On the other hand *JBP* has a far more practical and utility-oriented tendency than is generally understood. We cannot agree that Grotius was merely an idealist or visionary who naïvely stressed the significance of justice. See 3.1.3; 11.5.3.

[80] See Kasai 1984: 44.

3.2.2. Unjust Causes and Doubtful Causes

(1) *Unjust Causes: II. xxii*

According to this way of thinking, any war waged other than for the just causes enumerated in II. i–xxi is inevitably unjust, and there would appear to be no need for further discussion. However, Grotius takes up some specific causes of war that have been historically controversial, and clarifies why he considers them unjust. This can be explained by his consistent concern for the practical viewpoint. The list of unjust causes discussed is of course not exhaustive, nor are the causes referred to always consistent with the overall logical structure of *JBP*. On the other hand, since they address issues diametrically opposed in terms of political conflict, they serve to reveal Grotius's political inclinations.

First, Grotius regards as unjust those wars waged under the pretext of the 'discovery' of things already held by others, and of the denial of the ownership of 'peoples deprived of reason'. These causes were relied on, either independently or in combination with other causes, in the acquiring of territories through the 'discovery of the New World'. Whether these causes were just or not was a crucial issue both in theory and practice, and was fiercely debated.[81] In *Mare Liberum*, published in 1609, Grotius had already disapproved of these grounds for acquiring territories.[82] In *JBP*, he maintains this position, claiming that the notion of discovery applies only to those things that belong to no one, and that ownership (*dominium*) requires neither moral or religious virtue, nor full intellectual capacity. It is therefore impermissible to claim for oneself by right of discovery that which is held by another, 'even though the holder may be wicked, may hold wrong views about God, or may be dull of wit'. Although he concedes that peoples wholly deprived of reason may not have ownership, he very much doubts that any such peoples exist.[83]

In *Mare Liberum*, Grotius had criticized those who recognized the title to universal jurisdiction (*titulus universalis imperii*) of the Holy Roman Emperor or of the Catholic Church.[84] This negative attitude is maintained in *JBP*. The title to universal jurisdiction

[81] See Schmitt 1950: 54–66, 69–109; Taijudo 1955.
[82] Grotius 1916 ⟨1633⟩, II. See also Ito 1973.
[83] II. xxii. 9, 10.
[84] Grotius 1916 ⟨1633⟩, III.

claimed for the emperor is not always in the interests of humanity: even if it were, profit cannot constitute a just cause of war, because the right to rule (*jus imperii*) cannot come into existence except by consent or through punishment (*ex consensu aut poena*). As for the title claimed for the church, Grotius argues that religious power is valid only in the salvation of souls, and as such does not apply to secular matters.[85] Furthermore, it is not permissible to rule certain peoples by force on the pretext that it is for their own good, because by nature no one is a slave.[86] One can feel in Grotius's rejection of these claims the pulse of the youthful Netherlands repulsing Spanish political domination, and carving the modern age out of a medieval Europe dominated by the spiritual authority of the pope and the Holy Roman Emperor. This is Grotius the humanist and rationalist standard-bearer of the 'secularization of natural law'.

On the other hand, Grotius did not regard a subjugated people's desire for freedom as a just cause of war, and thereby sanctioned the *status quo* in Europe based on the traditional order of social status and feudal privilege. The notion that a person or a people is by nature free can be valid only with regard to the law of nature that precedes all human institutions. True, no one is a slave by nature. But this does not mean that man has the right never to be enslaved. Thus 'those who from a legitimate cause have come into personal or political slavery ought to be satisfied with their status'.[87] Grotius lists consent based on free will, as well as defeat in war, as legitimate grounds for entering into slavery. This argument entailing the abandonment of freedom, i.e. the enslaving of a free man on the basis of consent (*ex consensu*), is ultimately used as a basis for the formation of the state.[88] This is a manifest example of the 'modern' concept of law justifying the existing political institutions based on the traditional social order.[89]

For Grotius there was nothing contradictory in this duality—in

[85] II. xxii. 13 and 14. [86] II. xxii. 12. [87] II. xxii. 11.

[88] I. iii. 8(1); II. v. 31; III. viii. 1(1).

[89] Rousseau vehemently criticized this argumentation (1915 ⟨1762⟩: 27–31), while Borkenau regards it as 'the most significant proposition in Grotius' law of nature'. In other words, Grotius evaded the problem of the conflict between rule and formal law, a fundamental question of the theory of state, and [ended up] supporting the feudalistic form of rule in a civil manner by unilaterally raising contract, one of the two basic categories, above rule, the other basic category (Borkenau 1934: 145, trans. by Onuma).

combining hostility towards medieval authority with the normative approval of the existing order. The European (dynastic) states system itself, which continued to exist even after Grotius's time, had this duality. It included the 'free' Netherlands ('free' used here as an extension of the medieval *privilegium*) and was essentially based on the principle of the dynastic and patrimonial state. While a state structure based on the traditional social order may have been reorganized in the development of absolutism, it never ceased to exist.[90]

At the same time, we must keep in mind that Grotius developed his arguments within the framework of a *general theory* of war. This is important when we compare Grotius with Vitoria. For Vitoria, who lived in the age of 'discovery', the situation of the American continent was new and posed a very real problem. There people lived in a manner different not only from that of European civilization but also from that of 'infidels' or 'pagans' already known to Europeans. Most importantly, they were being brought under European domination, as it were, before Vitoria's own eyes. The problem of the just causes of war that Vitoria took up in *De Indis* was closely related to the actual wars waged by the Spaniards against the Amerindians. Thus, Vitoria's argument reflected the actual relations between Europe and non-Europe.

Grotius is far less conscious than Vitoria of these relationships. The Spanish domination of the Amerindians on the American continent was no longer a decisive issue. It had become a domestic one in that the 'New World' was already under Spanish domination. Thus the process leading up to the Spanish domination of the 'New World' was significant for Grotius as one of the subject-matters in his general theory of war. Such causes as 'discovery' or 'lack of reason' were discussed as just or unjust causes of wars fought in the rivalry among European powers. Subsequent theories of international law retained this theoretical framework.

It is sometimes said that international law based on the natural-law doctrine was more universal than international law based on the positivism of the nineteenth century. This is true if the comparison is limited to these two. However, the 'universalism' referred to here is nothing more than the illusion of universalism. The 'universalism' of European natural-law doctrine was not valid in non-

[90] See 3.3.4.

European regions, where the overwhelming majority of humankind lived. Even the relations actually existing between Europe and non-Europe are basically abstracted from the domain of international law (although the case of Vitoria is somewhat different).

The unjust causes of war listed in *JBP* clearly demonstrate this feature of 'universalism' based on the natural-law doctrine. The question whether a war is just or not was treated merely as an issue among European powers contending with each other: who was entitled to rule territories which they had 'discovered' or colonized? On the other hand, colonial rule was treated as a domestic issue, not as an issue of international law. Whether it was lawful for European nations to wage war against non-European nations was hardly discussed. The converse question was never discussed, because it never occurred to European international lawyers that non-European nations should be subjects of international law. Thus the actual domination of non-European territories and peoples by European powers (i.e. the colonial system as a whole) was rendered unquestionable under international law and thereby tacitly accepted.[91] This issue is discussed in more detail in the Appendix.

(2) *Doubtful Causes: II. xxiii*

As noted earlier, Grotius asserts in principle the self-evidence of natural law. He concedes, however, that 'certainty is not to be found in moral questions in the same degree as in mathematical science'.[92] He thus provides guide-lines on the course of action to be taken when the cause of war is doubtful.

First, as a general guide-line where the cause of war is doubtful from the standpoint of one of the contending parties, Grotius suggests these precepts: 'Hold aloof from a doubtful matter'; 'If . . . there is doubt on both sides, that which is the safer is to be adopted.'[93] In short, 'When in doubt, refrain from war.' This precept is valid since wars inflict terrible injuries even upon the innocent.[94] This conclusion is an expression of Grotius's funda-

[91] On the basis of the right of national self-determination and the concept of positive peace, the United Nations has repudiated the claim that colonial rule is a domestic matter. This UN practice constitutes a fundamental criticism of the basic structure of modern Eurocentric international law.

[92] II. xxiii. I. This again indicates Grotius's practical orientation.

[93] II. xxiii. 2(2) and 5(I).

[94] II. xxiii. 2, 4, 5, and 6.

mental belief in the proposition 'Thou shalt not shed blood', which is maintained throughout *JBP*.

Although Grotius concedes that there may be doubtful causes, they should be rare, having regard to the principle of the self-evident nature of natural law. As a result, the measures he suggests for avoiding war when the cause is doubtful are quite insufficient. He lists conferences, arbitration, the drawing of lots, and duels between representatives of contending parties as methods for avoiding war.[95] However, even with regard to arbitration, which is believed to be the most effective of these peaceful means of settlement, he presents hardly any substantial discussion. He admits that those who are more powerful often scorn arbitration,[96] and responds by attempting to illustrate how many monarchies throughout history have resorted to arbitration, and by arguing that Christian nations are especially bound to pursue arbitration. As for conferences, the drawing of lots, and duels, he simply mentions these in passing.[97]

Grotius is fully aware that the pursuit of profit is in fact a cause of war. Yet he stands aloof and passes judgement on war only from the viewpoint of justice. He disregards the alternatives of restraining war by delving into its political, economic, and social causes, and effecting necessary changes in domestic institutions or in international systems. He seeks to restrain war on the assumption of the maintenance of *status quo*,[98] by explaining and judging realities from the normative viewpoint of various kinds of law, the Bible, and other sources. This is the alpha and omega of his method of restraining war. So-called peaceful means of settling international disputes are limited to cases where the causes are doubtful, and his discussion is wholly insufficient in its content,[99]

[95] II. xxiii. 7, 8, 9, and 10.

[96] II. xxiii. 8 n. 2.

[97] II. xxiii. 7, 9, and 10.

[98] When there is doubt about whether a particular cause of war is just, Grotius requires both parties to find conditions under which war may be avoided, but also insists that the burden of proof rests more with the party demanding *change* (II. xxiii. 11). This also reflects Grotius's tendency to support the *status quo*.

[99] To regard Grotius as an advocate of 'peaceful settlement of international disputes', especially of arbitration (e.g. Matsukuma 1985: p. ii) is questionable. Although Grotius was committed to the value of peace, he sought to achieve this goal through his just-war doctrine, not arbitration. See also Edwards 1981: 125–8. However, Edwards does not seem to be fully aware that so-called peaceful means of settling disputes were for Grotius himself an exceptional means for avoiding war. See also Kingsbury and Roberts 1990: 27–8.

thus revealing the limitations inherent in his method, despite his deep commitment to peace.

As noted earlier, Grotius concedes that certainty is not to be found in assessing the justness of war in the same degree as in mathematics. Thus he must face the question 'can a war be just for both parties?' While insisting that a war, in principle, cannot be just for both parties, he acknowledges that such a situation may exist due to unavoidable ignorance. Furthermore, from the viewpoint of its legal effects, war can be just (*justum*) for both parties.[100] The notion of the 'laws of war' under the law of nations in Book III is based on this assumption. Specifically, the rights of war, i.e. rights to kill an enemy and to destroy an enemy's property are conferred upon both parties to formal wars, regardless of the legitimacy of either party's claim to a substantive just cause.[101] In the process of shifting towards the non-discriminatory view of war which came to prevail in the nineteenth and early twentieth centuries, international lawyers came to inherit Grotius's 'laws of war' based on this assumption by separating them from the just-war doctrine, a tragic 'inheritance of Grotius' which will be discussed later.

3.2.3. Specific Just Causes

After presenting his general enquiry into the just causes of war in II. i. 2, Grotius provides a catalogue of specific just causes in II. i. 3–18 and II. ii–xxi. Here we deal with causes based on defence (II. i. 3–18) and wrongful acts (II. xvii) as well as rights under the law of nations (II. xviii–xix), as part of 'that which others owe us'. Other substantive causes will be examined in later chapters.

(1) *Defence: II. i. 3–18*

In Book I it was demonstrated that a war waged against imminent attack is permissible. This right of self-defence is not based on the unjustness of attack but on the fact that each individual is by nature his own defender. This right is recognized as valid even when the assailant is not responsible for the act. Even the use of

[100] II. xxiii. 13.
[101] III. iv, esp. iv. 2. See also II.4.2.

force on a third party other than the assailant—the so-called right of necessity—is permissible *under natural law* if there is no other recourse. In the last analysis, however, such use of force is prohibited by the 'law of love (*lex dilectionis*)', especially as set forth in the Gospel.[102]

Counter-attack by force is not permissible if the danger is merely assumed; it is allowed only when the danger is immediate and certain (*presens et certum*), and there is no other way it can be averted.[103] As long as these conditions are satisfied, the rights or legal benefits that should be protected by a defensive war include not only life and body, but also chastity, fidelity, and even property. Even a disproportionate counter-attack (e.g. killing a robber in defence of property) is permissible.[104] The disproportion in value between property and life is offset by 'the favourable position of the innocent party and the odious role of the robber'.[105]

As far as natural law is concerned, virtually the only exception to the lawfulness of self-defence is when the assailant is a ruler whose preservation is useful to the state. This is because natural law obligates people to fulfil not only the dictate of corrective justice, but in certain cases also to perform acts exemplifying self-control, bravery, and other virtues. Therefore, if one's assailant is a ruler whose life is useful to the entire nation, one is not allowed to kill him. Grotius's rejection of the right of resistance against superiors (I. iv) is maintained even in the case of self-defence against imminent attack by a ruler.[106]

The argument concerning self-defence outlined above is developed with private war in mind, but in principle it can also be applied to public war.[107] However, as Grotius himself admits, since there are no higher courts presiding over supreme rulers, wars between these powers will continue with no end in sight. This

[102] II. i. 4(1). This is an example of a multi-layered normative structure serving the aim of minimizing violence, which will be elaborated in ch. 11.

[103] II. i. 5. See also II. i. 17.

[104] II. i. 6, 7, 11–13.

[105] II. i. 11.

[106] II. i. 9. This apparently contradicts Grotius's own concept of natural law, which basically involves rights and obligations in the strict sense, and is distinguished from religious, ethical, and moral virtues. However, since he regards the existence of a ruler as an important condition for keeping the peace, Grotius is not much troubled by his inconsistency here.

[107] II. i. 16.

tendency is reinforced because public powers[108] possess the right to wage war not only for defence but also for punishment.[109]

To avoid this consequence, he seeks to limit the causes of (public) defensive war by banning war to weaken the growing power of a neighbour and war waged by 'one who has himself given just cause for war [to his enemy]'.[110] He also seeks to limit the possibility of punitive war through various techniques discussed under the cause of punishment in II. xx.[111] These attempts at limitation clearly show his delicate and difficult position, recognizing the realities of war and the weakness of absolute pacifism on one hand, and yet seeking to minimize the disaster of war by all means on the other.

(2) *The Obligation to make Restitution for Wrongful Acts: II. xvii*

As noted in the table cited at the beginning of 3.2.1, rights that justify restitution against injury are 'that which belongs to us' (II. ii–x) and 'that which is owed to us' (II. xi–xix). The latter is subdivided into three sources: agreement (II. xi–xvi), wrongful act (II. xvii), and law, specifically, the law of nations (II. xviii–xix).[112] The wrongful act here refers to an act of causing damage through a fault (*culpa*), whether of commission or omission. The obligation to make restitution arises under the law of nature. This obligation includes compensation by payment of damages as well as the restoration of the *status quo ante* (*restitutio in integrum*) and other compensatory measures.[113] It is enforceable by the court, and as such constitutes a just cause of war. In a formal war, however, some injuries are considered legal as regards their external effects under the law of nations. Thus an obligation to make restitution arising from a wrongful act is treated somewhat differently. If one party captures something in a formal war, the other party is not entitled to demand its return, even if the former lacks a just cause,

[108] In I. iii. 1, one who wages public war is defined as an 'author (*auctor*) with jurisdiction (*juridictio*)'. In I. v. 1, he is referred to as 'public power, in most cases supreme public power (*potestas publica, maxima summa*)'. The lack of precision of Grotius's definition may be explained by the historical realities of the distribution of power. See 3.3.4.

[109] II. i. 16. [110] II. i. 17 and 18.

[111] See ch. 7, esp. 7.2.2.2, 7.2.3, 7.2.4, and 7.4.

[112] II. i. 2; xvii. 1; xviii. 1. Kelsey *et al.* trans. *ex maleficio* in II. i. 2, as 'in consequence of a *criminal* act' (emphasis added), as a subcategory of 'that which is owed to us', following the phrase 'by contract'. This is not correct, for war as punishment is not discussed here. It should be trans. as 'wrongful act'.

[113] II. xvii. 1–5, 12–17, and 22.

and therefore his act of seizure may be considered as wrongful from the viewpoint of justice.[114]

The legal rights that serve as grounds for demanding restitution for injury must be rights in the strict sense of the term. A mere aptitude (*aptitudo*) is not enough.[115] If such rights are violated through the fault of another and thereby damage is caused, the obligation to make restitution will include compensation for any loss of property, and loss or expense incurred as a result of the injury, and any loss of future profits. Protectable legal benefits include not only life, person, and property (including intangible property), but also honour, reputation, and the like. Reparation for violations of these rights must also be allowed. Furthermore, a person who has forced another to contract by deceit or under duress has an obligation to free the victim from his contract.[116]

In addition to one whose wrongful act directly violates the rights of others, there are also those who may be liable for the damage such an act causes by virtue of their own acts or omission. These include those who order the act, who give consent, aid, or advice in carrying it out, or who fail to fulfil their duty in preventing the wrongdoer from committing the act. Grotius states that the order in which these people are held liable is as follows: (1) one who by command or otherwise has impelled the perpetrator to commit a wrongful act; (2) the perpetrator; and (3) others who are involved in the act. Thus the ruler of a state is liable for an act committed by his subject, and the master of a slave or animal for an act of his slave or animal, if the ruler or master is at fault.[117] Having developed this theory of liability, Grotius gained the reputation as the founder of the *culpa* doctrine in international law. Moreover, his claim has been understood as a theory of state responsibility based upon tacit approval (*patientia*) of a wrongful act by a state. This theory was generally accepted until the end of the nineteenth century, but is now criticized by many writers.[118]

Space does not allow a detailed examination of the problem here, but a brief comment is in order. It is not helpful in evaluating a theory to ignore either the historical circumstances or the theoretical

[114] II. xvii. 19. [115] II. xvii. 2(2).
[116] II. xvii. 2–5, 12–17, and 22.
[117] II. xvii. 6–10, 11, 20–1.
[118] See e.g. Tabata 1938: 757–76; 1973: 418–21; Brownlie 1979: 437–40; Yamamoto 1982: 78–103.

assumptions on which it was based. Grotius presented his theory as the antithesis of the notion of collective responsibility which was a characteristic of medieval Germanic law. He expounded it without drawing a sharp line between private persons and states. Moreover, he advanced his theory as part of a just-war doctrine. It is not difficult, then, to understand why his doctrine incorporates both the *culpa* principle and the concept of *patientia*. It may have been valid in later centuries to argue that private persons are the subjects of national law, and states the subjects of international law, and that the two are therefore responsible on completely different planes. By the nineteenth century, the right to commit acts of violence had been monopolized by the state and a sharp line was drawn between private persons and states. But it is difficult to fault Grotius on this account, for such assumptions were not made in his time.

In evaluating the *culpa* doctrine, we must take into account the fact that it was supported for nearly three centuries after Grotius. The 'secular age', which Grotius helped to carve out, was in broad perspective an age when a system of capitalistic economy permeated the world. True, Grotius himself lived in the age of mercantile capitalism, the earliest stage of capitalism, and his own view of man and society fell basically within the traditional framework of pre-modern Europe. In this sense we can say that Grotius was not a Grotian. Yet the secularization of law advanced by Grotius constituted one of the key elements in the capitalist development that followed. Even the scholars who criticize Grotius's *culpa* doctrine would not deny its historical significance. Their criticism should be understood as indicating that his doctrine is not appropriate to today's conditions.

(3) *Rights under the Law of Nations: II. xviii–xix*

In terms of system, II. xviii–xix correspond to the substantive rights which are based upon *lex*, the third source of that which is owed to us. However, Grotius actually takes up here only rights under the law of nations, as suggested in the table at the beginning of 3.2.1. The most important right under the law of nations is the right of legation (*jus legationum*). Ambassadors or legates are representatives exchanged between supreme rulers. But if there is a civil war and the two sides are so nearly equal that it is doubtful which side is in control, representatives sent by both may also be recognized as ambassadors. The receiving state cannot reject these ambassadors without just cause, and must respect their inviolability. The obligation to respect inviolability does not apply to a third state: even if a third state fails to respect it, this will not constitute a violation of the law of nations.[119]

According to Grotius, an ambassador may be rejected if there is any problem (1) with the sending state, (2) with the ambassador himself (the case of an atheist is cited), or (3) with the reason for sending him (e.g. if there is a strong suspicion that the ambassador is sent to incite the people of the receiving state).[120] This is clear enough. By contrast, there are differing views on the question to what extent the inviolability of ambassadors must be recognized. Grotius regards this lack of agreement as an unavoidable result of the fact that the law of nations does not arise from specific reason or rationality (*ex certis rationibus*) but is based on the will of nations (*ex voluntate gentium*). His own opinion is that ambassadors are immune from the jurisdiction of the receiving state. Since ambassadors are regarded as representing the supreme ruler of the sending state, they are generally treated as if they were outside the territorial jurisdiction of the receiving state. In principle, the receiving state cannot punish an ambassador even if he has committed a serious crime; the most it can do is to send him back to the sending state and demand that he be punished there. This exemption also extends to the members of staff of the embassy. The movable goods of the ambassador are likewise placed outside the jurisdiction of the receiving state. These privileges are recognized not only when the sending state and the receiving state are at peace, but also when they are at war. This is because not only do many problems arise in war which cannot be dealt with except through ambassadors, but peace itself can hardly be made by any other means.[121]

Grotius states that violation of the right of legation has constituted a just cause for war throughout history.[122] However, since diplomatic envoys at this time tended to play the role of 'high-ranking spies', and were often regarded as such, their diplomatic privileges were not yet fully established. For example, just after

119 II. xviii. 2(1) and (3), 3(1), 4(5), and 5.
120 II. xviii. 3.
121 II. xviii. 4, 6, 8, and 9.
122 II. xviii. 11.

Grotius was born, the Spanish ambassador to England, Mendoza, was engaged in a plot to dethrone Queen Elizabeth. There was a strong public opinion calling for the application of English law to punish him. Gentilis had to make every effort to persuade the English government not to bring Mendoza to trial. As Grotius himself admits at the beginning of this argument, there were various conflicting views on diplomatic privileges of the time. Thus, Grotius contributed to the establishment of diplomatic privileges by asserting as a fictitious notion the idea that ambassadors were as if outside the territory of the receiving state (*quasi extra territorium*).[123]

This provides a clue to Grotius's standards for expounding certain rules as rules of natural law, or of the law of nations. He regards natural law as originating in the social and rational nature of man. While drawing a sharp line between natural law and the law of nations in terms of their sources, he recognizes, along with arguments a priori, arguments a posteriori as a method of proving the existence of natural law. Indeed he relies heavily on the latter.[124]

As long as human communities coexist and have to maintain a certain level of relations, the right of legation is to be recognized. From the principle of man's social nature and the necessity of exchanges between nations, as well as from the weight of the historical materials which demonstrate the point a posteriori, it would not have been surprising for Grotius to expound the right of legation as a right guaranteed under natural law—especially if we contrast the 'self-evident nature' of the specific rules that Grotius discusses almost *ad nauseam*, from II. ii–xv. Many of the latter leave us in doubt as to why they are self-evident, yet he does not hesitate to claim that they are rules of natural law. Since Grotius recognizes nature (*natura*) in man-made institutions and incorporates them into natural law,[125] any existing institution has the possibility of being sanctified as part of natural law.

Nevertheless, the right of legation, together with the right of burial, is classified as a right under the law of nations. This is due to the historical situation noted above. The various rules had not yet fully developed into societal norms shared by his contemporaries as part of their normative consciousness. Similarly, after discussing

[123] II. xviii. 4(5). See also Nussbaum 1954: 95, 111.
[124] See 3.1.2.(1).
[125] I. i. 10(4).

the right of burial and citing other rights under the law of nations, Grotius states: 'For although all these rights are in some degree derived from the law of nature, yet from human law they acquire a kind of support, either against the uncertainties of conjecture, or against certain exceptions which otherwise natural reason seems to suggest'.[126]

As noted earlier, Grotius claims that the diversity of views concerning the inviolability of ambassadors is due to the lack of any distinct reason on which the rule of inviolability should be based. Since that rule is based on the will of nations, diversity inevitably exists.[127] This is not a very convincing argument. Even the law of nature, which is believed to arise from definite reason, is characterized by a lack of agreement as to its content no less serious than in the case of the law of nations. Everywhere in *JBP* Grotius had to grapple with divergent views, and he exerted enormous effort to establish his own view as the only 'natural' one. It is difficult to deny that the expression 'there are as many laws of nature as there are advocates of natural law' also applies to Grotius. Although in an over-simplified manner, Borkenau clearly points to Grotius's weakness:

> To say that the law of nature is directly self-evident amounts to a pure fiction . . . If Grotius tries to protect the law of nature, he is compelled to make every effort to deduce it from nature. But if he does this all of his views will be negated. For anything that needs to be proved cannot be self-evident.[128]

Nevertheless, for Grotius himself there was a difference of degree in the light of the standard of self-evidence. And this standard of self-evidence was guaranteed on the basis of the framework of the common sense discussed earlier.[129] True, among the individual rules, which Grotius claimed to be self-evident, some would not generally be so regarded. But on the whole, these rules were accepted and adhered to in his age, as well as in subsequent ages, due to their common-sense nature. This point requires further elaboration.

[126] II. xix. 6.
[127] II. xviii. 4(2).
[128] Borkenau 1934: 148, trans. by Onuma.
[129] See 3.1.3.

3.2.4. Realistic and Vulnerable Features of Grotius's Theory

As noted in 3.2.1(4), Grotius's 'secularization of natural law' took the form of a combination of the theoretical independence of law from religion and its substantial dependence. A key to understanding the overwhelming success of *JBP* lies in the fact that it consistently maintains a delicate balance between its mutually conflicting elements by mobilizing the most comprehensive materials and knowledge through a normative method. But this balance is fragile precisely because it cannot be maintained without the utmost subtlety.

One of the characteristics of Grotius's approach to the problem of war and peace is its unsatisfactory treatment of the means of 'peaceful settlement of disputes'.[130] Such means should be resorted to only when the causes of war are doubtful, a situation which he regarded as exceptional. Therefore, peaceful means of settling disputes were not expected to perform a substantial role. This is because he carried out his work on the assumption that to catalogue the just causes of war in a precise, specific, and comprehensive manner constituted a workable scheme for restraining the outbreak of war. This in turn was based on the premiss that since man is a rational and social being, aware of the actual disadvantages brought about by wars waged for unjust causes, he would be compelled to wage only just wars once a specific and comprehensive catalogue of just causes was compiled.

Fukuda once explained the intricacy and complexity of natural law characteristic of the continental natural-law school led by Grotius as follows: it has the tendency to 'cling to the view that natural order still exists even at a time when the medieval system of social status has clearly lost its self-evident nature, and the institutions corresponding to that view have evidently collapsed'.[131] It is certainly true that the law of nature advanced by the continental school constituted a huge and intricate 'system' of specific substantive rules. However, Grotius had to have such a specific and comprehensive set of substantive rules to achieve his fundamental objective of minimizing violence. And it is an exaggeration to say that Grotius 'tried to arrange the existing social order, without modification, as the substance of natural law' when 'the institutions

[130] See n. 95 and accompanying text.

[131] Fukuda 1971: 28 and 31.

corresponding to that view [that a natural order still exists] have evidently collapsed'.[132] As recent studies on absolutism clearly demonstrate, the medieval system of social status had not yet wholly lost its self-evidence in Grotius's time. Grotius certainly did try to 'arrange' the existing social order into the content of natural law. In so doing, however, he sought normatively to *re*arrange the existing order by *selecting* the features which should be preserved, thereby seeking to restrain outbreaks of war.

To catalogue the just causes of war thus constituted Grotius's most important task. As a matter of principle, these just causes had to be separated from religion because Europe was in the midst of religious wars. A catalogue of just causes which included 'true religion' would have been meaningless if a conflict occurred as a result of different interpretations by different religious sects. On the other hand, a rule from which were abstracted all traditional normative—including religious—contents could in no way have regulated the actual behaviour of Grotius's European contemporaries. Consequently, only religious and ethical norms *established as societal norms* had to be relied on. Moreover, for Grotius, expelled from political life in his own country, war could be regulated only through the study of jurisprudence (Prol. 25–6, 28, 30)—more accurately, through his multi-layered normative structure.[133] To that extent, constructing a general theory of law was of decisive importance. Yet it was not in itself the goal. It was no more than the most important *means* of restraining war available to Grotius.[134]

This being the case, the various religious and moral elements had to be introduced when this was deemed necessary to realize the lofty goal 'Thou shalt not shed blood', even if this led to inconsistency in his system. Moreover, as long as supreme governing power (*summum imperium*) was a necessary and useful institution for maintaining order and guaranteeing peace, the use of force against it had to be restricted as much as possible. It is on these bases that a defensive war against a third party and against an act of violence by a ruler, both presumably permitted under the law of nature, are prohibited by the 'law of love'. Likewise, the right to force virtues

[132] Ibid. 28. [133] See also II.4 and II.5.

[134] This constitutes a decisive difference from Pufendorf: constructing a general theory of law was itself the purpose of his major work *De Jure Naturae et Gentium libri octo*.

other than justice on others is permitted as part of governing power.[135]

One can also find the supremacy of the imperative 'Thou shalt not shed blood' in the relationship between rights under the 'laws of war' and the moderations (*temperamenta*) developed in Book III. In order to regulate the conduct of wars between supreme rulers and to secure peace based upon *faits accomplis*, Grotius goes into great detail in listing the rights under the laws of war that should be granted to those engaged in formal wars (III. iii–ix). But he sets forth *temperamenta* on a grand scale in an effort to restrict even the execution of these rights as much as possible. His statement, 'I must retrace my steps, and must deprive those who wage war of nearly all the privileges which I seemed to grant, yet did not grant them',[136] vividly indicates his intentions. And the rules and principles that Grotius claimed in the *temperamenta* included various religious and ethical norms which constituted societal norms for his European contemporaries.

The question remains to what extent Grotius *consciously* developed this systematic argument. Whatever the answer, one cannot deny that the conclusion follows from the logic inherent in *JBP* itself. Moreover, as noted earlier, one of the main reasons for *JBP*'s success was that it was a comprehensive work containing specific norms which incorporated traditional normative concepts, and as such, conformed to the realities of his day.

On the other hand, the realistic features of Grotius's thought are not limited to its conformity to traditional institutions and norms. His realism lay also in its conformity to what could be anticipated as the basic characteristics of the emerging political and social structures of Europe. His basic attitude of liberating law from religion conformed to the period of capitalism, of nation states, and of secularization, and constituted an indispensable element of this period, which was to continue for more than three centuries. Similar things can be said of his *culpa* theory, his non-discriminatory attitude in granting the rights of war to both parties to formal wars, and the 'voluntarism' of his theory of agreement. These features, conforming to what was anticipated for the future, clearly contradict the aspects of his thought which conformed to traditional features.

135 II. i. 9.
136 III. x. 1(1).

Later ages naturally came to accept the Grotius who espoused the former.

However, as Grotius came to be thus 'accepted' or 'inherited', his fragile 'system' gradually became unravelled. As a result, the intentions he himself had in constructing his 'system' were betrayed, its decisive weakness exposed. As noted earlier, just causes, the cataloguing of which is supposed to constitute the basic scheme for restraining wars, were regarded as 'self-evident'. What actually served to guarantee this self-evidence was common sense, or social convention, including its traditional normative contents. Likewise, the right to wage a defensive war against a superior or against a third party, as well as the right of belligerents to kill, injure, or destroy, were to be permitted under the law of nature or under the law of nations, and were denied only by means of the law of love and other lofty virtues. There was neither means nor logic in Grotius's theory to enable law in the strict sense to restrict these wars independently and by its own authority. From the eighteenth century on, as the secularization of societies and the separation of law and morals proceeded in Europe, the influence of the traditional moral values of Christianity and of other accepted ethical values, which guaranteed his fragile 'self-evident' law of nature, were reduced. With this change in the spirit of the era, the normative effectiveness of Grotius's theory of natural law was likewise reduced, not only as a domestic politico-legal theory, but also as a theory to regulate and restrain wars between nations—which Grotius strove so hard to achieve.

No doubt Grotius would have wanted to prevent his catalogue of just causes of war and of the various rights under the laws of war from being cut off from religion and moral virtues, and treading an independent course. And yet his theory was accepted in later periods primarily in terms of the independence and secularization of law, with his commitment to peace being treated more as a personal propensity. This was certainly not what he intended. But, however cruel it might be, it was the virtually inevitable consequence of his theory.[137]

[137] So long as the 'revival of the just-war doctrine' following World War II is considered from the viewpoint of Grotius's intention in seeking to regulate war through the application of law and justice between political powers, it appears to be a legitimate successor to Grotius's theory. However, to talk of revival or succession while virtually ignoring the differences between the historical reality of Grotius's

3.3. Authors of War

3.3.1. Authors of War in General

According to Grotius, the author of war is in some cases a private person (*privatus*), in other cases a public power, most often the supreme public power (*potestas publica, maxime summa*). In the former case, the war is a private war (*bellum privatum*), in the latter, a public war (*bellum publicum*). A public war is a formal war (*bellum solenne*) when it is declared, and has certain legal effects according to the law of nations.[138] If one of the belligerents is a private person and the other a public power, the war in question is a mixed war. This is nothing more than a classification, and hardly plays a substantial role in Grotius's later discussion. For instance, a war of subjects against their rulers is a mixed war, but a state of mixed war does not have any particular legal significance in itself. The legal significance and effects associated with wars of subjects against rulers derive from the relations that already exist between rulers and subjects.

There are three possible ways in which one may actually wage war: as a principal (*principalis*), as an auxiliary agent (*abjuvans*), or as an instrument (*instrumentum*). These are classified in *JBP* as follows:

Classification of Those Who Engage in War

1. On authors of war in general: I. v
2. When war is waged for the sake of others not for oneself: I. v. 2–4
   (*a*) As an auxiliary agent: II. xxv
   (*b*) As an instrument: II. xxvi
3. When war is waged for oneself as a principal (general cases: no detailed discussion)

3A. War of subjects against a ruler as an especially problematical case: I. iv

time and that of the 20th cent. is far too one-sided. Conspicuous examples include (1) the differences between the coexistence of multi-layered independent powers prevalent in 17th-cent. Europe and the monopoly of legitimate violence by states in the 20th cent.; and (2) the remnants as societal norms of medieval morality and religious consciousness in the former and their virtual disappearance in the latter.

[138] I. v. 1; I. iii. 1(1) and 4(1); III. iii. 1. In III. iii, Kelsey *et al.* repeatedly trans. *bellum solemne* as 'public war'. This is not only misleading, but incorrect. Here Grotius discusses various features of formal war, not public war.

The principal author of war is the one whose right has been violated. According to Grotius, 'by nature (*naturaliter*) everyone is the defender of his own rights; that is the reason why hands were given to us'.[139] Grotius does not provide a substantial explanation of authorship of war as a principal. He understands war as that which starts when a lawsuit ends, or the extension of a lawsuit. Therefore, those who enjoy substantive rights and can sue in their own right have the status of authors of war who wage war as principals. The doctrine of substantive rights, developed in Book II, can be understood as having been formulated principally with a view to those who wage war or bring lawsuits on their own behalf, i.e. as principals. Those who wage war as auxiliaries or instruments share the just causes that their principals possess.

Thus Grotius discusses the question of authorship of war only in connection with individual substantive rights,[140] and does not deal with it in its entirety. Likewise, although Grotius discusses in I. iii the question of public power and supreme governing power, in order to clarify the authorship of public war and of formal war, he does not provide a sufficient explanation of the relationship between just causes of war and authorship of war. Consequently, many important problems are buried under a complex and intricate body of discussion of individual substantive rights. Grotius may well have regarded authorship of war as a principal as too obvious and natural to require any explanation. The only case he thought it necessary to explain was where the lawfulness of war was in doubt because of some deficiency in the qualification of the principal author. This is why he discussed separately the question of resistance by subjects against a ruler.

3.3.2. War of Subjects against Superiors: I. iv

(1) *Historical Background*

Europe was ravaged by religious wars in the sixteenth and seventeenth centuries. Out of this religious passion emerged a group of passionate writings which advocated the use of force against tyrants, and insisted on the legitimacy of overthrowing them.

[139] I. v. I.

[140] On the capacity to own property or to exercise the right of ownership, see e.g. II. iii. 6; II. v. 2; II. xxii. 10(1). On the exercise of reason as a requisite for acts in the law, see II. xi. 5(1). On the question of capacity to inherit, see II. vii. 16.

Certain of these anti-monarchical doctrines occupied an important position in the spiritual and political life of Europe during this period. The well-known *Vindication against Tyrants* (*Vindiciae contra tyrannos*) appeared in the midst of the Huguenot War under the pseudonym Stephen Junius Brutus. Francisco Suárez, esteemed as a leading theologian, wrote *Defense of the Faith Against the Errors of the Angelican Sect* (*Defensio fidei*) in 1613 at the request of Pope Paul V. Since this book denounced the power of absolute monarchs, it was immediately banned in England and France.

The issue of the right of resistance was also debated in the Netherlands, in relation to its independence from Spain. The edict of the States General promulgated on 26 July 1581 was in fact the declaration of independence of the Netherlands. It began with the statement: 'It is common knowledge that the prince of a country is appointed by God to be the head of his subjects to protect and shield them from all iniquity, trouble, and violence . . .'. It pointed out that if a monarch fails to protect his subjects and deprives them of their perennial freedom, privileges, and customs, they should not recognize him as their monarch. It cited numerous evil deeds committed by Philip II, and stated that the Netherlands' subjects were treated not as subjects but as enemies. On these grounds it declared that Philip II had naturally forfeited *ipso jure* the throne of the Netherlands, and that the Netherlands no longer recognized him as its supreme ruler.[141] The edict thus relied upon the right of resistance, a doctrine which was fiercely discussed at the time. There was no way Grotius could avoid tackling it directly. Still, he exercised extreme care in his treatment of it.[142]

(2) *Significance of the Term* Bellum

The first characteristic of Grotius's treatment of this problem is that he uses the phrase 'war (*bellum*) of subjects against superiors'

[141] 'Edict of the States General of the United Netherlands by which they declare that the king of Spain has forfeited the sovereignty and government of the aforesaid Netherlands, with a lengthy explanation of the reasons thereof, and in which, they forbid the use of his name and seal in these same countries', 26 July 1581, Kossman and Mellink 1974: 216–28.

[142] e.g. Grotius must have taken into account the fact that Suárez wrote a strongly anti-monarchical *Defense of the Faith*, which greatly offended the secular powers in England and France. Despite the fact that he must have read Suárez, Grotius did not even mention his name in the Prolegomena. Scott attributes this to the fact that Grotius, then financially dependent on Louis XIII, did not want to be associated with Suárez (1944: 20*a*). However, Tuck warns against overestimating the late Scholastic school's influence on Grotius (1979: 58–9).

as his title for I. iv, and adheres to it throughout.[143] Europe in his time was still undergoing a historical process through which legitimate violence came to be monopolized by the state. Thus independent bodies at various levels still existed as distinct powers, although they were gradually being stripped by absolutist monarchs of their authority to rule others and of the means of enforcement (*Zwangsapparatus*).[144] Under these circumstances, Grotius regarded as 'war' all conflicts involving the use of force between various levels of powers, including 'private persons' (*privati*) and states. This is clearly demonstrated in his use of 'war' for subjects against superiors.

(3) *Grotius's Attitude towards the Right of Resistance*

Secondly, while vague about the legitimacy of resistance against a superior, Grotius stresses the virtue of obedience and thereby reveals his penchant for maintenance of the *status quo* between ruler and ruled. Although he admits that one must not carry out an order issued by a ruler which is contrary to natural or divine law, he stresses that one must not resist it by force.[145]

Grotius begins with a discussion of a tyrant who, having the legitimate title to rule, rules his subjects unjustly (*tyrannus quoad exercitium*). Characteristically, he mobilizes a range of authorities to support his argument that a war against a superior is not permitted. These include natural law, the Hebrew law (not as a special law addressed to the Hebrew people but as a general law), the law of the Gospel, and the traditional usages of early Christians. The bases of his argument also vary widely. They include the usefulness of secular power and its conformity to the will of God, the expectation of salvation through obedience even to unjust rule, the fact that unjust rule is exceptional, the natural tendency of man to submit

[143] I. iv (Lat. 79–93). Grotius usually uses the term *bellum*, although according to context he sometimes uses such expressions as 'resist by force (*vi resistere*)' (Lat. 80). Kelsey *et al.* trans. *bellum* as 'rebellion' or 'to rebel against' in the headings of I. iv. 2–6, where Grotius constantly uses the term. This is incorrect as well as misleading, particularly because they correctly trans. *jus belli* as 'the right to make war' in the headings of I. iv. 8–14.

[144] Goubert, who has made insightful observations on the 'state' system under French absolutism, avoids using the conventional term *état* in the title of his textbook on the French 'state' system from 1600 to 1750, using *pouvoirs* instead (1973: esp. its 'Positions'). What is true in relation to 18th-cent. France, where centralization had advanced more than in Germany, Poland, or the Netherlands, is true *a fortiori* for many European nations 100 years earlier. See further 3.3.4.

[145] I. iv. I(3).

to power and authority, and the analogical inference from the obligation of a slave to obey his master.[146]

Grotius then refutes the argument advanced by the Monarchomachs, who claim that a subordinate ruler (*magistratus inferior*) is entitled to resist a monarch. Grotius says that a subordinate ruler may be a public person (*publica persona*) in his relation to those subordinate to him, but is only a private person (*privatus*) in his relation to one who holds the supreme power (*summa potestas*). All governmental authority (*omnis facultas gubernandi*) possessed by the subordinate ruler is subject to the latter. Thus whatever he does contrary to the will of the supreme ruler (*voluntas summi imperantis*) is deprived of public authority and is regarded as a private act.[147] The Monarchomachs justified the right of resistance against the king by treating a subordinate ruler not as an organ of the king but as an organ of the state or kingdom. By contrast, Grotius repudiates the right of resistance traditionally accorded subordinate rulers by incorporating them into a hierarchical legal order, with the supreme ruler at the apex.[148]

Must one obey this law of non-resistance even in case of extreme and imminent danger? Despite hesitating at times, Grotius basically advises submission in this world, i.e. martyrdom, so that eternal salvation might be attained.[149] In this way, while prohibiting the execution of an order contrary to natural or divine law, Grotius seeks to resolve the question of resistance against tyrants *quoad exercitium*, not through disobedience but through submission and eternal salvation. He goes on to illustrate cases where the law of non-resistance would not be violated, i.e. where active resistance would be permitted. They are: (1) when a free people (a people under their own rule) resists its chief; (2) when a supreme ruler abdicates supreme governing power; (3) when a king alienates his kingdom or places it in subjection to another; (4) when a king tries to destroy his own people; (5) when it is provided as a condition of granting supreme governing power to a ruler that the subjects be released from the duty of obedience under certain conditions; (6)

[146] I. iv. 2 and 7. [147] I. iv. 6(1).

[148] This reasoning calls to mind Bodin (1577: 318, 333). Grotius adopted a normative approach with 'justice' as its core, which is radically different from Bodin's order-oriented approach characterized by the statement 'even a tyrant is a sovereign'. But he ended by reaching many of the same conclusions. See also Sasaki 1973: 104–9, 123–7.

[149] I. iv. 7.

when a king who possesses only a part of the supreme governing power tries to usurp the part that does not belong to him; and (7) when the freedom of resistance is reserved in the original agreement between the ruler and the ruled.[150]

Grotius proceeds to discuss the question of resisting a tyrant without title (*tyrannus absque titulo*). Here again he is reluctant to approve of anyone resisting a usurper, so long as the latter manages to maintain order. However, just as Grotius admitted a certain number of exceptions in the case of tyrants *quoad exercitium*, he approved the use of force to resist the usurper: (1) if the usurper gained governing power (*imperium*) by waging an unjust war and maintains his rule merely by force; (2) if a positive law exists which allows people to resist such a usurper; and (3) if the authority to resist is granted by the true possessor of supreme governing power (*qui jus verum imperandi habet*).[151]

As this discussion makes clear, while Grotius generally denies the right of resistance, in certain exceptional cases, he allows active resistance both against tyrants *quoad exercitium* and against tyrants *absque titulo*. Indeed, it might be argued that these exceptions were not as limited as his basic principle seemed to suggest.[152] Consequently, various interpretations of Grotius's view of non-resistance came to be advanced. At one extreme is Lauterpacht's opinion that the principle of non-resistance is merely theoretical.[153] At the other is Figgis's opinion that the exceptions are so narrow that it may be doubted whether any case but that of the Netherlands ever fell within it.[154] Between the two extremes are various interpretations, such as that resistance is permissible under natural law but not under the law of the Gospel,[155] or that Grotius solved the question in a 'tactful, comprehensive, and legally persuasive way'.[156]

It is true that Grotius cites as many as ten cases of justified resistance against both types of tyrants. Hence it is an exaggeration to doubt whether any case but that of the Netherlands ever fell

[150] I. iv. 8–14. [151] I. iv. 15, 16–18, 19.

[152] See Wolzendorff 1916: 254; Ottenwälder 1950: 95.

[153] Lauterpacht 1975*b*: 356. [154] Figgis 1916: 185.

[155] Ottenwälder 1950: 97. He cites in support III. vii. 7, but misinterprets the relevant passages as saying that resistance is permitted under natural law but not morally. It should be interpreted as saying that resistance by force is neither permissible nor pious.

[156] Edwards 1981: 129–35, at 130, rejecting Lauterpacht's claim as 'an unfortunate overgeneralization' (ibid. 132).

within the cases in which resistance is justified. However, in six of the seven cases where Grotius allows resistance against tyrants *quoad exercitium*, the supreme ruler is not a true ruler or has abdicated the supreme power. The one remaining case relates to the situation where there is a positive municipal law that clearly allows subjects to resort to active resistance.[157] Thus, Grotius's fundamental attitude towards the legality of armed resistance by subjects against a supreme ruler under natural law is one of denial. The cases he cites are for the most part those where a supreme ruler actually *loses* his supreme governing power. The only case where supreme governing *power* was regarded by Grotius as lost was one with which even the anti-Monarchomach Barclay would agree.[158] Furthermore, the three cases where he allows subjects to wage war against a usurper are limited to situations where it is patently clear that the usurper does not hold true supreme governing power. Subjects who wage such a war are not taking up arms against a supreme ruler in the true sense of the term.

Grotius himself suggested this when he proceeded from the principle of prohibiting armed resistance to discuss cases where resistance is permissible. In dealing with his seven cases, he states: 'We said that resistance cannot rightly be made to those who hold the supreme governing power. There are certain points which we now ought to bring to the reader's attention, in order that he may not consider those guilty of disobeying this law who in reality are not guilty [of disobeying the law of non-resistance]'.[159] In other words, those seven cases are not *exceptions* to his principle, because they do not involve resistance toward a supreme ruler in the true sense of the term. Thus it is not appropriate to construe the relationship between the principle of non-resistance and the seven cases as a principle subject to exceptions. Moreover, the three cases where Grotius allows the right to resist a tyrant *absque titulo* do not contradict any such principle. Even such typical anti-Monarchomachs as Bodin and Barclay recognized resistance against a tyrant *absque titulo*.

While persistently denouncing any form of support for or involvement in any manifest and grave violation of natural law, Grotius was always reluctant to grant his approval to the right of

[157] I. iv. 8–14. [158] See I. iv. 11. [159] I. iv. 7(15).

active resistance.[160] Rather as a humanist, a devout Christian, and a seeker of negative peace, he believed that man should seek a solution at an individual level through passive disobedience, including as its most extreme manifestation, martyrdom. His intention is also revealed in I. iv. 20, the last section of the chapter on the 'war of subjects against superiors'. Here he states: 'in case of a controversy the private individual ought not to take it upon himself to pass judgment, but should accept the fact of possession'.

On the other hand, if we attend to the cases where Grotius approved of active resistance not from the purely theoretical viewpoint of natural law but from the viewpoint of the positive law of his time, we can see that he was not as restrictive as his anti-Monarchomach tone suggests.[161] Moreover, as noted earlier, he was rather hesitant in asserting the principle of non-resistance. It is thus not necessarily meaningful to ask whether Grotius approved or disapproved of the right of armed resistance, and to demand a clear-cut answer. In understanding the basic features of *JBP*, it is important to recognize the duality in Grotius's principle regarding the right of resistance, a *duality* that gives rise to conflicting interpretations, especially his ambiguous attitude toward the relationship between secular power and God.

(4) *Grotius's Seemingly Modern but Fundamentally Traditional Framework*

This brings us to the third characteristic feature of Grotius's view of the right of resistance, i.e. the seemingly modern but actually tradition-bound feature of Grotius's theory of the state. On one hand, Grotius states: 'men joined themselves together to form a civil society (*societas civilis*) not by command of God, but out of their own free will (*sponte*), being influenced by their experience that isolated households (*familia*) are vulnerable to attack. [From] this origin state power (*potestas civilis*) is derived . . .'.[162] In Prol. 15 and II. v. 24(1), he also refers to *promito* and *pactio* in the context of the formation of the state (*civitas/societas civilis*). Thus it cannot be denied that his theory of the state involves some contractual features based on human design.

[160] Thus to say that Grotius is closer to the Monarchomachs than to the anti-Monarchomachs in his attitude towards the right of resistance, or that he is more supportive of the right of resistance (Ottenwälder 1950: 95), cannot be sustained.

[161] See Wolzendorff 1916: 256–60.

[162] I. iv. 7(3).

On the other hand, in requiring obedience to the supreme ruler, Grotius assumes that the power of the state exists for the sake of public peace and order, and stresses that this power is both taken for granted and natural in character.[163] Moreover, as is evident from the expression 'isolated households are vulnerable to attack', he has in mind households, which in themselves contain a superior–subordinate relationship, as a constituent unit of a civil society.[164] The power of a head of a household over its members (wife, sons and daughters, and slaves) is already given and regarded as natural, although it appears to be based on the principle of contract. The obedience of a subject to a king is based on the same principle as that of family members and slaves to the head of the household.[165]

One can also see the same characteristics, seemingly modern but fundamentally tradition-bound, in the relationship between the secular power and God. It is true that Grotius provides a secular basis for the power and authority of the state, as noted earlier. On the other hand, he often cites with approval writers who base the power of the state on the will of God, and relies on their authority as a basis for demanding obedience to state authority.[166] Furthermore, the phrase 'men joined themselves together to form a civil society' cited above as exemplifying the contractual composition of states is immediately followed by the statement: 'and so Peter calls this an ordinance of man. Elsewhere, it is *also* called a divine ordinance (*divina ordinatio*), because God approved an institution which was beneficial to mankind.'[167] For Grotius, power justified in a secular manner must not contradict the will of God. Here one can clearly see the *hypothetical* nature of the secularization of natural law by Grotius. In other words, there exists a *de facto* agreement or concordance between the conventional composition of political power and its conformity to the will of God.

In this way, Grotius justifies the secular power of the state again and again by expounding its conventional origin based on the free will of the people, by stressing its natural and given characteristics, and by claiming its conformity to the will of God. But Grotius does not justify everything done in the name of the secular power of the state. He fully acknowledges that a ruler who is supposed to be just may actually rule unjustly. Since the law of non-resistance applies

[163] I. iv. 2(1), 4(3)–(5).

[164] II. v. 1, 8, and 27.

[165] I. iv. 4(6).

[166] I. iv. 3, 4(1), 6(3), 7(9) and (15).

[167] I. iv. 7(3) (emphasis added).

to a true supreme ruler, nothing will be done to correct the unjust rule, unless there is a positive law that permits resistance. It is true that those who patiently subject themselves to such an unjust rule are promised 'eternal salvation'. However, can such a solution be acceptable to Grotius, who separated the problem of war and peace from religion, and adopted secular justice as the ultimate standard of judgement? The answer can no longer be found in the notion of the 'war of subjects against superiors'. It must be sought in the domain of 'war for the sake of others'—more specifically, in the lawfulness of war launched to save subjects of other rulers from unjust rule.

3.3.3. War for the Sake of Others

(1) *War for the Purpose of Assisting Others: II. xxv*

According to Grotius, one may wage war not only as a principal and for oneself, but also for the sake of others. To help others as much as possible is not only permissible but honourable.[168] First, since subordinate members of a family or subjects of a state can be regarded as if part of the ruler, it is lawful for the ruler to wage war for their sake if they possess just causes of war.[169] Grotius does not regard injury to a subject as necessarily injury to the state to which he belongs. Instead he discusses this situation under the category of war for the sake of others, such as wars fought for allies or friends. Allies, whether they are protected members or equal partners of mutual-assistance treaties, are on an equal footing with subjects in the sense that they should also be defended. Participation in war is permissible as long as it is provided in these treaties that when one party is engaged in a just war the other party is obligated to give assistance. Furthermore, if one can render assistance easily and without loss, one may wage war to assist one's friends even when such assistance has not been promised beforehand. Neighbourhood also constitutes a tie which binds men together and may summon them to mutual aid.[170]

These types of relationship, however, merely show typical cases where rendering assistance is permissible. As long as there are mutual ties among human beings, these constitute sufficient grounds for conducting a war for others, even in the absence of intimate

[168] I. v. 2(1). [169] II. xxv. 1(2). [170] I. v. 2(1); II. xxv. 4 and 5.

relationships.[171] Although with the formation of civil societies their rulers possess a certain power and authority over their own subjects, 'the exercise of the right of human society (*jus humanae societatis*) is not precluded' if the rulers commit a manifest wrong against their subjects, such as the persecution of Christians. The use of force to save others exposed to violence is, though not an obligation, thus permissible. Even if the subjects of a state are not allowed to resort to armed resistance, a ruler of another state may wage a war against a ruler of the former state. The prohibition of war against a ruler by his subjects arises from the fact that it is waged by *subjects*, and not from the substantive cause of war. In this way, a war waged in the name of 'human society' by a third party against a tyrant is justified. Grotius is aware that this justification is often used as a pretext for intervention based on selfish motives. But he adheres to his position, arguing that a right does not cease to exist because it is abused to some extent.[172]

Grotius's theory has a lacuna as a result of denying subjects the right of armed resistance, despite actual instances of unjust rule by a supreme ruler. Grotius tried to fill this gap by allowing a third party to exercise its right as a member of human society. It is obvious, however, that he failed. First, the intervention in question is regarded not as an obligation but a right that a third party *may* exercise. Thus there is no assurance that subjects suffering from unjust rule would be rescued. Secondly, as Grotius himself admits, he failed to provide any means of preventing the third party from exercising the right of intervention as a pretext to satisfy its selfish desires. Thirdly, one has to take into account various practical and utility-oriented factors before deciding to wage war for others. These factors are likely to have a restraining effect on decisions made from the viewpoint of justice. Fourthly, and most fundamentally, from the viewpoint of rectifying unjust rule, the very idea of denying subjects suffering from it the right of armed resistance

[171] I. v. 2(2); II. xxv. 6. Kelsey *et al.* trans. 'hominum inter se conjunctio' as 'the mutual tie of *kinship* among men' (emphasis added). This is misleading because the same term is used as a trans. of 'cognati' which has a different meaning. It is to be noted that Grotius, on one hand, overcame the narrowness of medieval European notion of universality by referring to the whole human society. On the other hand, he reveals his cultural mind-set by citing only the prosecution of Christians (not Jews or Muslims etc.) as a case where intervention is allowed.

[172] II. xxv. 8.

and granting the right of waging a war of intervention only to a third party is unnatural and unrealistic.

A war to assist others, even in the situations outlined above, is not permitted unconditionally. A prerequisite, common to wars in general, is that the party receiving assistance must have a just cause of war. This excludes treaties of alliance that would require assistance to any sort of war regardless of its substantive cause. Nor is one allowed to serve as a mercenary without due regard to the cause of the war in question. It is also impermissible to serve in the army merely for material profit, such as for plunder or for pay.[173]

But restrictions on a war of assistance do not concern only the justice or just cause of the party receiving the aid. War for the sake of others has traditionally been discussed not only as a question of the right to make war for others but also as a question of the duty to provide assistance to others whose rights are unjustly violated. Grotius denies this duty if there is a strong fear that one's own life or property may be endangered as a result of rendering the aid. This is because one may reasonably prefer one's own life and property to those of others. Furthermore, a ruler must not wage war for the sake of subjects unless this can be done without injury to the majority of his subjects, since the duty of the ruler concerns the whole rather than the parts. Indeed, when an enemy demands that a particular citizen, even if innocent, should be handed over, the state may abandon him if it lacks the power to resist the enemy.[174]

Grotius is pragmatic enough to value the lives of thousands above that of a single person, a position quite different from that indicated by the 'absurd' maxim *fiat iustitia ruat coelum*. His theory, while assuming the form of deduction from reason (proof a priori), is always given substance and specific shape by its practical and utility-oriented approach. Justice for Grotius is nothing other than justice within the framework of common sense, as is vividly demonstrated here.

Those who are Not Involved in War: III. xvii

Similarly, when others are engaged in war, a third party deciding whether to participate is to consider the matter not only in terms of justice, but also from a practical viewpoint. Hence it is possible for

[173] II. xxv. 9 and 10. [174] II. xxv. 2, 3, and 7.

a people to remain at peace while maintaining a degree of daily contact with the belligerents. On the other hand, the capitalist economy at this time was still in its primary stage ('merchant capitalism'). Commercial activities were not sharply distinguished from state activities, and were not well protected in time of war. Furthermore, the European armed forces had many mercenaries with little discipline, whose wages were often delayed. It was normal for belligerents to inflict violence without distinction on those not involved in the war, e.g. capture by regular warships and privateers, plunder of non-combatants by armies and mercenaries.[175]

While recognizing that it was not strictly necessary in terms of his normative system to discuss those not involved in war, Grotius was fully aware that 'in time of war on the pretext of necessity many things are done at the expense of those who are at peace'.[176] He stresses the principle, so far as the rights of belligerents are concerned, that unless the necessity is overwhelming, another's property should not be tampered with, and that 'more is neither to be taken nor used than necessity requires'.[177] He draws from history examples where military discipline was strictly maintained, and plunder punished, and cites two conditions for preventing harm to those not involved in war: appropriate wages and enforcement of military discipline. A king who fails properly to pay his soldiers, thereby inducing them to plunder his own or his neighbours' subjects, is responsible to those who are plundered.[178]

With regard to the attitude of a third party, when one of the belligerent parties has a just cause, it is the duty of those not involved in a war to do nothing to hamper its conduct of the war, and to refrain from doing anything to reinforce or assist one who wages an unjust war. However, when it is doubtful which party has the just cause, those not involved in a war must assume an impartial attitude towards both sides in permitting troops to transit or furnishing supplies to troops. The most desirable thing for those not involved is to remain friendly with both belligerent parties by

[175] Howard 1976: 2, 37, 42–52, 56; Jessup and Deák 1976 ⟨1935⟩, 10–13.

[176] III. xvii. 1.

[177] '[W]e must briefly repeat here what we have said elsewhere, that the necessity which gives any right over another's property must be extreme' (ibid). Here 'elsewhere' refers to II. ii. 10, where the question 'how it is permissible for one who is waging a just war to take possession of a place situated in a country free from hostilities' is discussed.

[178] III. xvii. 2.

making treaties with them and rendering to each the common duties of humanity.[179]

Thus, Grotius deduces the primary duty of those not involved in a war from his just-war doctrine: one must give assistance to the party waging a just war. Only when it is doubtful which party has a just cause does he qualify this by demanding those not involved to show impartiality. With the exception of the short description in III. i. 5, he does not discuss the various principles concerning capture and contraband in time of war (e.g. the principle that the flag covers the goods, *Consulato del Mare*, etc.).[180] Above all, he lacks a clear, comprehensive notion of neutrality. When discussing situations that would correspond to neutrality today, he merely refers to individual issues, using a variety of terms such as 'those who are of neither side in war', 'those who are not involved in war', 'those who are at peace', or 'those who keep out of war'.[181] One cannot discern here any notion of a neutral state possessing a fixed number of rights and duties according to the law of neutrality as an independent and comprehensive legal category.[182]

In later ages the law of neutrality emerged, transforming rules which according to Grotius were to be applied only in 'doubtful cases', into principles applied to neutral states in general. Some have cited Grotius as an authority in this transformation. However, his approach is fundamentally different from the later legal concept of neutrality, which was established as an important component of the non-discriminatory view of war. This concept of neutrality is based upon the strict distinction between an enemy and a neutral, as well as between state activities and private activities, and which eschews any legal judgement as to whether a war is just in its substantive cause. Thus, neutrality law is of little importance either in Grotius's own treatment—a natural outcome of his framework of the just-war doctrine—or in terms of his influence on later ages.

(2) *War Waged by Those as an Instrument of Others: II. xxvi*

So far Grotius had laid down guide-lines for those with complete freedom and independence to decide whether they should participate in war. It is also necessary to indicate the guide-lines for

[179] III. xvii. 3(1) and (3).

[180] Ishimoto 1958*a*: 75–99.

[181] See II. ii. 10; III. i. 5. See also Latin text of III. xvii (heading and text of s. 1; text of s. 2; heading and text of s. 3).

[182] For a similar view, see Grewe 1984*a*: 256–7.

those who lack such freedom, i.e. those who are subject to the rule of another. This is one of the traditional issues discussed repeatedly in the doctrine of Christianity: (1) whether it is permissible for Christians to serve in the military; and (2) assuming that it is permissible, whether it is permissible to fight in an unjust war.[183]

Grotius generally takes a negative attitude on these questions. First, subjects ought not to serve in the military if the cause of war is clearly unjust. It would be a crime to participate in an act that must obviously be avoided because of its cruel and inhuman nature, even if ordered by a superior to do so.[184] Secondly, when the just cause of a war is in doubt, Grotius is sceptical about the dominant view that one must obey the judgement of one's superior and perform one's military duty. This view contradicts the principle that when in doubt one must choose a safer course, i.e. the principle of avoidance of war (II. xxiii). Moreover, refusal to perform one's military duty does not necessarily constitute an act of disobedience. In the case of an unjust war, there is no disobedience in refusing to fight. Even if it were adjudged disobedience, the sin of disobedience is a lesser crime than homicide, particularly the killing of many innocent people. Since disobedience is encouraged even when the cause of war is doubtful, a subject must absolutely refuse to participate if he believes that the war in question is unjust. This is particularly true if the war is not a defensive war.[185]

In this way, subjects are encouraged to refuse participation in an unjust or doubtful war. A good ruler, for his part, should exempt from military service those who are not satisfied with the cause of the war, but may impose extraordinary taxes upon them instead. Moreover, avoidance of military service is to be admitted even if there can be no doubt with respect to the just cause of war, because it is not right to compel Christians to serve against their will.[186]

Lastly, when subjects are engaged in an unjust war, the enemy, although waging a just war, does not have a true and internal right (*jus verum ac internum*) to kill innocent subjects who are not responsible for the unjust cause. These are allowed to defend themselves. This does not mean that the war is just on both sides. The just cause is on the side of those who wage a just war. What is unjust, however, is the individual act of trying to kill those who

[183] For a concise treatment of the subject, see Miyata 1978: 30–74.
[184] II. xxvi. 3. [185] II. xxvi. 4(1)–(8). [186] II. xxvi. 5.

could properly be spared. Against such an act, even the subjects of those waging an unjust war are allowed to defend themselves.[187]

Grotius's views on participation in an unjust war appear inconsistent with his views on the right of resistance. Considered from the viewpoint of how subjects should act when ordered to engage in an unjust war, the two questions raise the same issue. Nevertheless, Grotius treats the right of resistance as part of the problem of war waged by a principal, while he treats participation in an unjust war as a problem of participation in war as an instrument, advocating obedience to an unjust order for the former, but disobedience for the latter. This apparent discrepancy bears on the relationship between the contemporary reality of various independent powers which could engage in war and the method he adopted to incorporate them 'systematically' into *JBP*. We will next examine this problem.

3.3.4. The Realities of War in Seventeenth-Century Europe and the Unsystematic, Comprehensive Nature of *JBP*

The Europe of Grotius's time was in a complex, transitional period. On one hand, the multi-layered independent powers (*pouvoirs intermédiaires*) based on medieval principles of social status were about to be integrated into centralized territorial states. On the other hand, this very process of integration was brought about by a *reorganization* of the principle of social status: some aspects of this principle were denied and others utilized (recall, for example, how absolutist monarchs expanded and strengthened their power by marriages and inheritance). A territorial state about to emerge as a unified body, at least in appearance, was often not fully integrated, with public and private elements not fully separated. This transitional character—in which the public institutions of the modern state retained patrimonial and private features—could be observed in every state institution in Grotius's age, including territoriality, judicial power, the bureaucracy, public finance, and local administration.[188] The status of those who wage war was no exception.

In medieval Europe, the right of 'private persons' constituted an

[187] II. xxvi. 6.

[188] Brunner 1968: 194–7; Oestreich 1969: 159, 183; Tochikawa 1984: 268–428; Naruse 1988: 38–43, 353–66.

inseparable part of law and order. Violation of this right in itself constituted an infringement of legal order. Private persons who vindicated their rights by self-help defended the legal order at the same time.[189] This medieval regime of decentralized power and authority had already disappeared by the time Grotius wrote *JBP*. The prohibition of private war, hardly achieved by the Peace of God and the Truce of God, came to be generally effective, and was accompanied by the establishment of absolutist powers, with a few exceptions such as Poland and Scotland. Armed conflicts gradually assumed the character of war between nations waged under royal authority.

On the other hand, the decentralized principle of social status remained influential in various respects, in particular in determining various aspects of the practice of war. For example, the War of Independence of the Netherlands was a war of alliance involving various provinces such as Holland and Zealand, although its aim was the formation of a single unified state. The armed forces basically belonged to each member province. While authority to command them was entrusted to the United Provinces, it was based on the consent of the provinces.[190] The Huguenot War and the Thirty Years War were, to use a modern expression, a mixture of civil and international war. Both were involved in the Netherlands' War of Independence, through intricate relations of alliance, inheritance, and marriages. The very fact that the nobility and various local powers were able to vie with one another for supreme governing power, or to engage in conflict with the king, reflects the fact that the means of violence were still shared. The king was basically the most powerful among the nobles, and armed forces formed under the royal authority had an aspect of an alliance of various armed forces led by nobles.[191]

Most of these forces were composed of mercenaries. Their commanding officers (*condottieri*), who appeared at the end of the European Middle Ages, were of varying stature, ranging from the near equals of monarchs, to minor nobles who served as commanders of small military units. Even in Grotius's age, these *condottieri* played an important role in European wars as professionals who offered their troops under contract and undertook wars for hire. The professional commanders naturally strove hard

[189] Kern 1956: 163, 169, 185–6, 192–3.

[190] Kurihara 1969: 79–81, 106–25.

[191] Goubert 1973: 114–21.

to minimize injury to their troops. Thus their general strategy and tactics entailed living off the enemy's country by avoiding decisive battles until the enemy's war funds dried up and its troops deserted, thereby forcing the enemy to accept conditions of peace unfavourable to it. This, coupled with the spread of strong fortresses made possible by the development of fortification techniques, served to prolong wars and to intensify the injuries inflicted on non-combatants.[192]

Despite the fact that 'money is the nerve of war (*pecunia nervus belli*)', a bureaucratic fiscal system capable of securing regular money from subjects had not yet been fully established. Monarchs who initiated frequent wars for whatever reasons—pursuit of material profits, honour, religious zeal, etc.—often found themselves unable to pay sufficient wages to their mercenaries or even to their own soldiers. Soldiers regarded plunder of battlefields as normal, even if they were being paid for their service. Plundering was all the more normal if wages were unpaid. The Sack of Antwerp by Spanish forces in 1574 (the Spanish Fury) is all too well known, but it stands out only because of its scale and thoroughness. Plunder was virtually synonymous with war.[193]

The situation was basically the same at sea. Except for decisive warfare involving large fleets, a situation that occurred only rarely, naval warfare in Grotius's day was a series of constant, paralysing operations directed at commercial activities on the high seas. Many of the participants in this 'warfare' were privateers, essentially indistinguishable from pirates. To build and maintain a navy required huge amounts of money, involving as it did an infrastructure of dockyards, shipwrights, pilots, cartographers, and ordnance experts. Monarchs incapable of bearing such a huge financial burden issued letters of marque to professional privateers and granted them a veneer of 'state' character. To this extent privateers assumed the status of those who wage 'public' wars, sometimes even becoming national heroes.[194]

Finally, the European wars of the day were largely tied to religious conflicts. Although religion in some cases was used as a pretext

[192] Howard 1976: 16–19, 24–7, 34–7. Also see Institute for the Study of Western History 1955: 119–58; Wijn 1970: 204–12.

[193] Howard 1976: 24, 29, 37. See also Yamauchi 1987; 1988.

[194] Howard 1976: 42–53. See also Otsuka 1969: 85. According to Andrews, 'Protestantism, patriotism and plunder became virtually synonymous' (1964: 16).

for waging war, in other cases religious zeal itself constituted an important cause of war. Other wars assumed the character of an armed resistance by various independent powers opposed to a royal authority bent on establishing a territorial state and on curtailing their power. Even though wars in sixteenth- and seventeenth-century Europe may in certain respects be characterized as international wars guided by *raison d'état*, one cannot deny that many of them, such as the Huguenot War, the Netherlands' War of Independence, and the Thirty Years War, assumed other complex features. In these wars, both royal authorities and those opposed to them resorted to employing mercenaries and privateers.

These are the wars that Grotius witnessed and condemned as wars that 'even barbarous nations would be ashamed of'. Thus he felt compelled to demonstrate that 'there is a common law among nations, which is valid alike for war and in war'.[195] It was wars such as these which were characterized by disorder and lack of discipline, partly public, partly private, and which were unbearable for non-combatants. The realities of war then are reflected in *JBP*, although Grotius was reluctant to admit that he was discussing contemporary issues.[196] He stressed the importance of *temperamenta* under the law of war, prohibited belligerent troops from plundering those not involved in war, and regarded the regular payment of troops and the enforcement of military discipline as the best policy for preventing plunder.[197] His own statements suggest the extent to which war was almost synonymous with plunder, with extensive injury and loss inflicted on the civilian population.

On the other hand, the transitional and complex character of war provided a difficult problem for him. Grotius dealt with the realities of war and sought to regulate and restrain them, but he could not digest them properly in his 'system' of law. In particular, the complex features of the authorship of war—partly centralized and partly decentralized, partly public and partly private—made a theoretical solution extremely difficult. Grotius tried to overcome this difficulty by introducing a comprehensive concept of war, and by then distinguishing between public and private war. In the end however, he failed, because he had to deal with wholly different phenomena according to the same principle: international wars

195 Prol. 28. 196 Prol. 58.

197 III. x–xvi, esp. xii; xvii. 1 and 2(3).

between absolutist states and lawsuits between private persons. This is revealed in his inconsistent treatment of subjects of a state in discussing: (1) the lawfulness of war in aid of subjects of other rulers, (2) prohibitions upon subjects participating in unjust war, and (3) requiring of subjects obedience to unjust rule.

As discussed in 3.3.3, according to Grotius, injuries inflicted on subjects may justify war waged to assist *others*.[198] In this sense, a subject is an independent power (*sui juris*) on an equal footing with an allied state. In addition, under the name of 'human society', Grotius accepts that wars may be undertaken to protect the subjects of other rulers from unjust rule.[199] Moreover, while subjects are prohibited from taking up arms against a supreme ruler, such armed resistance is regarded, at any rate, as a war (*bellum*) undertaken by one author of war against another. These features clearly reveal how far Grotius's image of the world departs from an international society comprised of sovereign states that have achieved a monopoly over legitimate violence, are mutually independent, and are obligated to refrain from interfering in the internal affairs of other states. His image of the world is nothing less than a multi-layered aggregate of independent powers, including not only states but also non-state actors on various levels.[200]

On the other hand, the world in which Grotius lived was no longer the medieval European society where each member of the society was considered a bearer of the entire legal order. Grotius himself denied the right of resistance on the part of subordinate rulers by treating them merely as private persons if they acted against supreme rulers.[201] Moreover, he claimed that in an ordinary situation where the courts are functioning normally, private persons are allowed to resort to force only for self-defence.[202] Subjects (referred to as *instrumentum* of war in II. xxvi) are literally nothing more than instruments in large-scale wars waged between absolutist states.

Thus subjects of a state assume an ambiguous character considered from the viewpoint of the authorship of war. They are mere

[198] II. xxv. 1. [199] II. xxv. 8(2).

[200] See Oestreich 1969; Brunner 1968: 242–80, 281–93; Goubert 1973; Corvisier 1976: 14–22; Naruse 1979: 3–60; Ninomiya 1979: 183–233; Tochikawa 1984: 268–428. Also see the references cited in these works.

[201] I. iv. 6(1).

[202] II. i. 16. Also see I. iii. 3(6) and (7); I. iii. 2.

instruments in a war launched by a supreme ruler against others, but nevertheless possess complete capacity as authors of war in their relation to other subjects, to supreme rulers of other states, and even to their own supreme ruler. But their 'war' is considered unlawful in relation to others as long as the courts are functioning normally, and in relation to their own ruler at all times, due to their non-transferable personal status.[203]

These ambiguous characteristics inevitably raise the problem of 'system' in *JBP*. As noted earlier, it would be appropriate to discuss the problem taken up in II. xxvi, as a continuation of I. iv, as far as the problem itself is concerned: an order to participate in an unjust war leads to the question of the lawfulness or otherwise of a refusal to obey such an order, which in turn leads to the lawfulness or unlawfulness of resisting it by force. Indeed, some of the materials Grotius uses in the two chapters are the same (e.g. the armed forces of Emperor Julianus).[204] Nevertheless, the problem is partly discussed in Book I in the form of 'war waged for oneself' and partly in Book II in the form of 'war waged for others'.

For Grotius himself, the justification for this treatment lay in these two classifications of war: 'war waged for oneself' versus 'war waged for others', and furthermore, as subcategories, 'war waged for others as an auxiliary agent' versus 'war waged for others as an instrument'. However, this leaves open the question whether such classifications are properly integrated into his discussion. Even if this is answered in the affirmative, it remains problematic that wars of subjects against superiors were discussed in I. iv, before this classification is set out in I. v. This is a rather manifest defect for a book written by such a mature jurist as Grotius.

However, we must remember that, although Grotius organized *JBP* as a treatise on jurisprudence, establishing a distinctive arrangement of natural-law doctrine, let alone 'international-law'[205]

[203] II. xxv. 8(3).

[204] I. iv. 5(2); II. xxvi. 3(4).

[205] In the intellectual history of Europe before Grotius the term *jus gentium* was used in an ambiguous and complex manner, both in its relation to natural law (*jus naturae/lex naturalis/jus naturale*) and to the common nature and content of municipal laws. In citing earlier theories and historical records, Grotius tries to use the term *jus gentium* as precisely as possible, classifying it into four cases: (1) when it signifies natural law; (2) when it signifies the law of nations properly so called, based on the consent of all nations; (3) when it signifies *jus gentium* under Roman law; and (4) when it signifies common rules found in many domestic laws of European or

doctrine, was not his primary objective. Rather, it was the practical purpose of regulating and restraining war, or minimizing bloodshed. As noted earlier, the question whether subjects should obey or resist if their ruler rules them unjustly had long been a doctrinal problem for Christianity. In the early seventeenth century, when the stable medieval order was about to collapse, it also became an important practical and political issue. Consequently, although he took extreme care in treating this problem, he had to discuss it not only from a systematic but from a practical viewpoint. This is one of the reasons why the 'war of subjects against superiors' is discussed in detail in I. iv, before I. v, where the authorship of war is taken up as a general theme of discussion.

Furthermore, the authors of war are those who wage war as principals, and who are also the subjects of the substantive rights discussed in Book II. The discussion in II. i–xxvi, is generally based on this 'self-evident' assumption. The only cases discussed independently are those exceptional cases where the lawfulness of war waged by someone as a principal is questionable because of particular characteristic features such as subordinate position (I. iv), or where war is waged not for oneself (II. xxv–xxvi). It seems, at first glance, curious that the general theory of the authors of war (I. v) is expounded after the distinction between public and private war (I. iii) and the question of war against superiors (I. iv) have been examined. However, this 'general theory' is offered merely as a supplement, with the exceptional cases where war is made for others examined later in separate chapters. Thus, it may not be proper to treat I. v, as a general theory of the authors of war, and I. iv, and II. xxv–xxvi, as specific explanations.

It is also difficult to present a coherent interpretation of the two (seemingly) conflicting statements on the lawfulness of war after the establishment of courts. On one hand, Grotius says that the freedom to wage war is restored when the judiciary is not available (I. iii. 2). On the other hand, he justifies private war after the establishment of courts by emphasizing the lawfulness of self-defence and limiting the Gospel's prohibition on violence to

Christian nations. Grotius sometimes allows himself to be influenced by conventional usage and fails to adhere to his own classification. But it is clear that he did not use *jus gentium* solely to designate international law in the modern sense of the term. See also Hrabar 1925: 551; Ago 1983: 389, 391; Onuma 1987: 405–43, esp. 435–7.

vengeance motivated by private interest (I. iii. 3). Accordingly, private persons are not permitted to wage wars of restitution or of punishment. Although he sometimes reaffirms the latter position (e.g. II. i. 16), he develops his whole argument in Book II on the assumption that *any* subject of law, including a private person, is entitled to file a suit, and hence to wage war of any kind if the judiciary is not available. Here again, from the systematic viewpoint, one cannot deny that there is an apparent weakness.

But if we consider who were the actual authors of war at the time, we must ask how realistic it would have been to propose such 'logical' interpretations. It is only when a judicial system capable of remedying violations of rights is available that one is prohibited, as a private person, from exercising the right to use force for restoring property or inflicting punishment, which one possesses as an inherent right. When these preconditions are lacking, the very classification into private and public persons loses its significance. The author of war in question is in fact an independent power (*sui juris*) with its own authority and means of violence. It becomes a 'private person' only when it subjugates itself (or is effectively subjugated) to a higher authority. In Grotius's age the military structure of an absolute state system itself was still dependent on a decentralized structure comprising these independent powers. Since *JBP* had the practical aim of regulating and restraining war, Grotius had to incorporate this historical reality,[206] at the price of considerable strain and even inconsistency in his normative system.

It is true that one of the main reasons for the inconsistency of his 'system' lies in Grotius's very equation of war with a lawsuit, and the associated normative approach to all types of conflict, from legal disputes between private persons to large-scale wars between absolutist states. But what makes *JBP* so important in the history of ideas is precisely this 'transcendental' nature of a law which places justice above all other things and evaluates reality from its standpoint.[207] Thus, the only way left to Grotius was to give specific form and substance to the idea of justice by introducing 'common sense', i.e. concrete ideas, senses, and emotions shared by his contemporaries, thereby enhancing the persuasiveness of his argument. This Grotius actually did with resounding success.

[206] It cannot be denied, though, that Grotius, under the influence of European antiquity, tended to over-emphasize the power of the head of household.

[207] Cassirer 1932: 322–5.

The seventeenth century was characterized by a strong desire for 'system', a desire Grotius himself expresses in the Prolegomena.[208] And it is often said that Grotius wrote the first systematic treatise on international law. From his use of concepts such as *bellum*, *imperium*, and *jus*, however, it is clear that Grotius did not conceive of international law as a law regulating the relations between states vested with sovereignty. Among the norms which regulate the relations between independent powers, natural law is given superior status, while *jus gentium* in *JBP* has merely a secondary status. Thus to translate *jus gentium* as 'international law' is incorrect and misleading. 'International law' in *JBP* is composed of natural law, the law of nations (*jus gentium*), the divine law, and other supplementary norms.[209] Even establishing a theory of international law *in this sense* is not the primary object of *JBP*. Nor is *JBP* a systematic treatise. Although one can say that *JBP* is a comprehensive treatise on just-war doctrine based on a general theory of law, this does not mean that it is a systematic treatise of international law in the modern sense of the term.[210] The characteristic feature of *JBP* lies in its 'comprehensive but unsystematic' nature, guided by Grotius's strong desire for peace and to minimize bloodshed.

[208] Prol. 1 and 30.

[209] Onuma 1987: 405–43.

[210] Hrabar refers to *JBP* as 'un traité encyclopédique de droit où la nature toute particulière des relations entre Etats disparaît' (1925: 551).

4

State and Governing Power

4.1. Introduction

In the present chapter, we inquire into Grotius's theory of the state by examining his concept of state power (*potestas civilis*), supreme power (*summa potestas*), governing power (*imperium*), and other related concepts. Grotius's theory of the state has been variously assessed.[1] But in *JBP*[2] Grotius does not treat such themes as state and governing power as independent and self-contained subject-matter. He merely discusses them as incidental to the argument in *JBP* for the restraint of wars. For instance, the definition of the state in I. ii. is given for the purpose of distinguishing between private and public wars; the inherent nature of supreme governing power is taken up in I. iii. with a view to discussing who is properly entitled to resort to war; original acquisition, derivative acquisition, and extinction of supreme governing power, as well as agreements between supreme rulers, are discussed in Book II, which treats substantive just causes of war; and acquisition of supreme governing power by war is

[1] Takashima *et al.* (1962: 56–8) regard Grotius's doctrine not as a social-contract theory but as a theory of subjection by contract, which presupposes inequality among men. They criticize the ambiguity of the concepts of sovereignty and people in his theory and point out that reason (*ratio*) plays the role of a mediator between the ruler and the ruled. Meinecke (1957: 246–8) holds that Grotius sought to construct a theory of the state based on the law of nature. Cassirer (1962: 318–20) argues that Grotius's theory is a contract theory in which the state is founded upon man's sociability. Vorländer (1978: 83) claims that the state as described by Grotius is not a unified integral body but merely an aggregate of men. Link (1982: 80) observes that in Grotius's theory religion forms the basis of the power relationship of civil societies.

[2] The various kinds or branches of state power, governing power, and the like are discussed in particular in *De Jure Praedae Commentarius*, *De Antiquitate Reipublicae Batavicae*, and *De Imperio Summarum Potestatum Circa Sacra*. But Grotius does not consciously pursue the theory of the state in any of these works.

examined in Book III from the viewpoint of laws of war as well as *temperamenta*.[3]

It is true that there are several reasons why Grotius refers to the state, the supreme governing power, and concepts relating thereto in *JBP*. The first reason for this is to distinguish between public and private wars. He maintains that private wars may be permissible according to natural law. His scheme is to start with an explanation of rules common to all wars, private as well as public, and then to develop rules peculiar to the latter. Thus private war logically precedes public war.[4] Public war refers to a war waged by one (*auctor*) who has the competence (*jurisdictio*) to wage it,[5] i.e. one who holds the supreme power.[6] This is why Grotius has to discuss what constitutes supreme power and who holds it.

Secondly, under the law of nations, a war is considered formal if it is waged under the authority of those holding the supreme power of both belligerent parties. Grotius identifies formal legality with justness from the viewpoint of the law of nations.[7] Acts in a formal war are given the outward appearance of being just as long as they comply with the formal requirements of the law of nations, and the opposite party is not entitled to resort to a new war by invoking those acts as just causes.[8] Since the supreme governing power serves as the criterion for deciding whether these external effects are allowed, it is necessary to clarify the concept of supreme governing power.

Thirdly, many wars fought in Grotius's day were caused by disputes over the right of succession to the throne or over territorial titles.[9] Given his desire to regulate and restrain war by establishing reasonable rules, it was essential for Grotius to be clear about the attributes of supreme governing power and its consequences (e.g. the effect of an agreement between supreme rulers), together with acquisition, succession, and extinction of that power.

Fourthly, it is necessary to explain which body holds supreme governing power—thereby establishing relations of superior and

[3] Link also says that Grotius does not describe a self-contained theory of the state (1983: 11–17).

[4] See 3.1.1. See also Ito 1965*a*: 396, 409.

[5] I. iii. 1(1).

[6] I. iii. 4(2); I. iii. 5(7); I. v. 1.

[7] I. iii. 4(1); III. iv. 1 and 3. See also III. iii. 1, 5, and 11.

[8] Kasai 1984: 52–3. [9] See 5.3, 5.5.2.

inferior—in order to restrict war or resistance by inferiors against superior as much as possible. For Grotius, this signifies the denial of legitimacy to civil wars, which might lead to the destruction of the state as perfect association. For a war to be just, not only should the substantive cause be just, but it should be waged by one with the authority to wage it.[10]

Given these reasons, it is not necessary for Grotius to explore the theory of the state as an independent subject. In this sense, there are intrinsic limitations in any study of Grotius's theory of the state as formulated in *JBP*. Nevertheless, such a study is both necessary and useful. Modern international law is conceived as a law that regulates relations between *sovereign states* and Grotius is often called 'the father of international law'. To understand properly the significance of Grotius in the history of international law, we cannot avoid the question of how Grotius comprehended the state, and whether we can trace the modern concept of sovereignty in *JBP*. In evaluating Grotius's theory of the state, we adopt the social-contract theory advanced by Hobbes, Locke, and Rousseau as our frame of reference. This is because, first, they advanced their theory of the state by abstracting man from all existing social institutions[11] and sought to demonstrate the inevitability of the formation of the state on this assumption of the state of nature. The concept of social contract was thus introduced to explain the formation of the state as an artificial entity, instead of the existing state being accepted as given. Although Hobbes, Locke, and Rousseau each projected a different image of the state, it was the mode of thinking characteristic of these thinkers that paved the way for the development of the theory of the state in modern political thought. Secondly, Grotius himself based his concept of the state on consent. Whether or not his theory of the state has anything in common with the social-contract theory advanced by Hobbes, Locke, and Rousseau constitutes one of the key questions in examining the 'modernity' of Grotius.

[10] Grotius 1950 ⟨1604⟩ (Eng. 59); Ito 1965*a*: 402–3. Ito thinks that in this regard Grotius was influenced by Gentilis.

[11] As Marx argues in many of his writings, such a view of man abstracted from all existing social institutions was actually a view of man in bourgeois society.

4.2. The State

Borkenau praises Grotius for basing the state on a purely secular foundation. On the other hand, he criticizes him for failing to articulate the concept of sovereignty and concludes that he evaded the problem of the conflict between rule and formal law, which is a fundamental question of state theory (*bürgerliche Staatslehre*).[12] Three issues are raised here which are central to the study of Grotius's theory of the state: the basis of the state, the question of sovereignty, and the contradiction between power and law. With regard to the third issue, Grotius himself says that one aspect (*species*) of the state is the association of law and governing power (*consociatio juris atque imperii*), another the interrelation between those who rule and those who are ruled (*relatio partium inter se earum quae regunt et quae reguntur*): in his view the political scientist studies the latter, the jurist the former.[13] In other words, Grotius consciously excludes from consideration the relation between ruler and ruled, the central problem of state theory, claiming to confine himself within the realm of jurisprudence. But however much Grotius may seek to confine his concern to the realm of law, problems such as relating to governing power and resistance to authority cannot be avoided. Otherwise, any theory of law would be nothing but an ideological tool justifying the existing structure of power.

4.2.1. The Basics of the State, Civil Society, and People

Grotius defines the state (*civitas*) as 'a complete association (*coetus*) of free men, joined together for the enjoyment of rights and in the common interest'.[14] He gives no definition of *coetus* here, but in another context he explains that the causes of the original acquisition of rights over persons are birth, consensus, and crime. The original acquisition of rights over persons based on consensus is further divided into association (*consociatio*) and subjection. The state is classified as a form of association.[15] To this extent, Grotius

[12] Borkenau 1934: 141–51.

[13] II. ix. 8(2).

[14] I. i. 14(1); I. iii. 7(1). For a discussion on the influence of *coetus* in this definition, see Jellinek 1960: 159 n. 37.

[15] II. v. 17–26.

is consistent in maintaining that the state is based on the consensus of free men.

Grotius uses the term civil society (*societas civilis*) interchangeably with state (*civitas*). For example:

> as civil society was instituted in order to maintain public tranquillity, the state acquires over us and our possessions a greater right, to the extent necessary to accomplish this end.[16]

> in the first instance men joined themselves together to form a civil society. . . . out of their own free will, [and from] this origin state power (*potestas civilis*) is derived.[17]

Furthermore, Grotius uses the term people (*populus*) also interchangeably with the term state (*civitas*). For example: 'An association in which many heads of households unite into a single people and state (*populus et civitas*) gives paramount authority to the corporate body over its members. This in fact is the most perfect society.'[18]

Judging from these expressions, we can say that Grotius bases the state on consent or consensus. To that extent, we can place him within the contract theory of the state in its broadest sense. But the contract theory of the state in this sense has been widely shared in European political thought ever since Ancient Rome. We should take care before identifying Grotius's theory with the social-contract theory of Hobbes, Locke, and Rousseau. On the other hand, Grotius's identification of the state with civil society or people reveals that he failed to take into account sufficiently the nature of the state as an organized political power whose *ultima ratio* is legitimized political violence. He was not fully aware of the artificial character of the state. This suggests that he still retained the way of thinking in which society was not conceptually separated from the state.[19]

[16] I. iv. 2(1).

[17] I. iv. 7(2) and (3).

[18] II. v. 23.

[19] Murakami 1979: 2–14, 50–64. See also Brunner 1974: 74–9, 123–41. Murakami describes the history of legal ideas (*Rechtsideengeschichte*), centring on the state using the framework of the transition from a theory in which state (*civitas*) and civil society (*societas civilis*) could not be distinguished to that in which those two concepts became clearly separated. His book is of great value in examining Grotius's theory of the state. On the other hand, Marx regarded the concept of civil society (*bürgerliche Gesellschaft*) distinct from the state as his basic methodological category and constructed a theory which still holds true to a large extent. In this theory he

As noted already, Grotius seeks to comprehend the state only within the framework of the general theory of the law (*jurisprudentia*).[20] He finds the origin of municipal law in the rule of natural law that demands observance of agreements, and explains compliance with municipal law by arguing that those who unite to form a certain body, or who subordinate themselves to authority, explicitly or tacitly promised to obey the decisions made by the body or authority.[21] The state is thus treated mainly in its legal aspect, substituting obedience to municipal law for subjection to power.

4.2.2. The Formation of the State

(1) *Who Constitutes the State?*

If the state is 'a complete association of free men', what does Grotius mean by free men? According to his terminology, freedom (*libertas*) constitutes a sub-category of power (*potestas*), and refers to the power over oneself. In other words, freedom means not to be subject to another's rule.[22] In another context, Grotius draws a distinction between the freedom of individuals and that of an entire people. Individuals are free if they are not subjected to any other's rule. An entire people is free if it governs itself so that it is not placed under any ruler, whether king or aristocracy.[23] The freedom of an entire people can be spoken of only after the formation of a people or state. Here the freedom of individuals is in question, and the concept of free men as those who constitute the state is tautological: it means nothing but persons who are not under anybody else's rule. But Grotius rejects the view that freedom is by nature a human attribute, arguing that this can only be said according to the law of nature which precedes the introduction of any human institutions. While men by nature are not slaves, they do not have the right never to become slaves, and in this sense no one is inherently free.[24] The status of free men is a relative concept. Along with children and youths belonging to a family, slaves, and

classified the incessant metamorphosis from civil society into capitalistic society on one hand and the basic structure which gives rise to a legal and moral expression of civil society on the other (1947: 39–152). In this sense, it is instructive to compare Murakami's history of legal ideas and Marx's theory of civil society. For a discussion of Marx's theory on civil society, see Hirata 1969 and 1971.

[20] II. ix. 8(2). [21] Prol. 15. [22] I. i. 5.
[23] I. iii. 12(1). [24] II. xxii. 11.

retainers (*subditi*), Grotius cites citizens (*cives*) in their relation to the state as an example of those who are under the rule of another. He then compares them with independent powers (*sui juris*).[25] In other words, while citizens may be free in their relation to one another, they are in a subordinate position in their relation to the state. On the other hand, citizens usually have rights over their wives and paternal rights over their children. Thus Grotius's free men do not include wives who are under the power of their husbands, children and youths who are subject to paternal rights, and slaves who are subject to their masters. Rather, a free man is a head of household (*paterfamilias*), traditionally considered the member of a civil society.[26] In short, the free men who form the state are not human beings defined only by the fact that they are not subject to others; they are already historically defined by the established institutions of household and social order, including serfdom and slavery. Moreover, the relativity of this freedom, as opposed to the modern notion of absolute freedom, signifies that even a free man, i.e. the head of a household, stands under the governing power of a people as a whole or that of a king. This line of thinking enables Grotius to formulate a theory of the state using the head of the household as a model,[27] according to which the king or the state is analogized to the head of the household. Grotius's argument that the freedom of relatively independent persons may be alienated or abandoned can also be used as grounds for justifying slavery by consent. Although Grotius may have based his concept of the state on consent or consensus, it is logically possible to ground it, not on the concept of association, but on subjection as classified by Grotius himself. The case, described below, where a people subjects itself to another, and ceases to be a people, confirms this possibility.[28]

(2) *Conditions Prior to the Formation of the State*

In what condition does Grotius believe men lived prior to the formation of the state? We can deduce from his discussion of

[25] II. xxvi. I. Also see Link 1983: 23.

[26] II. v. 23. In this sense, Grotius's image of a 'free man' is Aristotelian. See Naruse 1984: 19–20.

[27] Tanaka 1984: 80–1.

[28] I. iii. 8(1).

the primitive community of things[29] that he has in mind an idea of the state of nature of a sort. In II. ii. 23 and II. xxii. 11, Grotius recognized that men have natural freedom before human institutions and laws are introduced. There appear to be stages in the state of nature, reflected in such expressions as 'not . . . in the original state, but in the state which followed the introduction of ownership and preceded all civil laws',[30] and 'the law of nature which existed before states were organized . . . in places where men lived in groups called families and not in states'.[31]

With regard to the right of ownership (*dominium*),[32] the transition from a primitive community of things to the institution of *dominium* is realized through division. Since the subject of the initial division is the family,[33] the family must have been formed before introduction of *dominium*. Grotius does not seem to assume an original state of nature where the family has not yet been formed. This is because the family is the most natural group, and also because his main historical material derived from biblical descriptions in which the family (Adam and Eve together with their children) was present almost from the beginning. Grotius even acknowledges that selling and buying and marrying already existed in the state of nature.[34]

Grotius does not seem to regard the introduction of *dominium* as a theoretical transformation, but rather as a natural historical process. It was the simplicity of human life and mutual affection that supported the primitive community of things. But simplicity was lost when men gained knowledge, in particular, of good and evil; harmony based on mutual affection was destroyed as human ambition enlarged; and division was initiated when human beings greatly increased in number.[35] Grotius treats the transition from primitive community to division of property merely as a factual process.

Thus, instead of emphasizing their institutional aspects based on human will, Grotius understands both the family and *dominium* as

[29] II. ii. 2. The phrase *status naturae* is found in II. v. 15(2), and *status naturalis* in II. vii. 27(1).

[30] II. viii. 1(1).

[31] II. xx. 40(4).

[32] For a discussion on the relation between *dominium* and *imperium*, see 5.1. Also see Tanaka 1984: 68–76.

[33] II. ii. 2(3). [34] II. ii. 19–21. [35] II. ii. 2(1)–(4).

given, in the sense that they have come into existence as a result of a natural process of development. This also applies to the formation of the state. Except for the brief mention of 'association' in his definition, he provides virtually no explanation of the process through which the state was instituted. Although Grotius has a certain image of the state of nature, he does not enquire into its substance.[36] He does not see the transition from the state of nature to the civil state as a theoretical transformation, and thus fails to confront the question why the state had to be instituted, much less contrasts the state of nature and the civil state as did Hobbes or Rousseau. Since Grotius finds the inherent nature of man in the desire for social life, it may be a matter of course to comprehend the various forms of human groupings (the family, associations of various kinds, the state) as a continuum. But if such an approach is followed, there is nothing inevitable in the state of nature as a premiss for the formation of the state. This is at once cause and effect of Grotius's lack of a theory of man deprived of all institutional garb.[37] The significance of the state of nature for Grotius lay merely in: clarifying the partial continuation of the primitive community of things, thereby establishing the freedom of such areas as oceans; enabling those rights that could be realized through judicial procedure after the establishment of the state to be pursued by war in the state of nature; and providing the grounds for exercising the right of punishment.[38]

4.2.3. People

Grotius often speaks of a people (*populus*), but his meaning is not necessarily clear. Citing Plutarch and Paulus, he argues that a people constitutes an integral whole because it possesses a single spirit (*spiritus*) or a single essential character. The spirit here means the full and perfect association of civil life (*vitae civilis consociatio plena atque perfecta*), whose first fruit is *summum imperium*.[39] Grotius uses the term people and state almost interchangeably when he

[36] Rousseau criticized Grotius for failing to arrive at the conception of the state of nature despite being aware of the need to trace his argument back to it (1964: 132).

[37] See 1.4.2.

[38] II. xx. 8(2)–(5). If we put his Thomistic thought aside, Rommen is right in drawing a distinction between Grotius and thinkers from Pufendorf onwards on the grounds that they have a different understanding of the state of nature and contract (1971: 76–110).

[39] II. ix. 3(1).

refers to the formation of the state by heads of households,[40] as well as to laws governing the mutual relations among peoples. On the other hand, when Grotius asks whether the bearer of *summum imperium* is the king, the senate, or the people,[41] the people is clearly understood as a concept distinct from the state. A people in this context constitutes the subject of democracy (*democratia*) as opposed to monarchy or oligarchy. The people is none other than an aggregate of citizens (*cives*) or free men, i.e. heads of households.

Another point relates to the cases of monarchy by which royal power is held as a usufruct. In such cases Grotius states that royal power is conferred by the will of the people. It would follow, as Rousseau pointed out,[42] that the people must have been formed before the establishment of royal power. This does not require a dual-contract scheme, consisting of a social contract followed by a contract of subjection.[43] If a people as a whole has not been formed it would be meaningless to say that the people may choose its own form of government.[44] It would be necessary to show that a people as the potential subject of democracy constitutes an integral whole, but Grotius does not show this. He says that there are cases in which a king may in his own interest place a 'people' that has lost its existence as a state together with its *imperium* under *imperium herile*, a power similar to a master's power over his slaves. But once a people loses its *imperium*, it should be no longer a people, but merely an arithmetical sum of a large number of persons.[45] We cannot avoid concluding that Grotius does not sufficiently enquire into what makes a people an integral whole.

4.2.4. The Contract Theory of the State

According to Grotius, rights over persons (*jus in personas*) can be acquired by birth, consent, and crime. The consent is classified as association and subjection. He cites marriage and society (*societas*) as examples of association, and adult adoption and voluntary slavery as example of subjection. The state (defined as an association in which heads of households unite together) is the most

[40] II. v. 23. [41] I. iii. 8–24.
[42] Rousseau 1964: 360.
[43] Hanga (1981: 37) finds in Grotius a theory of dual contracts. I cannot agree.
[44] I. iii. 8(2). [45] III. viii. 2(1); II. ix. 6.

perfect society.[46] To this extent, Grotius maintains his view of the state as an association. If the association itself were understood as a kind of agreement, it would be possible to place Grotius in the genealogy of social-contract theory of the state in a broad sense.[47] Indeed, in some passages, one may read that civil society is formed on the basis of a pact (*pactum*).[48]

On the other hand, there are cases where a people may subject itself to the rule of another by ceasing to be either a people or a state, whether as a result of being conquered by a victor who waged a just war, or spontaneously surrendering itself to a ruler or another people.[49] In these cases there occurs subjection of a people as a whole to another. In addition, in I. iii. 8, Grotius says that it is possible for each person to subject himself to the rule of another.[50] In this case, a state is formed on the basis of individual subjection. Thus he leaves open the possibility of subjection leading directly to the formation of an autocratic state.

Grotius seeks the origin of municipal law in a rule of natural law which requires strict observance of agreements. There, he argues that those who have associated themselves with some group (*coetus*), or have subjected themselves to a ruler, have promised, explicitly or tacitly, to obey the decision of the majority of the group or that of the ruler. This agreement can be interpreted, not as a contract to form a state itself, but as consent to obey the will of the state or its ruler. Moreover, Grotius assumes that the content of the promise is the same in the case of association as of subjection.[51] This implies that Grotius based the observance of municipal law derived from state power, not the formation of the state itself, on consent or agreement.

It could be argued that, for Grotius, limiting himself to the realm

[46] II. v. 1, 8, 17, and 23.

[47] As an example of such understanding, see Nerseshantz 1986: 74–5. Cassirer (1962: 318–20) says that Hobbes and Grotius are fundamentally opposed as to the position of contract in their respective theories. See also Troeltsch 1925*a*: 342; Brimo 1978: 100.

[48] II. v. 24(1).

[49] I. iii. 8(3)–(6); I. iii. 12; II. ix. 6; III. viii. 2. Derathé considers Rousseau's criticism of Grotius on this point one-sided (1986: 61–8).

[50] See also I. iii. 8(5), whose last sentence includes the word *homines*. The situation would be the same if a supreme ruler resorted to war against private persons other than subjects, e.g. against pirates (I. iv. 1(1)), and gained control over them.

[51] Prol. 15.

of law, there would be no significant difference between providing the theoretical grounds for the formation of the state and for the binding force of municipal law. In this sense, it is possible still to place Grotius in the genealogy of the contract theory of the state.[52] But it cannot be denied that there is a significant difference between founding the state itself on contract and consenting to subject oneself to municipal law. A Japanese historian contrasts the artificial character of Hobbes's state theory[53] with the natural character of the state since Aristotle.[54] According to this scheme, it is obvious that Grotius adheres to the latter view. True, Grotius uses the expression 'artificial bodies' (*corpora artificialia*),[55] but by no means emphasizes the artificial character of the state. Rousseau regarded the social contract as the only legitimate ground for political power, and repudiated sovereignty gained through force.[56] Compared with the clarity of Hobbes and Rousseau, Grotius's theory lacks logical consistency. This is why we hesitate to classify Grotius's state theory as a contract theory of the state in *modern political philosophy*.[57] What we can say is that Grotius does not tackle the theory of the state with an awareness of the need to dismantle a *given* state or society, trace it back to the hypothesis of the state of nature, and reconstruct it, starting with an enquiry into the essential nature of human beings.[58]

4.3. Supreme Governing Power

4.3.1. State and Civil Power

As discussed earlier, Grotius defines *summum imperium* (supreme governing power) as the first fruit of the association of civil life (*vitae civilis consociatio*), which constitutes the essential element or

[52] Cassirer 1962: 225. See also Cassirer 1919: 99, 120–5.
[53] Hobbes 1839: 171–96. [54] Naruse 1984: 96–100. [55] II. ix. 3(1).
[56] Rousseau 1964: 354–64.
[57] Gierke (1968: 100–15) regards Grotius's theory of the state as a theory of social contract, together with that exposed by Althusius. But his understanding of social contract is fundamentally different from ours, for he does not count Hobbes among social-contract theorists.
[58] Thus D'Entrèves's assessment of Grotius (1970: 53–63) is persuasive. He contrasts Grotius with Hobbes, Locke, and Rousseau, the most noted proponents of the social-contract theory in its proper sense, arguing that the appearance of that theory marked the introduction of individualism. D'Entrèves does not count Grotius among social-contract theorists in the narrow sense of the term.

the bond which binds the state together.[59] Grotius equates *summum imperium* with *summa potestas*. Before examining the content of *summum imperium*, it is necessary to recall the underlying concepts.[60] 'Power' (*potestas*) is included in the second meaning of the concept *jus*, i.e. 'right', when *jus* is comprehended in its subjective sense. 'Power' is a sub-category of *facultas*, a right in the true sense as distinguished from aptitude (*aptitudo*), which is included in the second meaning of *jus*.[61] Power is divided into power over oneself, i.e. liberty (*libertas*), and power over others (which includes paternal rights and the right of a master over his slaves). The state or civil power (*potestas civilis*) which serves as the basis of *summa potestas* or *summum imperium* is included under the category of power over others. He defines it as the moral capacity of governing a state (*facultas moralis civitatem gubernandi*),[62] and goes on to enumerate the elements of state power with a series of fine distinctions.[63] The matters over which the ruler governs through his own capacity concern either general interests or particular interests. The latter relate to law-making on secular as well as sacred matters.[64] The former is divided into what is exclusively public, including the making of peace or war and concluding treaties of alliance, on one hand, and exacting taxes and exercising the right of eminent domain, on the other, and what is related to private interests, including the judiciary. The ruler may also govern through others, such as subordinate rulers (*magistratus*) or other agencies, e.g. ambassadors (*legati*).

Grotius comprehends the sum total of all these functions and competences as state power.[65] But he does not indicate which of

[59] II. ix. 3(1). Grotius develops his argument by comparing artificial bodies (*corpora artificialia*) to a natural body. Hanga traces this to the organic theory of the state (1981: 33).

[60] See further 2.2.1, esp. Table 1.

[61] I. i. See also 2.2.2.

[62] I. iii. 6(1); I. i. 14(1).

[63] Before enumerating various elements of state power, Grotius cites several works which refer to legislation, judiciary, and appointment of public officials. Haggenmacher claims that Grotius's view here is similar to the modern concept of the separation of powers (1983: 538–40). But since Grotius makes no attempt to categorize the elements of the state power, we cannot accept this view.

[64] In his own writing Grotius recognizes the priority of secular powers even in regard to sacred matters, as far as peace within the state is concerned. Grotius 1970 ⟨1690⟩, esp. 1–22. See also Villey 1975: 607–8, and Midgley 1975: 143.

[65] I. iii. 6(2).

these functions or competences constitute the essential elements of state power.[66] State power in the European Middle Ages consisted of a range of powers with judicial power at its core. Bodin, by contrast, defined sovereignty as absolute and perpetual power, with legislative power at its core. He understood legislative power as the right of the sovereign unilaterally to command his subjects on all social relationships, arguing that the fundamental attribute of sovereignty is that it is absolute and indivisible.[67] There is no trace of this view in Grotius. Even if a state lacks one or the other of the functions and competences included in his list of the constituent elements of state power, this does not necessarily mean that it ceases to be a state. Subordinate rulers in *JBP* are supposed to share state power with the supreme ruler at the outset. Thus Grotius does not accept the indivisibility of supreme power. Instead of understanding *summum imperium* as an integral and exclusive power, he comprehends it merely as a power higher than others in a series of powers. This reflected the reality since the European Middle Ages when political power was shared at a number of levels.[68] But he is not committed to overcoming this reality on the theoretical level.

Rather, while lacking as it does the ultimate aspect of the raw physical power of the state, Grotius's concept of power can be reduced to *facultas*, and *facultas* to *jus*, which implies justice. The power of the king includes both paternal rights and the rights of a master. The obligation to pay taxes prevails over the obligation to pay private debts.[69] Legitimization of actual rule is thus built in to state power itself: dominance based on the power of the state is regarded by Grotius as natural and self-evident.

4.3.2. *Summa Potestas* and *Summum Imperium*

Grotius points out that power is supreme if its actions are not subject to the *jus* of another and therefore not invalidated by the latter's will.[70] With regard to others, power comprises the right over persons (*jus in personas*), such as paternal rights or the rights of a master over his slaves.[71] Indeed Grotius includes rights of the

[66] In I. iii. 19, Grotius uses the term 'the very law of supreme governing power (*jus ipsum summi imperii*)', but does not develop it.

[67] Bodin 1576: 145. See also Sasaki 1973: 101–4.

[68] See 3.3.4. See also Bendix 1977: ch. 2.

[69] I. i. 6. [70] I. iii. 7(1). [71] I. i. 5.

state over its subjects in the category of rights over persons.[72] The terms *summum imperium* and *imperium* are used interchangeably with, and in place of, the term *summa potestas*.[73] But Grotius occasionally uses the term right of ownership (*dominium*) over persons, as in the rights of parents over their children in the period of 'imperfect judgement' and of a husband over his wife.[74] *Imperium* is primarily a power over persons, but secondarily extends over land or territory (*territorium*), or even over a part of the sea.[75] When a king subjugates the subjects of another state he has conquered in his own interests, he acquires what Grotius calls *imperium herile*, that is, a power over the community as a whole which is equivalent to that of a master over a slave. It is distinguished from the usual form of governing power (*imperium civile*): those under *imperium herile* do not constitute a state but a large family (*magna familia*).[76]

What are we to make of this jumble of concepts?[77] *Imperium* originally referred to the rights of those in the highest public offices in Ancient Rome, the totality of such rights and powers,[78] imperial power, or the empire itself.[79] Thus *imperium* can at least be understood as power with a public character. In contrast, the concept of power (*potestas*) includes paternal rights and the rights of a master over his slaves, in addition to the public powers which accompany

[72] II. v. 1–5, 23, and 27.

[73] In *JBP*, Grotius uses (*summa*) *potestas* and (*summum*) *imperium* almost without distinction. A symbolic example is found in Prol. 33, where Grotius says he will explain the inherent nature of *summum imperium* but defines its corresponding term *summa potestas* in I. iii. Generally speaking, the term (*summum*) *imperium* is used more frequently after I. iii. 10(5). There are also cases where Grotius uses these terms in different combinations, like *imperium et potestas* (I. iii. 8(5) and (10)) and *imperii potestas* (I. iii. 21(6)). The use of *potestas publica* is somewhat wider. In *De Imperio Summarum Potestatum Circa Sacra*, *summa potestas* and *summum imperium* are distinguished (Grotius 1970 ⟨1690⟩, 1–3). See Haggenmacher 1983: 537–8. Examples of somewhat misleading trans. into English by Kelsey *et al.* are 'public authority' for *dominium civile* (I. iii. 8(6)), 'supreme power and authority' for *summum dominium* (I. iii. 8(16)), and 'dominion' for *imperium* (I. iii. 24).

[74] II. v. 2(1) and 11. Grotius uses the term *dominium* also for slaves (III. vii. 7). But since slaves are regarded as things according to the law of nations (III. vii. 5(2) and (4)), to that extent there is no inconsistency.

[75] II. iii. 3(1) and 13.

[76] III. viii. 2(1).

[77] For a detailed discussion on the relation between *imperium* and *dominium* (and the significance of the concept of *dominus*), see Tanaka 1984: esp. 75–82.

[78] Meyer 1978: 86–125.

[79] Mitteis = Lieberich 1981: 28–34, 58–65, 144–65, 219–31.

public office.[80] Powers held by feudal lords and knights in the European Middle Ages, although formally derived from the king, were substantially independent and imposed limitations on the king's power.[81] Even in the age of absolutism, when the concept of *summa potestas* was emerging with the attributes of independence from any other authority and of supremacy, there still remained governing powers at various levels.[82] These bearers of *imperium* appeared as 'private persons' *vis-à-vis* their superiors, but as 'public persons' with public power *vis-à-vis* their inferiors. Against this historical background, Grotius regarded the supremacy implied in *summum imperium* and *summa potestas* as a matter of relative priority in a hierarchy of bearers of *imperium* on various levels. Grotius's concept of *summa potestas* or *summum imperium* cannot be equated with the concept of sovereignty, singular and absolute.

Grotius claimed to have paid the utmost attention to the definitions and interrelation of the various concepts used in *JBP*,[83] but he none the less treats *summa potestas*, *summum imperium*, and *imperium* as equivalent to one another without first defining *imperium*. Nor does he adequately investigate the consequences of ownership (*dominium*) over persons, of *imperium* over land, or of *imperium herile*. Grotius failed to re-examine the confusion of concepts he had inherited,[84] and did not pay much attention to distinguishing public power from private rights.

4.3.3. Bearers of *Summa Potestas*

The bearers of *summa potestas* may either be common (*subjectum commune*) or particular (*subjectum proprium*). The former is the state,[85] the latter one or more persons, depending on the laws and

[80] Meyer 1978: 90–1; Kaser 1986: 68–70, 257–9.

[81] Kern 1968: 105–20. But his view of 'the eternal Middle Ages' is questionable. See also Hartung 1980: 9–51; Mitteis = Lieberich 1981: 97–117, 195–207.

[82] Merzbacher 1982: 55–8; Oestreich 1982: 240–3.

[83] Prol. 56. See also Prol. 40–1; I. iii. 10; II. xx. 41–3.

[84] Murakami 1979: 80–3.

[85] Had Grotius carefully analysed the proposition that the state is a common or regular bearer of *summum imperium*, he might have developed a concept of state sovereignty. But this point is not developed at all. Thus we cannot accept Hinsley's claim that Grotius made a conscious attempt to harmonize the theory of sovereignty formulated by Bodin with the dualistic theory of civil society (1986: 138–9). See also Haggenmacher 1983: 539–40.

customs of each nation.[86] On the basis of this distinction, Grotius discusses who the particular bearers are by refuting the doctrine of popular sovereignty.

(1) *Refutation of the Doctrine of Popular Sovereignty*

In identifying the ultimate bearers of *summum imperium*, Grotius first comments that this depends on the laws and customs of each nation. But this is not the end of the matter, since his discussion turns to refuting the doctrine of popular sovereignty, according to which *summa potestas* always resides in the people[87] and peoples are entitled to punish kings who abuse their power. But Grotius's refutation is fraught with logical inconsistencies. He argues as follows: (1) in some cases a people will subject itself to another voluntarily; (2) it is possible to acquire *imperium* by waging a just war; (3) there are various forms of government and some kings have the same rights as those held by the people as a whole; (4) not all kings hold power on the basis of the will of the people; (5) not all governments are constituted for the benefit of the governed; even if this were the case, a king who rules badly should not be removed by the governed, but can be punished only by God.[88] Thus Grotius failed to grasp the essence of the issue. Whatever the actual form of government might be, it is the ultimate source of power—apart from divine will—that is being enquired into, whether in the doctrine of popular sovereignty advanced by the Monarchomachs[89] or by Althusius,[90] or in the theory of sovereignty constructed by Bodin.[91] But Grotius confuses the problem of the legitimacy of power with that of the form of government, and develops his criticism of the doctrine of popular sovereignty only at the latter level. Whether *summa potestas* or *imperium* or sovereignty resides in a king or the people is a problem of principle, not of the actual state of affairs in a particular community. It is irrelevant to

[86] I. iii. 7. For a discussion which points out the contradiction in Grotius's theory of the state while comparing this description with the mode of argument Grotius uses later, see Nerseshantz 1986: 75–7.

[87] Derathé says that Grotius was not opposed to popular sovereignty, stressing the phrase 'without exception' (1986: 67–8). But at least in *JBP*, Grotius is extremely reluctant to support the doctrine of popular sovereignty.

[88] I. iii. 8.

[89] Treumann 1976: 73–87, 98–105. But his assessment of Grotius's contract theory (pp. 101–2) is problematic.

[90] Gierke 1968: 26–8.

[91] Sasaki 1973: 99–130.

the claim of popular sovereignty to show that a monarchical system exists and that the people benefit from it.[92] Thus Grotius does not directly address the problem raised by the Monarchomachs and by Bodin.

Furthermore, the reasons he gives to refute the doctrine of popular sovereignty reveal the pre-modern features of his view of the state. This is illustrated by his proposition that since each person has the right to enslave himself, an entire people also has the right to subject itself by completely vesting *imperium* in one or more persons.[93] Other illustrations are the idea that some people are more suited to being ruled than ruling, which Grotius deduces from Aristotle's theory that some men are by nature suited to being slaves; the idea that it is possible to constitute a government whose aim is not the interests of the ruled but solely that of the ruler, but which cannot for this reason alone be called tyrannical; and his attempt to legitimize royal power by divine will.[94]

After rejecting the doctrine of popular sovereignty, Grotius also rejects the doctrine of mutual dependency between the king and the people: the view that a people must subject itself to a king if he governs well, but the king must subject himself to the people if he governs badly. Grotius argues that the people cannot deprive a king of his *imperium* even under a bad government, and that the judgement whether a king governs well or badly may itself precipitate a clash between king and people, with great disturbance to public tranquillity.[95] Thus, in order to avoid a war of resistance or a civil war, Grotius rejects both the doctrines of popular sovereignty and of interdependence between king and people.

(2) *Forms in which* summum imperium *is held*

After criticizing the doctrine of popular sovereignty, Grotius offers two cautions about how to determine where *summum imperium* resides in each nation. First, one should not be misled by synonyms and the outward appearance of things. A ruler may have the same power under two or more different names, or may have different powers even if they are called by the same name. Secondly, it is necessary to draw a distinction between the right itself and the forms in which it is held (*modus habendi jus*).[96] On the basis of this

[92] I. iii. 8(5), (10)–(11).

[93] Rousseau criticized this proposition (1964: 355–6).

[94] I. iii. 8(1), (4), and (14)–(15).

[95] I. iii. 9.

[96] I. III. 10–11.

distinction, Grotius goes on to enumerate various forms in which *summum imperium* is held.

First, a ruler may hold *summum imperium* in the form of a perfect right of ownership (*in pleno jure proprietatis*), i.e. as his patrimony (*in patrimonia imperantis*): such a patriarchal monarchy arises when a ruler acquires *imperium* after conquering his enemy in a just war, or when another people, of its own will, subjects itself unconditionally under to the rule of another. A patriarchal monarch may, if he wishes, transfer his *imperium* without the consent of the people. To justify such a form, Grotius distinguishes the freedom of a people (*libertas civilis*), which is lost when the people comes under the rule of a king, from individual freedom, arguing that the transfer of the former does not necessarily mean the subjection of individual members of the people to the transferee but rather the transfer of the perpetual right of governing them as a people. He thus insists on the admissibility of such a transfer. Subordinate rulers may likewise hold *imperia non summa*, as in the form of full proprietary right with the right of transfer.[97]

Secondly, kings usually possess *summum imperium* in less perfect or less complete form, i.e. as a usufruct. When royal power is conferred by the will of the people, it should be presumed that it would be contrary to the will of the people for the king to transfer his *imperium* to another king or people.[98] Such a form does not involve rejecting hereditary monarchy, because people may have transferred power to a king and his lawful successors.

Thirdly, *imperium* may be held as a temporary right (*jus temporarium*). The Roman dictator, whose term of office was clearly fixed, is an example.[99] If a king holds *imperium* under the proviso that he will lose his throne if he breaks his oath, his *imperium* approaches a temporary right.[100]

These three modes of holding *imperium* are closely connected with the question of the derivative acquisition of *imperium*, or of succession to the throne as a substantive cause of war.[101] In the first, patriarchal, form, the king or the people as a whole may transfer *imperium*,[102] and the transfer may not be invoked as a just

[97] I. iii. 11(1), 12, and 14. [98] I. iii. 13.

[99] I. iii. 11(1). See Meyer 1978: 86–9, 128–9.

[100] I. iii. 16.

[101] Another point is the mode of appointing regents (I. iii. 15).

[102] II. vi. 3.

cause of war. Moreover, as between the first and the second, a different rule is applied to intestate succession.[103] With regard to the third, temporary, form, derivative acquisition by inheritance is excluded. On the other hand, Grotius's theory of the forms of holding *imperium* has little to do with the theory of the forms of government, much less with the theory of the state. Grotius himself, notwithstanding the distinction between the forms in which *summum imperium* is held and *summum imperium* itself, declares that the essence of *imperium* is the same, irrespective of the form in which it is held: the only difference is in the degree of majesty or dignity.[104] Logically, there should be a difference between the first form and the second with respect to the admissibility of resistance when the governing power is to be transferred. But Grotius is unclear even on this point.[105] Thus, there is no compelling reason to develop a theory of the forms of holding *imperium*.

While the threefold classification is properly concerned with the form in which *imperium* is held, in developing his argument Grotius shifts his attention to the forms in which royal power is held. This shows his real intention, despite his apparent neutrality as between forms of government. Opposed to the doctrine of popular sovereignty, he seems to regard monarchy, the most common contemporary form of government, as the basic model in his theory of the state. His attitude to popular government—except that found in European antiquity—is much less favourable.[106] Thus, his theory of the forms in which *summum imperium* is held provides, in effect, a rationalization of monarchy, including the absolute monarchy which was being established in his time.[107]

(3) *Division of* Summum Imperium

Grotius refuses to treat *summum imperium* as indivisible, claiming that there are mixed forms of government as a result of the division

[103] II. vii. 12–37.

[104] I. iii. 11(2).

[105] Compare II. v. 31; III. vii. 7; III. viii. 2; II. iv. 14, with each other.

[106] Hanga notes Grotius's class-consciousness by referring to the compromise between the burghers of the Netherlands and the feudal aristocracy, and the deference he pays to the French king, his patron (1981: 36, 38–40). Hanga's argument is too schematic to be acceptable. In this theory of forms of government, Grotius does not attach much importance to aristocracy. See Link 1983: 24.

[107] Eikema Hommes 1979: 95–7.

of *summum imperium*.[108] Although the governing power of Rome (*Romanum imperium*) was a unity, the East was ruled by one emperor and the West by another; in the Roman interregnum the people and the nobility exercised *imperium* jointly.[109] Since Grotius's concept of state power is merely the sum of the various powers, and the supremacy of *summum imperium* is nothing more than relative priority among those who share *imperium*, it is only natural that division of *summum imperium* or *imperium* should be possible. Grotius fails clearly to distinguish between the theory of *imperium* and the forms of government: his theory of *summum imperium* thus retains much of what Hinsley calls dualism.[110]

(4) *Superiority of Others and* Summum Imperium

Grotius admits that *summum imperium* may be vested in one who pays tribute or who is bound by an unequal alliance and acknowledges the superiority of the other party.[111] But here he traps himself in a vicious circle: one who does not subject himself to another is free; *summum imperium* is indispensable to the freedom of a people as a whole; an unequal alliance does not necessarily mean subjection to the power of the other party; therefore, even one who is bound by an unequal alliance has *summum imperium*. A vassal bound by a feudal law is also regarded as a party to an unequal alliance. Protectorates, through the metaphor of private patronage, are said to possess *summum imperium*, too. On the other hand, if one party to an unequal alliance is much stronger than the other, and the treaty of alliance contains a clause consolidating this power, the stronger party will gain *imperium* over the weaker, or, at least, there will occur a division of *summum imperium* with the result that the latter's *imperium* is shared. Again this is a natural outcome of Grotius's refusal to recognize the indivisibility of *summum imperium*. After the theory of indivisible state sovereignty came to be established, vassals bound by feudal laws or protectorates were regarded as not having sovereignty. By contrast, Grotius's argument mirrors the contemporary political situation, when various forms of power such as feudal lords, *Länder*, and cities coexisted subject to complex relations, of alliance and feudal contract.

[108] For a discussion on Rousseau's criticism on this point, see Derathé 1986: 261–74.

[109] I. iii. 17–20. See also II. ix. 11.

[110] Hinsley 1986: 138.

[111] I. iii. 21–3.

4.4. The Right of Resistance and Subordinate Rulers

4.4.1. The Right of Resistance

Grotius adopts an extremely negative stance towards the right of resistance.[112] To recognize a right of resistance is contrary to the purpose for which a state is formed, i.e. the maintenance of public peace. He admits that all men by nature have the right of self-defence in order to ward off injury. But civil society is instituted to maintain public peace, and as such a state has a prior claim over us and our property to the extent necessary to accomplish this end. From this Grotius deduces the proposition that the right of self-defence men once possessed should be denied in principle after the formation of the state.[113] Although Grotius regards the state as based not on divine will but on human will, in denying the right of resistance,[114] he does not hesitate to invoke, among other precepts, Hebrew law, the law of the Gospel, and the teachings of early Christians.[115] This apparent contradiction reflects his desire to affirm and maintain the existing order.[116] His priorities are revealed in the question whether one should choose freedom or peace. While admitting this is a difficult choice,[117] Grotius opts for peace, arguing that in the final analysis life (*vita*) is a higher value than freedom.[118] In this sense, as Meinecke says,[119] Grotius occupies a significant place in the history of pacifism. Given this sense of order and value, rebellion was for Grotius the worst possible outcome. It is more prudent to have peace even with injustice or subjection than to cause domestic disturbance for the purpose of seeking justice or freedom. The Netherlands' War of Independence[120] was

[112] According to Tuck, Grotius adopted a more liberal position in *De Jure Praedae Commentarius*, but abandoned this stance after publishing *De Imperio Summarum Potestatum Circa Sacra*, taking a more restrictive view towards the right of resistance (1979: 64–5).

[113] I. iv. 2(1).

[114] I. iv. 2–5. While saying that autocracy contains the concept of injustice (*injustitia*) (I. iii. 8(14)), Grotius advises submission to injury (*injuria*) incurred by the ruler. Indeed, he does not approve the right of resistance except in very limited cases (I. iv. 8 ff.). For detailed discussion, see 3.3.2.

[115] I. iv. 3–6. [116] I. iv. 4(5). [117] I. iv. 19(2).

[118] II. xxiv. 6(1)–(2). The argument that it is better to be a slave than to die and the notion of slavery as the price to pay for nourishment and other necessities of life (II. v. 27(2); III. vii. 5–9) are consequences of this choice.

[119] Meinecke 1924: 283. For a criticism of Meinecke's view, see Eikema Hommes 1979: 96.

[120] Vansomeren 1965: 69–99.

justifiable rather as war of secession based upon necessity than as a rebellion.[121] Grotius's assertion that the right of resistance should be accepted only if its exercise does not cause innocent people harm, or the nation to fall into great confusion,[122] also reflects his commitment to 'peace and order'.

If this rejection of the right of resistance reflects a commitment to peace, it also symbolizes his pre-modernity. Hobbes's self-preservation, Locke's property, and Rousseau's freedom constitute the supreme values in their theoretical systems: it was by fully explaining these values that they constructed their respective theories of the state. Thus resistance against those who oppose these values is approved as a matter of principle. In contrast, for Grotius there are hardly any values of greater importance than the tranquillity of the state. Since peace is the greatest value, submission is preferable to resistance. The image of freedom of Grotius is far distant from that of Rousseau.

4.4.2. Subordinate Rulers

As noted earlier, subordinate rulers are from the first envisaged in Grotius's concept of state power. But subordinate rulers have a double character in relation to the right of resistance: as private persons *vis-à-vis* their superiors and as public persons *vis-à-vis* their inferiors. As long as their authority derives from *summum imperium*, any act contrary to the will of the supreme ruler is denied a public character.[123] This two-sidedness reflects the realities of Grotius's age with the coexistence of intermediate and local powers.[124] But Grotius seems to be inclined to incorporate subordinate rulers into the hierarchical system of the state, which is consistent with his rejection of the right of resistance traditionally allowed to subordinate rulers. The twofold character of subordinate rulers was being overtaken in the process of their integration into the bureaucratic system of the state, although it is not clear how much Grotius was aware of this.[125]

4.5. Conclusion

From the standpoint of the law-governed state (*Rechtsstaat*), Gierke claims to detect a modern element[126] in Grotius's distinction be-

[121] See II. vi. 5–6. [122] I. iv. 7(2). [123] I. iv. 1(2) and 6.
[124] Gierke 1968: 143–52. [125] Ibid. 352–4. [126] Ibid. 287.

tween the acts of a supreme ruler carried out as such and those carried out as a private person, with the corollary that only the former are exempt from the binding force of municipal law.[127] It is true that Grotius criticized the claim that the formation of the state or civil society was based on the direct will of God, and found the source of state power in human will.[128] In this sense, it can be said that he founded the state on a secular basis, eliminating the secular authority claimed by the pope or the church in the European Middle Ages,[129] as well as by Calvinist theocracy.

However, when Grotius rejected the right of resistance, he did not hesitate to legitimatize the state by the will of God, advocating submission to state power.[130] We should be cautious about claiming modernity for Grotius's theory of the state simply because of its secular elements.[131] At any rate, it is difficult to gain an overall understanding of Grotius's view of the state, because he does not develop a theory of the state as an end in itself, nor does he always discuss the state, *imperium*, and related concepts in a consistent way.

Grotius seeks to avoid both absolute pacifism and the unconditional confirmation of the *status quo*. Instead, he adamantly adheres to the values of peace, the antithesis of war,[132] by pursuing the regulation of war through legal means. A thorough inquiry into the theory of *imperium* or of the state might have been an obstacle to this goal. Thus there is a close connection between Grotius's overall aim and his scattered discussion of the various problems concerning state and *imperium*. The refinement of the modern theory of the state since Hobbes, on one hand, and the quantitative increase in the rules of positive international law, on the other, led to the abandonment of the legal regulation of the substantive causes of war, and the adoption of a non-discriminatory view of war. The theory of sovereignty played a major role in this development. But, in the science of international law, that development was a process through which the state became more and more formalized,[133] the

[127] II. xiv. 1–2.

[128] I. iv. 7(3).

[129] Grotius 1970 ⟨1690⟩, 2–9.

[130] I. ii. 7(2)–(3); I. iv. 3–6.

[131] Link, recognizing both new and old elements in Grotius's theory of the state, describes it as an old wineskin filled with new wine (1983: 11–35).

[132] See 3.1.1.

[133] For a discussion on its significance and limitations, see Jellinek 1960: 162–73, esp. 169 n. 53.

subject of various rights under positive international law, while its political character, with legitimate violence as its *ultima ratio*, slipped into the background. In this process, the question 'what is a state?' was increasingly abandoned by international lawyers.

Thus it may be possible to talk about Grotius's theory of the state if we consider the theory of the state simply as a conceptual definition. But in the deeper sense of an attempt to found a basis for the state, through an enquiry into the nature of human beings apart from any social institutions, there is no theory of the state in Grotius. For that it is necessary to turn to Pufendorf's theory, systematized in *De Jure Naturae et Gentium*, the outstanding successor of Grotius as well as of Hobbes.

5

Dominium and *Imperium*

5.1. Introduction

In *JBP* Grotius elaborates two kinds of rights as grounds for claiming the restitution of things[1] (*recuperatio rerum*), one of the three just causes of war. These are that which belongs to us (*quod nostrum est*) (II. ii–x), and that which is owed to us (*quod nobis debetur*) (II. xi–xix).[2] This chapter will focus on the former: what belongs to us.

According to Grotius, some things belong to us as rights common to all men (*commune hominum jus*), others by our own right (*nostrum singulare jus*). A right common to all men is one deriving from a primitive state of community (*primus status rerum communium*), and surviving even after the introduction of *dominium*. It holds good over things or, in some cases, over acts.[3] Our own right consists of *dominium* and *imperium*.[4] *Dominium* is usually equated with the right over things, and *imperium* with the right over persons, but in Grotius's system they are not so clearly distinguished. Although *dominium* is primarily a right over things, the rights of parents over infants, or of a husband over his wife, are also classified as *dominium*.[5] Likewise, *dominium eminens* (the right of eminent domain) is a right that a state holds not only over things belonging to its subjects but also over the subjects themselves.[6] On the other hand, although *imperium* is primarily a right over persons, it is secondarily a right over things, i.e. over land and parts of sea.[7]

[1] Grotius limits things to corporeal things (*res corporales*). II. ii. 1. See also II. iii. 2.

[2] There are three sources of the latter: agreements, wrongful acts, and law (see 3.2.1). On this classification, see also Coing 1982*b*: 253–4.

[3] II. ii. 1. [4] II. ix. 1. See also II. v. 1; II. x. 1(1).

[5] II. v. 2(1) and 11. The Belgian theologian Leonardus Lessius (1554–1623) also recognized both *dominium* over things and *dominium* over persons such as slaves (Krause 1982: 73).

[6] I. iii. 6(2). For further discussion, see 5.9.

[7] II. iii. 4(1) and 13(1).

Grotius sometimes uses the expression *proprietas* or its adjective *proprius*. Historically, *proprietas* and *dominium* are not identical concepts. For example, the Glossators used *proprietas* only to connote the relationship of things belonging to a person, whereas they used *dominium* to mean the power (*Herrschaft*) held by an owner.[8] Grotius does not recognize any essential difference between them, commenting instead that jurists call 'proprietas' 'dominium'. Yet nowhere in *JBP* does he define either *proprietas* or *dominium*.[9] In I. i. 5, he merely states that *facultas*, which is one aspect of *jus* as a moral quality, includes *dominium* in addition to power and obligation.[10]

5.2. The Evolution of *Dominium* and Rights Common to All Men: II. ii

5.2.1. The Evolution of *Dominium*

Relying on the Bible, Grotius divides into three periods the process by which *dominium* came into being: the period symbolized by 'the tree of life' (the primitive state of community); the period symbolized by 'the tree of knowledge'; and the period symbolized by 'the tower of Babel'.[11] According to Grotius, common ownership (*communio*) belongs not to the law of nature in itself (*simpliciter*) but to the law of nature in relation to particular institutions (*pro certo rerum statu*). Accordingly, common ownership is not invariable, but can be altered by the introduction of *dominium*.[12] While the Essenes and some tribes in America live without the institution of *dominium*, such cases are rare.[13] By a natural historical development, common ownership—first of movables, later of land—was abandoned and *dominium* was instituted.[14]

8 See Willoweit 1974: 139–42.

9 See Feenstra 1978: 227–8. In *Mare Liberum* he uses *proprietas* and *dominium* in a different way. *Dominium* there has two meanings: something which is one's own (*proprium quid*), and the faculty to make proper use of common property in a primitive state of community (Grotius 1978 ⟨1618⟩, 33–4). See also n. 16.

10 Power here means freedom in its application to oneself, paternal rights or rights of a master over his slaves in its application to others.

11 II. ii. 2(1), (2), and (3).

12 I. i. 10(7). The distinction between these two laws of nature will be explained later.

13 II. ii. 2(1).

14 II. ii. 2(4).

Grotius thus explains the development of *dominium* as history.[15] But he also demonstrates its development at the level of law. *Dominium* arises out of a kind of explicit agreement (*pactum*) by way of division (*divisio*), or an implicit agreement by way of occupation (*occupatio*).[16] In short, the primitive state of community was first modified by an implicit agreement about occupation.[17] Then, things were divided and, as a result, *dominium* came into being over things which had been common to all men. Thereafter, *dominium* came to be acquired only by way of occupation of those things that were not divided.[18]

The late Scholastics were concerned with the question whether the state of community is merely permitted according to natural law or dictated by it, and if the latter, whether it is possible to change the state of community and introduce *dominium*.[19] Grotius explains the development of *dominium* at the level of history and of law, but fails to connect the arguments he presents at these two levels. At the level of history there is no explanation at all of division or occupation. The notion of occupation and division based on a human agreement is nothing more than a fiction justifying the *status quo* with respect to property holdings.[20] Grotius's theory of the development of *dominium* thus serves to reinforce the existing order of ownership and government by justifying instances of inequality of ownership resulting from division or occupation.[21]

[15] See 4.2.2(2).

[16] In *Mare Liberum*, Grotius states that all forms of ownership (*proprietas*) originate in occupation. Moreover, this occupation is not based on consent (Grotius 1978 ⟨1618⟩, 40). Thus the basis of ownership is completely different from that found in *JBP*. In *Inleiding tot de Hollandsche rechtsgeleertheyd* (s'Gravenhage, 1631), Grotius argues that, according to reason, inanimate things belong to the one who occupies them. Here he also treats ownership (*eigendom*) as something originating in deliberate human action, and not as something based on consent (Grotius = Lee 1926: 81, 83 (II. iii. 2)).

[17] II. ii. 2(5).

[18] II. ii. 3(3); II. iii. 1. According to Grotius, there are two categories of corporeal things which are not subject to *dominium*. Included in the first category are those things, such as the sea, which by nature cannot become subject to *dominium*. Included in the second category are those things, such as lands, islands on the sea, wild animals, fish, and birds, which by nature can be subject to *dominium* but have not been made so because no one has yet occupied them (II. ii. 3(1) and (2), 4, and 5).

[19] See Seelmann 1979: 112–26.

[20] See Cocceji 1744: 438; Villey 1976: 189. See also Tuck 1979: 77, 89.

[21] For a similar view, see Murakami 1979: 83.

5.2.2. Rights Common to All Men

Rights common to all men can be regarded as a revival of the primitive right that all men held in the state of community.[22] The existence of these rights can be assumed, not from the law of love, but from the fact that those who originally introduced *dominium* intended to depart as little as possible from natural equity (*aequitas naturalis*).[23] As an example of a right common to all men, Grotius cites the right to conclude a contract which binds a people to sell its crops only to the other party.[24] He had in mind the Netherlands' monopoly on the spice trade with the Moluccas, which at the time was a controversial issue for the Netherlands in its relations with England.[25]

If these rights common to all men, which continued even after *dominium* came to be instituted, were over-emphasized, the institution of *dominium* would be threatened. For instance, if a person wishes to pass over a part of the land, a river, or the sea which is under the *dominium* of some other nation (*populus*),[26] he should seek their prior permission. However, Grotius argues that, when refused, a person may demand the right to pass as of right.[27] This leads to the conclusion that, although various conditions may be imposed on passage for the protection of the owner, the passage itself may be mandated by force.

On one hand, Grotius regards *dominium* as a right that can be disposed of at the discretion of its owner.[28] On the other hand, he admits a wide range of rights common to all men. Yet he fails to elaborate the connection between the two in a coherent way, assuming instead that a kind of predetermined harmony exists and that no contradiction will arise. Despite this assumption, it is possible that some contradiction do arise between them.[29]

[22] II. ii. 6(2).

[23] II. ii. 6(1) and (4).

[24] II. ii. 22–4.

[25] See Pauw 1965: 67; Oudendijk 1970: 40.

[26] See 4.2.3. for discussion of the different meanings of *populus*. Here Grotius apparently used the term synonymously with 'nation' or 'state'. See also II. v. 23.

[27] II. ii. 13(3).

[28] II. ii. 20; II. vi. 1(1).

[29] See Brandt 1974: 40–1. Tuck argues that *JBP* is Janus-faced, speaking the language both of absolutism and liberty, as shown in the defence of voluntary slavery and of resistance *in extremis*, and that Grotius is thus both the first conservative rights theorist in Protestant Europe and also in a sense the first radical rights theorist (1979: 71, 79–80, 143). Tuck cites as an example of this bivalence

5.3. Original Acquisition of the Right over Corporeal Things II. iii and iv

'Our own right' can be acquired either through original acquisition or through derivative acquisition. This distinction is based on Roman law, but its content is modified considerably in *JBP*. In discussing original acquisition, Grotius distinguishes the acquisition of rights over corporeal things from the acquisition of rights over persons. We discuss the former in this section.

5.3.1. Occupation

Original acquisition (*acquisitio originaria*) of rights over corporeal things takes place either through division or through occupation. Since only acquisition through occupation is possible after the primal division of things, the discussion here is limited to occupation. It should be noted that Grotius placed 'occupation', not 'discovery', at the centre of his argument. As is well known, Spain and Portugal claimed rights based on papal grant and discovery. By contrast, England, France, and the Netherlands, which lagged behind the Iberian powers in acquiring colonies, based their colonial claims on the theory of occupation, by analogy with Roman law. In this sense, his theory was highly controversial.[30]

According to Grotius, both *imperium* and *dominium* may be acquired over things belonging to no one (*quae proprie nullius sunt*), by a single act called occupation.[31] Grotius does not say this explicitly, but he is referring only to the occupation of unoccupied land.[32] *Imperium* acquired by a people or by its ruler extends over occupied land and over inhabitants on the land, and may not be transferred to subjects or to foreigners. In contrast, *privatum plenumque dominium* (absolute ownership of private property) over land[33] acquired by a people or by its ruler can be transferred to

Grotius's modification of the principle of private property (79–80). It is true that the revival of the ancient right of using things (*jus illud pristinum rebus utendi*), i.e. of rights common to all men *in extremis*, might lead to the notion of 'inalienable rights'. But the contrast of the defence of private property and common property does not necessarily correspond to the two tendencies, radical and conservative, postulated by Tuck.

[30] See e.g. Schmitt 1950: 96–109; Taijudo 1955: 98–9. See also Dreier 1987: 161.

[31] II. iii. 4(1) and 19(2).

[32] See II. viii. 9(1).

[33] II. iii. 19(2). For the concept of *privatum plenumque dominium*, see also 5.9.

subjects or to foreigners. But even if *privatum plenumque dominium* over land is transferred to private persons, a people or its ruler will retain *dominium generale* (ultimate or residual ownership) over that land. Thus *dominium* transferred to private persons is dependent on this *dominium generale*. As a result, when these persons abandon their *dominium*, or when they cease to exist, their land reverts to the people or its ruler.[34]

A different principle applies to movables. Natural law recognizes the right of private persons to occupy movables (e.g. wild animals, fish, birds) found on the land or maritime territory of a state. However, municipal law may restrict this right.[35]

While both people or its rulers and private persons are entitled to *dominium*, Grotius imposes the limitation that according to the law of nature only persons possessed of reason are entitled to *dominium*. Those who do not possess reason, such as children and the mentally handicapped, cannot have *dominium*. According to the law of nations, however, such persons may acquire or enjoy *dominium*, although they may not exercise it (e.g. by alienating their property).[36] In order to understand this section without contradicting Grotius's basic premisses, we have to interpret it as follows. First, the term 'nature' in 'contrary to nature (*contra naturam*)' or 'outside nature (*praeter naturam*)' should not be understood as natural law in general, but as mandatory natural law. Secondly, Grotius believes that a deliberate act based on reason is necessary only when one exercises or alienates *dominium*. Thus, natural law (mandatory natural law) limits only the exercise and alienation of *dominium* to those who possess reason, not its acquisition or enjoyment. Human volitional law can not make provision contrary to this natural law. But since the acquisition and enjoyment of *dominium* belongs to the domain of permissive natural law, human volitional law can lay down its own rules instead. The law of nations allows even children and the mentally handicapped to acquire and enjoy *dominium*.[37]

5.3.2. Occupation of the Sea

While rivers may be originally acquired by occupation,[38] oceans or the main parts of the sea are not subject to *dominium*. It is a man-

[34] II. iii. 19(1) and (3).
[35] II. ii. 5; II. iii. 5. See also II. viii. 2–7.
[36] II. iii. 6. See also II. v. 2(2); II. xxii. 10(1).
[37] See also Reibstein 1958: 359. [38] II. iii. 7.

made institution (*institutum*), not natural reason, that prohibits the sea from being occupied lawfully. However, according to the law of nature, it is possible to occupy a part of the sea which is, as it were, shut in by lands, such as bays and straits. An act of the will (*animi actus*) manifested by an overt act (*externus actus*) is required for such occupation, and the sea will revert to common use as soon as the possession (*possessio*)[39] resulting from occupation ends. This occupation does not give those who occupy some part of the sea the right to impede innocent passage.[40]

Unlike the case where *dominium* and *imperium* are acquired at the same time, it is more likely in the case of 'a part of the sea' that only *imperium* will be acquired, without *dominium*. As long as *imperium* is established, an occupied part of the sea is a territory, though *dominium* does not extend over it.[41] Here Grotius uses the expression, 'a part of the sea' (*pars maris*, *portio maris*), instead of 'a part of the sea which is, as it were, shut in by lands (*pars maris quae terris quasi clausa sit*)' such as bays and straits. He seems to envisage only coastal or littoral areas as falling within the intermediate categories, *pars* or *portio maris*.[42] Grotius refers to two specific methods of establishing *imperium*: one through the medium of persons (e.g. where a warship is stationed), the other through that of territory (e.g. where those sailing along the coast can be constrained from the land).[43] Although under natural law anyone may engage in fishing in these areas of the sea, this may be restricted by the municipal law of a coastal state. In the negotiations between England and the Netherlands in 1610, 1613, and 1615 there were severe disputes over the question of trade monopoly, herrings, and whales. Grotius took part in the last two meetings as a member of the Dutch delegation. Thus the right to prohibit fishing had considerable practical importance.[44]

According to Grotius, foreigners may occupy waste or unused land directly, and acquire *dominium* over it.[45] But this principle does not apply to a part of the sea. A part of the sea may become a territory by occupation, but it is only *imperium*, not *dominium*, that will be acquired by such occupation. *Privatum plenumque dominium*

[39] Kelsey *et al.* trans. both *possessio* (II. iii. 11; II. iv. 2 and 9) and *occupatio* (II. ii. 4; II. iii. 11 and 12) as possession. This is inappropriate because Grotius generally draws a distinction between *possessio* and *occupatio* except in II. ii. 10.

[40] II. iii. 8–12. See also II. ii. 13(1).

[41] II. iii. 13(1).

[42] See Oudendijk 1970: 47–8, 51.

[43] II. iii. 13(1) and (2).

[44] See Pauw 1965: 43–64; Oudendijk 1970: 33–40.

[45] II. ii. 17.

does not extend to parts of the sea which are not shut in by lands. Consequently, *privatum plenumque dominium* may not be transferred to subjects or to foreigners; Grotius does not discuss whether foreigners could acquire *dominium* over such parts of the sea, but presumably they could not. Gentilis had already distinguished between ownership (*proprietas*) and the right of jurisdiction and protection (*jurisdictio et protectio*), on the grounds that the latter is permitted for the sea but the former is not, and it has been suggested that Grotius was influenced by this view.[46] But Gentilis's right of jurisdiction and protection do not fully correspond to Grotius's *imperium*.

Mare Liberum is often quoted in discussions on Grotius's theory of the freedom of the seas. Opinions are divided on whether there is a volte-face between *Mare Liberum* and *JBP*.[47] In the former, Grotius argued that, except for small inlets, every part of the sea is free.[48] *Mare Liberum* was written to justify the capture of the Portuguese merchant ship *Catalina* by the United East India Company. It emphasized the freedom of the seas to counter the Portuguese claim. In contrast, Grotins argues in *JBP* that, even if the main parts of the sea are by nature not subject to *dominium*, *imperium* over some parts of the seas (by implication, but not expressly, limited to coastal areas) is recognized fairly extensively. To this extent, there are differences in emphasis between *Mare Liberum* and *JBP*.[49]

5.3.3. Abandonment of *Dominium* and *Imperium*, and Occupation

According to Grotius, prescription in the strict sense (*usucapio et praescriptio*) is a matter of municipal law, and hence does not apply to those who are not subject to the same municipal law. If this were the case, disputes between kingdoms or over borders of kingdoms would never cease. He thus introduces the theory of 'assumed abandonment and resultant occupation' (*derelictio praesumta et eam*

[46] Ito 1984: 180–3. See also Knight 1925: 94–5; Pauw 1965: 32.

[47] e.g. Fulton 1911: 342–50; Pauw 1965: 67–76; Oudendijk 1970: 40–52; Lauterpacht 1975*b*: 362; Ito 1984: 187–9. See also Roelofsen 1983*a*: 5–15.

[48] Grotius 1978 ⟨1618⟩, 45–6, 50.

[49] On the controversy over the freedom of the sea which arose after the publication of *Mare Liberum*, see Fulton 1911: 350–77; Alexandrowicz 1960: 162–82; Oudendijk 1970: 67–91; Ito 1977: 1–16; Ito 1984: 69–160.

secuta occupatio). If a person possesses something belonging to another for a long time, the latter is assumed to have abandoned it. Property which is assumed to have been abandoned may be acquired through possession for an extended period.[50] According to Grotius's theory of intention and representation, intention is inferred not only from express words but also from action or inaction. To assume that something has been abandoned by inaction, the owner must for a long time (ordinarily beyond human memory) acquiesce in his property being possessed by another person. For this principle to be valid, the owner must act with knowledge and not be prevented by duress from objecting.[51]

Without such an assumption, however, the possession of a thing for an immemorial period may bring about a transfer of *dominium* in accordance with the law of nations, provided possession is not interrupted or called into question by an appeal to arbitration. In other words, according to the law of nations *dominium* may be alienated even if the original owner has no notice of the alienation, or if he has been prevented from objecting by duress.[52] A king may acquire *imperium* over another king, or a free people *imperium* over another free people, by long possession.[53]

As a matter of logical structure, it is difficult to regard long possession as giving rise to original acquisition by occupation subsequent to assumed abandonment. True, strict conditions are imposed on this original acquisition under natural law. But this natural law is merely permissive, so that it is possible to modify those conditions by the law of nations. Thus original acquisition may be admitted in a fairly wide range of cases. In boundary disputes, it would be convenient for a powerful monarch to claim that *dominium* and *imperium* can be acquired merely by showing long possession and the absence of any claim to arbitration in the mean time. Especially if duress were permitted, this would be an ideal legal tool for powerful nations to deprive powerless nations of their territories. Grotius seems to have thought that his rules would assist in regulating and restraining wars, but they might well justify conquest instead.

50 The heading of II. iv, and II. iv. 1 and 2.
51 II. iv. 3–7.
52 II. iv. 9.
53 II. iv. 11.

5.4. Original Acquisition of the Right over Persons: II. v

Rights over persons are of three kinds: those acquired by birth (*generatio*), by consent (*consensus*), and by wrongful act (*delictum*).

5.4.1. Rights over Persons Acquired by Birth

Rights acquired by birth are rights held by parents over their children. The right of the father is superior to the right of the mother on account of the superiority of sex.[54] While parental or paternal rights are usually regarded as a form of *imperium*, they are also a form of *dominium*. This, together with the fact that there are cases where the right of a husband over his wife is referred to as *dominium*,[55] indicates how extensive the domination of the head of the household over the family members was, and how strongly Grotius's notion of *dominium* was coloured by its *Herrschaft* nature.

Grotius uses the expression *sui juris* to describe children in the third period when they have left their parents and are living an independent life.[56] In this period, children are independent of parental control, though they are still expected to show affection and respect towards them.

5.4.2. Rights over Persons Acquired by Consent

(1) *Association*

Rights over persons acquired by consent derive either from association (*consociatio*) or subjection (*subjectio*). There are public associations (a state as an association formed by a people, and an association between peoples) and private associations.[57] Marriage is a private association, formed by the cohabitation of a man with a woman in which the latter is placed under the protection of the former.[58]

Grotius presents the principle of majority rule in decision-making as a principle applicable to all associations.[59] However, this

[54] II. v. 1. [55] II. v. 2(1) and 11.

[56] II. v. 6. [57] II. v. 17.

[58] II. v. 8. Grotius draws a distinction between the requirements of marriage under natural law, and those under divine volitional law and the law of the Gospel based on a natural sense of honour (*honestas naturalis*). In fact, however, this distinction is rather arbitrary, an arbitrariness which probably reflects the social realities of Grotius's age, which could not always be explained by standards of 'reason'. (See Dilcher 1984: 324–5.)

[59] II. v. 17–20 and 22.

principle of majority rule is not suitable for marriage, which is an association of two persons. Instead, at least in matters relating to marriage and domicile, a husband has *imperium* over his wife, and there is a unilateral obligation of *fides* assumed by a wife towards her husband. Decisions made by the husband bind his wife. To regard Grotius's theory of marriage as paving the way for the recognition of the equality before law of both spouses, and for divorce based on mutual consent,[60] is thus unacceptable.

Against the background of this general principle of association, Grotius defines a state as the most perfect society, established as an association in which many heads of households unite into a single people. He remarks that a state has a paramount authority (*maximum jus*) over its subjects, but does not indicate the specific contents of this authority. Nature prohibits subjects to leave their country in large numbers, for it would cease to exist if this were allowed. However, withdrawal of private persons is different, and a state has no legal claims against exiles.[61] These are the only points Grotius makes about the state: he does not present any general theory of the state.

As this analysis demonstrates, Grotius's concept of association is multi-layered, consisting of marriages, households, private bodies (*collegia*), cities, provinces, municipalities, states,[62] alliances, and the society of nations.[63] Even the state, which Grotius considers the most perfect society, is definitely not the modern sovereign state, with which independent powers with the authority to rule over others and the means of enforcement cannot in theory coexist. The power of a head of a household over his wife, children, and slaves is called *imperium*, as is the *imperium* of a state over its subjects. The distinction between the various associations mentioned is not an essential one, but is only a matter of degree. This is why in the opening passage of I. i, Grotius declares that he does not intend to treat controversies among 'states' but controversies among 'those who are not held together by a common bond of municipal law', such as private persons belonging to different nations, kings, nobles, or free peoples.[64] The society of nations[65] envisaged by

[60] As does Dufour 1972: 250–1. [61] II. v. 23–5.
[62] II. xiv. 5; II. xviii. 2(1); III. viii. 1(1).
[63] On this point, see e.g. Vollenhoven 1931: 4–13.
[64] I. i. 1. See also 3.1.1(1), esp. n. 3.
[65] Grotius refers to the society of nations by such phrases as 'that universal

Grotius is not an international society consisting only of states but a society of men, consisting of kings, peoples, and other independent powers. Nor is it a world state (*civitas maxima*) as conceived by Christian Wolff, which consists solely of individual nations and could itself be regarded as a single state.[66]

(2) *Subjection*

In addition to the associations referred to, rights over persons acquired by consent include rights acquired by subjection. These can be divided into two types: public and private.[67] The noblest form of private subjection is adult adoption,[68] the basest, slavery. Complete slavery is lifelong service which a slave owes in return for nourishment and other necessities of life. There is nothing unjust or cruel about it if the conditions are within certain limits.[69] Although no man may consent to alienate the right to his own life, the right of life and death over slaves is recognized where municipal law so provides and where the king has unlimited power.[70] There is very little basis for the view that Grotius's description of slavery is based on humanistic considerations.[71] To Rousseau the abandonment of liberty means the abandonment of man's qualification as man, his rights, and even his obligations; hence it is contrary to his inherent nature. No wonder Rousseau severely criticized Grotius's approval of slavery based on consent.[72]

According to Grotius, the children of slaves may not escape from their master if they have not yet compensated at least for the indebtedness they owe their master for nourishing them.[73] However, it is impossible for children to give consent when they are not even regarded as having reason and are considered to be under the control of their parents. Likewise, marriage, an unequal association

society' (*magna illa universitas*) (Prol. 17), 'the mutual society of nations' (*mutua gentium inter se societas*) (II. viii. 1(2)) and 'that greater society of nations' (*major illa gentium societas*) (III. xxv. 1). He also uses the phrase 'that community which binds together the human race, or binds many nations together (*illa [communitas] quae genus humanum aut populos complures inter se colligat*)' (Prol. 23) and the phrase 'human society' (*societas humana*) (II. viii. 26; II. xxi. 3(2)).

[66] Wolff 1972 ⟨1749⟩, s. 9, 10, etc.

[67] II. v. 31. [68] II. v. 26. [69] II. v. 27. [70] II. v. 28.

[71] As an example of such an interpretation, see Lauterpacht 1975: 356.

[72] Rousseau 1964: 355–6.

[73] II. v. 29(2).

dominated by the husband's *imperium*,[74] cannot be recognized in reality as an association formed by the free consent of man and woman.[75] Finally Grotius put more emphasis on the paramount authority given to the corporate body over its members than on the aspect of consent on which a state is based.[76] There are thus many difficulties in Grotius's assertion that association is based on consent. This consent is rather a constructive or nominal basis for justifying human institutions, and Grotius's theory of association is properly characterized more as an aspect of natural order than as dependent on consent.[77]

5.4.3. Rights over Persons Acquired by a Wrongful Act

Grotius ends his analysis of the original acquisition of rights over persons with a brief discussion of rights over persons acquired as a result of some wrongful act committed by them. Subjection without consent arises for those who have the right to exact punishment as a result of some wrongful act. In this case, a war of restitution is allowed against a third party who has violated this right. There is also the possibility of launching a punitive war against the wrongdoer.[78]

5.5. Derivative Acquisition: II. vi and vii

5.5.1. Derivative Acquisition by Act of Will

According to Grotius, derivative acquisition (*acquisitio derivativa*) takes place either by an act of will or by operation of law (*lex*, i.e. natural law, the volitional law of nations (*lex gentium voluntaria*),[79]

[74] Grotius regards associations between brothers, subjects, friends, and allies as social relationships without inequality, and those between father and children, master and slave, king and subjects, God and men as unequal social relationships (I. i. 3(2)). There are also unequal alliances (I. iii. 21).

[75] See Wieacker 1967: 297; Dufour 1972: 223–4, 241–2, 251.

[76] II. v. 23 and 24(2). See also Gierke 1902: 101.

[77] For a similar view, see Riedel 1975*a*: 744–6; Riedel 1975*b*: 233–4. See also Fukuda 1971: 28.

[78] II. v. 32.

[79] Generally, the expression *jus gentium voluntarium* (I. ii. 4(2); II. iv. 9; II. viii. 1(1); II. xii. 26(1); II. xviii. 1; III. i. 5(5); III. ii. 2(1); III. iii. 12, etc.) is used rather than *lex gentium voluntaria*, but there is no difference between the two.

or municipal law). Acquisition by act of will refers to voluntary transfer of *dominium* or *imperium*.[80] It is the nature of *dominium plenum* (absolute title to property)[81] under natural law that the holder is allowed to alienate his right. The requirements for alienation are (1) an act of the will (*actus internus voluntatis*) of the giver and his manifestation of this will (*signa externa*); and (2) an expression of the will of the receiver to accept the offer (*voluntas accipiendi cum suo* [i.e. accipientis] *signo*). Delivery as a necessary element for alienation is required only by municipal law, and is improperly treated as a requirement of the law of nations. Although many municipal laws require delivery, this is a mere coincidence or concordance.[82]

Like *dominium*, *imperium* can be alienated according to the will of the holder, but the requirements differ depending on whether the holder is a king or a people. A king may have *imperium* in the form of *dominium plenum*. Or he may be entrusted with *imperium* as a usufruct granted by the will of his people, in which case the latter is the holder of *imperium*.[83] In the former case, the king may alienate his *imperium* by satisfying the conditions required for the alienation of *dominium*.[84] In the latter case, however, the people are presumed not to have permitted the king to alienate his *imperium*.[85] Subject to this basic distinction, Grotius classifies the alienation of *imperium* into six cases:[86] (1) alienation of *imperium* in its entirety; (2) alienation of *imperium* over a part of a people or withdrawal of a part of a people from the state[87] (the former is admitted for the purpose of establishing a state, the latter out of necessity;[88] but it is

[80] II. vi. 1(1). Kelsey *et al.* trans. *acquisitio derivativa* in the headings for II. vi and II. vii as secondary or derivative acquisition of property, thus giving the impression that these principles are limited to corporeal things. However, *acquisitio derivativa* is not so limited. In II. vi and II. vii Grotius discusses the derivative acquisition of rights over both corporeal things and persons.

[81] *Dominium* is incomplete if there is something less than this full capacity (see Grotius = Lee 1926: 85 (II. iii. 10–11); also I. i. 5). The distinction between complete and incomplete capacity holds good also over *imperium* (see II. vi. 7).

[82] II. vi. 1 and 2. [83] I. iii. 11(1). [84] II. vi. 3.

[85] I. iii. 13(1). [86] II. vi. 3–13.

[87] Grotius cites the example of a city that surrendered after being surrounded by an enemy nation. This principle can also be applied to a region within a nation that secedes and declares its independence. In all likelihood, Grotius had in mind the Netherlands' War of Independence.

[88] In case of extreme necessity some things are reduced to the domain of pure natural law (*merum jus naturae*) (II. vi. 5), which can be understood here as the law of nature in the primitive state of community (I. i. 10(7); II. viii. 1(1)).

doubtful whether the latter can be regarded as a case of alienation of *imperium*);[89] (3) alienation of part of a territory such as uninhabited or deserted land; (4) conditional alienation; (5) alienation of inferior jurisdiction (*jurisdictiones minores*), and (6) alienation of a people's hereditary property, specifically, of the rights to acquire alluvial additions, to levy tax, to confiscate property, and the like. Such alienations are valid only if there are no laws that increase or decrease the power of a king or a people.[90] They can thus be understood as requirements under permissive natural law.

It has been argued by some that Grotius acknowledged the right of self-determination because in certain cases he required the consent of the people (or a fraction of the people) as a condition for alienating territory.[91] This is wrong, as his reasons for accepting the institution of slavery demonstrate. National consciousness at the level of a people had not yet emerged, and any resemblance to the right of self-determination is fortuitous.

5.5.2. Derivative Acquisition by Operation of Law

Grotius acknowledges that derivative acquisition may take place under the law of nature, the volitional law of nations, and municipal law. He treats only the first two, on the grounds that derivative acquisition under different municipal laws is too varied and that disputes arising from war cannot be settled by municipal law.[92]

Derivative acquisition under natural law extends to constructive payment of a debt (*expletio juris*), certain cases of self-help, and intestate succession. Grotius merely refers to the definition of constructive payment of a debt[93] and self-help in cases where the courts are not available. But he discusses intestate succession in great detail. This is because most contemporary wars were wars of succession arising over disputed questions of inheritance.[94] Although Grotius states in the Prolegomena that he wrote *JBP* without considering the controversies of his time,[95] he did not

[89] Grotius uses the word *alieno* (alienate) in the heading and the word *recedo* (withdraw) in the text of II. vi. 5. Although a part may withdraw from the whole on grounds of necessity, necessity does not include the right to alienate (II. vi. 6). Thus it would be difficult to regard secession as a form of alienation.

[90] II. vi. 13.

[91] See e.g. Lauterpacht 1975: 361.

[92] II. vii. 1.

[93] II. vii. 2(1).

[94] See Naruse 1970: 73; Trevor-Roper 1970: 267–8, 290.

[95] Prol. 58.

consistently maintain this attitude. In the section on succession, it is obvious that he sought to present standards for settling contemporary disputes over inheritance, particularly the succession of kingdoms. In fact, he cited examples of succession close to his own age, in addition to those from ancient times.[96]

(1) *Succession by Private Persons*

Grotius traces the origins of intestate succession to the natural assumption that the deceased intended to have his heirs inherit his property.[97] On the basis of this assumption and of the duty to support one's family, property held by the parents should be inherited by lineal descendants, rather than by lineal ascendants.[98] These principles concerning succession by private persons belong to the permissive, not to the mandatory natural law. Thus, positive laws and agreements may establish different rules of succession. Except for cases in which he rejects the validity of certain municipal laws,[99] Grotius adheres to his original policy of not discussing municipal law in detail, and states only general principles of private succession. But these principles cover only a limited range, thus leaving wide scope for diversity in the rules of municipal law.[100]

(2) *Succession of Kingdoms*

Grotius explains succession to kingdoms in great detail. He first draws a distinction between those kingdoms whose kings have an unrestricted *dominium*, i.e. patrimonial kingdoms (*regnum patrimoniale*), and those whose kings are merely vested with usufructuary rights. In the former case, adopted children are not to be excluded from being heirs; the eldest child, whether male or female, succeeds to the throne if the kingdom is indivisible. In patrimonial kingdoms each king may decide freely who should succeed.[101] In usufructuary kingdoms it is not the king but the people who decides succession. But it is possible to make kingdoms hereditary (*regnum hereditarium*) by the consent of the people.

[96] II. vii. 22(1) and 27(2). [97] II. vii. 3. [98] II. vii. 5.

[99] II. vii. 11(1); e.g. municipal laws such as those of England, Brittany, and Sicily, under which the goods of shipwrecked persons may be confiscated by the state treasury, are contrary to mandatory natural law (II. vii. 1).

[100] Grotius remarks in *Inleiding* that there are various local laws in the Provinces of Holland and West Friesland which are still not unified (Grotius = Lee 1926: 187 (II. xxvi. 12)).

[101] II. vii. 12 and 13.

Grotius then sets out detailed rules covering various kinds of succession and related issues such as disinheritance and abdication. None the less, his treatment of this issue is neither fully satisfactory nor entirely systematic. A first difficulty is as follows: while succession by private persons is understood to be based on permissive natural law, it is not clear whether this is the basis for succession to kingdoms. In many cases he acknowledges the existence of laws and customs that differ from these general principles,[102] but nowhere does he clearly state that these principles themselves are allowed for by permissive natural law. Rather he states explicitly that the principle that the eldest child is given preference if patrimonial kingdoms are indivisible is based on the law of nations,[103] and that among various forms of derivative acquisition by operation of law, those treated in II. vii are based on natural law and the volitional law of nations.[104] Furthermore, he illustrates three kinds of right created by the volitional law of nations: rights by virtue of long possession, rights arising from intestate succession, and rights arising by an unequal contract.[105] We can thus surmise that the general principles applicable to succession to kingdoms are based on the volitional law of nations. A basic aspect of Grotius's thought is that principles which are self-evidently rational should be treated as part of the law of nature. However, disputes over succession to kingdoms were serious and frequent, and the principles he describes were not self-evident in this sense. It is thus more likely that Grotius treated his general principles of succession as arising, not from the law of nature, but from the law of nations.[106]

A second difficulty is Grotius's distinction between patrimonial and usufructuary kingdoms. Although central to his treatment of succession, Grotius does not clarify the basis on which the distinction should be drawn.[107] As a result, the principles related

[102] II. vii. 14, 29, and 34.

[103] II. vii. 13. [104] II. vii. 1. [105] II. xix. 6.

[106] The law of nations here may be understood as the law of nations properly so-called (see II. viii. 1 and 26). However, its principles may be changed by municipal laws, by custom (II. vii. 14 and 29), or by royal command (II. vii. 13). They are not necessarily principles of universal validity.

[107] Grotius states that some kings come to hold *imperium* with *dominium plenum* when they have acquired their kingdom in a just war, or when a people have subjected themselves without reservation to avoid some greater disaster (I. iii. 11(1)). It is not clear what actual case he had in mind, nor whether these are the only cases where *imperium* is combined with *dominium plenum*.

to usufructuary kingdoms may well have no clear or defined application.

Thirdly, according to Grotius, judicial jurisdiction belongs only to a superior. But there are no superiors with respect to succession to *imperium*, especially to supreme governing power. Thus neither the king nor the people in control of the kingdom can make a final decision on succession. If a dispute arises over succession, the disputing parties should agree to arbitration. But this is not compulsory,[108] and thus no one is authorized to render a final decision on such disputes. Although he originally intended to put forward standards of legal interpretation for settling those disputes that might actually take place with respect to succession,[109] it is doubtful whether his standards could effectively solve actual problems.

5.6. Acquisition under 'the Law of Nations': II. viii

After discussing original and derivative acquisition, Grotius examines those matters traditionally treated by Roman jurists as causes or grounds for the acquisition of *dominium* under the law of nations.[110] These are occupation of *res nullius*;[111] treasure trove; alluvion; breeding of animals; specification and blending of materials; planting, sowing, and building; acquisition of fruits;[112] and delivery.[113] Except for the breeding of animals, these matters

[108] II. vii. 27. See also II. xxiii. 8.

[109] Indeed he thought that consideration of the principles he expounds would make it 'easy to settle disputes concerning the right to kingdoms': II. vii. 24.

[110] Concerning this, see Harada 1975: 106–17; Kaser 1983: 112, 116, 120–4.

[111] The heading for II. viii. 5, states that 'it is not contrary to the law of nations (*jus Gentium*) that wild animals should be the property of kings'. Considering the content of II. viii. 5, it should be the law of nature, not the law of nations, that is invoked here.

[112] In Roman law, a life tenant and a bona fide possessor having a just cause (*ex justa causa*) acquire ownership over fruits when they are separated from the principal (in the *Pandects* a bona fide possessor is bound to make restitution of fruits that still remain: see Harada 1975: 109–10; Kaser 1983: 121–2). However, according to the late Scholastics, a possessor, whether in good faith or in bad faith, is obligated to make restitution of the fruits (Nufer 1969: 19). Grotius apparently adheres to this theory. See also II. x. 4–6.

[113] II. viii. 2–25. Wieacker warmly approves Grotius's view that delivery is unnecessary, i.e. his adoption of the principle of consent (*Konsensprinzip*), claiming that it exerted an influence on the study of private laws in France and on various codes of Germany (Wieacker 1967: 293). See also Ourliac and Malafosse 1971: 342. However, in *De Jure Praedae Commentarius*, Grotius affirms delivery *brevi manu* (1964 ⟨1604⟩ (Eng. 141)).

were generally regarded as the causes or grounds for the acquisition of *dominium* under Roman law. But Grotius argues that principles different from Roman law exist under natural law with respect to each of these except delivery,[114] and that delivery itself is merely an institution established by municipal law, which is not required under natural law. The natural law referred to here is not natural law in itself (*simpliciter*), but natural law in relation to particular institutions (*pro certo rerum statu*), that is to say, not natural law in the primitive state of community, but natural law in the state that existed after the introduction of *dominium* but before the establishment of municipal law. As is shown by the case of the occupation of *res nullius*, municipal laws may make different provision from natural law in relation to particular institutions.[115] The distinction between these two types of natural law is used to give flexibility to natural law.[116] By arguing that natural law in relation to particular institutions is open to modification by positive laws, Grotius secures a similar flexibility to that arising from the distinction between mandatory and permissive natural law.

The causes or grounds for the acquisition of *dominium* under the law of nations, as presented by Roman jurists, are treated as belonging to permissive natural law and thus as open to variation by municipal law. It was wrong for the Roman jurists to identify them with the law of nations, for they happened merely to be principles common to many peoples, and any people may freely change them.[117] In contrast, the law of nations properly so-called (*jus gentium proprie dictum*) is concerned with the mutual society of nations, and incorporates the bond of human society.[118] It is common to all nations regardless of time and place. Grotius mentions here only the acquisition of *dominium* by right of a belligerent in a formal war as a cause for acquiring *dominium* under the law of nations properly so-called.

Since various municipal laws existed with respect to the issues discussed in this chapter, it would have been impossible to hammer out a law of *dominium* common to various nations beyond time and place, let alone to formulate a 'self-evident' general principle based

[114] In II. viii, Grotius takes a rather negative view of Roman law, stressing that its principles constitute merely one of many municipal laws. However, he is eclectic in adopting or rejecting Roman law according to his own standard. See also Krause 1982: 148, 197; Villey 1975: 613, 617.

[115] II. viii. 1(1) and 5. See also II. ii. 5; II. iii. 5.

[116] I. i. 10(7). [117] II. viii. 1(2). [118] II. viii. 26.

on pure standards of reason. Consequently, Grotius could not treat the issues discussed in this chapter as part of mandatory natural law, the law of nature in itself, or the law of nations properly so-called, but only as matters limited by their own time and place, that is, as the law of nature in relation to particular institutions limited in time and place.

5.7. Extinction of *Dominium* and of *Imperium*: II. ix

Dominium and *imperium* may be extinguished by the abandonment or extinction of the person in whom *dominium* or *imperium* resides. With regard to abandonment, Grotius merely refers to the principle that *dominium* ceases to exist when the intention to assert *dominium* terminates. Extinction occurs when a person dies intestate without an heir.[119] Grotius analyses in particular detail the extinction of peoples or states. He understands a people (*populus*) as an artificial entity with a single body (*corpus*) and a spirit, i.e. a full and perfect association of civic life, the first product of which is supreme governing power. Just as a river remains unchanged though the water running in it changes constantly, so a people remains unchanged though its membership changes from one generation to another. But the people ceases to exist if the body is broken up, or if its form or spirit disappears.[120] As an example of the extinction of a people, Grotius discusses the celebrated question: 'Who is the present holder of those rights which once belonged to the Roman Empire?'[121]

In *Inleiding* he had only discussed the extinction of *dominium plenum*, distinguishing extinction, death of the owner, abandonment, escape of wild animals, delivery, crime, act of authority, and prescription.[122] By contrast, in *JBP* Grotius does not distinguish the extinction of *dominium* from the extinction of *imperium*: moreover, the causes of extinction are limited to abandonment and extinction of the subject in whom they are vested. The extinction of *dominium* and *imperium* of peoples or states is discussed in much more detail than that of private persons. These features suggest that we should not take Book II of *JBP* as an independent theory of private law.

[119] II. ix. 1–3. [120] II. ix. 3–6.
[121] II. ix. 11. See further, Goez 1958: 281–377.
[122] Grotius = Lee 1926: 221–3 (II. xxxii. 2–8).

5.8. Obligations Arising from *Dominium*: II. x

The obligations in II. x are those which third parties owe to the owner of a thing (*res*).[123] Grotius mainly relies on the restitution theory advanced by the late Scholastics. He deals only with obligations arising from *dominium* and does not refer to obligations arising from *imperium*.[124]

The first obligation is that the possessor of a thing belonging to another is bound to make restitution of it and its fruits to the owner, regardless of whether he acted in good faith or not.[125] Secondly, where the property of another has been consumed in the course of making a profit, there is an obligation to make restitution of that profit to the owner of the property. It is contrary to equity (*aequitas*) that the possessor of property should profit from it at the expense of the owner.[126] The general principle is that a person who has been enriched is bound to make restitution of any gain he has made from another's property.[127]

Grotius claims to be concerned only with natural-law obligations.[128] However, since the obligation here arises from permissive natural law, municipal law can lay down different rules. Thus, the possessor of property whose owner is unknown is not bound to transfer it to others (e.g. the poor), but municipal law may provide such an obligation.[129] A receiver of money for a dishonest and immoral purpose is not obligated to make restitution of it under natural law, but may be so obliged in some municipal laws.[130]

5.9. Conclusion: Grotius as the 'Father of Private Law Theory Based on Natural Law'

According to Wieacker, Grotius constructed his international law (*Völkerrecht*) on the basis of natural law, and thereby succeeded in formulating international law as a general theory of law. As a

[123] The owner of *res* has not only a right over it, but also a right over persons (*jus in personas*). Kelsey *et al.* wrongly trans. *jus in personas* as 'persons' (II. x. 1(1)).

[124] Grotius discusses the duty that a subject owes to his ruler in I. iv, in the form of the question whether it is permissible for the former to resist the latter.

[125] II. x. 1(2)–(5). [126] II. x. 2.

[127] See Nufer 1969: 41–4. [128] II. x. 9(1).

[129] II. x. 11. The Scholastic school emphasized the obligation of the possessor of unclaimed property to give it to the poor, or to the Vatican. Vitoria opposed this, arguing that one may keep it until the true owner appears (Otte 1964: 79–80).

[130] II. x. 12.

result, his international law became a model for private-law theory based on natural law (*natürliches Privatrecht*). Through Pufendorf, Thomasius, and Wolff, Grotius influenced even details of the natural-law-oriented codes of many European countries including Germany. He also influenced the jurisprudence of the Pandectists, and modern European theories of private law.[131] Other scholars praise Grotius even more highly, calling him 'the father of private law theory based on natural law'.[132] For a number of reasons, this judgement cannot be sustained.

First, as Wieacker himself recognized, Grotius develops his 'private law theory' in Book II in connection with the just causes of war. His main concern is to enumerate the just causes of war, not to develop theories of ownership, contract, and so forth in themselves.[133] Thus, the reason why he discusses marriage and succession in such detail is that they were major causes of war. The factors cited as causes for the extinction of *dominium* and *imperium* were closely related to war. By contrast, he hardly discusses such matters as the requirements for the assignment of property or the specific forms of wills,[134] although they are important in the field of private law.

It is in *Inleiding* that Grotius develops a theory of private law, rooted in the positive laws of the Provinces of Holland.[135] This work is composed of three parts: (1) 'Of the Principle of Law and of the Legal Condition of Men'; (2) 'Of Real Rights (*Beheering*)'; and (3) 'Of Personal Rights (*Inschuld*)'. II. ii–x of *JBP* correspond

[131] Wieacker 1967: 290.

[132] Thieme asserts that, while people may object to calling Grotius 'the father of international law', no one opposes calling him 'the father of private law theory based on natural law' (Thieme 1954: 19, 21–2). See also Wolf 1963: 280–1; Feenstra 1973: 399–400; Krause 1982: 9; Hofmann 1987: 68, 73.

[133] II. ii. 1. The view advanced by Vollenhoven (1931: 100–29; 1934: 420), that in Book II Grotius treats the international law of peace and in Book III the international law of war, cannot be sustained. Book II should be regarded as treating the substantive causes of war. For a similar view, see also Ago 1983: 381–2; Haggenmacher 1983: 547–68; Haggenmacher 1985: 127.

[134] II. vi. 14(1).

[135] For the view that *Inleiding* is an important work in the field of private law, see Augé 1968: 102. According to Lee this work ceased to be a practical guide and went out of print at the beginning of the 19th cent. when a positive law of the Netherlands was enacted (Grotius = Lee 1926: p. viii), but *Inleiding* continues to have a significant influence in South Africa and Sri Lanka (Lee 1930: 29, 38). Gellinek states that 221 of the 508 legal terms used in *Inleiding* are still used today (1983: 110). See also Feenstra 1983*a*: 494–6; Smidt 1984: 179–93.

roughly to (1) and (2), and II. xi–xix to (3), but their contents differ considerably. For example, Grotius states in *Inleiding* that the complete title to property (*vollen eigendom van enckele zaken*) is acquired either by possession (acquisition of *res nullius*, acquisition by consent of the previous owner, acquisition of fruits, and prescription), or by non-possession (specification and alluvion): II. iv–x. This division is different from that between original and derivative acquisition in *JBP*.

Secondly, whether Grotius's theory can be regarded as a theory of private law is itself open to question. It is doubtful to what extent Grotius distinguishes clearly between public law and private law, or between public and private persons or capacities. According to Grotius, a people or its king acquires *imperium*—in which is included *jus eminens* (ultimate or radical title)—and *privatum plenumque dominium* by their initial occupation of land, and thereafter the latter right is distributed to private persons individually.[136] Here one may argue that Grotius distinguishes between *imperium* and *dominium*, and between public and private persons. However, this is not necessarily true. *Dominium* is not conceived as a merely economic, private-law kind of right. Indeed, *imperium* and *dominium* are not clearly distinguished as legal concepts.

Italian jurists from the twelfth century onward introduced important changes in the concept of ownership (*dominium*) under Roman law as a right over things. They distinguished protection (*protectio*), i.e. *dominium* based on governing power (*dominium secundum imperium*) on the part of the ruler, from private ownership (*proprietas*), i.e. *dominium* based on private ownership (*dominium secundum proprietatem*) on the part of others. Thus they made a sharp distinction between protection in public law and private ownership. But they also formulated the concept of *dominium* as a higher concept which included both governing power (*imperium*) and private ownership, and which thus had both public law and private law elements. According to this concept, *dominium* was not simply an economic right to use and dispose recognized by private law: it assumed a political and public-law character. Even in more modern times, this political character (*Herrschaft*) did not disappear, though it was weakened. It was not until Hegel that this political character was eradicated and the modern concept of

[136] II. iii. 4 and 19(2).

ownership was clearly formulated, with the power to use and to dispose of property as its central element.[137]

Grotius's concept of *dominium* retains many medieval features. He says that *dominium civile* (civil authority), i.e. the power to govern (*jus regendi*), can be acquired in the same manner as *dominium privatum* (ownership of private property) is acquired by a formal war,[138] and compares *dominium civile*, as *imperium*, with *dominium privatum*. *Dominium civile* overlaps with the *imperium* held by a people or its king.[139] Reflected here is the European medieval distinction between *dominium secundum imperium* and *dominium secundum proprietatem*.[140]

According to Grotius, a people or its king has *dominium eminens*, or *dominium supereminens* (the right of eminent domain) over subjects and their property.[141] By this right, a state is empowered to use, destroy, or alienate anything belonging to its subjects, if the public interest requires it and some compensation is paid.[142] A state may also take from a subject a right he acquired as a result of a vow sworn to him, or, if there is no right, forbid him to receive anything in accordance with such a vow.[143] This *dominium (super)eminens* is equated with the *jus eminens* which is included in *imperium*, and is distinct from *privatum plenumque dominium* or *dominium generale* held by a ruler over the land. Thus it constitutes a part of *imperium*,[144] although Grotius calls this right *dominium eminens*, a form of *dominium*. Once again this reveals the *Herrschaft* character of his concept of *dominium*.

137 See Brunner 1965: 244; Murakami 1979: 80–113.

138 I. iii. 8(6). According to Grotius, the *dominium privatum* that a private person can acquire directly is limited to movables captured in a formal war (III. vi. 12).

139 *Dominium publicum* (public ownership) as mentioned in II. ix. 12 also contains elements of both *imperium* and *dominium*.

140 However, Grotius does not distinguish between *proprietas* and *dominium* in *JBP*. In this sense, he is not necessarily using medieval concepts without qualification. See 5.1.

141 I. iii. 6(2); III. xix. 7. Grotius classifies capacity or power (*facultas*) as that which is common (*vulgaris*) and that which is superior (*eminens*), and defines the latter as the power which the community exercises over its members, or over the property of its members, for the sake of the common good (I. i. 6).

142 II. xiv. 7; III. xx. 7(1).

143 II. xiii. 20(3). *Dominium (super)eminens*, as formulated by Grotius, is different from the modern notion of expropriation. Grotius's theory of *dominium (super)eminens* was criticized from the time it was first introduced, and was abandoned in the 19th cent. A new conception (expropriation or *Enteignung*) arose in its place (Schwab 1975: 95–9).

144 II. iii. 19(2). See also Link 1979: 167–77.

Grotius often contrasts *dominium civile* or *dominium (super)eminens* of a people or its king with *dominium privatum* as private property rights, thus giving the impression that the latter has a non-political and private-law character. However, this *dominium* transferred to private persons by a people or its king remains dependent on *dominium generale*.[145] In *JBP* Grotius's concept of *dominium* is not a purely private right, and *imperium* and *dominium* are not clearly distinguished.[146]

Imperium extends primarily over persons, and only secondarily over land (or parts of the sea).[147] However, *imperium* as a right over persons is not limited to rights held by a people or its king. Parents, especially fathers, have *imperium* over their children, i.e. paternal rights (*patris imperium*, *imperium paternum*).[148] In marriage, the husband is regarded as the head of the wife.[149] The rights of a father over his children and of a husband over his wife are treated as a form of *imperium*.[150]

As Gierke pointed out,[151] Grotius divides the acts of a king into those done in his capacity as a king and those done as a private person, and states that municipal law is applicable only to the latter. Grotius thus seems to draw a clear distinction between public and private capacities.[152] However, the supreme governing power held by a king, and expressed by such terms as *summum imperium*, *summa potestas*, or *dominium civile*, is not an exclusive power. The power of the king ranks higher than the power of a head of the household (*patria potestas*) or of a master over his slaves

[145] The doctrine of divided ownership continued until the beginning of the 19th cent. when it was rejected by Thibaut, but it had been rejected by the humanists even before him (Wagner 1938: 32; Wiegand 1976: 118, 126). Thus it is problematic to relate the structure of Grotius's *dominium generale* held by a people or its king and *dominium* held by private persons, directly to the doctrine of divided ownership (in this regard, see Feenstra 1978: 229–30; Tanaka 1984: 78).

[146] For a discussion on the confusion between ownership (*Eigentum*) and *Herrschaft* from the European Middle Ages until the end of the 18th cent., and Grotius's failure to draw a distinction between them, see Schwab 1975: 76–9, 95–6; Link 1979: 168; Günther *et al.* 1982: 39–41.

[147] II. iii. 4(1) and 13(1). See also 5.1.

[148] II. v. 1 and 3–5.

[149] II. v. 8(1).

[150] See III. viii. 2(1). With regard to slavery, Grotius uses only the word *jus* in II. v. 27–9. However, it is possible to refer to the right or power over slaves (I. i. 5) as either *imperium* or *dominium* (under the law of nations) (II. xxvi. 1; III. vii. 5(2) and (4)).

[151] Gierke 1902: 287.

[152] II. xiv. 1(2). See also II. iv. 12(1).

(*dominica potestas*),[153] but these powers are merely located in a hierarchical order of independent powers, and are not different in character.[154] Grotius does not imply that the power of the king is the only public power, and that powers held by others such as the head of a household are private powers. His concept of supreme governing power is thus not to be identified with the modern concept of sovereignty. Nor is it correct to see an independent theory of private law in *JBP*, either as a matter of Grotius's intention or as emerging from the logical structure of his theory.

On the other hand, having regard to his influence over later generations, it cannot be denied that his thought contains some forward-looking elements which had a certain impact on later private-law theory, though not necessarily in a way he expected. Examples include the formulation of *dominium* on the basis of human agreement, the general theory of intention and representation, and marriage as an agreement between man and woman.[155] But because of the vulnerable features of Grotius's 'system' of natural law, *JBP* came to be treated by subsequent ages not as a systematic theory aiming to regulate and restrain war by means of law, but as containing a number of specific rules whose value was independent of his overall system.

In II. ii–x, Grotius attempts to formulate his system of natural law, relying mainly on Roman law[156] and on the theory of restitution advanced by the late Scholastics,[157] although subject to his own criterion of 'reason'. In this attempt, he defines the domain of permissive natural law as one which is open to change through volitional law. This technique is extensively used in the argument concerning 'that which belongs to us', especially in relation to

[153] I. i. 6. See also Cocceji 1744: 82; Grotius = Barbeyrac 1746: 42.

[154] See 4.3.1 and 2. See also Wolf 1963: 282.

[155] See Wieacker 1967: 290; Schwab 1975: 95–6; Feenstra 1983*a*: 489, 496–8; Feenstra 1983*b*: 461–5; Gellinek 1983: 120.

[156] The distinction between original and derivative acquisition is based on Roman law, and much of its content is derived from it. Grotius extends this distinction not only to *dominium* but also to *imperium*. Even with regard to *dominium*, however, he does not necessarily follow Roman law without qualification. For example, he excludes specification, one of the modes of original acquisition under Roman law (II. iii. 3), and he includes in derivative acquisition forms of succession that belong to a completely different category under Roman law. See also n. 114.

[157] See e.g. Nufer 1969: 68–78; Feenstra 1973: 377–402.

municipal law.[158] Moreover, he draws a distinction between the law of nature in itself and the law of nature in relation to particular institutions, which has the same effect as the distinction between mandatory and permissive natural law. Thus, though some rules are introduced as laid down by natural law, they are not invariable, since it is possible to provide different rules by volitional law. Grotius's practical approach, based on his recognition of the existence of various municipal laws, required such a vulnerable framework of natural and volitional law. Thus his system of natural law incorporated existing rules and institutions of or among states into natural law.[159] The basis for distinguishing between existing rules and institutions which reflect natural law and those which reflect volitional law is their degree of 'self-evidence'. This argument is developed in as comprehensive a manner as possible, so as to attain multifold restraints upon war,[160] even at the risk of undermining the systematic basis of his theory. Under such constraints, it is not surprising that *JBP* reflects a very vulnerable 'systematic' theory of private law.[161]

158 I. ii. 6(2); II. ii. 5 and 24; II. iii. 5, 6, and 10(3); II. iv. 9, 10(3); II. v. 5, 9, 11, 13, and 14; II. vi. 13; II. vii. 11(1); II. x. 11–12. See also II. v. 7, 8(1), 10(2), 24(1), etc.

159 See Fukuda 1971: 28.

160 For a similar view, see Grewe 1984*b*: 177; Behnen 1986: 95.

161 For a similar view, see Landsberg 1898: 4. Pufendorf, who is generally regarded as heir to Grotius, treats war in only one chapter (VIII. vi) of his principal work, *De Jure Naturae et Gentium*. He does not catalogue the just causes of war (1934 ⟨1688⟩, VIII. vi. 3). *Dominium* is discussed in IV. iv–ix, agreement (*pactum*) in III. iv–ix, V, etc.). He did not intend to formulate a theory of war, but to build a system of natural law regarding moral entities (*entia moralia*) in general. See also Denzer 1972: 67–74, 152–5, 218–21.

6

Agreement

6.1. Introduction

Apart from his contribution to the development of international law and of modern natural-law theory, Grotius has also been highly regarded for his contribution to modern contract law. In particular he is said to have put an end to the protracted dominance of Roman law, which attached great significance to the formalities of contract, and for having contributed to the birth of a new theory based on the mutual assent or 'meeting of minds' of the parties.[1] Although there is some justification for this view, Grotius's theory of agreement should not be considered the prototype of later voluntaristic theories which emphasized the autonomy of the will and even treated customary international law as a tacit agreement. One of the characteristics of *JBP* is its emphasis on reason and its reluctance

[1] This theory has various names: the will theory (*Willensdogma* or *Willenstheorie*) in the broad sense of the term, voluntarism (*voluntarisme*), or consensualism (*consensualisme*). There are subtle differences in the content and scope of each of these concepts, depending on where and when they were used (e.g. see Rieg 1957: 125–9, for a discussion on *Willensdogma* and *le principe de l'autonomie de la volonté*; Kitamura 1983: 169–70, for a discussion on *Willensdogma* and *consensualisme*; and Kinoshita 1985: chs. 2 and 3, for the relations between the European *Willenstheorie* and the common-law theory of contract; see also Hoshino 1972 and 1983). Nevertheless, there is a basic common feature, the recognition of the legally binding force of agreements based only on mutual assent, as opposed to the doctrine which requires agreements to be in a certain form or to be at least partly implemented. In this study this emphasis upon the will of the parties will be referred to as voluntarism. As to Grotius's role in the birth of modern contract theory, see Pothier 1861: no. 4, 22 *et passim*; Seuffert 1881: 130–1; Hironaka 1964: 31–9; Wieacker 1967: 287–301; Augé 1968: 101; Arnaud 1969: 9–12, 207–8; Ourliac and Malafosse 1969: 113; Gierke 1981: 101 n. 70; Hoshino 1983: 7, 13. Although voluntarism has not been so influential in common-law countries as in continental Europe, Grotius has been referred to as one of the key figures who contributed to the change in contract theory from formalism to voluntarism. Through Pothier (whose *Traité des obligations* was highly regarded) and other exponents of voluntarism, he had a certain, though indirect, influence on common-law theory as well. See Pound 1959: 455–7, 462; Kinoshita 1985: 48, 50–1.

to accord any overriding or privileged status to the will of the parties.

Grotius is also considered, at least by some scholars, to have adopted a contract theory as the basis for his theory of the state, and thus to have been an originator of social-contract theory.[2] Others deny this, pointing out that he does not construct a theory of the state by starting from the concept of the state of nature in which morally indifferent individuals exist outside any social or political framework.[3] Moreover, while referring to contract as the basis for the establishment of the state, he provides little by way of argument in support of such a contract. He discusses the binding force of agreements for the first time in II. xi, as part of his account of specific substantive rights capable of justifying war. The binding force of an agreement between heads of households to form a state is not singled out for attention. The issue is dealt with at the general level of the popular normative consciousness of the binding force of agreements. Thus Grotius's 'contract theory' must be examined in relation to the *whole* structure of *JBP*.

Grotius's theory of agreement in *JBP* is set out in II. xi 'On Promises' (*De Promissis*), II. xii 'On Contracts' (*De Contractibus*), II. xiii 'On an Oath' (*De Jurejurando*), II. xiv 'On Promises, Contracts and Oaths of the Supreme Rulers' (*De Eorum qui Summum Imperium Habent Promissis et Contractibus et Juramentis*), and II. xv 'On Treaties and Sponsions' (*De Federibus ac Sponsionibus*). One of the central questions here is the relationship between II. xi, which argues for the binding force of promises (*promissio* and *promissum* are used interchangeably), and II. xii–xv. Is the treatment of the binding force of promises in II. xi to be regarded as presenting a general theory of the promises and agreements dealt with in detail in II. xii–xiv? If so, why does Grotius argue for the binding force of *promissio* rather than of *pactum* in II. xi? How is the binding force of promises related to the proposition *pacta sunt servanda*, which many international lawyers have regarded as a timeless, universal principle?

This chapter seeks to comprehend Grotius's theory of agreement as it relates to the whole structure of *JBP*, focusing on II. xi–xiv, and discussing the issues outlined above. First the history of the

[2] See e.g. Gierke 1981: 100–1, 101 n. 70; Scheltens 1983: 45 n. 6.

[3] See e.g. Fukuda 1971: 17–19, 29–32. For a discussion of 'social contract', see also Gough 1936: 2–6; Inoue 1984.

concept of the binding force of agreements will be discussed, followed by an outline, and then an evaluation, of the theory of agreement in *JBP*.

6.2. The History of the Concept of the Binding Force of Agreements

6.2.1. *Nudum Pactum*[4] under Roman Law

Classical Roman law had a closed system of contract law. Contracts enforceable by a right of action (*actio*) under the civil law were limited to verbal contracts (*contractus verbis*), literal contracts (*contractus literis*), real contracts (*contractus re*), and consensual contracts (*contractus consensu*). Consensual contracts were limited to sale and purchase (*emptio, venditio*), lease and hire (*locatio, conductio*), partnership (*societas*), and mandate (*mandatum*). No binding force was attributed to any other form of agreement. 'Nuda pactio obligationem non parit: sed parit exceptionem' (D. 2. 14. 7. 4) was a basic principle of Roman law. It is referred to here as the *nudum pactum* principle.

Roman law, however, did not consistently maintain a rigid formalism. To begin with, a consensual contract, one of the limited classes of contracts enforceable by a right of action, was in its substance a bare or formless agreement. The fact that legal effects were accorded to consensual contracts as early as the second century BC has been said to be 'a unique phenomenon in the history of comparative law',[5] to be contrasted with the characteristically strict formalism of the ancient law of obligations. With the acceptance of consensual contracts and the relaxation of the strict formality of agreement by way of stipulations (*stipulatio*), the formalism of Roman contract law gradually declined.

The *Corpus Juris Civilis* recognized that, when one party performed his promise, an obligation of counter-performance arose for the other party. It included this obligation in the category of real contracts. Four kinds of innominate contracts (*do ut des*, *do ut*

[4] *Nudum pactum* has been translated into English in various ways: simple, formless, informal, bare, naked for *nudum*, and agreement, pact, promise for *pactum*. *Nudum pactum* itself was used interchangeably with *nuda pactio*. In this ch. the terms 'formless' or 'bare' agreement will be used.

[5] Harada 1975: 182.

facias, *facio ut des*, and *facio ut facias*) were thus recognized. The *Corpus Juris Civilis* also accepted the legally binding force of certain types of agreement, although they were not recognized as consensual contracts: these included *pactum adjectum*, *pactum praetorium* (*constitutum*, *receptum*), and certain types of *pactum legitimum* (*compromissum*, *donationis pactum*, *pollicitatio dotis*).[6] The acceptance of these agreements suggests that the closed system of Roman contract law no longer fitted the economic realities, and that formalism was about to collapse.

Despite this, the *principle* of formalism was maintained. Maine stated that 'if the technical language of the Romans had been as plastic as their legal theories, these Pacts enforced by the Praetor would have been styled new Contracts, new Consensual Contracts'.[7] But these changes were brought about by accepting a limited number of agreements as exceptions to the existing system of contract law. The *nudum pactum* principle continued to exist under Roman law throughout its history. Most studies of the principle *pacta sunt servanda* by international lawyers fail to attend to this point. Quoting Cicero and other ancient authorities, they tend to conclude without thorough analysis that *pacta sunt servanda* has been recognized 'since time immemorial'.[8] This view is refuted by more recent studies of Roman law and its history.[9]

On the other hand, we should not over-emphasize the importance of the *nudum pactum* principle. It is true that the principle was consistently maintained until the *Corpus Juris Civilis*, and that

[6] For discussion of the process through which legal protection came to be accorded these agreements, see Mikazuki 1946*a*: 117–28; Mikazuki 1946*b*: 318–23; Hironaka 1974: 158–237. The recognition of consensual contracts was supported by (1) the expansion of the territory of the Roman empire and the consequent increase in the number of non-Roman citizens; and (2) the brisk commercial and trading activities that served to create, from an economy based on rural communities, a Roman knightly class, the only capitalist class able to bear comparison with modern capitalism in terms of its rationalistic character. One proof of this is the fact that consensual contracts appeared as an institution under the *jus gentium* in Roman law, which regulated relations (especially transactions) between Roman and non-Roman citizens and between non-Roman citizens. See Weber 1925: vii. 3, and 4.

[7] Maine 1870: 32.

[8] e.g. Whitton 1934: 159–62; Wehberg 1959: 775–7; Kägi 1961: 710–11. The question raised in the text is not sufficiently discussed even in recent works (e.g. Lachs 1982: 364–6).

[9] See e.g. studies compiled in *Archives de philosophie du droit*, 13 (1968), and Hironaka 1974.

it survived for almost ten centuries thereafter, despite repeated challenges.[10] This survival, however, does not mean that the principle dominated the law of contract. A *nudum pactum* might lack legally binding force in the sense that it could not be enforced by a court, but it was legally protected in the sense that it could give rise to a right of exception or of defence (*exceptio*).[11] A payment made on the basis of a *nudum pactum* was valid and could be a defence to a claim for unjust enrichment on the part of the creditor. In addition, it is said that in the legal life of Rome, *nudum pactum* made up only a small proportion of all agreements. Under the vulgar law of the post-Classical Age and the *Corpus Juris Civilis*, a right of action came to be extended to most contracts and the formality of *stipulatio* came to be more and more relaxed. As a result, the only agreement that continued to be classified as *nudum pactum* and thus as unenforceable was an agreement which the parties themselves did not seek to make enforceable.[12]

Furthermore, if the view 'that the binding force of a contract could be *constituted* on the basis of men's will' was 'absolutely unknown',[13] this does not mean that the normative consciousness that promises should be kept was not shared by the society at large. Even in Rome where the *nudum pactum* principle prevailed, this popular sense of the binding force of agreements existed. The *Digest* itself states, at the beginning of II. xiv 'Agreement', that 'there is nothing more appropriate to man's faith than for people to observe what they have agreed upon between them', and links this with 'natural equity' (*aequitas naturalis*). In *De Officiis*, Cicero lists justice as one of the four virtues, the basis of which is 'good faith' (*fides*), i.e. the obligation to keep one's promises.[14] Although he cites various cases where a promise need not be kept, these are treated as exceptions.[15] In considering the legal culture of Rome we should not overlook the importance of this concept of *fides*, which

[10] One reason for its survival was that the vigorous commercial and economic activity of the Roman empire declined and was not renewed throughout the long period of the European Middle Ages.

[11] For a different view, see Diósdi 1981: 123.

[12] Kaser 1979: 159; Diósdi 1981: 124.

[13] Hironaka 1964: 27 n. 17 (emphasis in original).

[14] Cicero 1913: I. vii. 20 and 23 (Lat. 20 and 24).

[15] Ibid. I. x. 32 (Lat. 32); III. xxiv. 92 (Lat. 368). The phrase 'pacta et promissa semperre servanda sint' (ibid.) is often cited as the source of *pacta sunt servanda*.

was later to become one of the bases for recognizing the legally binding force of agreements in general.

It is true that the *nudum pactum* principle later became an object of fierce controversy, at times attacked, at other times supported, as a basic principle of Roman contract law. But we have to avoid adopting a larger-than-life image of this notion, underestimating the strength and prevalence of the popular normative consciousness that promises should be kept, just as we should avoid over-emphasizing the 'since time immemorial' principle, *pacta sunt servanda*.

6.2.2. The Theory of Agreement in the Law and Practice of Medieval Europe

For a number of reasons the *nudum pactum* principle maintained its hold in medieval European legal thinking. One reason, of course, was the continuing influence of Roman law; another was the predominance of formal and real contracts in Germanic law.[16] Furthermore, the commanding authority of Aristotle was also a ground for denying the binding force of a *nudum pactum*, for according to his concept of *synallagma*,[17] actual performance by a contracting party was needed for an agreement to be binding. Under the English common law, as well, formal and real contracts tended to predominate.[18]

However, as commerce developed it became obvious that the *nudum pactum* principle could not respond to the extension of economic activities beyond the boundaries of local communities. Moreover, the failure to keep promises was a sin under Christian doctrine: canonists were persistently critical of Roman law's denial of the binding force of a *nudum pactum*.[19] Thus that principle gradually lost its sway.

Within the Roman-law tradition, Azo, one of the leading Glossators in the twelfth century, admitted that natural obligation could arise from *nudum pactum*. Accursius argued that as long as an

[16] Mikazuki 1946*c*: 385–92; Bärmann 1961: 32–5.

[17] For various views at different times on *synallagma*, see Seidl 1932: 1322–4; Benöhr 1965.

[18] Pollock 1876: 116–26; Plucknett 1956: 628–36; Simpson 1975: pt. I, esp. 185–90.

[19] On the attitudes of the various canonists towards *nudum pactum*, see Spies 1928: 35–138; Chévrier 1929: 14–183; Söllner 1960: 243–59; Bärmann 1961: 35–42.

agreement reflected a consensus it was not to be regarded as a *nudum pactum*.[20] Scholars began to doubt how common the *nudum pactum* was in reality.[21] Among the Commentators, the view came to be generally accepted that natural obligation arose from all agreements, whatever their form, although opinions differed on their specific effects. Merchants asserted that even a *nudum pactum* should be protected by the right of action. Bartolus, a representative Commentator, remarked that it was contrary to equity (*aequitas*) not to accept the legally binding force of a *nudum pactum* in a court of commercial matters, and this gradually became the dominant view.[22] While maintaining the doctrine that only a vested agreement (*pactum vestium*) gave rise to a right of action, Bartolus accepted the binding force of agreements generally by regarding agreements with *causa* as being vested under canon law.[23] All these were attempts to solve the problem within the framework of the *nudum pactum* principle. Yet, compared with the view of contract that prevailed in the classical age of Rome, and even with that found in the *Corpus Juris Civilis*, the arguments of the Commentators constituted a real step towards establishing agreement based on mutual assent.

The practical effect of customary law was working in the same direction, under the pressure of economic needs. It is said that in France from the thirteenth century, a legal custom came to be generally adopted whereby an agreement of the contracting parties created a binding obligation, although the expression of their will to be bound had to be outwardly indicated either before a witness or in writing.[24] The binding force of bare agreements came gradually to be accepted also in Germany, on the authority of a statement in the *Sachsenspiegel* (I. 7): 'Anyone who has guaranteed or entered into an agreement concerning some matter should fulfil it, or if he has promised something, he should definitely keep it.'[25] In England the need for the security of commercial activities gradually brought about a relaxation in the formal requirements of contracts and the protection of simple contracts, especially in equity.[26]

[20] Seuffert 1881: 39–43; Hironaka 1974: 141–2.
[21] Chévrier 1929: 177–8.
[22] Seuffert 1881: 61; Hironaka 1974: 242–3.
[23] Söllner 1960: 247–53.
[24] Kitamura 1976: 1771–2; Kitamura 1983: 172–3.
[25] Kubo *et al.* 1977: 44.
[26] Kinoshita 1985: 100–5.

6.2.3. The Attitude of the Church

The same position was also promoted by the canonists. From the twelfth century, it was argued that anyone who broke a promise would ultimately be subject to excommunication for committing a grave sin, and, secondly, that the right of action under canon law extended to bare agreements: *ex nudo pacto actio nascitur*. The first of these arguments, endorsed by Huguccio in the twelfth and by Innocent IV in the thirteenth century, came to be almost unanimously accepted. The second argument did not gain the same degree of acceptance, but was supported by influential canonists from the thirteenth century onwards, and eventually gained a considerable degree of acceptance.[27] Baldus stated that it was the common opinion of the canonists that the right of action in canon law extended to *nudum pactum*.[28] In England, too, canonists played an important role in recognizing the legally binding force of informal agreements.[29]

This attitude must have had great significance, given the role the church played in contemporary European life. The ecclesiastical courts had jurisdiction over lawsuits that overlapped with the jurisdiction of the secular courts. Creditors whose right of action was not recognized under secular law were able to compel their debtors to keep their promises by suing in the ecclesiastical courts, with the ultimate sanction of excommunication.[30] The phrase 'May peace be preserved, may agreements be observed'[31] in the decree of Gregory IX was often cited, and was influential in establishing the notion of the binding force of agreements regardless of their form.

A number of theologians who directly preceded Grotius and

[27] Spies 1928: 35–138. [28] Söllner 1960: 247.

[29] Plucknett 1956: 304; Simpson 1975: 321–3; Kinoshita 1985: 104.

[30] Considering the relative unimportance of the *nudum pactum*, how much practical significance could this have had in people's lives? Spies directs his attention to the relationship between two developments in France: (1) the jurisdiction of the ecclesiastical court was abolished in 1539; and (2) in the early 16th cent., the binding force of agreements in general came to be generally accepted. He argues that because people could no longer seek redress in the ecclesiastical court, the secular courts came to accept the binding force of agreements in general (1928: 217–19).

[31] 'The Bishop Antegonus said: "Agreements (*pacta*) entered into shall have binding force, and those who have been sued due to their failure to obey them shall be disciplined by the Church." All in attendance said: "May peace be preserved, may agreements be observed (*Pax Servatur, pacta custodiantur*)"': *Corpus Juris Canonici*, 1695, Decreta. Gregor. IX, lib. 1, tit., xxxv, *De pactis*, cap. i.

who are believed to have influenced his contract theory, including Vitoria (1483–1546), Molina (1535–1600), Suárez (1548–1617), and Lessius (1554–1623), acknowledged, not fully but to a certain extent, the binding force of *nudum pactum*.[32] They argued that the reason for the negative attitude of Roman law towards *nudum pactum* was that it sought to limit the range of litigious conflicts, and that there was no distinction between bare and vested agreements (i.e. those giving rise to a right of action) under natural law, or under *jus gentium* in Roman law. Like other canonists, both Molina and Lessius affirmed that canon law accorded a right of action to an agreement with cause (*pactum cum causa*).[33]

Finally, it should be noted that the *nudum pactum* principle, the criticisms of it, and the attempts to overcome it involved the issue whether agreements in general ought to be legally protected by the right of action in municipal courts. In other contexts, such as agreements between kings, where the right of action was not the issue, it was possible to discuss the binding force of agreements or promises independently of the *nudum pactum* principle. The idea that prevailed in such cases was that agreements and promises were binding. This idea, in its simplest and most basic sense, was widely recognized, since without it there could be no negotiations and no stable relations between individuals or communities.

This does not mean that the principle *pacta sunt servanda*, as understood today, has always been accepted as a universal principle. The abstract notion of a subject or bearer of law, presupposed by the modern notion of *pacta sunt servanda*, did not exist in many pre-modern societies. The binding force of agreements was limited to those whose observance of the agreement could be guaranteed

[32] On the theories of contract formulated by these theologians, see Diesselhorst 1959: 20–30, 106–11.

[33] Issues such as formalism in Roman contract law and its decline, *causa* in the formative process of the will theory, and the significance of and interrelations between these concepts are complicated because the concepts are ambiguous and their content differs subtly depending on the time and the claimant. For a study of these intricate interrelations of *causa*, see Söllner 1960. The shift from formalism to voluntarism does not simply mean that the element of formality was removed so that mutual assent came to be regarded as the essence of contract. On one hand, *causa*, i.e. the substantive basis of agreements, was considered a sufficient condition for a legally binding agreement. On the other hand, with the gradual transformation and relaxation of the formal requirements, the existence of *causa* came to be regarded as a new form of 'vesting (*vestitus*)'. In this way, the sharp theoretical contrast between the Roman law jurists and the canonists was mitigated (Chévrier 1929: 174–83; Söllner 1960: 252–3).

by some sanction common to the parties, whether in the form of a material or religious sanction for non-observance, or by the existence of some independent authority, secular or spiritual, which could play the role of guarantor. And yet, the fact remains that the idea that promises should be kept has been widely accepted,[34] both for practical and for ethical reasons.[35]

6.2.4. The Significance of Agreement in European Culture

In addition to such universal societal requirements, the Old Testament spirit of a 'covenant between man and God' was a mainstay of European life. Covenants were considered sacred. Aquinas and Gratianus, dominant figures in the intellectual life of medieval Europe, taught that promises even between enemies must be kept.[36] Thus in both legal and political domains the binding force of promises and agreements came to be recognized. Vows to God, the feudal contract that supported the *Lehen* system, the contractual basis of various state theories since Cicero, treaties between kings, all assumed the binding force of promises or agreements in the naïve or simple sense of the term.[37] Had these agree-

[34] The validity in the pre-modern period of contracts affecting personal status (Weber 1960: 111; see also Schmitt 1928: 67 ff.) can be explained only by this wide popular acceptance of the binding force of agreements in general. Indeed, the modern state has so increased its functions that men now do things by virtue of their status as citizens and as those subject to its territorial jurisdiction which they formerly did by agreement (Cohen 1933: 554).

[35] Hironaka, Villey, and others have rightly denied the allegedly timeless and universal nature of the *pacta sunt servanda* principle by pointing out its link with modern capitalism, individualistic thinking, and the idea of natural law (see Villey 1962: 271–83; Hironaka 1964: 3–58; Villey 1968: 1–11; Hironaka 1974). Scholars in common-law countries have demonstrated the even more limited hold of the principle there (Horwitz 1977: 160–210; Atiyah 1979). But this does not contradict the universal consciousness of the binding force of promises in the naïve sense. Moreover, in its naïve sense of popular normative consciousness, the subtle difference between the binding force of 'promises' and of 'agreements' does not matter. For a similar view, see Cohen 1933: 554–5; Havinghurst 1961: 9–20. See also Höbel 1954: 328; Pound 1922: 137–8.

[36] Taube 1930: 347–54; Gough 1936: 26–7; Jellinek 1976: 201–3; Schildenberger 1970: 140–6; Jomparto and Kuwabara 1985: 9–11.

[37] Some have argued that treaties were either conceived as a form of agreement intermediate between *nudum pactum* and fully binding agreements (Phillipson 1911: 381; Chauveau 1891: 120), or required a certain form by virtue of the *nudum pactum* principle (Chailley 1932: 96–7; see also Bergfeld 1968: 174–7). However, it is unlikely that the compatibility between the *nudum pactum* principle and the binding force of treaties was seriously discussed, partly because treaty-making was usually

ments been considered *nuda pacta* because they did not fit within the categories of contracts under Roman law, and thus unenforceable, both accepted religious and social theories, and the social and political relations based on them, would have been undermined.

It was generally accepted in medieval Europe that in exercising their power, kings had to observe their promises, because even they were subject to God and the law.[38] The contract theories attributed to Hooker and Marsilius of Padua were tenable only on the assumption of the normative consciousness of the binding force of agreements. This intellectual tradition led to the notion of a contract between a king and his people, advocated by the Monarchomachs,[39] some of whom described the contract as a mandate (Salamonius), or an agreement by stipulations (Brutus), others simply as an agreement (Buchanan, Mariana). But none of the Monarchomachs gave any extended technical treatment of this issue: it is unlikely that they were concerned with the problem of consistency or compatibility of their theories with the *nudum pactum* principle.

The binding force of agreements was not always unconditionally affirmed in each of these contexts. Those who denied subordinate rulers the right of resistance strenuously attacked the contract theory of the Monarchomachs. But even the anti-Monarchomachs did not attack the idea that promises must be kept. They merely asserted (1) that a king was for various reasons not bound by an agreement with his subjects, (2) that a people or a subordinate ruler could not be a party to such a contract, or (3) that the people had alienated its rights precisely by entering into an agreement to that effect. For example, according to Barclay, a leading anti-Monarchomach, the power of the monarch was grounded in an agreement with the people. It was precisely because the people had effectively alienated their rights by this agreement that royal power over them was unconstrained.[40]

Machiavelli argued, from the viewpoint of expediency, that a

accompanied by the making of pledges or oaths, and partly because agreements between states did not raise any issue of enforceability before the domestic courts.

[38] Gierke 1881: 619–20 n. 279. See also Gough 1936: 21–72; D'Entrèves 1939: 130ff.; Kern 1956: 188; Wieacker 1967: 268.

[39] See Treumann 1895: 53–64; Sasaki 1973: 24–42; Yamashita and Maruyama 1977: 40–3, 48–9.

[40] See Treumann 1895: 39.

king was not necessarily bound by his promises. It is precisely because of the intellectual tradition described above that this was seen as such a bold, even deviant, approach. Machiavelli became a target of fierce criticism and attack, even by those (such as Bodin) who themselves rejected important features of the medieval intellectual tradition. While seeking to minimize the traditional constraints on kings by asserting a theory of sovereignty, Bodin repeatedly stressed that even a king should strictly observe a promise, especially one which pledges his faith (*foi*).[41]

To summarize, the *nudum pactum* principle was limited in its scope to the domain of enforceability by way of legal action. Even in this domain, by Grotius's time that principle had gradually lost its dominant position. But the issue remained controversial. Even in canon law, which consistently fought against the *nudum pactum* principle, there was continuing controversy between those who affirmed that legal protection should be given to *nudum pactum* and those who insisted that it should be limited to an agreement whose binding force was recognized by secular law. Even among the former, the dominant view was that there had to be a cause (*causa*) for a binding agreement. Among Roman law jurists, the *nudum pactum* principle retained its hold. Conanus (1508–1551), whom Grotius chose as the target of criticism in developing his argument, was a good example.

6.2.5. Conanus's Theory of Agreement

Conanus (Conan) did not recognize the binding force of *nudum pactum*, and vehemently criticized canon law and law merchant for adopting the contrary view. While his argument is based on Aristotle's doctrine of justice and his concept of *synallagma*, it is close to modern ideas of the separation of law from morality or religion. According to Conanus, justice is either general or special. General justice has to do with whether a man is virtuous (*honestus*) by nature or in his relationship with God. It corresponds to natural law properly so-called. This is a question that philosophers and theologians, rather than lawyers, must address.[42] Thus natural law for Conanus means nothing more than moral precepts. Promises

[41] Bodin 1577: 616 ff.

[42] This is based on Ogawa 1985: 809–10. I am indebted to Ogawa's study, which compelled me to revise my earlier view of Conanus, which had been based on Bergfeld 1968: see Onuma 1983.

should be kept as a matter of this general justice. Even if the other party fails to keep his promise, a virtuous man is expected to keep his. Conversely, a virtuous man should not force the other party to keep his promise if he is unwilling to do so. Thus, as long as promises are treated as an issue of general justice, although it may be praiseworthy to keep a promise, no relationship of rights and obligations exists between the parties.[43]

By contrast, special justice is a question specifically for jurists. It corresponds to the law of nations and to municipal law. Here its significance lies in the role it plays in negotiations or transactions, i.e. in maintaining and facilitating social life. Whereas virtue is the lodestone of general justice, utility (*utilitas*) is the key to special justice. Men enter into transactions to make up for what they each lack. Thus it is necessary to maintain order in bargaining, and it is here that the concept of *synallagma* becomes important.[44]

The concept of *synallagma* in Aristotle is both ambiguous and comprehensive. Along with intentional or voluntary exchanges of consideration, such as selling and purchasing, lease and hire, or guarantee, it includes unintentional or involuntary exchanges such as theft, adultery, murder, or defamation. At its core is the existence of specific acts between the parties involved, and the demand for restoration of the original state of affairs disturbed by those acts. In other words, a condition different from the original one, whether positive or negative, results from a certain act of one of the parties *vis-à-vis* the other party. This leads to the demand, from the viewpoint of expletive justice, that the original state of affairs be restored. This is called *synallagma*.[45]

Based on this approach, Conanus, while recognizing that consensual contracts are convenient and even indispensable for carrying out transactions and that they can thus form the basis for mutual reliance on another's future conduct, argued that binding force was accorded to innominate contracts only when *synallagma* was involved.[46] Furthermore, on the basis of Digest 2. 14. 7. 2 and 50. 16. 19, he maintained that *synallagma*, typically established by actual performance, constituted the basis of the other party's obligation. As long as this view was adopted, the binding force of

[43] Ogawa 1985: 811–12. [44] Ibid. 807–9.

[45] This interpretation of *synallagma* is mainly based on Despotopoulos 1968: 115–27. See also Benöhr 1965: 8–16.

[46] Ogawa 1985: 807–8.

nudum pactum had to be denied, for a mere promise could not bring about an actual state of affairs different from the original.[47]

Conanus's sharp distinction between law and morality (or religion) is similar to Grotius's theory, which in principle made law independent of religion or morality. However, this independence of law from religion or morality coexisted in Grotius with a common content of the two systems. In order to accomplish his paramount aim of restraining war, Grotius could not ignore the actual regulatory power of religion. In the realm of the theory of agreement, he had to reject the legal principle *nuda pactio obligationem non parit* by relying on the popular normative consciousness of the binding force of agreements (a consciousness which was legal, moral, and religious at the same time). To relegate the binding force of *nudum pactum* to the realm of morality could not be tolerated.[48] Thus he chose Conanus as his principal opponent in seeking to establish the legally binding force of agreements in general.

6.3. Grotius's Theory of Promise and Agreement[49]

6.3.1. ON PROMISES (*DE PROMISIS*): II. xi

Grotius begins his discussion of the obligation that arises from promises with a refutation of Conanus's theory of agreement. According to Grotius, Conanus asserted that (1) neither under the law of nature nor under the law of nations is any obligation created by those agreements which do not involve *synallagma*; (2) nevertheless, if giving effect to such agreements, apart from the promise involved, is consistent with honesty and some other virtue, it is honourable to comply with them; (3) the binding force of agree-

[47] Bergfeld 1968: 172–3.

[48] Pound rightly says that '[t]o the jurists of the seventeenth and eighteenth centuries no distinction between natural obligation and civil obligation was maintainable, since all natural rights or obligations must for the very reason that they were natural be legal also' (1961 ⟨1922⟩, 142).

[49] In II. xi–xiv, Grotius does not strictly distinguish between *promissio*, *promissum*, *pactio*, and *pactum*. For instance, in II. xi. 5, he uses *promitto* in the title ('the possession of reason on the part of the promisor (*in promittente*) is requisite'), but in the text he uses both *promissio* and *pactum*. Similar terminology is found throughout *JBP*. According to the Digest, the term *pactum* is derived from *pactio* (D. 2. 14. 1. 1). As a rule, Kelsey *et al.* trans. *pactum* or *pactio* as agreement and *promissio* or *promissum* as promise. They sometimes also trans. *pollicitatio* as promise (e.g. the text of II. xi. 14).

ments does not derive from the agreements themselves but from the formal contractual instrument (*contractus*) in which they are contained or to which they are added, or from the delivery of the object of an agreement; and (4) agreements which have the force of an obligation according to positive laws (*leges*), such as those containing stipulations, derive their force from the fact that positive laws render obligatory what would otherwise only be honourable.[50]

Grotius refutes Conanus on three levels. First, his theory would mean that agreements between kings or peoples have no force unless such agreements were put into effect by one party. Secondly, positive laws can be characterized as agreements common to a people or nation. Conanus himself accepts that positive law can accord binding force to agreements. If so, why cannot the intention of each person to be bound have the same effect? Thirdly, ownership of property (*rei dominium*) can be transferred by an act of will sufficiently manifested. If so, it should be possible to transfer the right to demand the delivery of property (the right being less than ownership itself) or the right to do something.[51]

Grotius goes on to distinguish three ways of speaking about things yet to come: (1) an expression of a mere intention concerning something in the future; (2) a sort of promise (*pollicitatio*) which is binding on the promisor but which confers no legal right on the other party; and (3) a perfect promise which clearly manifests the intention to confer a corresponding legal right on the other party. The third has an effect similar to the alienation of property: a promise to give (*promissio dandi*) corresponds to the

[50] II. xi. 1(1) and (2). In his understanding of Conanus, Grotius uses the phrase 'jure naturae ac gentium', and claims that Conanus asserted proposition (1) as described in the text. However, given Conanus's own terminology, this is not necessarily accurate. Even Conanus recognized the binding force of promises without *synallagma* under his pure natural law (which corresponds to Grotius's 'higher virtue'). However, because natural law is clearly *law* for Grotius, it is understandable that he should interpret Conanus in such a way. See further n. 48 and 6.2.5.

[51] II. xi. 1(3). Grotius quotes various authorities to reinforce his view that observance of promises is an obligation enjoined by natural law. He cites passages from Roman law such as 'nothing is so in harmony with the good faith of mankind as that men should keep the agreements that they have made with one another' (D. 2. 14. 1), and 'the man who according to the law of nations ought to pay, and on whose good faith we have relied . . . is indebted by the law of nature' (D. 50. 17. 84. 1). Also cited are European classical authorities such as Cicero (who in *De Officiis* refers to the observance of promises as a foundation of justice), Horace, and the Platonists (II. xi. 1(4) and (5)).

alienation of property, a promise to perform (*promissio faciendi*) to the alienation of some portion of human freedom.[52]

Finally Grotius relies on the Bible to assert that 'God Himself, who cannot be bound by any established law, would act contrary to His nature (*natura*) if He did not make good His promises'.[53] Thus the obligation to keep one's promises is understood to arise from the nature of 'immutable justice, which is common to God and to all beings possessed of reason'.[54] Grotius clearly seeks the ultimate basis of the binding force of promises in the self-evidence of natural law, i.e. the dictate of right reason. This is an example of his rationalistic framework, although this rationalism is reinforced and substantiated by the practical argument that transactions or relations between men are impossible unless binding force is accorded to agreements.[55]

Grotius proceeds to examine the conditions required for a perfect promise. The most important requirements seem to be that the promisor is not subject to intellectual disability and that the other party accepts the promise made.[56] The first requirement is axiomatic, since the binding force of promises is based on natural law, which assumes rationality.[57] The second requirement means that a promise gains objective existence as an agreement by being clearly expressed through the external act (i.e. a sufficient indication of will) of the promisor and accepted by the other party.[58]

Grotius recognizes as far as possible the validity of promises despite defects that may be present (e.g. intimidation or duress),

[52] II. xi. 2, 3 and 4. [53] II. xi. 4(1).

[54] Ibid. [55] Prol. 15; II. xvi. 1(1). See 6.4.

[56] II. xi. 5 and 14. Before acceptance, a promise may be revoked because the right has not yet been transferred (II. xi. 16). Roman law forbids the revocation of a promise (*pollicitatio*) before its acceptance, but this is merely a provision of positive law, not of natural law (II. xi. 14).

[57] Fundamentally, possession of reason is required by natural law as a condition for acquiring and retaining ownership. The law of nations in the common interest introduces the provision that minors and intellectually handicapped persons should be able to acquire and retain ownership. However, the exercise of that right is limited to those who possess reason (II. iii. 6; II. v. 2). The promises of the intellectually handicapped, children, and others who lack reason are thus void. The age at which the capacity of minors to make promises is accepted differs from one municipal law to another. There are also certain laws which declare certain promises of wards and minors void, but this is purely a matter of municipal law, and has nothing to do with natural law (II. xi. 5).

[58] II. xi. 11. Although Grotius himself uses 'promise' and 'agreement' interchangeably (see n. 49), the scheme 'promise plus acceptance constitutes agreement' is inherent in his argument.

while seeking to overcome any resulting hardship by other means (e.g. postliminy, compensation for damage, return of excess profit).[59] With regard to duress, Grotius recognizes the validity of a promise even if made under the influence of fear, on the basis that, unlike the case of mistake, an agreement (*consensus*) does actually exist. He argues that the one who has been intimidated should be released, not because the promise was void but because of the damage that should otherwise be wrongfully caused.[60] Performance of a promise based on a cause contrary to natural law cannot be required (because a wrongful cause would defile the sanctity of a promise). But if the promise has already been performed, the wrongfulness is separated from the promise itself, and the binding force of the promise has effect.[61] Even a promise made without a cause is valid under natural law, as is a promise made to obtain something which was already due before the promise (a promise which is made for a non-existent cause).[62]

In an age when Roman law maintained its dominant influence, some scholars supported a compromise position, that binding force should be accorded even to bare agreements provided there was a cause (*causa*). By contrast, Grotius asserted that even promises lacking *causa* had binding force, a clear indication of his thoroughgoing emphasis upon will (*voluntas*). However, his theory of agreement is not to be understood merely within the context of voluntarism. Grotius's rationalistic framework, with the dictate of right reason at its core, directs human beings as subjects (bearers) of will and their mutual relations, including agreements. Thus, the relations between the voluntaristic framework and the rationalistic framework (and, as will be shown later, the practical and utility-oriented approach) constitute the crucial point in understanding Grotius's theory of agreement.

6.3.2. On Contracts (*De Contractibus*): II. xii

After discussing promises, Grotius proceeds to discuss contracts by first classifying 'acts of men which are useful to others'. In this classification three main points emerge. First, 'acts of men which are useful to others are contracts, with the exception of purely charitable acts (*actus mere benefici*)'.[63] In addition, acts of mixed

[59] Exceptionally, a promise is void when a promisor makes a promise on the basis of an assumption of fact which is wrong (II. xi. 6).

[60] II. xi. 7. [61] II. xi. 9. [62] II. xi. 10 and 21. [63] II. xii. 7.

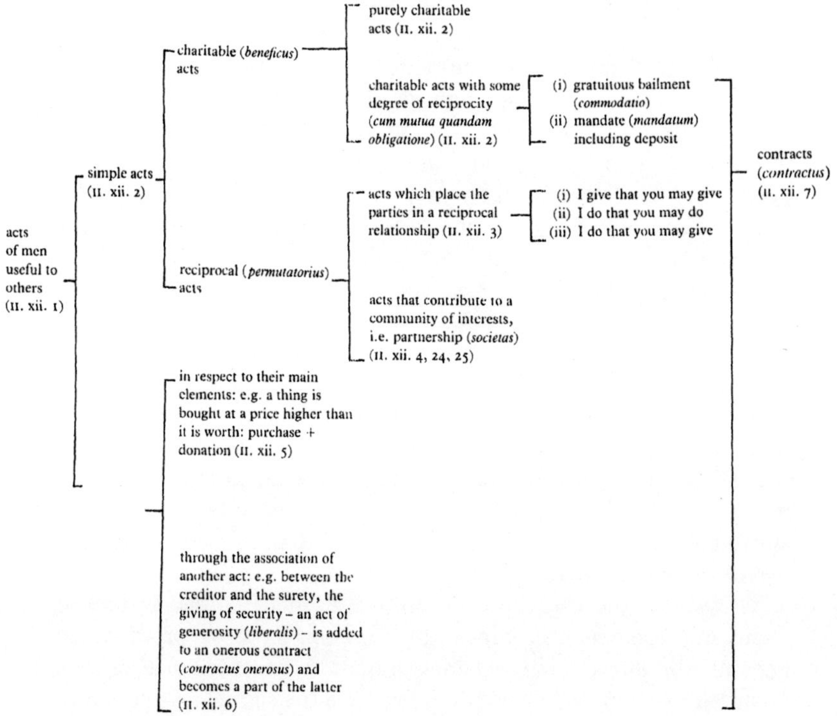

FIG. 6.1. Acts useful to others

character are classified as contracts, even though they may involve charitable acts: so too are charitable acts which involve some degree of reciprocal obligation (*cum mutua quadam obligatione*).[64] Thus in *JBP contractus* is a comprehensive notion with a concept of reciprocity in the broad sense at its core. Since this reciprocity does not require a strict mutuality of obligations, various gratuitous acts (gratuitous bailment, mandate, and deposit in trust) are included in contracts (although donation is not).[65]

Secondly, with regard to 'acts which place the parties in a

[64] II. xii. 2, 5, and 6.

[65] II. xii. 2. Had Grotius given absolute status to the mutual assent of the parties in the establishment of a contract, donations could have been included in the category of contracts. That donation was not so characterized reinforces the view that Grotius's theory was not exclusively based on the principle of voluntarism.

reciprocal relationship' (reciprocal acts except partnership), Grotius adopts a classification which according to Roman law was merely a subcategory of innominate contracts: (1) 'I give that you may give'; (2) 'I do that you may do'; and (3) 'I do that you may give'. He omitted the fourth type of innominate contract, 'I give that you may do'.[66] Thirdly, he repudiates the Roman-law distinctions between nominate and innominate contracts, or between agreements enforceable by action and those which are not, asserting that 'natural law ignores those distinctions'.[67]

Grotius's contract theory is voluntaristic in the broad sense, because it excludes the formalism of Roman law and acknowledges the establishment of a contract based on the mutual assent or the agreement of will. On the other hand, the will must be that of a rational person, and as such is subject to the limitations imposed by natural law as the dictate of right reason, a reason guided and substantiated by practical and utilitarian considerations.[68] This is manifested in the definition of acts which he claims to be the starting-point of his contract theory as 'acts of men which are useful (*utilis*) to others'.

Thereafter, the classification Grotius adopts is basically one of form and convenience. Since the binding force of promises in general has already been demonstrated, whether an act can be regarded as a contract or not does not have the significance it had in Roman law. What is important is that, since a contract is defined in terms of reciprocity, an equitable relation (*aequalitas*, *aequitas*) between contracting parties is demanded of all forms of contract (*in contractibus natura aequalitatem imperat*).[69] This is a central requirement imposed by the principle of rationalism, which qualifies and counterbalances the voluntaristic features of Grotius's contract theory.

By the time of Justinian, the closed system of Roman contract law, including its exclusive classification of contracts, had already lost its significance. Innominate contracts, consensual contracts,

[66] II. xii. 3(1). According to Pufendorf, the fourth type was omitted because it is contained in 'I do that you may give' (1934 ⟨1688⟩, v. ii. 9). But he does not provide any particular justification for this view. See also Grotius = Barbeyrac 1724: I. 418 n. 2.

[67] II. xii. 3(3).

[68] See 6.4.3.

[69] II. xii. 8. In many cases Grotius uses *aequalitas* to express equitable relations between parties, fairness, or equity, but sometimes he uses *aequitas* (e.g. II. xii. 13(2)).

and certain bare agreements occupied important positions outside the traditional classification of enforceable legal acts. Against that historical background, Grotius borrowed the classification and terminology of Roman law, except for 'I give that you may do', as a classification of reciprocal contracts. This reflects both his innovativeness in respect of principle, manifested by the assertion of the binding force of agreements in general, and his reliance on traditional terminology, notions, materials, and sources.

We have already noted that in the 'secularization of natural law' Grotius broke away from the tradition of medieval Europe (the spiritual dominance of Christianity) in principle, while relying heavily on its substance.[70] What is important for Grotius is not the separation of law from religion, the construction of an independent legal system *per se*, but the construction of a legal system that will serve the practical aim of restraining war. Thus, his break with the tradition of medieval Europe was not limited to the relation between law and religion. It also involved the continuing influence of Roman law. Moreover, he constructed his theory of agreement by adopting, at least partly, the teachings of Christian moral theology, which emphasized the binding force of promises, and by using the Bible as a key authority.[71] This also reveals that the independence of law from religion is a *hypothetical* proposition. On the other hand, Grotius did not slavishly follow the tradition of medieval European thought but modified the classifications and terminology of Roman law for his own purposes. For example, while sale and purchase, and exchange, were clearly distinguished under Roman law as consensual and innominate (real) contract respectively, Grotius included both under the category 'I give that you may give'.[72]

This willingness to vary or reject Roman-law categories is a product of Grotius's fundamental attitude of according binding force to agreements in general, including *nudum pactum*. Roman contract-law classifications depended on enforceability in court. In Grotius's theory of agreement, this is not significant, for the binding force of agreements in general has already been demonstrated. For Grotius, only a classification suitable to the actual

[70] 3.1.4.

[71] II. xi. 4(1). This is one of the main factors responsible for the misunderstanding of the 'religious basis' (Diesselhorst 1959: 39–40) of Grotius's theory of agreement. This point will be discussed in 6.4.

[72] II. xii. 3(4).

needs of contract was useful. 'Contracts, which the Roman law jurists called innominate, are neither less natural nor less ancient [than nominate contracts] . . . [T]he exchange of commodities, which is reckoned among the innominate contracts, is both simpler and more ancient than purchase'.[73] To be sure, Roman law, which distinguished sale and purchase from exchange, was comparatively rather exceptional. Grotius was thus able to remark that '*in accordance with nature* we shall refer to all those contracts placing the parties in a reciprocal position to the three classes which we have mentioned, without making any distinction between the nominate and the innominate'.[74]

Grotius argues that *aequalitas* is required in contracts by natural law, first with respect to antecedent acts (*actus procedaneos*, which includes the actual course of negotiations and the relationship between the parties so far as it has some significant impact on their contract), secondly with respect to the act of making the contract itself, and thirdly with respect to the thing about which the contract is made.[75] With regard to an antecedent act, *aequalitas* in knowledge of the facts is necessary. Hence a party is required to point out to the other any defects in the object of the transaction so far as they are known to him. Grotius argues that these rules are not only established by Roman civil law, but are consistent with the nature of the act of contracting.[76] However, Grotius's view was in fact contrary to Roman law, under which fraud was permitted in sale and purchase.[77] Thus, the obligation to make known the facts is based on his own rationalistic natural-law theory, and on his claim that there is a closer association between contracting parties than ordinarily obtains in human society: from this it follows that mutual obligations arise which are more stringent than those ordinarily obtaining.[78] This obligation to make known the facts does not exist if the other party is aware of the fault in question, because the parties are then on an equal footing.[79]

With respect to antecedent acts, *aequalitas* is also required as regards freedom of the will. Where fear is unjustly inspired in

[73] II. xii. 3(3) (Lat. 229).
[74] Ibid. (emphasis added).
[75] II. xii. 8.
[76] II. xii. 9.
[77] D. 4. 4. 16. 4.
[78] II. xii. 9(1). See also Wieacker 1967: 296.
[79] II. xii. 9(3).

concluding a contract, it should be removed.[80] In II. xii. 8, Grotius states: 'The law of nature enjoins that there be equitable relations between parties in contracts, and in such a way that the party who receives less acquires a right from the inequitable position (*ita quidem, ut ex inaequalitate jus oriatur minus habenti*).' Here the effect of *aequalitas* seems merely to be that the party who is at a disadvantage must be given a chance to recover what he has lost. This interpretation[81] is consistent with Grotius's basic premiss that promises are as far as possible to be recognized, and that any inequality or disadvantage that may arise is to be redressed by other means. However, in II. xii. 10, he cites with approval a case where a contract was annulled because it was made under the influence of fear unjustly inspired. In II. xi. 7, he says that a person who unjustly arouses fear is under an obligation to release the promisor, not because the promise is void but because the fear was unjustly occasioned. The same point is made in II. xvii. 17. Thus the *jus* accorded in II. xii. 8 to a disadvantaged party includes the right to escape from the contractual obligation.[82]

Aequalitas in the act of making a contract, the second area where Grotius calls for equitable relations between parties, is not required in a charitable contract (*contractus beneficus*) such as a mandate, but must be observed in a completely reciprocal contract (*contractus permutatorius*). Thus if either party has promised to pay in excess of what is reasonable, the excess amount is not to be considered a donation. Persons making contracts of this kind do not usually have such an intention, and it should not be presumed that they did.[83]

Aequalitas in the object of a contract is the third area where Grotius enjoins equitable relations between the parties. When there is *inaequalitas* in the thing in question (e.g. when there is a latent defect or a mistake in the price) this should be corrected, even if both parties are without fault (*culpa*) in the transaction. The reason

[80] II. xii. 10.

[81] This is probably the interpretation of Grotius = Barbeyrac 1724: II. 421.

[82] Grotius states that, according to the law of nations, *inaequalitas* between contracting parties is permissible so far as external effects are concerned. For there would be no end to disputes if it were permissible to withdraw from an agreement on account of its *inaequalitas* (II. xii. 26). This implicitly shows that *under natural law* Grotius admits the right to withdraw from a contract when there is an inequitable relation between contracting parties.

[83] II. xii. 11(1).

why Roman law limited the correction of *inaequalitas* to grave cases was to prevent a multitude of lawsuits. Those who are not subject to a municipal law (as is the case in relations between states) should not follow such a rule.[84] Even in charitable contracts he requires *aequalitas* to some extent.[85] For example, a mandatary ought to be compensated for the expense and loss incurred or suffered as a result of the mandate. One who simply borrows something without charge is under an obligation to compensate the owner if he loses the thing. This is not only because of the lender's right of ownership, but because the borrower has benefited or profited from the loan. These rules accord with Roman law but they are derived from the principle of natural equity (*ex aequitate naturali*).[86]

This requirement of *aequalitas* is consistently maintained in the subsequent discussion of specific problems concerning contracts, including sale and purchase,[87] prices, monopolies, money as a means of exchange, lease and hire, insurance, interest, and partnership. Grotius's theory of price first appears in the context of the discussion of sale and purchase, and again in the discussion of monopoly and of lease, hire, and employment. The most natural measure of the value of a thing is the need for it, but other factors such as man's penchant for the luxurious, the scarcity of things, and the labour and expenditure of the dealer should also be taken into account. In the final analysis, a thing is valued at the price generally offered within a certain range.[88] It is impermissible to profit by establishing monopolistic prices which are higher than the current range of prices, by preventing adequate supplies of goods

[84] II. xii. 12(2).

[85] II. xii. 13(1). In the title Grotius mentions not only partly charitable acts but also purely charitable acts: 'What *aequalitas* ought to be in acts that are purely charitable acts, or partly charitable acts (*in actibus mere aut partim beneficis*).' But in II. xii. 2 he had declared that he would not treat purely charitable acts in II. xii, and in II. xii. 13 he discusses only acts that are partly charitable.

[86] II. xii. 13(2). Kelsey *et al.* trans. *aequitas naturalis* as natural justice. In the context this is not a mistranslation.

[87] With regard to sale and purchase, ownership may be transferred at the time the contract is made even if there is no delivery. But this does not require the conclusion that if an object has been sold twice the first buyer always has priority. In such cases the sale is considered effective which is accompanied by a transfer of title either by delivery or in some other way (II. xii. 15). Scholars have disagreed over the binding force of dual sales (see Grotius = Barbeyrac 1724: II. 429 n. 6; Pufendorf 1934 ⟨1688⟩, V. v. 5; Wieacker 1967: 297).

[88] II. xii. 14.

from being imported by violence or fraud, or by buying up all the goods available so as to sell them at an unfair price.[89]

With regard to interest, Grotius recognizes the validity of an agreement by which a person who has lent money receives, within a reasonable limit, compensation for the loss he has suffered from not being able to use that money himself. Municipal laws which stipulate substantive interest rates on such loans are contrary neither to natural law nor to divine volitional law, if they are within reasonable limits. However, municipal laws that exceed the limit can grant only impunity, not rights, to those who exact interest. And charging interest is not permitted to Christians.[90]

With regard to partnership, it is not unjust to form a partnership in which a partner who takes upon himself the risk of loss is entitled to share more in any profit than a partner who does not, for *aequalitas* is maintained in such a case. However, it is against the nature of a partnership for one of the partners to share in the gain but be immune from loss. Nor is it just to form a partnership in which a partner is forced to bear the risk of loss but is not allowed to share in the gain. Such an arrangement is contrary to the nature of partnership, according to which all partners should share in the gain.[91]

Thus while recognizing contracts based solely on mutual assent, Grotius imposes rigid restrictions on the freedom of the contracting parties by insisting on the importance of *aequalitas*. In effect he reformulates, from the viewpoint of *aequalitas*, the requirements he had developed for the validity of promises from the viewpoint of the freedom of rational men.[92] Contracts which are contrary to the requirement of *aequalitas* are denied binding force. Grotius's theory of contract is thus rooted in his natural-law theory, which concedes a dominant position to reason, expressed here by the substantive value of *aequalitas*. This is far from a pure theory of voluntarism in which freedom of will is dominant. Thus one can understand Wieacker's insistence that Grotius's contract theory follows the Aristotelian, Thomist tradition, which requires *aequalitas* as a touchstone of the justness of contracts.[93]

[89] II. xii. 16. [90] II. xii. 20–2. [91] II. xii. 24(3).
[92] See e.g. II. xi. 6 with II. xii. 9 and 13; and II. xi. 7 with II. xii. 10.
[93] Wieacker 1967: 295.

However, with the exception of fraud and the violation of the obligation to make known a fault in a contract, Grotius ultimately retreats from his requirement of *aequalitas*, arguing that *inaequalitas* in agreements is considered as *aequalitas* as far as external acts are concerned. Thus it is impermissible to enforce *aequalitas* upon the parties to an agreement under the law of nations. *Inaequalitas* in agreements between kings, states, or peoples cannot constitute a ground for waging a just war. This acceptance of *inaequalitas* is for the practical reason of restricting disputes that would otherwise arise, especially between those who lack a common judge who could determine a just price. Disputes would be unavoidable if one could withdraw from a contract on the grounds of *inaequalitas*.[94] Grotius's voluntarist law of contract, restricted by the requirements of *aequalitas* under natural law or the principle of reason, is thus *ultimately directed* by the practical consideration of the need to minimize disputes.

6.3.3. On Oaths (*De Jurejurando*): II. xiii

In medieval Europe an oath was a bond that guaranteed the fulfilment of contracts and treaties, and had an important effect in putting an end to disputes.[95] The practice of concluding a contract by oath-taking and of inserting expressions of oath in treaties is believed to have continued until the eighteenth century.[96] Reflecting this historical importance of oaths, II. xiii is even longer than II. xi (promises) and II. xii (contracts).

The conditions of the validity of oaths are the same as for promises. Both are binding expressions of will, and thus both the capacity to reason and expressed intention are required. An oath

[94] II. xii. 26. This section reveals Grotius's thinking not only on the status of the rules discussed in II. xii, but also on the relations between the law of nature and the law of nations in general. The rules so far discussed were rules of natural law, unless otherwise indicated. However, most of these rules belong to the permissive domain of natural law. In this domain one is required by natural law to observe volitional law, as long as it is not contrary to the mandatory natural law. Thus the comment in the text does *not* constitute a permission to change the rules of natural law by agreement contrary to natural law. It is merely a rule which differs from a 'natural' rule (in the sense of the rule one is inclined to adopt within the permissive range of natural law). It is clear that volitional law cannot be contrary to natural law: e.g. it is impermissible to change the rules about fraud, or the obligation to make known the facts, by agreement based on the law of nations.

[95] II. xiii. 1(1) and 13(1).

[96] See Pothier 1861: no. 103; Idman 1913: 21 (cited by Taube 1930: 349).

taken as a result of fraud is not binding, if it is clear that the oath-taker would not have agreed if he had not been deceived. Neither are oaths to perform unlawful or impossible acts binding.[97] On the other hand, an oath is a promise with God both as witness and as judge: '"God be my witness" and "God be my judge" . . . amount to the same thing. For when a superior having the right to punish is called as a witness, punishment for faithlessness is at the same time asked from him.'[98] An oath thus has unique features because it involves God. Unlike other promises, no tacit condition can absolve one who has taken an oath. Oaths to perform an unlawful act and oaths which obstruct a greater moral good both lack binding force, for it is man's duty to God to advance towards goodness, and man does not have the power to deprive himself of either the capacity or freedom to perform good deeds.[99] An oath should be sworn with God as one's witness, but it may also be sworn in the name of other things related to God, and even in the name of 'false', i.e. non-Christian, gods. In the latter case, although the oath-taker acts 'mistakenly', he nevertheless possesses a sense of piety towards divinity in the general sense of the term.[100]

Provided these requirements are satisfied, an oath is valid *vis-à-vis* the whole world, because it is taken not only in relation to the other party but also to God. An oath given to a pirate, a robber, a tyrant, or even to those who have broken good faith, is binding. Although public enemies are treated differently from pirates under the positive law of nations, this difference is irrelevant in relation to God. Similarly, even if one is forced to take an oath out of an unjustly inspired fear, the oath-taker will be obligated in respect of God to keep the oath, although no right will be created for the other party. If *aequalitas* is not properly observed in a contract and thereby its obligations are not recognized, it will none the less have to be fulfilled if an oath has been taken, since faith (*fides*) in God has to be observed. But since an oath is an act which a person pledges to God exclusively, the heir of the oath-taker is not bound by an oath if the contract itself is void.[101]

The binding force of oaths is limited by the power of rulers over those who took the oaths—a king over his people, a father or

[97] II. xiii. 2, 4, 6 and 8. [98] II. xiii. 10.
[99] II. xiii. 3(3) and 7. [100] II. xiii. 11 and 12.
[101] II. xiii. 14, 15, 16, and 17.

master over the members of his household, a husband over his wife. In other words, subjects are not permitted to bind themselves without the approval of those who rule over them. The latter, moreover, can deny those under their rule any rights they have gained through an oath, by virtue of the right of eminent domain, thereby forbidding one who has taken an oath to receive anything by it.[102] This reflects the lack of independence of 'individuals' in *JBP*.

Logically, the argument that those subject to a rule cannot bind themselves without the approval of their rulers is applicable not only to oaths but to all other self-binding acts (assuming liabilities under contracts, concluding contracts for the formation of the state, etc.). In the theory of promise and contract developed in II. xi and xii, anyone who is capable of reason should be able to make a promise or conclude a contract. In its actual application, however, only heads of households as independent powers, not individuals in general, are deemed so qualified. And even the head of a household is subject to the restrictions imposed by the king's right of eminent domain. It is clear that the modern notion of private property as an absolute right to use or dispose of one's own assets freely, according to one's own will, was not yet seen in *JBP*.

Finally, Grotius examines the teaching of Christ, 'Swear not at all' (Matthew, 5: 34). Although Grotius did not equate biblical teachings with natural law, he frequently cited the Bible as expressing lofty virtue, or as proof of the existence of natural law, with the aim of restraining war. He thus could not ignore a biblical phrase which, if literally interpreted, would render oaths void. He sought to solve this problem by limiting Christ's injunction to 'the promise of a future uncertainty'. This phrase is an admonition to avoid indiscriminately taking oaths that are difficult or impossible to keep, and instead to strive to keep one's own word without taking oaths.[103] While this may strengthen the proposition that all promises, including oaths, should be observed, in no way does it

[102] II. xiii. 20. Kelsey *et al.* use the term 'sovereignty' here for *supereminens dominium*. This is questionable, considering the problem of the concept of 'sovereignty' in Grotius. Kelsey *et al.* themselves trans. the same words as 'eminent domain' in II. xiv. 7. It is not always clear whether Grotius distinguished *eminens dominium*, *supereminens dominium*, and *jus eminens* from each other, but it seems likely that he did not.

[103] II. xiii. 21.

contradict it. By thus excluding the literal interpretation of the biblical phrase, he incorporates it into his theory of oaths. On the other hand, he approves the customs of various countries that observe Christ's command literally, and allows the same effect to alternative ceremonies as to oaths.[104] This is an illustration of his flexibility of interpretation in pursuit of the general principle that promises are binding.

6.3.4. On Promises, Contracts, and Oaths of Supreme Rulers (*De Eorum qui Summum Imperium Habent Promissis et contractibus et juramentis*): II. xiv

Grotius next discusses the theory of agreement on the part of supreme rulers, with particular emphasis on the promises of kings. In considering these, he adopts a basic distinction between what a king undertakes as a private person and what he undertakes as a king, in his capacity as a supreme ruler. The promises, contracts, or oaths of a king in his private capacity are not only subject to the law of nature and the law of nations, but are also regulated by municipal law and even by local laws. By contrast, since municipal law does not stand above a king acting in his capacity as a supreme ruler, he is not bound by it. But if a king was not given complete rights by the people and is subject to municipal law, his acts as such may also thereby be regulated and rendered void to the extent that they are contrary to municipal law.[105] Whether particular acts of a king are undertaken by him in his capacity as a private person, and are thus subject to municipal law, is up to him to decide. If he expresses no intention, his intention must be judged from circumstances. When a king acts with the intention not to be bound by municipal law, his acts are 'judged only by natural law (*ex mero jure naturali*)'.[106]

In contrast, when a king concludes a contract as a private person he is obligated even to his own subjects, not only by natural law

[104] II. xiii. 22. [105] II. xiv. 1(2) and 2–6.

[106] II. xiv. 2(2). This rather misleading statement was presumably made to stress that the acts of a king are not regulated by municipal law. Given Grotius's system of laws, the acts of a king or other supreme ruler would be regulated by the law of nations and divine law, as well as by natural law.

but also by municipal law. This is because 'a true and proper obligation arises from a contract of a king, which he entered into with his subjects'. According to Grotius, 'such is the nature of promises and contracts we have shown above; and this holds even between God and man (*ea enim est et promissorum et contractuum natura, ut supra ostendimus: etiam inter Deum et hominem*)'.[107] This is an application of the general principle of the binding force of promises asserted in II. xi. 4. However, it is not permissible for subordinates to compel by force the one to whom they are subject. Accordingly, a king who places himself under an obligation to his subjects by concluding a contract with them cannot be compelled to fulfil his obligation.[108] In other words, subjects are not permitted to enforce their contractual rights by filing a lawsuit or by resorting to war.

Conversely, a right gained by subjects against rulers can be taken away as a punishment or by the right of eminent domain in the public interest, in which case, if possible, compensation should be paid. This right of eminent domain applies only to subjects, not to foreigners.[109] From a systematic viewpoint, it is not necessarily appropriate to discuss eminent domain as part of the theory of contract or of oath.[110] Grotius develops his theory of the right of eminent domain here due to his propensity to touch upon any topic that may be related to war or litigation, even at the cost of deviating from the main topic. Such examples are found throughout *JBP*, demonstrating its unsystematic and all-inclusive nature.

Finally, Grotius discusses whether the contracts of a king are binding on his successors. Two cases need to be distinguished: (1) where the next king succeeds to the kingship and all his possessions; and (2) where the next king succeeds only to the kingship, or to the kingship and some of his possessions. In the former case, the successor is bound by his predecessor's promises and contracts. In the latter case, the successor is bound only indirectly, through the state as intermediary.[111]

[107] II, xiv. 6(2).
[108] Ibid.
[109] II. xiv. 7 and 8.
[110] Grotius touches on the right of eminent domain in I. iii. 6(2) and II. iii. 19(2), but he clarifies its content only here and in II. xiii. 20(3).
[111] II. xiv. 10, 11, and 12.

6.3.5. Grotius's View of Promises and Agreements in Other Chapters

So far we have discussed Grotius's theory of promise and agreement as set out in II. xi–xiv. In this section we survey his treatment of promises and agreements in other chapters, having regard to the basic problem outlined in 6.1. The argument in II. xi–xiv, can be assessed only if we take into account Grotius's view of promises and agreements in the broad sense, manifested in his discussion of a variety of forms including treaties (*foedus*), sponsions (*sponsio*), consensus (*consensus*), conventions (*conventio*), and faith (*fides*), most of which are discussed in other chapters than II. xi–xiv.

(1) *Treaties and Faith with Enemies*

Grotius believed that although war could arise from breaches of private conventions, this was more frequently the case with public conventions.[112] Thus it was essential to discuss public conventions between supreme rulers (treaties in the broad sense of the term). In II. xvi ('On Interpretation'), he similarly focuses on treaties. In Book III he discusses in detail faith (*fides*) between enemies, especially peace treaties and truces. His discussion of these agreements confirms the characteristic features of his theory of promise and agreement.

In II. xv and xvi, and III. xix–xxiv, *promissio*, *promissum*, *pactio*, *pactum*, *consensus*, and *conventio*, and their respective verb forms are, in principle, used interchangeably among themselves and with such terms as *contractus*, including its verb form, *foedus*, and *fides*. The difference between these various terms is almost negligible. The only exception is that while, in *promissio* and *promissum*, emphasis is placed on the acts of one of the parties to the agreement, in *pactio* and *pactum*, emphasis is placed on the results agreed upon by both parties.

The term *fides* is used in the titles of most of the chapters and sections in III. xix–xxiv. This is probably because agreements with enemies were usually accompanied by oaths, given the difficulties in securing compliance, and in traditional nomenclature such agreements were accordingly referred to as, or together with, *juramentum*

112 II. xv. 1. Here, the terms *conventio* and *contractus* are used synonymously.

or *fides*.[113] However, except when it is necessary to distinguish promises and agreements from the oaths which accompany them,[114] the terms *promissio*, *promissum*, *pactio*, *pactum*, and *conventio*, and at times their respective verb forms, are used interchangeably with *fides*.[115]

The general requirements for a binding promise basically apply to treaties. Thus treaties with 'those who are strangers to the true religion (*his qui vera religione alieni sunt*)' or pagans (*profani*), as long as they are rational beings, are also permissible under natural law.[116] Even pirates are human beings, and as such relations with them are regulated by natural law. '[F]rom this follows [the proposition] that agreements must be kept (*ex quo nascitur ut pacta servanda sint*).'[117] This emphasis on the binding force of promises is also maintained in the case of faith with enemies. A promise is binding even with an enemy since 'the obligation to speak the truth arises from a cause (*causa*) which was valid before the war and may, perhaps, in some degree, be removed by the war. But a promise in itself confers a new right (*at promissio per se jus novum confert*)'.[118] With regard to the so-called principle *rebus sic stantibus*, Grotius adopts a very restrictive approach, although he concedes that this principle may be recognized under certain conditions. To this extent the voluntaristic character of Grotius's theory of agreement is confirmed by his approach to treaties and keeping faith with enemies.

However, Grotius does not accord any privileged status to the autonomy of the will, disregarding the procedural and substantive justness of agreements. His 'voluntaristic' attitude is further directed by the rationalistic framework of natural law which enjoins justice. Thus, whether to participate in a war according to a treaty of alliance ought to be decided by considering the just causes of war. No aid should be given to an unjust belligerent, even by an

[113] Such terms as *fides* and *juramentum* are used in the argument of Gratianus and Bodin for the observance of agreements even with enemies and bandits. See Bodin 1577: 617 ff.; Taube 1930: 350; Sibert 1956: 39–40.

[114] e.g. III. xix. 5 and 8.

[115] See the titles and text of III. xix. 1, 2, 13, 14, 15, 16, 17, 18; III. xx. 1; III. xxi, xxii; III. xxiii. 1, 6, 7, 8; III. xxiv. 1; III. xxv. In III. xxi. 5, *contractus* is used even to express an agreement of *induciae* (truce).

[116] II. xv. 8–10.

[117] III. xix. 2(2). This is the only place in *JBP* where the proposition *pacta sunt servanda* appears virtually without alteration.

[118] III. xix. 1(3).

ally. Natural law, the standard for judging the justness of a war, cannot be annulled by concluding agreements, i.e. treaties of alliance.[119] Furthermore, although an agreement to engage in a combat (*certamen*) to bring a war to an end is generally not permitted, it is permissible in the exceptional case when the unjust belligerent is about to gain a victory and the wholesale massacre of innocent people is almost certain to follow.[120] Grotius's rationalistic concept of justice is always subject to common-sense considerations, in the interests of minimizing bloodshed.

(2) *Promises and Agreements in Relation to Rights over Persons*

Since Grotius discusses treaties and faith with enemies in II. xv and III. xix–xxiv, after demonstrating the binding force of promises in II. xi, it is possible to argue that the former presupposes the latter. By contrast, state contracts, slave contracts, and the like, which are based on consent (*consensus*), are discussed virtually without reference to II. xi. The binding force of these promises or agreements is virtually taken for granted.

Grotius divides rights over persons based on consent into rights based on association (*consociatio*) and rights based on subjection (*subjectio*).[121] The first category involves rights and obligations between persons in which members of a society recognize the binding force of a law applicable to that society and promise to abide by it. These are the cases of agreement (*pactum* or *consensus*) on the basis of which a husband has authority over his wife, a state as a form of public association has authority over its members, and the law of nations has binding force over nations. The second category involves rights and obligations between persons who by subjecting themselves to another recognize that their relationship is one of subordination and promise to abide by it. Examples are the cases of consent (*consensus*) where subjects submit to state power as a form of public subjection, adopted adults submit to their father, and slaves submit to their master (the latter two are cases of private subjection).[122] This division of rights over persons is not particularly helpful in determining their specific legal relationship. For example, although marriage is 'the most natural association (*consociatio maxime naturalis*)',[123] its specific content is that the wife

[119] II. xv. 13. [120] III. xx. 43(4). [121] II. v. 8(1).
[122] Prol. 15, 17; I. iii. 8(3)–(7); II. v. 8, 23, 26, and 27; III. i. 8(2).
[123] II. v. 8(1).

is entirely subject to her husband. Grotius thus emphasizes the element of subordination based on consent not only in the case of *subjectio* but also of *consociatio*.

(i) The State Grotius discusses the state under different titles in I. iii and iv; II. v, vi, and vii, and elsewhere, and does not treat it under any separate title. He defines the state (*civitas*) as 'a complete association of free men, joined together for the enjoyment of rights and for their common interest'.[124] He also remarks that 'an association (*consociatio*) in which many heads of households (*multi patres familiarum*) unite into a single people and state (*in unum populum ac civitatem coeunt*) gives paramount authority (*maximum jus*) to the corporate body over its members. This in fact is the most perfect society (*quia haec perfectissima est societas*)'.[125] Thus Grotius's view is not very different from the Aristotelian view of the state as the most perfect society, with heads of households as its constituent members. Those who form a state are not morally indifferent individuals but heads of households who already have governing power, a political and social institution, over family members. Grotius lacks a methodological notion of the state of nature, which would have been required if the formation of the state had been regarded as a radical change from one condition to another (instituted society). *JBP* certainly contains descriptions of the condition of man prior to the institution of the state. However, this development is not seen as a change in principle, but rather as the natural historical development based on the principle of sociability.[126]

Rather than basing the formation of the state on agreement or contract, Grotius tends to appeal to the concept of agreement, including tacit agreement, as the basis for submission to municipal law. Just as the essential feature of marriage, 'the most natural association', is the submission of a wife to a husband, so in the case of the state as a public association, he emphasizes not the formation of a state by members with equal status, but the submission of subjects to a supreme ruler once a state is established. This is a natural consequence of the fact that, even when he deals with a state or marriage as an association, he regards it as a subconcept

[124] I. i. 14(1). [125] II. v. 23.

[126] For a similar view, see Gierke 1913: 384. See also 4.1.2.(2); Scheltens 1983: 50.

of 'a right over persons based on consent (*jus in personas ex consensu*)'.[127]

In addition to the formation of a state based on the association of heads of households, Grotius recognizes the mode of state formation where a large household grows into a state.[128] Examples are public subjection, where a people surrender to a man, or several men, or to another nation. Also included in this category are cases where a people live under a head of a household possessing great estates, upon condition that they submit to his rule, or where a head of a household owning a great number of slaves sets them free, upon condition that they submit to his rule.[129]

Since the first example includes an unconditional surrender of one nation to another, there seems to be lacking not only a contract of association but also a contract that limits the arbitrary power of the ruler. In the second and third examples, the only requirement for the formation of a state is that heads of households who wish to take up residence in a large estate, or freed slaves, should recognize that the owner of the estate or the one who formerly owned the slaves is the ruler of the state. Even if one calls this arrangement a 'contract', it is a far cry from the general notion of a contract where parties of equal standing have mutual rights and obligations. Moreover, such a conception of contract contradicts Grotius's own view of contract, which emphasizes reciprocity and *aequalitas* between the contracting parties.

Thus Grotius's view of the state is not based on a social-contract theory properly so called, according to which morally indifferent individuals, on an equal footing in the state of nature, establish a state by agreement. Nor does it necessarily involve a contract limiting the arbitrary power of the ruler.[130] But this does not mean that Grotius's view of the state altogether lacks a contractual basis. When he says that a state must obtain the consent of the people

[127] See II. v. 8.

[128] I. iii. 8(3). See also II. v. 31.

[129] Although Grotius himself discusses only the first of these examples as a form of public subjection, considering his own definition of public subjection the last two should also be included.

[130] Gough 1936: 77; Fukuda 1971: 17–32. Although there is a concept in *JBP* similar to a contract to restrict the arbitrariness of the rules (see I. iv. 12 and 14), it is problematic to talk about the significance of contract or social contract as the basis for Grotius's 'right of resistance', as do Wolzendorff 1916: 247–61 and Ottenwälder 1950: 94–5.

who live in an area of the state before alienating that part of the state, Grotius declares that 'this body (*corpus*) of which we are treating [i.e. a state] is in fact of a different kind [from the natural body] since it was formed contractually from compact (*voluntate contractum*)'.[131] He also says that in forming a state it may be agreed that citizens reserve the right to withdraw.[132] Moreover, 'men joined themselves together to form a civil society not by command of God, but out of their own free will (*homines non Dei praecepto, sed sponte . . . in societatem civilem coiisse*)', because isolated households were vulnerable to attack.[133] Thus although he does not clearly adopt a social-contract theory as the basis for the formation of the state, he nevertheless treats the issue of subordination to state power in terms of the agreement or consent of the ruled. In so doing, he does not think it necessary to demonstrate the binding force of this agreement or consent. He simply assumes it as self-evident.

In the Prolegomena Grotius states that 'the mother of municipal law is that obligation which arises from mutual consent' and that this obligation 'derives its force from natural law'.[134] This is because those who have associated themselves with others or with some group, or have subjected themselves to a man or to men, 'had either expressly promised, or from the nature of the transaction must be understood impliedly to have promised, that they would conform to that which should have been determined either by the majority, or by those upon whom authority had been conferred'.[135] This argument is developed immediately after the statement that 'it is necessary that among men there be some method of obligating themselves one to another, and no other natural method than this [*the observation of agreements*] can be imagined'.[136] The binding force of the agreement is thus grounded in the self-evidence of natural law, supported by practical considerations. In the case of a state as a form of public subjection, the validity of the consent of the ruled is also taken to be self-evident. Thus in both types of state, the state as public association and as public subjection, Grotius relies on the self-evidence of the binding force of promises.

(ii) The Law of Nations, Marriage, and Slavery The assumption that the binding force of agreements is self-evident manifests itself

131 II. vi. 4. 132 II. v. 24. 133 I. iv. 7(3).
134 Prol. 16. 135 Prol. 15. 136 Ibid.

also in the law of nations, in the association of husband and wife, in slave contracts, and in the agreement legitimizing ownership, all of which are based on agreements or promises. These are all discussed before the basis for the binding force of promises is demonstrated.

Public association between states, nations, or peoples is given various names: that great world (*magna illa universitas*), that community which binds together the human race, or which binds many nations together (*illa (communitas) quae genus humanum aut populos complures inter se colligat*), the mutual society of nations (*mutua gentium inter se societas*), human society (*societas humanas*), or that greater society of nations (*major illa gentium societas*).[137] The common interests of various nations are found in this aggregate. It is the (voluntary) law of nations (*jus gentium* (*voluntarium*)) which takes into consideration this common interest (*utilitas*) and which applies by mutual consent to all states or to the majority of states (*inter civitates aut omnes aut plerasque ex consensu*).[138] When there is a law in many nations that, by chance, contains the same provisions, this law is sometimes called *jus gentium*. But this terminology is wrong. The law of nations properly so-called is necessarily based on consensus common to nations (*consensus communis*) and includes the mutual obligations between nations.[139] The binding force of the law of nations is thus based on agreement between nations, supported by considerations of utility. The binding force of agreement as such is considered to be self-evident, or to be derived from natural law: no further proof is given.

Marriage, the most natural association, is defined as the cohabitation of a man with a woman in which the woman is placed under the man's protection.[140] Such an association is observed among certain animals. However, because man is an animate being endowed with reason, there is added to this the faith (*fides*) by which the woman binds herself to the man. The obligation to observe this faith is a unilateral one from the wife to the husband. The government of the household is not held in common because of the difference of sex. Since the wife becomes a member of the husband's household, the husband rules over the wife not only in matters related to marriage but also in general matters of domicile. A

[137] Prol. 17, 23; II. viii. 1(2) and 26; II. xxi. 3(2); III. xxv. 1.

[138] Prol. 17. The terms 'law of nations (*jus gentium*)' and 'volitional law of nations (*jus gentium voluntarium*)' are used synonymously.

[139] III. i. 8(2) and (5). [140] II. v. 8(2).

woman consents to subject herself to the rule of her husband out of her own free will. But once she has given her consent, the husband retains forever governing power over his wife irrespective of her will. In this sense, a husband-and-wife association has the same characteristics as the association of the state.[141]

As this reveals, no reciprocal relationship of rights and obligations between husband and wife is recognized. What is emphasized is the unilateral power of a husband and the unilateral submission of a wife, her obligation to keep faith.[142] The binding force of promises is important, for it is the wife's consent at the time of the marriage that constitutes the basis of her submission in the association of marriage.[143] And yet the binding force of this promise, which is to be demonstrated in II. xi,[144] is ultimately regarded as self-evident.

Among rights over persons based on consent, there are many types of private subjection. Grotius discusses the case of slaves in most detail. Complete slaves, the most typical, are those who owe 'lifelong service in return for nourishment and other necessaries of life'.[145] Grotius assumes agreement as the basis for subjection to this form of slavery. This is evident from the fact that, in addition to discussing this issue as part of 'the rights over persons based on consent', he cites with approval the words of Dio of Prusa that 'innumerable persons, though free, give themselves into slavery to serve by means of contract (*ex contractus formula*)'.[146] This contract is justified on the argument, based on considerations of utility, that to be assured of a stable supply of food is more desirable than the loss of freedom, because there is no assurance that people such as day-labourers always have enough to eat. A similar argument is used to justify conquest and patrimonial monarchy. A weak person who ought to become a slave is analogous to a people threatened with destruction, a person who ought to be a master (a head of a household) to a conquering state or a supreme ruler.[147] It is evident that Grotius's view of the household has the same basic structure as his view of the state.

[141] II. v. 8 and 23.

[142] See Dufour 1972: 244–5.

[143] Wieacker states: 'Grotius cites marriage as an example of association (*consociatio*). Marriage was for Grotius a corporation (*Korporation*), not a contract (*Vertrag*)' (1967: 297; Wolf 1963: 282 is of the same view). Wieacker is right as long as the relationship between husband and wife is not reciprocal. But this does not deny that the basis of this relationship is based upon consent. See II. v. 10(1).

[144] Ibid. [145] II. v. 27(2). [146] II. v. 27(1). [147] I. iii. 8(3).

In a number of chapters before II. xi, various other forms of promises and agreements are mentioned. These include the promises of a king to his subjects or to God, the promises of a head of the household to his family, the promise of a husband to his wife, treaties of alliance, feudal contracts, and agreements on which ownership of things is based.[148] In some cases Grotius affirms the binding force of these agreements, in others he either qualifies or limits it. But he never denies their binding force as such. For example, when a supreme ruler makes a promise to his subjects concerning matters of government, that promise is valid as a promise. But it does not mean that the ruler thereby ceases to be supreme. Similarly, even if a head of the household promises something to his family, or a husband to his wife, this does not mean that their power, deriving from their status, thereby ceases.[149] In all these cases the binding force of promises as such is assumed as self-evident.

6.4. Evaluation of the Theory of Agreement in *JBP*

6.4.1. The Importance of Will in *JBP*

Grotius played an important role in establishing a modern theory of contract based on mutual assent by rejecting the traditional Roman-law principle *nuda pactio obligationem non parit*. In refuting Conanus, Grotius did not stop at compromise arguments (such as that a *nudum pactum* is obligatory if it has a just cause, or that a *nudum pactum* is obligatory under natural law although the right of action does not arise from it). He demonstrated the binding force of a promise in the most general form, characterizing it as an expression of the will of rational beings, and asserting that it is the dictate of natural law that a promise ought to be observed. In the sense that a promise is a key element common to all forms of agreement, the argument as to the binding force of promises in II. xi is also valid for the agreements referred to in II. xii–xv, III. xix–xxiv, as well as elsewhere in *JBP*. Although earlier scholars had expressed doubts and criticisms of the *nudum pactum* principle, Grotius was the first to refute the principle in a general, thorough,

[148] I. iii. 16, 21, and 23. *Proprietas*, or ownership over things, is not a 'right over persons based on consent'. But it is based on a kind of agreement (*pactum*), either expressed, as by division, or implied, as by occupation (II. ii. 2(5)).

[149] I. iii. 16(1).

and convincing way. In this sense, he succeeded in providing the historical basis for the modern voluntarist theory of agreement, the thoroughgoing form of which is the will theory of the nineteenth and early twentieth centuries.[150]

6.4.2. The Limited Scope of *Pacta sunt servanda*

However, to regard Grotius as an advocate of the voluntarist school of contract theory is one-sided. The argument in II. xi does not clearly embody the principle *pacta sunt servanda* as a general proposition. Nor does it necessarily constitute the basis for the binding force of *all* agreements. There are several reasons for this.

First, Grotius emphasizes the importance of *aequalitas* in contracts. He requires *aequalitas* in the negotiations between the parties, in the act of making the contract, and in its object, to a much greater degree than modern theories, which stress party autonomy.[151] For example, he insists on the obligation to disclose any defect and the obligation of one who has received payment exceeding the just price to return the excess. The validity of mutual assent, if there is *inaequalitas* under natural law, is thus denied. It is clear that Grotius does not admit that the freedom of the will has an absolute status. Agreements are binding because they are based on the will of rational beings, rather than because they are based on the will itself.

Secondly, Grotius's theory of promise is not clearly formulated as a general theory of agreement. True, the argument as to the binding force of promises in II. xi can be applied to various forms of agreement in *JBP*, and as such can be characterized as a general theory of agreement. But it is also treated as a specific theory of 'bare' promise, on the same footing as other forms of promise such as contract and oath.[152] While II. xii ('On Contracts') and II. xiii ('On Oaths') thus have a structure parallel to that of II. xi, there is no attempt to demonstrate separately their binding force. This is

[150] See n. 1.

[151] Horwitz stresses the difference between the earlier equitable theory and the voluntaristic theories of the 19th cent. (1977: 160–210). Although his reference is made in the context of American law, where the influence of Grotius's theory of contract is much smaller and only indirect, one can see many features of what Horwitz calls the traditional equitable theory in Grotius.

[152] See e.g. the parallel usage of promises, contracts, oaths, and the like in the text of II. xiii. 1(1), 2, and 3(5), the title and text of II. xiv. 1(1), 6(2), 9, and 10.

partly because they are premissed on the argument in II. xi. But there is another factor: since their binding force had traditionally been recognized, Grotius did not need to demonstrate it. Traditionally, *contractus* was always accepted as giving rise to a right of action. The binding force of oaths was accepted, because it involved God or some other sacred element. Accordingly, it would have been enough for Grotius to demonstrate in II. xi the binding force of the particular class of agreement known as *nudum pactum*.

Grotius is not consistent in his term for the most general and comprehensive notion of agreement. Sometimes he uses *pactum*, sometimes *conventio* or *pactio*.[153] One reason for this inconsistency was the status of oaths, which, as we have seen, were still important in Grotius's time. Although an oath might contain a promise with God as its witness, it might have been doubted whether it could really be called an agreement. It was only when oaths had lost their importance, and a completely secular theory of agreement came to be accepted, that a general theory including all forms of promise could be expressed as the binding force of agreements in general: *pacta sunt servanda*.

Finally, having regard to contemporary socio-economic factors, it was difficult for a sophisticated general theory of agreements to be established. Hironaka argues that the approval of the binding force of agreements in general came to be established in the process by which contracts as a legal mode of commodity exchange came to be a basic element of social relations. He further claims that onerous contracts played a vital role in establishing the principle *pacta sunt servanda*.[154]

It is true that the Netherlands played an important role in the development of early capitalism. However, it is difficult to characterize (as Hironaka claims) early seventeenth-century Europe as an age when 'contracts as a legal mode of commodity exchange came to be a basic element of all social relations'.[155] There is no trace in Grotius of the later primacy of onerous contracts. In *JBP* the argument about the price of goods appears only in the context of a

[153] In II. xv, Grotius cites Ulpianus's distinction between public and private conventions (*conventio*) without alteration, and uses *conventio* as the most comprehensive concept of agreement. However, he further divides public conventions into three categories: treaties (*foedus*), sponsions (*sponsio*), and others (*pactiones aliae*). Thus besides *conventio, pactio*, a synonym of *pactum*, is used as a general concept of agreement.

[154] Hironaka 1964: 14–39. [155] Ibid. 34–5.

rather dispersed discussion of various specific contracts. That primacy was not recognized even by Pufendorf, who gave much more attention to onerous contracts than Grotius.[156]

6.4.3. The Structure of the Theory of Agreement in *JBP*

(1) *Self-Evidence of the Binding Force of Promises in the Ordinary Normative Consciousness*

To gain an overall understanding of the theory of agreement in *JBP*, it is necessary to determine how the argument as to the binding force of promises in II. xi relates to the discussion of the various agreements that appear prior to this chapter, taking into consideration the intellectual history of promises and agreements in Europe. Of primary importance is the fact that the argument in II. xi does *not* necessarily constitute the basis on which Grotius earlier discussed the various types of agreement.

The *nudum pactum* principle certainly occupied a dominant status in the history of contract in Europe before the seventeenth century. But it did not affect *every* agreement in social life. Its principal importance lay in the domain of law where a right of action was an issue. State contracts, feudal contracts, and other agreements were not necessarily within the scope of the *nudum pactum* principle. That they were binding was generally considered to be self-evident. To abide by these agreements was in most cases to pledge one's faith (*fides*). Thus they remained important both in the day-to-day life of Europe, and, through the invocation of God in oaths, from the viewpoint of the salvation of the soul after death.

Had Grotius intended to establish a general theory of the binding force of agreements applicable to all agreements and promises, that general theory should have constituted the basis of the binding force of state contracts, feudal contracts, slave contracts, and the other agreements discussed prior to II. xi. But this was not the case. It is true that consent is treated as the basis of associations, such as the state and marriage, and of relations of subjection, such as those involving slaves and adopted adults. Feudal contracts were also counted among agreements. Obedience to municipal law was based on the agreement of the constituent members of the state.

[156] See Pufendorf 1934 ⟨1688⟩, III. iv, and v; V. i, ii, and iii.

The law of nations was considered to be based on agreement between nations. But these agreements are discussed mainly in II. v, where the original acquisition of rights is examined, rather than in II. xi, where the theory of promise is discussed as a form of derivative acquisition of rights. The binding force of these specific 'agreements' is not demonstrated in any coherent way.

This is not to say that no account is given of why such agreements are binding. Grotius stated in Prol. 8 that 'the obligation to fulfil promises (*promissorum implendorum obligatio*)' is, together with the abstention from that which belongs to another, the restoration to another of anything of his one may have, restitution for any damage incurred through one's fault, and the exaction of punishment, characterized as 'the source of law properly so-called'. And in Prol. 15, he stated that 'it is a rule of natural law to abide by agreements (*verno cum juris naturae sit stare pactis*)' on the grounds that 'it is necessary that among men there be some method of obligating themselves one to another, and no other natural method than this [*the observance of agreements*] can be imagined (*neque vero alisa modas naturalis singuli potest*)'. Actually, the basis of the binding force of promises, which is demonstrated in II. xi, is nothing more than this dictate of natural law, which is substantiated by considerations of practicality and utility.

(2) *The Self-Evidence of the Binding Force of Promises in II. xi and its Substantive Basis*

Grotius bases his argument for the binding force of promises in II. xi on three grounds: (1) the practical argument that if agreements between nations are not binding, serious consequences would follow; (2) the logical argument that since municipal law can be characterized as an agreement of the people, and since Conanus admits the binding force of municipal law, it is inconsistent not to recognize the binding force of agreements; and (3) the analogy from the voluntary transfer of ownership based on natural law. Ultimately, Grotius's argument is based on the self-evidence of natural law, reinforced by an appeal to numerous precepts from the Bible.

It is simplistic to conclude (as Diesselhorst does)[157] that Grotius's theory of promises has a 'religious basis' merely because he con-

[157] Diesselhorst 1959: 39–42.

cludes his demonstration by relying on the Bible. In *JBP*, although law is independent from religion in principle, it is dependent on it in substance. Grotius uses the Bible as the source not only of religious norms and divine volitional law, but also of natural law.[158] This natural law should be 'self-evident', but it is not convincing to say merely: 'Proposition X (e.g. agreements are binding) is a self-evident dictate of reason.' It is necessary to *demonstrate* why and how natural law is 'self-evident', i.e. to give evidence of its self-evidence! Hence the use of biblical precepts, many of which express ideas *generally accepted* by his European contemporaries as societal norms, and which were for that reason more likely to pass as self-evident.

On the other hand, it is wrong to regard Grotius's use of the Bible merely as an embellishment (as Olivecrona does).[159] Olivecrona himself states that for Grotius the force of a promise stems from the promisor's will, and that there is in that effect a 'psychological basis' for him to be obligated to do what he promises.[160] This is none other than the popular normative consciousness of promises and agreements which Grotius ultimately relied upon to demonstrate the 'self-evidence' of the binding force of promises and agreement. In II. xi he sought the ultimate basis for the binding force of promises in a rule of 'immutable justice, which . . . is common to God and to all beings possessed of reason'.[161] However, while the self-evidence of natural law can be formally 'demonstrated' by biblical precepts, no substantive basis for it is given. Its substantive basis is the very fact that Grotius's contemporaries held in common, though not articulated in legal terms, the normative consciousness that promises must be observed. This normative consciousness is reinforced by the practical consideration that human relations would be impossible if promises need not be fulfilled. This is not spelt out in II. xi, but is shown *indirectly* in the statement that agreements between nations would have no force (a situation at all costs to be avoided) if the binding force of agreements in general (including *nudum pactum*) were not recognized.[162]

[158] See 3.1.4. [159] Olivecrona 1971: 289–90.

[160] Ibid. 288. Olivecrona uses metahistorical and highly abstract terms to discuss the popular normative consciousness that supports the binding force of a promise. What is important is to clarify what he calls the 'psychological basis' of the binding force of agreements.

[161] II. xi. 4(1).

[162] II. xi. 1(3). This argument must have provided an important basis for the

In this way, the substantive basis of the self-evidence of natural law, the ultimate ground for the binding force of promises in II. xi, is provided by Grotius's framework of common sense, including the practical and utility-oriented approach which underlies the whole argument in *JBP*. When Grotius says in Prol. 15 that the observance of agreements is a rule of natural law, he asserts that 'it was necessary that among men there be some method of obligating themselves one to another, and no other natural method can be imagined'. In II. xvi. 1, he points out more specifically that 'if natural reason itself does not dictate that one to whom a promise has been made has the right to compel the promisor to do what the right interpretation suggests . . . the matter would have no outcome, a condition in which moral affairs are held to be impossible (*quod in moralibus pro impossibili habetur*)'. The self-evidence of the binding force of the agreements (state contracts, feudal contracts, marriage, and slavery) discussed prior to II. xi, as well as of promises, discussed in II. xi, is supported by common sense, including the practical argument that life would be impossible if the binding force of promises and agreements were not accepted.

(3) *Problems in Grotius's Method of the Theory of Agreement*

Grotius rejected the *nudum pactum* principle by making use of the popular normative consciousness that promises should be observed, thereby paving the way for the establishment of *pacta sunt servanda* as a 'universal' legal principle. This involved a break with the past. According to this popular sense of the binding force of promises, the *nudum pactum* principle had had a certain status: in the context of the right of action under Roman civil law, it was admitted to be a basic principle. However, we must remember that Grotius's 'system' embraces all forms of dispute, from lawsuits between private persons to wars between states, and that it comprehends all these issues within a *legal* framework and seeks to reach a *legal* solution. There was thus for Grotius no area left for the *nudum pactum* principle to operate as a legal principle.[163]

'self-evidence' of the binding force of agreements, for any man of common sense would agree that it would be disastrous for the binding force of treaties to be denied. But this argument was particularly important for Grotius himself, given his stringent need for a principle of the binding force of treaties. Without it his paramount aim of restraining war (whether by truce, peace treaty, or alliance) would never have been accomplished.

[163] See also n. 48.

A more serious problem exists in the relations between the autonomy of the will, the precepts of natural law which restrict this autonomy, and the practical approach which guides and substantiates the rules of natural law. The theory of promises and agreements developed in II. xi–xiv involves three propositions: (1) agreements are given a wide range of operation since they are based on the autonomy of the will; (2) this autonomy is restricted and directed by natural law, whose core is the concept of *aequalitas* as between parties to the agreement; and (3) this whole framework is itself guided and substantiated by the practical purpose of minimizing the outbreak of disputes.

However, 'rights over persons based on consent', although they may be based on agreement, do not presuppose the requirements discussed in II. xi–xiv. Those who give such a consent are not assumed to be of equal standing. The relations between unequal parties are merely *explained* and *justified* by reference to agreements. Harsh agreements, such as slave contracts and the subjection of a conquered people to the rule of the conqueror, are not subject to ethical restrictions based on natural law. They are justified on the basis of the simple utility-oriented proposition: 'It is better to be a slave than to die.'

A similar gap between Grotius's advocacy of the deductive method of proof relying on the 'self-evidence' of natural law and his substantiation of the abstract dictates of right reason by an appeal to common sense can be found in his treatment of Roman law. In various respects, he relied on Roman law to formulate and develop his contract theory: examples include (1) his arguments about mistakes, fraud, duress, and the acceptance of promises; (2) his classification of innominate contracts as part of his classification of contracts; and (3) his reliance on Ulpianus in classifying the various forms of *conventio*. But his attitude towards Roman law is highly selective. The provisions and rules of Roman law, like the writings of the Stoics and the Bible, are merely materials for the construction of his theory, and no privileged status is accorded them. Natural law as the dictate of right reason, being substantiated by an appeal to common sense, is throughout the frame of reference or guiding principle. Even rules apparently derived inductively from Roman law (as well as the positive laws of various countries) are to be deductively based on the dictates of right reason.

(4) *Duality of Grotius's Theory of Agreement*

Grotius's theory of agreement came to perform a dual role in modern legal theory. On one hand, it helped to shatter the closed, formalistic contract theory derived from Roman law, and paved the way for the modern theory of contract based on mutual assent. Grotius's theory also established a firm basis for treaties, whose binding force had been accepted but the theoretical basis of which was precarious because of its uncertain relationship to the *nudum pactum* principle. In this sense, it is understandable that later scholars came to associate Grotius with the *pacta sunt servanda* principle, even if that association was strictly incorrect.

On the other hand, his theory of agreement continued to be located within a view of the binding force of promises that emphasized the importance of *fides*, a view prevalent in contemporary Europe. He did not go beyond that tradition, but established within it the basis for the binding force of agreements in general. He assumed the traditional Aristotelian view of man as a social and political being, another prevalent view in Europe. It never occurred to him to dismantle and restructure the various existing groups (*corps*) and subject–ruler relations as human relations stripped of their socially-given nature. Existing groups and subject–ruler relations were explained either as associations or as relations of subjection, but in either case based on agreement or consent. They were thus explained as contracts based on the free will of rational beings. In this way, the entire existing order of multi-layered relations between ruler and ruled came to be justified in the name of natural law.

In the domain of international law also, Grotius did not provide the theoretical basis for the principle *pacta sunt servanda*. Nor did he regard treaties as such as a 'source' of international law. He merely reaffirmed the characterization of *jus gentium* as a tacit agreement between nations, a view often used in later ages for explaining customary international law within a purely voluntaristic framework. Even this 'independence' of *jus gentium* from natural law in *JBP*[164] is to be understood in a reserved and qualified

[164] In *De Jure Praedae Commentarius*, Grotius equated the primary law of nations (*jus gentium primarium*) with secondary natural law (*jus naturae secundarium*). Compared with this, one can certainly talk about the *relative* independence of *jus gentium* in *JBP*.

manner. First, some of the specific rules do not necessarily fall within the domain of international law. For example, although such rules as the eldest son's right of succession, or the validity of contracts lacking in *aequalitas* under *jus gentium*, are applicable to international relations, they are not limited to them. They can be regarded more as domestic rules. Secondly, the will of the parties which constitutes the basis of *jus gentium* is not an absolute will, independent of natural law. As has been indicated earlier, the will is qualified, first by natural law as the dictate of right reason, and secondly by considerations of practicality.[165]

In the field of the theory of agreement, like other fields, Grotius is often thought of as a great 'modernist'. But again this was not because he rejected the traditional view of man and of society. He was rather a great intermediary. While using tradition as a substantive basis, he formulated a modern theory in a general and comprehensive way, a theory that could be accepted both by his contemporaries and by later ages.

[165] Guggenheim fails to understand these critical features of *JBP* when he says that '[l]a grande originalité de la pensée de Grotius a . . . été d'établir une stricte separation entre le droit des gens et le droit naturel' and that '[p]our lui, le droit des gens exige *seulement* l'élément du consentement, tandis que l'élément de rationalité est reservé au droit naturel' (1958: 30, 42, emphasis added). Similar misunderstandings can be found in many authors, who tend to read *JBP* in too modernistic a way.

7

Punishment

7.1. Introduction

Punishment is 'an evil of pain which is inflicted because of an evil of action (*malum passionis quod infligitur ob malum actionis*)'. Grotius's theory of punishment is developed mainly in II. xx, which begins with this famous definition. Some have argued that this chapter marks the first appearance of the idea of criminal law in the modern theory of natural law.[1] But the theory of 'punishment' in *JBP* was not conceived with a view to constructing a self-contained, comprehensive theory of punishment. While Grotius's preference for systematic description[2] may have led him to discuss the general theory of law,[3] his theory of punishment was presented as an indispensable preliminary to advocating punishment (*punitio*) as one of the just causes of war, which is the main theme of *JBP*.[4]

Grotius advanced his detailed catalogue of just causes of war not in order to *approve* wars waged for those causes, but to *prohibit* as unlawful any war that did not have a just cause. Therefore, he had to be rigorous in determining the just causes of war.[5] This is why he regarded only serious crimes as an object of punishment, and thus as a just cause of a punitive war. It is misleading to interpret the chapter on punishment as an independent criminal-law theory. In it Grotius makes no distinction between crimes committed by states and by private persons, nor does he distinguish the punishment which should be inflicted on states from that which should be inflicted on private persons. He never treats states as having *monopolistic* or *exclusive* rights to punish or to wage a punitive war.

[1] e.g. Kimura 1966: 10.

[2] See Villey 1975: 597 ff.

[3] See Wieacker 1967: 297.

[4] Also, the 'theory of private law' set forth in Book II of *JBP* is developed only in relation to just causes of war undertaken in order to make reparation for violation of rights over life, body, property, etc.

[5] Prol. 28.

In his theory, the natural right of inflicting punishment is shared by states as well as by private persons.

Planitz states that the eighteenth-century period of the Enlightenment finally marked the end of the medieval approach to criminal law in Europe.[6] According to the theocratic criminal law previously adhered to, all governing powers, including the right to punish, originated in God. Crime was not only a violation of secular norms but also an infringement of divine law. Punishment was inflicted by God through ministers in whom He had vested the right of inflicting punishment.[7] By accepting God's punishment in this world the criminal could atone for his sin and ensure salvation in the next.[8] This meant that the severer the punishment the more effective its redemptive force. It could never be too severe. This idea, combined with the general notion of preventing offences by threats, made punishment extremely cruel.[9] A despotic criminal law was based on religious theory with law and religion inseparably combined. The Enlightenment school of the theory of punishment flatly rejected this. According to this school, the basis of the state's right to punish, which is monopolistic and exclusive, is a social contract based on man's free will. Punishment is a means to realize rational aims in the future, and retributive justice is to be viewed from a humanitarian standpoint. Thus the Enlightenment school emphasized utilitarian goals, but demanded retributive justice in order to maintain a rational balance between crime and punishment.[10]

But before this stage was reached, Grotius had already sought to do two things which were necessary if the medieval approach was to be dismantled: (1) to provide a secular basis for the right to inflict punishment and (2) to mitigate the severity of punishment. His 'secularization of criminal law' dealt the first blow to the medieval theory of criminal law. This chapter was the starting-point for later disputes over the theory of punishment.[11] But although Grotius has been often mentioned in the history of criminal-law theory, he has not been subjected to careful analysis.

[6] Planitz 1971: 259. See also Shoji 1972: 5.
[7] See Murakami 1979: 204. See also Fuwa 1950: 95.
[8] See Garçon 1922: 68.
[9] See Saiki 1938: 374–5. See also Garçon 1922: 68, 74.
[10] See Shoji 1972: 24–5.
[11] For a similar view, see Takigawa 1948: 78.

Publicists often comment that particular ideas were already apparent in Grotius, but fail to specify how and where those ideas were apparent.[12] In contrast to Grotius, Kant stressed punishment for its own sake from the viewpoint of the absolute dignity of the human character. He refused to allow punishment to be used as a means of achieving ends other than punishment itself. It was Kant's theory of punishment, not that of Grotius, which was the guiding theory in the nineteenth century. This situation continued until 1877 when Jhering developed his relativistic theory in *Zweck im Recht*.[13]

7.2. Punishment in General

7.2.1. Reasons for Punishment and Those Who Have the Right to Punish

Grotius first discusses the subject of punishment from the standpoint of the criminal himself. He then considers, from the standpoint of the person who exercises the power to punish the subject, the basis of that right. In doing so he relies on a form of a contract theory:[14] a person is deemed to have entered into a kind of contract (*contractus*) of his own free will,[15] under which he subjects himself to punishment if he commits a crime. As an Arminian advocating man's free will and the independence of reason, Grotius rejected the absolute sovereignty of God asserted by Orthodox Calvinists

[12] e.g. Fehr cites Grotius as the legal thinker who preceded Beccaria in liberating criminal law from theocratic views, but fails to elaborate or explain this argument (1952: 208).

[13] See Liszt 1905: 128 ff.

[14] II. xx. 2. Grotius cites Michael of Ephesus's annotation *On Aristotle's Nicomachean Ethics*, 5. 2: 'There is here a kind of giving and receiving which constitutes the essence of contract; for whoever has taken property or stolen anything else pays the penalty for it. . . . The ancients termed contracts not merely what men have willingly agreed to perform toward one another but also the things that are forbidden by the laws'.

[15] If the principle of legality is 'a way of preventing violation of rights by announcing in advance and by law a harm called punishment against an expected act of violation' (Yokoyama 1968: 88), Grotius's theory of 'criminal contract' can be regarded as the first step towards the establishment of that principle. For he assumes that, in making the contract to submit to a punishment if he commits a crime, an offender should be able to predict at the time of the crime what punishment he should receive in return. No one may conclude an agreement without knowing its substantive contents. Thus the established law should enable everyone to know in advance what constitutes a crime and what punishment may be exacted in response to it.

and their rigid doctrine of predestination. He replaced this concept with man's natural reason. God granted man free judgement and permitted him to exercise free will. Whether man wishes to be saved by God is a matter to be determined by free will.[16]

The next question is who is entitled to punish and why. To this, Grotius proposes the theory of the fictitious superior.[17] An offender by his very criminal act may be considered to have made himself inferior to *everybody else* who has not committed a similar crime, as if he had demoted himself from the class of men to the class of beasts, which are subject to men. Consequently, all other persons who have not committed a similar crime stand above the offender.[18] Thus anyone may punish the offender, just as Cain cried after killing his brother, 'Anyone who finds me shall kill me.' Such fictitious vertical relations between the criminal and the punisher apply only between those of equal status (brothers, subjects, friends, allies, and states). Among those who were originally in a superior–inferior relationship, the inferior is not allowed to punish the superior, even if the latter has committed an offence against the former (father against son, master against slave, or king against subject).[19] Although the idea that a superior had the right to punish was not new, Grotius's theory was obviously distinguishable. For example, Suárez thought that punishment was something 'given by the command of God' for the purpose of punishing wrongs.[20] Punishment among equals (e.g. equal states) required him to assume the existence of a certain superior authority: for Suárez, this authority was God. Accordingly, a state punishes another for a crime committed by the latter on the grounds that the former has superior authority as a minister of God. Thus the explanation given by Suárez involved the idea of a delegation of authority based on the Scholastic school of theology.[21] By contrast, Grotius, who rejects reliance on the authority of God, fictitiously raised to a higher rank all other persons of equal standing who had not com-

[16] See Matsushita 1959: 30. See also Jordan 1965: 322.

[17] II. XX. 3.

[18] Grotius quotes John 13: 7: 'Whoever of you is without sin . . . let him cast the first stone', and argues that this is a reference to a crime of a similar sort.

[19] See Vollenhoven 1926*a*: 27.

[20] Suárez 1944 ⟨1621⟩ (Lat. 805).

[21] Ito 1957*c*: 77–8.

mitted a crime, and thereby expanded the range of those with the right of punishment.[22]

In *JBP* the superior need not be God and can be a mere neighbour or neighbouring state. Thus, at least formally, *JBP* presented a theory of the right to punish not directly dependent on God's will.[23] Here, Cain's cry is a recognition of the fear of turning everyone into his enemy as a result of his own wrongdoing. Grotius sought to deter crime by generating the fear that one thereby risked turning the whole world into one's enemy.

7.2.2. Prerequisites for Exercising the Right to Punish

Although Grotius has generally been interpreted as an advocate of the retributive theory of punishment, it would be a mistake to take his definition out of context and exaggerate its importance. He uses the expression 'punishment in general means . . .', and does not view retribution as the best prescription for realizing justice. Following Aristotle,[24] he believed that certain things are good in themselves while other things are good only because of the purpose they serve or because they are needed. Punishment belongs to the latter category and is justified only if it generates a certain virtue or social utility.[25] This is why punishment may be pardoned or mitigated if there is no such reason. He rejects the notion of punishment for its own sake and instead asserts the idea of punishment for a purpose.

If the principle of absolute retribution is strictly applied,[26] there must be as many punishments as there are crimes. By contrast, punishment without purpose loses its justification, and the

[22] Grotius 1964 ⟨1604⟩ (Eng. 31); see also Ito 1965*a*: 397. Grotius rejects the theory of divine punishment, which he had adopted as the ultimate justification of punishment in *De Jure Praedae Commentarius*.

[23] See Prol. 11.

[24] Aristotle 1984: VII. xiii. 217–18.

[25] God may inflict punishment on human beings, his subordinates, for no other purpose than for its own sake. But because human beings are by nature equal, for one man to punish another who is his equal it is not enough merely to argue that punishment is necessary 'because a crime has been committed'. To justify punishment there must be some definite purpose, some 'good' or some 'necessity', such as preventing a crime or reforming an offender (II. xx. 4). See also Shoji 1983: 68–9.

[26] Kant argues that, even on the last day of civil society, the last murderer in prison must be executed (1922: 139–41).

opportunities to use it will be reduced to that extent if the principle of purposive punishment is accepted.[27] If this idea is applied to wars waged to inflict punishment, the rigid infliction of punishment, traditionally approved as a just cause of war, will be diminished proportionately, and the occasion for punitive war reduced as a result. Thus Grotius combines a weak retributive principle of punishment with a strong purposive principle of punishment.

Grotius lists three advantages or aims of punishment expounded by Plato and other philosophers: (1) the advantage to the criminal himself, i.e. correction; (2) the advantage to the victim, i.e. redressing the wrong and securing the victim's safety; (3) the advantage to the general public, i.e. denunciation.

Punishment for the advantage of the criminal himself[28] may be exacted under natural law by anyone who has not committed a similar crime. This punishment may not include the death penalty, unless there is no prospect of educating or curing the criminal and it is certain that by living he would only become worse. Since 'it would have been better for such a person to have never been born' (Mark 14: 21), dying would be a 'lesser evil' than staying alive. This is no longer punishment; rather, it is something closer to euthanasia adopted to free the criminal from an incurable disease. However, punishment for this end may be applied only in exceptional cases, because the decision as to whether the criminal's 'disease' is curable could be erroneous.

The second purpose of punishment is vindication (*vindicatio*) for the benefit or relief of the victim. This involves recovering the freedom, honour, or rights of the victim and protecting him from future injury by the same person. Although Grotius acknowledges that, according to the law of nature considered in isolation, it is not unlawful even for a private person (that victim or a third party) to exact this punishment, punishment by way of vindication should be carried out only for the purpose of removing the wrongdoer,

[27] According to the principle of purposive punishment, punishment is exacted not because a wrong has been committed but so that it will not be committed in the future. There is thus a possibility that a punishment even severer than the wrong could be exacted. Grotius may be open to criticism for not commenting on this possibility, but the significance of his reticence should be obvious if we bear in mind that his aim was to limit the exercise of the right to punish.

[28] Grotius's advocacy of punishment as education (*Erzielungstrafe*) was probably influenced by the new Protestant idea of punishment, an idea that did not serve the simple traditional purpose of frightening people into keeping within the law, but contributed instead to the purpose of reforming, educating, or rehabilitating the offender (Shoji 1972: 6–7).

incapacitating him from doing wrong, or reforming him. But vindication carried out by private parties goes beyond ensuring that the victim is not further harmed by the same offender, and turns into retribution. Therefore, after civil society was created ('as soon as numerous households (*familiae*) were united') and judicial jurisdiction (*jurisdictio*) was established, the power of vindication came to be vested only in civil society, and private persons were, in principle, no longer allowed to exercise the natural right of vindication.[29]

The third purpose of punishment is for the good of mankind in general. This punishment is exacted to deter crime in general by producing fear in people, so that they will avoid committing crimes. The right to punish for this purpose is granted to everyone under natural law, but after the state is established the exercise of this right is subject to municipal law (*jus civile*). Earlier theories generally regarded killing dangerous criminals as rightful (*innocens*) and necessary to defend society. Grotius argues that, even if a criminal is dangerous, he should not be killed if there is any possibility of reforming him in the future. Moreover, judgement in each case has to be carried out carefully and impartially, so the wisest arbiters should be chosen to act on behalf of the society.[30] He thus limits private rights to punish, which readily turn into retribution or revenge.

7.2.3. Mitigation of Punishment and Limitation of the Right to Punish by the Law of the Gospel

Grotius further limits the right to punish by invoking the law of the Gospel. Even if certain acts are allowed under natural law and municipal law, they may be forbidden according to divine law, which is a more perfect law and which promises rewards of the highest order. To obtain these rewards it is necessary to pursue virtues that transcend man's nature.[31] For example, although the law of nature permits murder for the sake of defending one's property, the law of the Gospel forbids this. In the latter, to be killed is regarded as more praiseworthy than to kill. Whereas under the law of nature men are not commanded to serve others at the risk of exposing themselves to danger, under the law of the Gospel

[29] II. xx. 8. See also I. iii. 2; II. ii. 5; II. vii. 27; II. v. 9; II. xxii. 11; III. xii. 1.
[30] II. xx. 9. [31] I. ii. 6.

men are so commanded. In other words, 'to live according to nature is the problem of him who has not yet become a believer'.

Of the first form of punishment, exacted for the benefit of the criminal, the right to discipline and to correct possessed by parents over children, masters over slaves, teachers over students, is not contrary to the Gospel. But to justify inflicting these punishments it is essential that they be useful for the person punished, by reason of his age or some other characteristic.

With regard to the second type of punishment, exacted for the benefit of the victim, vengeance for the sake of gratifying the victim is unlawful even according to natural law, and is of course forbidden by the law of the Gospel. Hebrew law not only forbids hatred harboured against neighbours, i.e. fellow countrymen (Leviticus 19: 17), but also demands that some form of kindness be shown even if they become enemies (Exodus 23: 4–5). The law of the Gospel expands the concept of neighbour to include all men and clearly prohibits retribution: '. . . love your enemies and pray for those who persecute you' (Matthew 5: 44). Similarly, Christ said: 'You have heard that it was said, "An eye for an eye, and a tooth for a tooth." But I tell you: If anyone slaps you on the right cheek, let him slap your left cheek too' (Matthew 5: 38–9).

This new teaching of Christ does not treat revenge as unlawful if it is taken justly, but urges forbearance and forgiveness. For Grotius, the right to take revenge resides only in God. Men should be patient and forbear until God takes revenge, thereby freeing themselves from the cycle of revenge and establishing in its place a cycle of forgiveness. It was to achieve this transition that the practice of demanding damages or banishing the offender was adopted as a replacement for corporal punishment.[32]

Grotius seeks to mitigate even the third form of punishment, exacted for the public good. He doubts the deterrent effect of capital punishment, and insists that publicly condemning criminals to long terms of imprisonment with hard labour is likely to be more effective in preventing crimes than the threat of capital punishment, as well as, from the standpoint of the supply of labour, more profitable for the state.[33] This argument is characteristic of Grotius as a utility-oriented advocate of the Enlightenment philosophy. Thus he plays a 'duet of love and calculation', mitigating the

[32] II. XX. 10. [33] II. XX. 12.

severity of natural law and compensating for the problems its rigid application may produce.

7.2.4. Mitigation of Punishment by Means of Pardon

After insisting upon the mitigation of punishment by the law of love, Grotius proceeds to present another mitigation theory, a theory of pardon,[34] by which he attempts further to mitigate the severity of punishment.[35] Pardon is a device stemming from the inherent human virtues of generosity and wisdom. Its essence is the forgiveness of crime. It embraces all instances where a prosecutor refrains from prosecution, a sentencing judge mitigates a penalty or imposes no penalty at all, or an official reduces a prison term or terminates the imprisonment itself after sentence has commenced. Thus, Grotius's notion of pardon is wider than the modern concept of the reduction or cancellation by the executive of a punishment imposed by the courts. Grotius does not clarify whether his demand for pardon constitutes a legal norm or merely a recommendation. Nevertheless, if people in general took it as a mandatory norm, and it served to deter war and mitigate its cruelty, Grotius's aim would be achieved. Any further explanation is unnecessary, and might even provoke an adverse reaction.

The Scholastic school had asserted that all crimes must be punished (since all crimes are equally evil). According to this view, pardon is an exemption from punishment which should have been imposed: 'the wise man . . . does what he ought to do'. Against this, Grotius argues that, even though a criminal deserves to be punished, and he who has the power to punish grants a pardon, and thus fails to punish, it does not follow that he does what he must not do. In other words, there is a discretion to exact punishment; the criteria for deciding whether to exact punishment or not lie in the purpose of each punishment.

Grotius goes on to distinguish between the period before the criminal law (*lex poenalis*) was created and the period after. In the

[34] Unlike Bodin, Grotius, and Pufendorf, Beccaria rejected the idea of pardon. On the basis that certainty of punishment is the best way to suppress crime, he criticized pardon as an institution that would undermine its effectiveness (1769: 175–7). Unlike Grotius, Beccaria adhered to Rousseau's theory of social contract and Montesquieu's separation of powers.

[35] II. xx. 21–7.

former, there was no need to exact punishment, and therefore a pardon could be granted, in the following cases: (1) where punishment would achieve no valid purpose (where few people knew the crime, and it was unnecessary, or even harmful, to disclose it by prosecuting the offender); (2) where there were other off-setting features (e.g. where the criminal had done something worthy of reward, thus off-setting the wrong he had committed); and (3) where the purpose of punishment could be attained by other means (e.g. where the victim was already satisfied with the offender's apology).[36] But even after the criminal law was created, a pardon could be granted in the form of the suspension of the criminal law. As a human volitional law that depends on man's free will, the criminal law may be suspended entirely or partially in respect of a particular person or conduct if there is a justifiable reason for doing so.[37] Such reasons include (1) where the punishment is unreasonably cruel in comparison with the crime; and (2) situations specific to the criminal, e.g. where his past achievements or future promise commend him to mercy, or where the criminal commits a crime through ignorance or some mental disorder. In these cases, the criminal is to be exempted from punishment.[38]

7.2.5. The Measures of Sentencing

Next Grotius examines the problem of sentencing.[39] Matters to be considered in connection with sentencing are the grounds on which punishment may be inflicted; and the purposes for which punishment is inflicted. No one in principle is subject to punishment disproportionate to the severity of the crime. On the other hand, the intention and motive of the criminal must be taken into account in determining the measure of punishment. Within these limits, a sentence should be imposed by reference to the advantages to be gained by exacting punishment. In addition, the sentence should vary depending on the scope, the degree, and the object of the injury or harm to other people and society. A crime which results in actual injury is more serious than an attempt, and the larger the number of victims the greater the culpability of the offence. The character of the criminal and his environment may also be included among the criteria for sentencing, because the ability to decide whether or not one should commit a crime differs depending on

[36] II. xx. 22.
[37] II. xx. 24.
[38] II. xx. 25 and 26.
[39] II. xx. 28–37.

one's physical condition, age, sex, and level of education, as well as one's personal circumstances at the time of the offence.

In certain cases it may be proper for an offender to be punished with a severity disproportionate to the crime. For example, it is just for a person who has pulled out an eye of another person to have his own eye pulled out and be subject to additional suffering. This is because it is unfair for an innocent person who has had his eye pulled out to be exposed to exactly the same danger as the offender.[40] However, from the standpoint of the one being punished, the lightest possible punishment is desirable. Although it will be necessary to impose a severe penalty for the purpose of making an example of the criminal and deterring others, punishment may be mitigated and even suspended indefinitely if there are no such extrinsic causes. Thus, Grotius quotes the examples of emperors who were lenient in sentencing and cites Isocrates's advice that 'punishments should be made less than the crimes deserve'. He agrees with Isaeus that, whereas penal provisions themselves should be strict, the punishments exacted should be milder.[41]

7.3. Punitive War

Grotius applies the theory of the fictitious superior also to punitive wars waged between those of equal status. This expands the number of those who may wage a punitive war. To offset this, he limits the crimes that may constitute a just ground for initiating punitive wars. Minor and habitual offences must be overlooked, and only serious offences are liable to punishment.[42]

Grotius does not specify the offences in respect of which a punitive war can be waged. However, the catalogue of substantive rights illustrated in Book II, violation of which may constitute a just cause of war, can also be used to determine the legal interests that should be protected not only by a war of restitution but also by punitive war. In fact, Grotius admits that, in many cases, wars of restitution based on wrongful acts may at the same time be punitive wars.[43] When this happens war will have a dual just cause, 'exacting punishment' and 'recovering damages', although Grotius does

[40] II. XX. 32. [41] II. XX. 36. [42] II. XX. 19 and 38.

[43] II. XX. 38. Grotius recognizes that the two rights to bring action may concur 'very often'.

not always distinguish civil wrongs from crimes.[44] He gives examples of cases where both civil action and criminal action arise (homicide, adultery, robbery, rape, perjury, and defamation). In these cases, not only is punishment inflicted on the offender, but the victim, the husband, or the bereaved family may sue for damages.[45]

7.3.1. Punitive War Exacted in Respect of Crimes against Men

The crimes catalogued in II. xx as just causes for waging a punitive war can be classified into two categories: crimes against men and crimes against God. Grotius applies the theory of the fictitious superior without modification to the question who may wage a punitive war in respect of crimes against men. The right to inflict punishment is vested not only in the victim but also in others who have not committed a similar crime. Grotius recognizes that his view differs from the earlier Scholastic theories of Vitoria, Vazquez, Covarruvias, Azor, and Molina.[46] They thought that the right to wage a punitive war was peculiar to state jurisdiction (*jurisdictio*), and strictly limited its use to the state with jurisdiction over the state that committed the crime, or to the victim state. In contrast, Grotius argues that the right to punish the offending state arises from the law of nature,[47] and rejects any such limitation on the right to punish. Private persons possessed the right to punish in the public interest under natural law before a state was established.[48] Thereafter, judges were appointed, who alone were given the right to take revenge on behalf of the injured. But the original freedom granted by nature of private persons before the establishment of the state may be revived in cases where the power of the state does not function.[49] Such natural freedom may still exist in its original form, because the relations between kings, peoples, or nations do not fall under a common jurisdiction. By arguing that the right of punishment is conferred on kings and peoples who themselves have not

44 See e.g. II. xvii. 11, where they are used indiscriminately.

45 II. xvii. 22.

46 II. xx. 40(4). The view advanced in *JBP* is also different from that advanced in *De Jure Praedae Commentarius*, where he had adopted the theory of jurisdiction espoused by the Scholastic school.

47 For a similar view, see Midgley 1975: 154; Ottenwälder 1950: 57. For a different view, see Ito 1965*a*: 429–30.

48 II. xx. 40(1). 49 II. xx. 8(4) and (5).

been injured, Grotius lifted all restrictions on those who could wage punitive wars, even though this ran counter to his paramount aim of minimizing war. This apparent contradiction must be examined from a number of perspectives.

First, Suárez, Vazquez, and others remained within the theoretical framework of the Scholastic school, and were content to determine to whom the right of punishment belonged by applying the theory of divine right. Since Grotius's law of nature was secular in character he could not rely on divine authority. This is the reason for introducing the theory of the fictitious superior. In order to overcome the difficulties inherent in this theory—the unlimited expansion of authors of war and the resultant increase in the outbreak of war—Grotius seeks to restrict and compress the justifications for punitive wars.

Secondly, Grotius thought it desirable for a third party to be the author of a punitive war. Since the exaction of punishment by the victim himself tends to be excessively cruel, it is appropriate for the purpose of ensuring impartiality to have a wise third party exact punishment.[50]

Thirdly, kings and peoples in Grotius's view are required not only to ensure their own individual interests but also to serve the interests of all mankind. A wise king is a friend not only to his own subjects, but to all of mankind.[51] Thus kings and peoples have an obligation to fight for the general good of mankind against acts that violate the law of nature or of nations, even if they have not been injured directly in any sense. Although this is not an absolute obligation (for natural law does not obligate them to fight a war for the sake of others at the risk of their own life and property),[52] Grotius states that 'the law of the Gospel orders it'.[53] Thus he places his ultimate hope of realizing justice on the faith of Christians waging wars as third parties to assist others. The traditional approach of individualism concerning the authors of war was changed in the direction of 'universalism' by Grotius's theory of the fictitious superior.

War waged by a third party is discussed in I. v, as war waged for the sake of others.[54] If state A were to infringe on state B's right, and B were to retaliate alone and defeat A, there would be no

[50] II. xx. 8(4) and 40(1). [51] Prol. 24; II. xx. 44. [52] II. xxv. 7.
[53] I. ii. 6. See also Prol. 50; II. xx. 10. See further Midgley 1975: 150ff.
[54] I. v. 2–4.

problem. But if B were defeated, justice would be silenced by force. Grotius had to admit war waged by third parties as a legal principle to fill the lacuna in justice thus created. The same holds true for wars waged for the sake of others as an intervention in their domestic affairs. Where the subjects of a certain state are suffering from the unjust rule of a despotic ruler, Grotius's system does not allow the inferior to wage war against the superior. Instead a third party may wage war against the tyrant for the sake of the latter's subjects.

Yet the involvement of volunteer states capable of crushing the strong and helping the weak is not institutionalized in Grotius's system, and it is only by chance that such a state may intervene. The examples Grotius gives are the great feats of legendary heroes such as Hercules and Theseus who freed people from tyrants with their unparalleled strength or intelligence.[55] Although the dangers of abuse of this right of intervention are manifest, Grotius was unable to conceive of any institutional safeguard for preventing them.[56] All he could do was to add certain qualifications in terms of the substantive just causes of punitive war. First, it is necessary to distinguish between violation of a state custom or of divine volitional law and crimes under natural law. This is to prevent punitive war from being conducted on the mistaken assumption that the offence in question is a crime under natural law when it is only a violation of some state custom or of divine volitional law.[57] Secondly, in natural law there are principles which are self-evident beyond doubt and principles which become apparent by deduction. Among the latter are laws and principles which are not so self-evident that all people can recognize them. Crimes committed by those incapable of such recognition should be excused.[58] Finally, he argues that wars undertaken to inflict punishment should be limited to crimes which 'are both atrocious and evidently wrong (*atrocissima et manifestissima*)',[59] in order to prevent war waged for the sake of others in circumstances where the justness of the war is doubtful. Only serious crimes such as disrespect for parents, homicide of a foreigner, cannibalism, and piracy justify punitive wars.[60]

These examples are consistent with the Scholastic idea of defending innocent allies and eliminating abnormal usages and practices,

[55] II. xx. 40. [56] See 3.3.3(1). [57] II. xx. 41 and 42.
[58] II. xx. 43. [59] Ibid. See also II. xxiii. 2, 4–6. [60] II. xx. 40.

as exceptions to the Scholastics' denial of the right of third parties to wage a war of assistance. Still there is a significant difference in that Grotius, albeit unsuccessfully, struggles to locate within his theoretical system as regular rights those rights which the Scholastic school recognized only as 'exceptions'. Again this difference stems from the fact that, while the Scholastic school ultimately sought support in 'divine punishment', Grotius had to treat the issue of who should wage wars of punishment in such a way that it could be settled without reference to God, at the level of logical necessity. On a more substantive level, however, Grotius was forced to adopt the solution of approving wars of assistance waged by third parties because he adhered to Aristotle's notion of a society based on superior–subject relations,[61] and denied subordinates the right of resistance against a despotic ruler.

Fourthly, Grotius sought to formulate a new theory concerning the authors of punitive war to deal with the turbulent political situation prevailing in Europe. The unity of the medieval Christian European world was collapsing, and the central position and authority of the emperor and of the pope were shaken to their foundation. Under the Scholastic theory of jurisdiction, a theory of punitive war cannot be based on the notion of a universal society or an international community. Tacitly accepting this view, Grotius posited the theory of the fictitious superior in an attempt to overcome the narrowness of the Scholastic theory, and to ensure (although by strained and implausible means) the relevance of his theory to his time.

The problem remains as to what 'universal' actually means in this theory. Grotius's 'universal' society is not a mere revival of the medieval 'universal' Christian world, by now disintegrated.[62] Nor is it a society comprised of individuals. Grotius's notion of society is comprised of households as a minimum constituent element and is thus not based on radical individualism. Nor is it conceived as a higher community that transcends individual states.[63] If that were the case, there would have been no reason to expound the concept of war waged for the sake of others in the first place. A superior would have been able to undertake punitive war on its own or order a subordinate to do so.

[61] I. i. 3. See also Fukuda 1971: 28.
[62] See also Ottenwälder 1950: 42.
[63] Eikema Hommes 1979: 87.

When Grotius referred to 'universal human society', what he had in mind, being constrained by the conditions of seventeenth-century Europe, was a 'world' virtually confined to Europe. The vast space outside and its vast numbers of inhabitants constituted a 'peripheral area' far removed from the 'centre'. Almost the only reason why the periphery had any meaning for the centre is that it provided a huge market for the latter's colonial activities and served as the object of its political, economic, and spiritual domination.[64] Grotius's concept of 'universal human society' helped to nurture the Eurocentric illusion of 'universality'. A clear distinction should be drawn between his concept and today's international society, which, at least nominally, subsumes all states and societies without discrimination on the basis of political, economic, cultural, religious, or racial factors. The 'universal human society' conceived by Grotius can only be understood as a 'world image' in which the social order prevalent in Europe was projected. To view Grotius's theory of punitive wars as a forerunner of modern collective security ideas[65] thus fails to take account of the enormous gap between the modern system and the basis of Grotius's 'universality'.

7.3.2. Punitive War Waged in Response to Crimes against God

Undoubtedly God can avenge an injury inflicted on Himself. But can men also do so? In responding to this question, Grotius abandons the dualistic mutual non-intervention doctrine according to which God disposes of His own affairs within His domain and men do the same within theirs. Instead, he supports a principle of mutual intervention where God's affairs and man's overlap. Just as God can exact punishment for crimes against men, so can men for sins against God. This reflects Grotius's deep attachment to the political utility of religion, as the element that binds men within political society and ensures the execution of its laws. Since words or acts of men that endanger religion, or deny the existence of God, are likely to prejudice the maintenance of legal order, they must be controlled by men too.[66] Natural law, which is supposed to exist

[64] Grotius devotes an entire section (II. xx. 49) to the question whether it is permissible to wage punitive wars against non-Christians who persecute Christians because of their religious beliefs. However, he never discusses the waging of wars of punishment against Christians who persecute non-Christians simply because of their 'paganism'.

[65] As does Vollenhoven 1926*a*: 28–31.

[66] II. xx. 44.

without God, cannot be maintained in its ultimate end without God. This indicates again the hypothetical nature of the statement in Prol. 11.

Grotius begins his discussion by asking what constitutes true religion (*religio vera*), a term widely used in European intellectual history only after the Reformation. It was used in two diametrically opposed senses, and at a time of religious and sectarian schism. The first involved a religious sect, professing to be the sole embodiment of the absolute truth, and using the term as a symbol to distinguish itself from other sects (the most striking example is the reformist sect of the Huguenot's National Synod).[67] The second was as a universal symbol uniting a number of divided sects into a single religion (the humanist usage).[68] Grotius adhered to the latter usage. He believed that only a Christianity reinterpreted and simplified according to 'reason' as advocated by the Stoic school could reunite the churches.[69]

Grotius presents certain universal principles of speculative philosophy as prerequisites for a religion to be a 'true religion'. They are: (1) that God exists; (2) that God controls human affairs and adjudicates upon them; (3) that there is only one God; (4) that God is invisible; and (5) that God is the creator of all things.[70] However, given his emphasis on the practical approach, Grotius acknowledges religious pluralism in discussing the just causes of waging religious wars, and refrains from demanding that all five principles be satisfied. He requires religions to meet only the first two, in order to guide people into maintaining and obeying the existing order. It does not matter whether there is one god or many. There are inherent elements common to all religions because even barbarian religions recognize these two principles.[71]

Thus, only atheism and blasphemy are unacceptable to Grotius, for they scoff at the proposition that men should fear God's wrath as a basis for complying with law and order. Any religion is approved as long as its doctrine urges subordinates to 'obey their superior'. Here religion is expected to have an ideological function

[67] See Sasaki 1973: 18 ff. [68] See Kato 1979: 7 and 14.

[69] See Villey 1975: 605.

[70] II. xx. 45. Grotius combines 'that God exists' and 'that there is only one God', thus proposing four, not five principles. Here the two are kept separate for the sake of clarity.

[71] II. xx. 46.

of maintaining, complementing, and concealing the existing order of relations between the ruling and the ruled.[72] Grotius, who approves of paganism while considering blasphemy a crime, differs radically from those who consider paganism a crime even more serious than blasphemy (e.g. Aquinas and Vitoria). While the earlier thinkers regarded religion from the viewpoint of belief in Christianity and its protection, at least in *JBP*, Grotius mainly valued religion from the viewpoint of political utility. So long as it is admitted that God exists and controls human affairs, Grotius is not concerned with the name or names of God or gods or the contents of His or their commands. Grotius's theology aimed to realize 'temporal peace': the role of the church was to contribute to order, peace, and progress in this world.[73] Paganism, heresy, or sects arising from disagreement with the other prerequisites do not constitute a barrier to the maintenance of political society and the execution of law, for they accept at least the proposition that men should fear God's wrath. Thus, while atheism and blasphemy can be punished by men, differences in religion or sect stemming from mistakes or differences in the interpretation of the law of God can be punished only by God. This is why differences in religion or sect are excluded from Grotius's catalogue of the just causes of punitive war. With this principle of tolerance, he seeks to exclude as unlawful the main cause of bloodshed in his age: wars among different religious groups or sects.

Grotius's principle of tolerance is different from the modern concept of tolerance as a condition for individual freedom of conscience.[74] It is closer to the theory of tolerance advanced by the *Politiques*, which arises from an awareness of the importance of maintaining the state order.[75] The *Politiques* regarded religion as 'the sole force that binds people to their obligations'.[76] Thus atheism could not be tolerated, lest it jeopardize the foundations of civil society. No doubt the policy of tolerating paganism and heresy was adopted out of political necessity;[77] for the *Politiques*, tolerance was not a virtue but a necessity.[78] Just as the aim of their policy of tolerance was to avoid religious wars, Grotius's principle of tolerance was indifferent to the content of Christian doctrine because of the need to exclude religious wars from the category of

[72] II. xx. 49. See also Grotius=Barbeyrac 1724: II. 628.
[73] See Villey 1975: 604. [74] See Figgis 1916: 101–2. [75] Ibid. 101.
[76] Pasquier 1966*b*: 65. [77] See Sasaki 1973: 58. [78] See Figgis 1916: 101.

just wars. In both cases, the state is deconfessionalized, but not free from religion.

It should be noted that Grotius makes no attempt to define a religious war. He professed to think about the problem of law apart from any specific facts and asserted that his deductions are by no means intended for the solution of present and future problems in real politics:[79] hence the composite character of religious wars, with their political, economic, and social factors all abstracted in Grotius's treatment. Such an abstract treatment of religious wars costs Grotius dearly. Although *JBP* may serve as a therapy for treating the symptoms of war, it can offer neither a prescription for removing the causes of war nor a perspective for paving the way for its regulation by changes in the *status quo*. To Grotius, the role of jurists is a modest one, namely, to terminate disorder and violence. It is too demanding to expect them to instruct people in all aspects of sharing. They are merely required to act in the capacity of an official or policeman when law is actually violated.[80]

Finally, a brief remark should be made on the connection between theism as an ideology for securing the effectiveness of law and the hypothetical deism presented in the Prolegomena. In a society without centralized means of enforcement (*Zwangsapparatus*), the authorities must rely heavily on ideological means for ensuring the compliance with law. Grotius not only admits that the utility of religion lies in its ideological character as an ultimate guarantee of the effectiveness of law, but also states that religion is more useful in the great community (*magna illa communitas*) than in a particular state.[81] While states are equipped with laws and ample means to execute them, and to that degree religion is replaced by law, in the great community there are fewer laws enacted by agreement, and only armed force exists to compel people to comply with law. Therefore it is necessary to rely primarily on piety and fear of God. This is why an offender against the law of nations is also characterized as having committed a sin against the law of God.[82] In Grotius's thought, God occupies a substantial position as a means of guaranteeing the effectiveness of law, despite his declaration in Prol. 11. But in addition to piety, Grotius finds public and private means of violence, as well as virtue and love, useful in

[79] Prol. 58. See also Cassirer 1932: 317–18.
[80] Villey 1975: 620. [81] II. xx. 44. [82] Ibid.

guaranteeing the effectiveness of law. In this sense the ideology in II. xx can be thought of as complementing the hypothetical deism of the Prolegomena.

Paradoxically, the utility of religion in a society gradually diminishes as laws and the means of their enforcement become more comprehensive and effective. Grotius first frees natural law from God, then reintroduces Him to ensure the execution of law. Is it likely that he would eventually banish God as no longer 'necessary' when laws become fully comprehensive and effective? This may be the case if the question is considered only from the viewpoint of the utility of religion for the purposes of law. However, under the system of law presented by Grotius, the denial of God tends to the denial of man created by God, and ultimately to the denial of natural law, as the dictate of right reason. It would signify the loss of the basis of Grotius's own system.

7.4. Conclusion

Grotius considers the maintenance of social order based on the social appetite of man (*appetitus societatis*) as the source of natural law. He presents five axioms as basic elements of natural law: (1) the inviolability of ownership; (2) the duty to make restitution for unjust enrichment; (3) the duty to fulfil contracts; (4) the obligation to make restitution due to wrongful acts; and (5) the liability to punishment for crimes.[83] These axioms are 'self-evident', not needing to be proved. Moreover, Grotius does not indicate any criteria for selecting them.[84]

He had already drawn a rough sketch of these five axioms in *De Jure Praedae Commentarius*, where he explains them in terms of three principles of common law which God had engraved into the mind of every person: (1) to obtain and to own those things which are necessary for self-preservation; (2) to refrain from injuring those things which belong to others; and (3) to abide by a promise. In *JBP* Grotius added punishment against crime to his list of

[83] Prol. 8.

[84] In fact, these axioms were subsequently incorporated one after another into the system of positive laws found in capitalist states (Matsushita 1959: 32; Wieacker 1967: 291 ff.; Villey 1975: 597, 621). Villey states that the origin of the main articles of the French civil code—Arts. 544 (inviolability of ownership), 1134 (performance of contract), and 1382 (compensation for damages)—lies in Grotius's 1st, 3rd, and 4th axioms (1975: 621).

natural-law axioms. The reason for doing so was probably that the paramount obstacle to peace was the international and national disorder triggered by religious differences. Grotius sought, by the stroke of his pen, to remove wars against heretics or religious sects from the area of legitimate secular wars of punishment, thereby making them unlawful on the ground that they are matters of God that no man can sanction. (It should be noted that there was no problem of wars waged against atheism.)

Religious wars for Grotius are not fought for the sake of God but for the sake of maintaining the social order. To maintain social order men need only to agree 'that God exists and that He controls human affairs', and therefore all forms of paganism and heresy are to be tolerated. Grotius's characteristic approach of choosing the lesser evil can also be seen in the way he treats other problems. He denies subjects the right to resist their superior in order to avoid the evil of rebellion and civil war,[85] argues that it would be wiser to force criminals to work than to execute them,[86] and insists that being enslaved is better than being killed.[87]

In establishing a general theory of law, Grotius did not specifically examine the inherent nature of man as the subject or bearer of rights. His law of nature is defined on the basis of what he considers the best elements of the inherent nature of man, i.e. social appetite, reason, and moral consciousness, in the traditional sense of these terms. While recognizing the existence of human impulses contrary to reason, which lead man to wage wars 'even barbarous nations would be ashamed of',[88] Grotius fails to explain why these evil elements do not also constitute part of the inherent nature of man,[89] or to locate them properly in his system of natural law. The assumption is that the causes of wrongdoing exist purely outside man; morality is the art of avoiding them. Crime is also understood as the result of the misuse of reason.[90] Grotius's law of nature, based on this naïve dogmatism regarding the nature of man, claims to be a deductive system. In fact, he seeks support or evidence for it in existing society, regarding the social relations that have emerged in history as the natural and universal order, and treating them as a direct expression of reason.[91] It never occurred to him to

[85] II. xxiv. 6. [86] II. xx. 12. [87] II. v. 27. [88] Prol. 28.
[89] See Tooke 1965: 207. [90] Ibid. 208.
[91] See Fukuda 1971: 44. See also Savigny 1828: 115.

eliminate the various independent powers below the level of the state from his theory, or to adopt a radical individualism.

This has a decisive influence on his theory of those who have the right to punish. Instead of treating this right as belonging only to the state, he takes it directly from the first axiom of natural law. Those who possess the right to punish are the independent powers at various levels. The state is merely the independent power that occupies the highest position in this successive order of coexisting powers. This multi-layered structure reflects the political structure in Europe, particularly the Netherlands of the early seventeenth century. The Netherlands did not possess a powerful central government, nor did it have a unified federal court. The Federal Assembly functioned as a forum of delegations from each province. Power was diffused not only from the republic to the member provinces, but also from the latter to their constituent nobles and towns.[92] The European states were, generally speaking, not modern states with power (including the right to punish) concentrated in a single authority. Thus the effective monopoly of the right to punish by the state, and its monopoly of the criminal law,[93] are not envisaged in Grotius.

The conspicuous method of restraining and mitigating war illustrated through *JBP*, namely, the tactic by which the freedom or right to wage war granted on one level is prohibited or retracted on another in a consistent manner, may be called the retractive method of argument. This method is very much in evidence in his discussion of punishment. Grotius recognizes in principle that, under natural law and the law of nations, certain crimes may constitute just causes for waging punitive war. He then limits the scope of those vested with the right to inflict punishment according to the purpose of each punishment. He does this by clarifying the advantages of inflicting punishment and excluding punishments without purpose as an object of war. Next, he seeks to mitigate punishment and to reduce the range of persons who have the right to punish, by stating that the punishment permitted under natural law or municipal law may be prohibited by divine law, because the law of the Gospel pursues a higher value. Furthermore, he restricts the exercise of the right to punish, and at the same time reduces the severity of its execution, by advancing his theory of pardon.

[92] See Kurihara 1969: 121–2.

[93] Shoji 1954: 162 ff.

Grotius never tires of devising means of avoiding the occurrence of war and mitigating its consequences, even at the risk of occasionally contradicting himself. His method may be compared to the game of *sugoroku* (a Japanese variety of *parchisi*) in which players never quite reach the final goal.

8

The Laws of War

8.1. Significance and Structure of the Laws of War

8.1.1. Difficulties Inherent in Just-War Doctrine

In *JBP*, Books I and II, Grotius lists defence, restitution, and punishment as the only just causes of war. To make this exclusive catalogue effective in restraining wars, he strives to clarify their content as much as possible. For unjust wars to be prevented it is necessary to avoid ignorance or misunderstanding about the just causes of war, matters which should be self-evident. At the root of Books I and II lies Grotius's conviction that it should be possible to arrive at sound judgement, overcoming obscurities and prejudice, through logical and systematic thinking.

The just-war doctrine requires (1) that a war should have a just cause and (2) that it should be conducted in a just manner, although individual doctrines differ as to the relationship between (1) and (2). Those who resort to war, into which innocent people may be drawn, are required to act with discretion and prudence. But beyond this the two requirements of just-war doctrine tend to conflict. It is true that a proper function of the just-war doctrine is to prevent unjust wars by limiting the right to wage war to those who have a substantive just cause. But that doctrine also affirms war based on just causes. This, in turn, tends to undermine efforts to regulate the actual conduct of war. The 'revival of Grotius' in the twentieth century not only constituted an important element in the 'outlawry of war', but was also utilized to generate antagonism against the enemy, as is evidenced by references to Grotius in support of the United States' *de facto* participation in the war against Germany from 1939 to 1941.[1] Conversely, the just-war doctrine tends to deny the unjust party all rights to conduct war.

[1] Onuma 1975: 121–57.

But it remains necessary to regulate the conduct of war for both belligerents, so as to mitigate the tragedy and brutality of war. It is difficult, however, to demand that those who have no just cause to wage war should conduct war rightly. This suggests that only those engaging in a just war can be obligated to act with restraint. Of course, such a conclusion cannot be accepted.

As far as Grotius is concerned, the first difficulty, the affirmation of just wars, is a problem that is already solved, at least in part. He repeatedly emphasizes that either as a dictate of right reason or as a matter of prudence war should be avoided as far as possible, even if one has a substantive just cause for waging it. Even an unjust enemy is to be pardoned. An unwinnable war, even if it would be a just war, should not be waged.[2]

The second difficulty, the inconsistency between an unjust war and compliance with the law of war, is the central problem Grotius has to solve in Book III. Where war has already broken out, it is necessary to restrain the conduct of both belligerents in order to limit the tragic consequences of war, and especially to prevent one war from becoming the cause of another. This involves introducing a non-discriminatory form of regulation of war, which is incompatible with the framework of just-war doctrine, since it tends to imply an affirmative answer to the traditional question whether a war can be just on both sides.

Grotius admits that, in relation to human problems, there are cases where it is impossible definitely to tell right from wrong due to man's 'insurmountable ignorance'.[3] But the argument about formal war in Book III is not limited to such cases. To generalize the ignorance that arises from the imperfection of man's reason is to weaken Grotius's conviction in that reason.[4] In Book III Grotius seeks to solve this second problem by provisionally shifting the level of his argument from the law of nature to the law of nations.

[2] II. xxiv. 1–9. See also III. xxv. 1(7).

[3] II. xxiii. 12.

[4] Schmitt points out that Grotius did not go even a step beyond the traditional just-war doctrine, which treats the justness of war solely from the viewpoint of substantive justice. He argues that Grotius even took a step backward to before Ayala and Gentilis, that the 'lives completely in the theological Middle Ages' (1950: 133). This assessment is not unjustified so far as the discussion of just-war theory in Books I and II is concerned. Precisely because of this, Grotius's discussion of formal war (*bellum solenne*) and moderation of war (*temperamenta*) in Book III is particularly important.

This theoretical manipulation allows scope for regulating the conduct of war on the part of both belligerents indiscriminately, without directly challenging the inconsistency of that regulation with the just-war doctrine based on natural law.

For Grotius, although the concept of right reason, which provides the basis for the law of nature, can be rigorously defined in theory, its specific rules are identified much more flexibly. His consistent concern for common sense, utility, and practicality in *JBP* plays an important role in mediating between existing institutions and natural law as a system of right reason.[5] The law of nations itself is established by the practical consideration of human reason, and therefore acceptance of its benefits serves to reinforce the bonds of human society. The argument advanced in Book III concerning the law of nations, under which a war may be fought 'legally' on both sides, is based on this argument. Grotius in effect side-steps any theoretical inconsistency.

Thus it would be a misunderstanding to consider formal war, moderation, and *fides* in war under the law of nations, which are the subjects of Book III, merely as problems of the positive law of nations, or of moral encouragement, and to interpret them apart from Grotius's framework of right reason. Grotius was certainly aware, on one hand, how easily men become slaves to violent emotions in time of war and lose their rational sense of respect for others.[6] But on the other hand, he hoped that belligerents would voluntarily terminate a war when they became aware of their own unjustness. The argument on the law of nations in Book III is not premised on the abandonment of the solution of conflicts by right reason, in cases where clouded human reason fails to deter the outbreak of war. Grotius has nothing to do with the simple dualism where by (1) the task of restraining war in advance is entrusted to the law of nature and (2) the task of regulating a war that has already commenced is entrusted to the law of nations.[7]

[5] The special characteristic of natural law in *JBP* lies in the effort to discover intermediate principles that are useful in deterring wars and regulating the conduct of war. See Stone 1965: 65–6, 68. Natural law as formulated by Grotius is based upon an autonomous moral discipline of law (Wieacker 1952: 176) which, through common sense and the balancing of practical considerations, flexibly incorporates as historically given the products of human experience into the system of natural law.

[6] Prol. 28, II. xxiii. 12(4).

[7] See Kasai 1984: 55–9.

8.1.2. The Structure of Book III

In III. ix, Grotius examines in detail the law of nature and the law of nations with regard to acts permitted in war. At the outset, he distinguishes between what is permissible without any preconditions (*nude*), and what is permissible in relation to a previous promise.[8] The latter is dealt with in III. xix–xx. The former is subdivided further into rules of natural law (III. i) and things which are permissible under the law of nations. In III. ii–iii, he justifies this theoretical side-step, and in III. iv he discusses the actual content of the law of nations with respect to the effects of formal war.

The effects of formal war can be classified as the effects of impunity (*impunitas*) and the effects of ownership (*dominium*). The former is subdivided into the right to kill or wound enemies (impunity relating to persons), dealt with in III. iv, and devastation and pillaging (impunity relating to things), dealt with in III. v. With regard to the latter, the right of acquiring things is examined in III. vi, rights over prisoners of war in III. vii, rights to govern (*imperium*) the conquered in III. viii and postliminy in III. ix. The theory of moderation in III. xi–xvi corresponds to the external effects examined in III. iv–ix and constitutes a discourse on internal justice. In III. x, Grotius attempts to reconvert the argument, which he earlier shifted to the level of the law of nations (formal war) in III. ii–ix, to the level of natural law, and seeks to diminish the effects of war under the law of nations in the interests of those who wage a just war. In this sense, the argument set forth in III. ii–ix concerning formal war under the law of nations may be read as a grand insertion in a continuing discussion of just-war doctrine under natural law elaborated in III. i and III. x. For Grotius, the framework of just-war doctrine which makes the concept of war a means of realizing law must always be maintained.

8.2. Rules of Natural Law

8.2.1. General Rules Regarding What is Permissible in War

Throughout Books I and II, Grotius attempts to break away from the medieval Scholastic just-war doctrine that defines just war as 'a

[8] III. i. 1.

war fought with just cause and in a just manner' by introducing his own definition, formulated exclusively from the substantive standpoint. As a result, the restoration or realization of justice becomes the most important object in his concept of just war, and the theoretical difficulties discussed in 8.1 are highlighted all the more. Once a just war commences, there is no principle which requires it to be stopped under natural law until justice is realized. Moreover, a victory by the unjust side should signify, from the viewpoint of natural law, merely an accumulation of injustice. This should result in the additional accumulation of the just causes on the part of those who would wage a just war. Since the realization of the object of war should be the only consideration in Grotius's concept of just war, it becomes extremely difficult for him to discuss restrictions upon the conduct of belligerents at the level of natural law.[9] The general rules of natural law which Grotius sets forth in III. i vividly reflect the theoretical difficulties inherent in his just-war doctrine.

At the beginning of III. i, Grotius introduces three general rules which are premisses for discussing what is permissible under natural law in a just war. The first rule is that all things necessary for attaining the purpose of war are permissible in war.[10] The term 'necessary' as used here refers to necessity of a moral nature: violence of all degrees is permissible, because in moral questions the end justifies the means. The balance between the severity of violence and the physical scale or conditions of rights violated will not be questioned, provided the violence is necessary to achieve the goal of preserving rights or restoring property. Even in a punitive war every form of resort to force necessary to exact the punishment should be permissible. Thus it appears that Grotius is leading up to

[9] According to the literal interpretation of *JBP*, *temperamenta* are addressed to those waging a just war (III. xi. 1). Bull argues that it is quite alien to Grotius to regard unjust belligerents as stripped of rights, thereby banishing them beyond the pale of international society. To deny rights to unjust belligerents is to adopt the logic of a religious combatant. He points out that it is also contrary to Grotius's concept of 'the great society of nations (*magna communitas gentium*)': Bull 1966: 600. But so far as the logical inclination of just-war doctrine is concerned, it would be more consistent for the rules of war to be addressed only to the just belligerent, with the unjust belligerent stripped of the rights of belligerency. By placing *temperamenta* after III. ii–ix, where he regards each belligerent as *justus* in the formal sense of the term, Grotius may well have intended to give *temperamenta* the *appearance* of an appeal to both parties.

[10] III. i. 2.

the most radical and thoroughgoing conclusion from his just-war doctrine.

However, Grotius drew this conclusion on the basis of his arguments on rights under natural law in Books I and II. Thus the very ends (the realization of those rights) justifying the means have already been restricted from the viewpoint of substantive justice embodied in a number of specific rules. The first general rule of natural law cannot be identified with the idea that 'necessity knows no law', a slogan associated with the doctrine of *raison d'état*. To do so would be to ignore the fact that Grotius wrote *JBP* to counter the argument that 'in the case of a king or state nothing is unjust which is expedient'.[11] Moreover, in Grotius's thought, a state or nation is not yet established as an entity distinct from its constituent individuals, and accordingly the double standard of *raison d'état* and human reason is alien to him.[12] Since natural law binds all men universally it regulates states or nations as well as the relations between them.

The second general rule is that the right to conduct war guaranteed by the first general rule may also arise even from causes which develop after the outbreak of war.[13] Thus the right to resort to war is allowed against, among others, subjects or allies of enemies, 'those who join in a war that is unjust out of ignorance', and those who join in bad faith in a war without a cause worthy of approval.[14]

The third general rule is that things not permitted according to the purpose of a war may nevertheless be done without committing evil where they are incidental to achieving that purpose.[15] Such acts as bombarding a pirate-ship with innocent people on board, or temporarily receiving property in excess in order to restore part of that property, are accordingly allowed. This permission, however, requires one to balance the good that is gained (e.g. exterminating pirates) and the incidental evil arising (e.g. endangering innocent persons). To invoke this rule in dubious situations, it is necessary

[11] Prol. 3.

[12] See also II. 6. 2., esp. 368 n. 68.

[13] III. i. 3.

[14] This second general rule coincides with the requirements for those who wage a war for the sake of others (II. xxv–xxvi). There, Grotius generally recognizes 'the right to assist in a just war' waged by another, but this is premised on the duty to judge whether one who wages the war—as a subject, or as an ally—has a just cause.

[15] III. i. 4.

to obey the demand of love (*caritas*) to favour that course which regards the interest of another more than one's own. This is essential to the interrelationships of men, who, unlike God, are inherently imperfect.[16]

8.2.2. Trade with the Enemy, Ruses, and Deceit

After introducing the three general rules of natural law, Grotius discusses some specific rules derived from them. The first involves the question what should be done to those who furnish enemies with supplies,[17] the second, the question of ruses and deceit.[18] The first question has to be considered on the level of natural law, because practices vary as to which of the two, the demands of war or a neutral party's freedom of trade, should take precedence: no established rules can be found in the volitional law of nations (*jus voluntarium gentium*).[19] Grotius sets up three categories according to the goods furnished.[20] In the case of military goods, the demands of war take precedence because the goods are inimical in character. By contrast, freedom of trade is protected for non-military goods. Things which may be used both for war and peace (e.g. ships or money) are treated differently depending on the degree of necessity to achieve the end of the war.

With regard to the second question, Grotius first asks whether ruses and deceit are inherently evil. This approach allows the possibility of moderating the first general rule of natural law, because it would not be permissible to resort to ruses and deceit if they are inherently evil, even to realize a just purpose in war. To this extent it is possible to discover in Grotius a residue of the Scholastic just-war doctrine that a just war should be fought justly. Grotius divides ruses and deceit into two categories: those which involve a negative action (dissimulation), and those which involve

[16] Since the ultimate goal of the just-war doctrine is to realize justice, the 3rd general rule of natural law should be deduced from it. Grotius, however, does not go so far as to accept the proposition *fiat iustitia pereat mundus*. He certainly does not doubt that war is morally proper as a means of realizing justice. On the other hand, war is abominable since it causes great suffering to innocent people (see II. xxiii. 6).

[17] III. i. 5. [18] III. i. 6–20. [19] III. i. 5(5).

[20] Lauterpacht regards the system of contraband as part of the Grotian tradition: 1975*b*: 349. However, contraband in modern international law was established along with the law of naval warfare and the law of neutrality. Schindler points out that neutrality is marginalized in *JBP*: 1967: 228, cf. III. xvii. It is simplistic to connect Grotius's statement in the text to the later concept of contraband in international law.

a positive action (pretence and falsehood).[21] Dissimulation is permitted: one is, for example, not required to notify facts to the enemy. With respect to positive acts of pretence and falsehood, Grotius makes a further distinction between acts whose significance is fixed by agreement (*ex conventione*), and acts where there is no such agreement. Ruses and deceit of the latter kind are allowed because they do not involve mutual obligations. For example, when one carries the same weapons and wears the same uniform as one's enemy, so as to be mistaken for an ally, there is no violation of obligation since there has been no agreement as to what constitutes the ally's insignia. Even if certain things have become accepted as a general custom (*consuetudo*), such a custom constrains no one if it is not established by universal consent (*consensus communis*).[22]

On the other hand, whether an action which has a specific significance under an agreement may be taken to deceive people depends on the circumstances. Grotius discusses this in detail as a general issue of falsehood (*mendacium*). In short, any term or phrase which has several meanings is permissible so long as it contains any element of truth. By contrast, no term or phrase is permissible if its tendency is to undermine the capacity of the opposing side to make rational judgements.

In III. i. 12–20, Grotius outlines a number of rules drawn from this general consideration of the natural law concerning falsehood. For example, it is permissible to make false statements to encourage people under certain circumstances, because an explicit or implicit understanding exists on the side being deceived. Those with a superior right (*jus supereminens*) may utter falsehoods for their own sake or for the public good. Honourable falsehoods to save the life of an innocent person or something of equal value are also permissible. Grotius clearly rejects the Augustinian tradition of generally prohibiting falsehood against enemies, on the ground that it is no more than an admonition for Christians. However, he adds that the liberty to tell lies does not extend to false promises or oaths, even in the case of enemies.

Grotius in principle approves ruses and deceit in war under natural law, so long as they are not prohibited by agreement. This is consistent with the first general rule of natural law, which permits all acts in a just war so long as they meet the standard of

[21] III. i. 7. [22] III. i. 8(2).

necessity and purpose. He is not entirely consistent, however: for example, in discussing cases where falsehood is permitted (III. xii–xvi), he bases his argument on the presumption that falsehood is prohibited under natural law. But the only cases where Grotius clearly prohibits falsehood against enemies are when promises or oaths are involved: this is grounded not on the inherent nature of falsehood, but rather on the inherent nature of promises and oaths. In the final analysis, Grotius permits falsehood against enemies, on the basis that the realization of the rights of others is universally regarded as more important than guaranteeing the freedom of judgement of the persons concerned.

8.3. The Scope and Application of the Law of Nations

8.3.1. Vicarious Responsibility

In III. ii and subsequent chapters, Grotius proceeds with his discussion at the level of the law of nations. III. ii is entitled 'How by the Law of Nature the Goods (*bona*) of Subjects may be Held for Debt of Their Rulers'. The question why subjects were bound by the acts of their rulers in war had to be answered before considering what was permissible in war, and against whom. Under natural law, no one is bound by an act of somebody else except in the case of inheritance of property. This is true for both private and public war. A state as conceived by Grotius, despite having full governmental authority, is essentially one of many multi-layered independent powers. Public wars are thought of as wars fought between supreme rulers. The latter should not have any right to sacrifice their subjects, who may have nothing to do with the causes of their rulers' wars. In discussing punishment in Book II, Grotius recognizes cases where subjects may be punished for a crime committed by their ruler. But he maintains that only subjects who have agreed to the crime are punishable, not those who opposed the crime but were out-voted.[23]

However, in Grotius's time, nations acted as integrated units in public wars. Subjects usually suffered harm and damage because of acts committed by their ruler. It would be contrary to Grotius's practical approach to ignore these realities, and not to provide a

[23] II. xxi. 7(2). See also II. xxi. 18.

legal explanation for them. This task cannot be achieved on the level of natural law, according to which man is responsible only for his own acts. Thus Grotius has to shift his argument to the level of the law of nations. According to Grotius, the law of nations introduced the principle that subjects may be held liable for the debts of their rulers:[24] the reason was a practical one, since the property of rulers, whose number is limited, is difficult to seize or arrest, but the property of subjects, whose number is usually large, is easy to seize and arrest. If seizure of subjects' property is allowed, it will become much easier to achieve the ends for which wars are fought. In this way, wars can be ended before they escalate in violence. Moreover, this principle is not so repugnant to nature that no one would disapprove of its introduction by custom and consent into human society. Members of the same society can maintain justice through domestic procedures, and thereby gain compensation for losses incurred as a result of another's act. Such institutional procedures are often not available to foreigners. Hence, it is not repugnant to nature to hold subjects liable for the debts of a ruler in exchange for the advantage of being members of the same society.[25]

Grotius demonstrates that customs which coincide with this principle are accepted in both perfect war (*bellum plenum*) and imperfect war (the so-called *jus repressaliarum*) in respect of seizure of persons as well as of property. The term 'perfect war' refers to wars between nations in which a formal declaration of war is made according to established practice. The term has the same meaning as *bellum solenne*, used by Grotius elsewhere. Imperfect wars are those that lack such formality, and in essence correspond to wars of reprisal. In either case, the liberty and property of those who have nothing to do with the acts that caused the war may be sacrificed. Grotius justifies this by reasoning from the principle of vicarious

[24] III. ii. 2.

[25] III. ii. 3–4. Grotius often resorts to this kind of argument when he affirms some usage or practice. However, it is doubtful how far this logic can apply to punitive wars. Grotius bases a punitive war on the fictitious argument that a person places himself in an inferior position by committing a crime (thereby establishing a superior–inferior relationship, a prerequisite for the existence of the power to inflict punishment). But it is highly questionable that the entire people to which a criminal belongs should itself be placed in an inferior position by his criminal act. This doubt is reinforced because he deals with punitive war rather differently from other types of war, requiring greater restraint in launching it.

liability. For Grotius the state, while it may be a perfect body politic, does not have the status of an absolute or unique entity, as the modern notion of the sovereign state suggests. His image of the state always overlaps with its constituent individual powers (heads of households, intermediate corporate bodies, etc.).

III. ii is subtitled 'On Reprisals'. Rights of reprisal exist only when *jus* is denied. Specifically, this occurs where (1) a judgement cannot be obtained against an offender or debtor within a reasonable time; or (2) a judgement rendered is clearly contrary to law.[26] Forceful measures are allowed in the latter case because foreigners are not subject to the authority of the tribunal that rendered judgement and there is no other course of action than war to realize the true right. In exercising the right of enforcement, one is not allowed to kill anyone other than the debtor. However, it is not prohibited to kill accidentally anyone who tries to hinder the enforcement action. Even in this case, one should abandon the enforcement of the right in accordance with the law of love if such accidental results can be foreseen.[27] Women and children are generally excluded as the objects of such enforcement. Reprisals require the supreme ruler's authorization. People integrated as a part of the state are compensated for this disadvantage with the advantage of becoming a member of a state. This is more or less comparable to the legal concept of a surety.[28] While the ownership of things seized is immediately transferred to the captor, a form of restitution is apparently expected between the debtor and the person whose property was the object of the reprisal. Thus, problems that arise between different peoples are reduced to those of restitution of rights among members of one state. As a result the chance of gaining restitution of rights through war is expected to be reduced, because private wars among members of the same states are already eliminated.

8.3.2. Formal War and the Declaration of War

In III. ii and the following sections, Grotius detaches the substantive just causes of war from his concept of just war. In III. ii, he recognizes that a just war under the law of nations can be extended

[26] III. ii. 5. In the age of imperialism a similar argument served to justify the exercise of the right of intervention by European nations in Asian, African, and Latin American nations, and to force the law of European nations on them.

[27] III. ii. 6.

[28] III. ii. 2(2).

beyond the person who actually violated the right of another, so as to involve all members of the state to which the violator belongs. At the beginning of III. iii, Grotius makes a decisive shift of argument:[29] 'a war is often called lawful not from the cause from which it arises, nor from the importance of its exploits, but from certain peculiar effects'.[30] These 'peculiar effects' are the legal effects which the law of nations confers on formal wars. As the title of III. iii, 'On War that is Just or Formal According to the Law of Nations (*De Bello Justo sive Solenni Jure Gentium*)' suggests,[31] *justus* here refers to 'legality' in the sense of meeting the formal or procedural requirements for war under the law of nations. Thus Grotius shifts the discussion from the substantive just causes of war under the law of nature to the formal legality of war under the law of nations. Despite this, he maintains the concept of 'just' war. Formal war (*bellum solenne*), which satisfies the formalities required by the law of nations, is just (*justus*) on both sides. Grotius is groping for ways to introduce a non-discriminatory view of war within the framework of a just-war doctrine. His law of nations was not necessarily a positive law clearly distinct from the law of nature, and this ambiguity enabled him to accept, and even to disguise, the shift in logic involved.

Grotius is aware of the logical gap that arises when he shifts his argument. He seeks to fill this gap by demonstrating the moral goodness of a commonwealth or state (*respublica*, *civitas*) or of a people (*populus*), and how they differ from a band of pirates or brigands, even if they commit an injustice.[32] According to Grotius, bands of pirates or brigands are formed to commit wrongdoings, whereas a commonwealth or state is formed to enable its members to enjoy their rights. Even foreigners are expected to be treated justly by it. A state formed to realize good ends does not lose its *raison d'être* just because it happens to commit an injustice. The initiation of an unjust war does not immediately defeat the main purpose of a state, the realization of law. However diseased a state may be, it is still a state so long as there remain tribunals and other

[29] Similarly, Haggenmacher points out the difference between the bilateralism of formal war in Book III and the bilateralism at the close of Book II (1983: 572).

[30] III. iii. 1(1). See also I. iii. 4; II. xxiii. 13(5).

[31] Kelsey *et al.* use the phrase 'lawful or public' for this title, but it should be trans. as 'just or formal'. The term 'formal' should also be used in the title of III. iv.

[32] III. iii. 2.

agencies necessary to enable foreigners to enjoy their rights in the same way as its members. Grotius goes so far as to state that 'even a gathering of pirates and brigands can be transformed into a state' if the purpose of their association is changed and a system for guaranteeing rights is established.[33]

In Grotius's usual formula, it is not necessarily repugnant to nature that the law of nations should distinguish between a group formed for the purpose of wrongdoing and a group that merely happens to commit an injustice. As a practical thinker, Grotius could not allow himself to be so meticulous about the substantive causes of war that he relegated the state, even when waging an unjust war, to the same level as a group of pirates and brigands. To do so would be to throw the baby out with the bath water. When a state happens to commit an injustice, it is necessary to remind its people of its essential moral goodness, which is indispensable if war is to be restrained by reference to substantive causes. While fully realizing that people in war are apt to behave irrationally, Grotius maintains his faith in reason, in the hope that one waging an unjust war will become aware of its injustice and desist. Being inherently good by nature, states are worthy of such expectations. For this reason, the rule of the law of nations, which recognizes special external effects only for formal wars waged between states or nations, is not in conflict with nature.

There are two prerequisites for a formal war: (1) it should have the support of the supreme power (*summa potestas*) on both sides, and be fought under their names; and (2) it should be publicly declared (*denuntiatio*).[34] III. iii is devoted to the second requirement.[35] First, Grotius confirms that a declaration of war is unnecessary for a just war under natural law.[36] The function of a declaration of war is to attract the benefit of the effects of the law of nations.[37] The cases where a declaration is not required are where

[33] III. iii. 3.

[34] III. iii. 4 and 5. In addition to *denuntiatio*, the term *promulgatio* is generally used, while the term *indicatio* or *edictum* is used when a war is declared unconditionally (*pura denuntiatio*), as when crimes are punished.

[35] For the first requirement, see I. iii. 4.

[36] III. iii. 6.

[37] But he goes on to say that if the benefit of the external effects of war is desired, a declaration of war is required even for just wars under natural law: III. iii. 12. This appears contradictory, since the notion of external effects is one of the law of nations, *not* of natural law.

one defends oneself from attack; where punishment is inflicted at the request of the criminal himself; and where the owner recovers property from one who is actually holding it. In short, they are limited to those where the harm or damage would be inflicted on those who have themselves violated another's rights. The purpose of a declaration of war is to ascertain clearly that the war is conducted by the will of the peoples or supreme rulers on both sides, and not on the private initiative of this or that member of a state. On the ground that a state is formed for a good purpose, the law of nations grants legal effects peculiar to it, irrespective of whether a war is just or unjust.

Grotius next examines the means of declaring war under the law of nations and under municipal law. For example, where property is seized in respect of a debt owned by someone else, a suit must be commenced or a default notice be given in advance.[38] A war declared against a ruler is at the same time declared against his subjects and allies.[39] If the war with the enemy to whom the declaration was made ends, and if another people or king is to be attacked because of the aid they furnished during the war, it is necessary to make a new declaration of war.[40] By the law of nations, war may be waged as soon as it is declared.

8.4. External Effects under the Law of Nations

8.4.1. Effects of Impunity

The effects that the law of nations attributes to a formal war are divided into the effects of impunity and the effects of ownership. The effects of impunity are discussed in III. iv and v: the right of killing enemies (*jus interficiendi hostes*) in III. iv, and the devastation and pillage of enemy property in III. v.

(1) *Significance of Effects of Impunity*

The effects of impunity mean that no question of punishment arises with regard to acts undertaken in a formal war: in this sense those acts are permissible. In discussing this issue, Grotius first considers the usual meaning of the expression 'to be permissible (*licere*)'.[41] The argument that something is 'permissible' because it is beyond

[38] III. iii. 6(2). [39] III. iii. 9. [40] III. iii. 10. [41] II. iv. 2.

the reach of human punishment is clearly different from the argument, maintained throughout Books I and II, that something is 'permissible' because it is not contrary to nature. Grotius distinguishes two usages of the term 'permissible'. The first is when something is morally wrong but not liable to human punishment; the second, when something is in itself not morally wrong. The second refers to acts whose avoidance is praised from the viewpoint of morality, but which are entirely licit under natural law (e.g. remarriage of a widow, or marriage of a confirmed bachelor who is expected to be single on some religious ground). By contrast, an example of the first usage of 'permissible' is adultery or theft, which are permissible in some countries. In this usage, what is 'right' and what is 'permissible' must be clearly distinguished.

Grotius identified two effects of impunity in a formal war: impunity of the act of violence against persons, on the one hand, and devastation and pillage of enemy property, on the other.[42] These effects were approved by the law of nations[43] because it would be dangerous for a third party to determine which belligerent has the just cause, as this would tend to involve other peoples in a foreign war. Moreover, even in a just war it is difficult to determine unequivocally the appropriate limits of defence, restitution, or punishment by external and objective standards. It is better to let the conscience of those actually engaged in the war resolve the problems than to rely on the judgement of others who are not involved. Grotius does not argue that it is impossible to decide whether a particular war is just or unjust. As a firm believer in human reason, he could never abandon the view that such a judgement is possible. Abstaining from judgement is justified for the practical reason of not involving innocent third parties.

(2) *Right to Kill or Wound Persons*

After these preliminary considerations, Grotius discusses the specific contents of the right to wound (including the right to kill) as an example of the effects of impunity with regard to persons.[44] For Grotius, killing or inflicting wounds on the wrongdoer himself in retaliation or revenge is in principle not prohibited under the law of nature. The problem is how far, beyond the permitted range of natural law, this right to kill or wound persons in a formal war is

[42] III. iv. 3. [43] III. iv. 4. [44] III. iv. 5–14.

extended under the law of nations. After pointing out that the right to kill and wound is generally called the right of war (*jus belli*), Grotius confirms that this 'right is simply a form of impunity'. It is permissible (i.e. not punishable) to kill or wound anyone in the enemy's territory, whether they bear arms or not. The same applies to foreigners who enter the enemy's territory after the outbreak of war. Foreigners who were in the enemy's territory before the outbreak of war are regarded as enemies if they do not leave within a reasonable time. Even if foreigners demonstrate no hostile intention of disturbing the course of military operations or of inflicting wounds upon those who wage war, they are not entitled to recover damages suffered during the war. This is to prevent human society from falling into the vicious circle of endless wars.

According to the law of nations, citizens of an enemy country are enemies wherever they may be found. When a war is declared, it is declared upon all citizens of the enemy. They may be killed with impunity wherever they may be. Grotius also affirms the right to kill or wound infants and women, captives, those who surrender unconditionally or whose surrender is refused, and hostages. At least under the law of nations, the right to kill or wound captives is permitted as a form of the right to kill slaves of war, a right which continues even after the peace treaty is concluded. Thus, the contents of the right to kill or wound persons are extremely severe, reflecting the realities of war from ancient times onwards.[45]

(3) *Restrictions on the Right to Kill or Wound Enemies*

Grotius then argues that the law of nations can limit the right to kill or wound as permitted by natural law. Here he elaborates on the prohibition of the use of poison, of assassination, and of rape. Neither the use of poison nor assassination is prohibited by natural law: so long as it is necessary for achieving just ends, it makes essentially no difference under natural law whether a person is killed by the sword or by poison. However, the use of poison was restricted in European practice under the law of nations, so as to prevent the danger of war from extending too widely.[46] The same is true of poisoning weapons or rivers.[47] The real reason why the right to kill or wound is restricted under the law of nations is that this is advantageous to supreme rulers. While kings are protected

[45] Grewe 1934*a*: 254–5. [46] III. iv. 15. [47] III. iv. 16.

more fully than their subjects from armed attack, they cannot be protected more than their subjects against poison. To keep the king's position secure, it became important to prohibit the use of poison as infamy. The same is true of the prohibition of assassination.[48] With regard to rape, while admitting that practices differ in various nations, Grotius leans towards prohibition on the grounds that it could never contribute to attaining the purposes of war.[49]

Grotius's conclusions may be convincing from a practical viewpoint. In discussing additional restrictions imposed under the law of nations, Grotius states: 'just as the law of nations . . . permits many things which are forbidden by the law of nature, so it forbids certain things which are permissible by the law of nature.'[50] But it is misleading to discuss the former and latter parts of the statement without any qualification as to the terms 'permits' and 'permissible'. 'Permits' in the former part refers to the effects of impunity. By contrast, 'permissible' in the latter indicates the permissive domain as contrasted to the absolute prohibition of natural law. In Grotius's system of law, human volitional law may incorporate additional restraints in the permissive domain. According to the first general rule of natural law, all that is necessary to realize just ends is permitted in a just war. But there could be nothing wrong with the law of nations introducing, for example, a prohibition of the use of poison in the permissive domain.

A different consideration compelled Grotius to discuss, side by side, matters on different theoretical levels, even at the risk of sacrificing theoretical consistency. Additional restrictions on the right to kill or wound have to be addressed to both belligerent parties. Hence, it is not sufficient to treat restrictions on the right to kill or wound enemies under the law of nations as additional restrictions imposed by human volitional law on the first general rule of natural law. Natural law only recognizes the right to kill or wound enemies to those who have just cause to wage war: this may result in the practical contradiction of appealing to the just side to exercise self-control while letting the unjust side do whatever it wishes, a conclusion which Grotius could never admit. Thus, in discussing the additional restrictions in the permissive domain of the natural law imposed by the law of nations, it is necessary at the

[48] III. iv. 18(4). [49] III. iv. 19. [50] III. iv. 15(1).

same time to introduce somehow the principal of non-discrimination of belligerents at the level of the law of nations.

Secondly, when Grotius discusses the restrictions on the right to kill or wound persons, he does not necessarily regard them as constituting part of 'the law of all nations (*jus gentium omnium*)', but rather of 'the law of more civilised nations (*jus gentium meliorum*)'.[51] The same idea is expressed differently elsewhere: 'this also is contrary to the law of nations, but of European nations, and of such others as attain to the higher standard of Europe.'[52] Grotius's concept of the law of nations is affected by a delicate mixture of a posteriori and a priori elements. Although the concept of natural law as the dictate of right reason should be a priori in its nature, he adduces evidence a posteriori in identifying and demonstrating its substantive content. On the other hand, although matters relating to the law of nations, as human volitional law, should be empirical or positive, he is not consistent in his empirical attitude. If there is no universal consensus, instead of denying the existence of the law of nations, he selects European practices as the substantive content of the law of nations.[53] Inherent in his concept of the law of nations is an element of an a priori value judgement concerning the relative value of various practices.

In Grotius's system of law, the concept of natural law as the dictate of right reason is clearly differentiated from Christian duty, which demands virtues higher than those demanded by reason, judged by a 'common sense' standard. On the other hand, Grotius actively incorporates, as part of the law of nations, existing practices of the European world that are fully consistent with his conception of reason. In his system, the content of natural law is based on the self-evident judgement of reason, the content of which is expanded or limited by human volitional law. Here, however, conformity with his concept of reason becomes the standard of judgement in identifying the rules of human volitional law.

It is within this cycle of flexible and resourceful thinking that Grotius turns the contents of his law of nations into something that does not contradict his rational judgement. The permissive law of nature and the law of nations are made into a mutually permeating system. In particular the discriminatory nature of just war under

[51] III. iv. 15(1). [52] III. iv. 16(1).

[53] Grotius sometimes alludes to Islamic law as well as to Chinese and Japanese practices, but only in passing.

the law of nature is overcome by means of this presumed harmony, vindicating his tactic of shifting the level of argument from the law of nature to the law of nations. The first rule of natural law that everything necessary to achieve the end for which a war is fought can be done justly, signifies the logical starting-point for piling up regulations based on reason, the element that permeates human volitional law.

(4) *Impunity of Devastation and Pillage*

After analysing in III. iv the effects of impunity with regard to persons, Grotius discusses in III. v the effects of impunity with regard to property. Since the law of nations permits even killing of enemies, there is nothing at all strange about devastating and pillaging enemy property. Such devastation and pillage are permitted even against the property of those who have surrendered.[54] Sacred things and places may be destroyed or laid waste as far as the law of nations is concerned.[55] Apart from their religious significance, sacred things may be used for human ends, and are therefore subject to public authority and law. Accordingly, the law of nations need not treat sacred things and places differently from other property in general. Similarly, consecrated objects do not belong to the dead: as they are owned by the living, they may be laid waste or pillaged under the law of nations.[56] However, the bodies of the dead should be treated carefully; to handle them carelessly would be contrary to the law of burial, which constitutes one of the rules of the law of nations.[57]

8.4.2. Effects of Ownership

The second effect recognized by the law of nations in a formal war is the right to acquire things (*jus acquirendi*) captured in war. In III. vi, Grotius discusses the right to acquire captured property, while in III. vii he discusses the right to enslave persons who have been captured, i.e. prisoners of war. The discussion on acquisition of governing power in III. viii is an application by analogy of the argument developed in III. vii.

(1) *Ownership of Things*

(i) Meaning of Dominium *in Terms of External Effects* According to natural law, the things that can be acquired through war are

[54] III. v. 1. [55] III. v. 2. [56] III. v. 3. [57] II. xix.

severely limited. In a war waged to recover property or damages, the things to be acquired are limited to things of the same value as that taken or lost. In a war waged to exact punishment, things to be acquired are limited to what will inflict loss not exceeding an equitable measure of punishment. By contrast, both belligerents in a formal war may become the owner (*dominus*) of things they have taken from their enemies without any limitations or standards of equity. This shift in argument from the law of nature to the law of nations raises serious doubts about the consistency of Grotius's system. He restricts himself to explaining that the possessors of booty should be protected in their possession by all nations, and hence that such a condition 'may be called ownership (*dominium*)' so far as its external effects are concerned.[58] In Book II, ownership was clearly distinguished from possession (*possessio*). But here possession is identified with ownership, even though this is qualified by the phrase 'so far as its external effects are concerned'. However, under natural law, the acquisition of ownership is strictly limited to specific causes. Transfer of ownership does not take effect by the mere transfer of possession. Grotius has to discuss again in III. x the obligation to restore ownership, but in terms of internal justice (*interna justitia*) or internal obligation (*interna obligatio*).[59] In this case, the obligation to restore ownership has nothing to do with restricting or nullifying any 'external effects'.

Although Grotius's non-discriminatory concept of formal war under the law of nations does not necessarily involve a capitulation to the reality that no common authority exists to judge the lawfulness of war, it does involve a compromise with reality. This generates considerable strain in Grotius's system of natural law. The logical gap appears most strikingly in III. vi–vii, where booty and prisoners of war are discussed. Here, paying hardly any attention to consistency with natural law, Grotius seems to restrict himself, in the manner of a positivist, to describe the actual practices of various nations.[60]

While the question of the right to kill or wound persons ceases to be a major question between enemies when actual combat ends, the

[58] III. vi. 2(1), in the section under discussion, Kelsey *et al.* wrongly trans. *bellum solenne* (formal war) as public war.

[59] See 8.5.

[60] Faced with this inconsistency, it is not surprising that Schmitt focused his criticism of Grotius's just-war doctrine on the section concerning the acquisition of ownership based on rights of war: 1950: 133–4.

question of booty and prisoners of war may very well be carried over to the post-war period, thus occasionally providing a reason for starting another war. Presumably Grotius had this in mind when he advanced the idea of what 'may be called ownership in terms of its external effects'. As long as there is no realistic hope of taking back booty and prisoners seized by the victor, it would be more practical to confer legal effects on the actual results at the level of the law of nations, divorced from the effect of natural law.[61]

(ii) Acquisition of Enemy Property by Right of War[62] The law of nations adopts the following principle regarding acquisition of enemy property in war. Assuming that the original possessors have lost hope of regaining what has been taken from them, things taken will be regarded as captured if they are brought within the borders of enemy territory. Grotius applies the same reasoning to persons: a person becomes a prisoner of war when he is brought within enemy territory. Ships and other things at sea are regarded as captured when they have been brought into docks or harbours in enemy territory, or to the place where a fleet is stationed. Territories are not considered captured simply because they are occupied. For territories to be so regarded, certain steps must be taken to ensure continued occupation: the building of defences such as permanent fortifications and trenches.

Changes in ownership by means of force should not be readily recognized. Property that does not belong to the enemy cannot be acquired even if it is actually held by the enemy or is within enemy territory. It is not an established rule of the law of nations that goods on board an enemy ship can be seized; rather, they are

[61] To combine this practical approach with an insistence upon a just result in accordance with natural law requires a recognition of the actual legal order as highly provisional. In commenting on truces, after noting that the majority opinion on the subject in his time tends to limit the duration of truces to a relatively short period, Grotius states: 'I may add likewise for twenty, thirty, forty, and even for one hundred years' (III. xxi. 1(3)). This can be read as confirming that peace as a lasting truce is a façade, essentially nothing more than a temporary condition, when seen from the level of human reason: see Kasai 1984: 59.

[62] In later ages booty or spoil came to be differentiated from prize in the law of naval warfare. Here, these terms mean merely transference of occupation as the basis of recognizing external effects. The term 'right of prize (*jus praedae*)' (III. vi. 1(2)) is also occasionally used, but since it is not fully developed in *JBP*, it is not clear how this term differs from the other two.

merely presumed to be part of enemy property. Enemy cargo on a neutral ship may be seized only when the owner of the ship agrees. Things that enemies have taken from others in a war may be acquired, because through external ownership (*dominium externum*) the law of nations first made the enemy the owner, and thus the subsequent acquirer.[63]

(iii) Attribution and Distribution of Booty Attribution and distribution of booty is an important problem for Grotius: it was necessary to prevent the outbreak of a new war over things seized in a previous war. The majority opinion of his time, relying on the rules of Roman law and other authorities, asserted the objects seized belonged to the person who captured them, but that the authority to distribute them among the soldiers was a matter for the military commander. Grotius, rejecting this view, states that it is possible to induce some established rules from agreements reached among nations on whether things taken belong to the entire people in whose name a war is waged, or to the individual person who actually captured them. According to the will of nations, enemy property is equated with ownerless property (*res nullius*), in so far as the mutual relations between enemies are concerned. As ownerless things become the property of those who gain possession by their own efforts, so they become the property of those who take possession of them through others. Grotius thus introduces a distinction between acts of war that are truly of a public character (*actus vere publicus belli*) and private acts (*actus privatus*) which are incidental to a public war. In private acts property is taken primarily with a private end in mind, whereas by public acts property is taken for the sake of the people. In the latter case, captured things come to be owned by an entire people or by the ruler in whose name a war is waged, for individual soldiers represent that people or their ruler, and do not act merely on their own behalf.

Seizure of territory is a public act of war, for it cannot be occupied without such public acts as the entry of an armed force. On the other hand, movables, if taken outside the scope of a soldier's duty, come to be owned by individuals who capture them. This is a regression from the position Grotius had adopted in *De*

[63] III. vi. 3–6.

Jure Praedae Commentarius where he stated that all booty captured in a public war belongs to the state.[64] Nevertheless, it is still an advance compared with contemporary practice under the mercenary system.

Grotius argues that there is no contradiction between the rule that booty is owned by an entire people and the practice of granting it to the soldiers on the decision of the military commander in chief. The right to decide on the distribution of booty, which custom vested in the commander (*imperator*), is based on the right to command and not because the booty came to be the commander's property.[65] But changes may be made in the right of booty by municipal law, by an act of state, or by 'custom rightly introduced'. Grotius thus approves the widely practised custom of granting booty to those (e.g. allies or wealthy subjects) who wage war at their own expense and risk. This is because allies naturally have the right to demand that they be compensated for losses arising from a joint public enterprise. The same is true of subjects who have volunteered their services.[66]

(iv) Application of the Law of Nations regarding Seizure of Booty If a dispute arises over property captured within the jurisdiction of a nation not involved in the war, ownership is to be decided by the laws and customs of the country of the captors. If this is impossible, then ownership of things taken by public acts committed in a war is to be adjusted by the common rules of municipal law (*jus gentium commune*).[67] According to the law of nations, enemy property may be captured even in a third party's territories, but only if this does not violate the law of the land.

(2) *Rights over Prisoners of War*

In III. vii, Grotius discusses the right to enslave prisoners of war. He assumes that, since slaves are regarded as property under the law of nations, there is no difference between the right to enslave prisoners and the right to acquire property taken in war, discussed in III. vi. Since no human beings are slaves by nature, or in the primary state of nature, the analogy of acquisition of property and

[64] Grotius 1964 ⟨1604⟩, 142, 156. [65] III. vi. 15.

[66] III. vi. 22–4.

[67] Kelsey *et al.* trans. *jus gentium commune* as 'common law of nations'. Judging from the context, the meaning is closer to the common rules of municipal law.

enslaving prisoners of war is somewhat curious. Captives come to be regarded as property only after they have been captured and become slaves. However, Grotius ignores this distinction.

There had been opposing views as to the right to enslave prisoners of war. Grotius did not take part in this controversy. Instead, he gave priority to the practical argument that, since it is permissible to kill enemies, the permission to enslave prisoners of war is tantamount to choosing the lesser evil, thereby avoiding the inhumanity and absurdity of a war of annihilation.[68] Grotius thus insists that the right to enslave prisoners of war under the law of nations endows masters with wider powers than over slaves under the law of nature. This conclusion is inevitable, since the right to kill enemies in war remains potentially valid, in the form of the right of the master over the life and death of a slave, even after the end of the war.

(i) War Slaves under the Law of Nations Grotius starts from the premiss that, in the primary state of nature, no human beings are slaves. But if the institution of slavery came into being by agreement or as a result of wrongful conduct, it could not be regarded as a violation of justice under natural law. In the law of nations, slavery is permitted to a larger extent, both with regard to persons enslaved and with regard to its effects.[69] Not only those who surrender themselves, or promise to become slaves, but all those captured in a formal war become slaves as soon as they are brought within the border. The children of prisoners of war also become slaves.[70] With regard to effects, not only does the property of slaves, including intangibles, belong to their master,[71] but the master's rights over prisoners of war are unlimited: anything done to a slave is permissible. But since this is so only in terms of the effect of impunity, municipal law may impose penalties for brutality on the part of masters towards their slaves.

According to Grotius, since there was no element of agreement

[68] Lauterpacht discusses Grotius as if he had based the institution of slavery on the requirements of humanity, goodness, and compassion: 1970: 356. But the proposition that those who have taken prisoners of war should 'enslave them instead of killing them' derives from the utility-oriented approach.

[69] Although Grotius recognizes extremely harsh effects as regards war slaves, he states that in his time prisoners of war had come to assume a role more of hostages to ensure the payment of indemnity than of slaves: III. vii. 9.

[70] III. vii. 1–2.

[71] III. vii. 3(2) and 4.

between captor and captive, the captor never promised not to kill his captive, but was completely free to do whatever he wished, including killing or enslaving him. The law of nations was introduced to maximize the advantage of enslavement and thus to induce captors to opt for enslavement rather than killing.[72] Hence, even after the war ends, the captor retains, in theory, the right to kill the captive. Grotius stresses the rationality of the law of nations by asserting that in civil wars many captives are killed because they are not governed by the law of nations: since neither belligerent can choose to enslave his captives, he is compelled to kill them.[73]

The law governing property can be applied to slaves because they are regarded as property. Thus it is possible to alienate rights over slaves. The same holds true for the children of slaves, for they would not have been born if their parents had been killed.[74] Similarly, the law governing booty is applied to the question whether slaves become the property of their individual captors or of the entire people.[75]

(ii) Escape of Slaves and Resistance to their Master Whatever their status under the law of nations, slaves cannot simply be subsumed under the law which governs captured property. Grotius discusses the problem of escape of captives by introducing the following distinction: if captives escape to their own people while the war is still in progress, they obtain their liberty by the right of postliminy; but if they flee to others, or to their own people, only after peace has been concluded, they must be restored to their master if the latter claims them.[76] This does not mean that slaves have an obligation not to escape: 'it does not follow . . . that a bond of conscience is also laid upon the captives'.[77] The issue concerns those 'rights which look only to an external judgement'. Even in the second case, where escape does not affect ownership, the recognition of the legal right of the master to the restoration of the captive does not imply the obligation of the latter not to escape.

This rule of the law of nations was established solely to avoid a

[72] III. vii. 5. [73] III. vii. 5(3).

[74] III. vii. 5(2). The difficulty that arises with regard to slavery based on agreement is how children of slaves can be made to inherit the slave status of their parents despite the fact that they are not able to grant consent on their own. This problem does not arise in relation to prisoners of war who become slaves.

[75] III. vii. 5(4). [76] III. vii. 6(1). [77] Ibid.

greater evil, even at the cost of violating natural equity. Grotius concludes that acts which contravene this rule should not too readily be regarded as crimes.[78] The right over prisoners of war is 'a right in respect to certain effects; it is a wrong, if we regard its intrinsic nature'.[79] The gist of the argument is that a change in the outward appearance of ownership as a result of a captive escaping and returning to his own people would nullify the external effect of the acquisition of ownership over captives as slaves. Thus the demand to restore a slave who has fled, or to exact punishment on the slave, cannot constitute a just cause for starting a new war. By contrast, the escape of a slave to someone other than his own people or their allies does not nullify the external effect of ownership under the law of nations. If that were recognized, some neutral third party would be embroiled in an unnecessary war by being forced to choose between judging the substantive just causes of war or stressing its external effects.

Certain rules prohibit anyone from trying to persuade slaves to desert their master's service. According to Grotius, this prohibition is just if it applies to slaves who are undergoing a just punishment, or who have made themselves slaves by voluntary agreement. It is, however, permissible by nature for persons to persuade slaves captured in war to resist passively. Hence this prohibition is meant merely to persuade slaves to endure, rather than engage in an act that may be contrary to the Christian spirit. On the question of active resistance on the part of prisoners of war,[80] Grotius rejects the right to resist their master's exercise of external rights. Mere escape and active resistance are completely different: if the right to resist actively were retained by slaves, the master's external rights would have no effect at all. Furthermore, if it were permissible to resist a master by force, it would also be permissible to resist by force a magistrate with the responsibility of protecting the master's external rights and their exercise.[81]

[78] III. vii. 6(4). [79] Ibid.

[80] III. vii. 7.

[81] Grotius explained this by analogy to the argument for rejecting the right of resistance against a supreme ruler (I. vi. 4(6)). But in the latter case active resistance is exceptionally permitted (I. iv. 8–14), including when a king has shown himself to be the enemy of his own people by trying to destroy them. In the case of war slaves, the prohibition against resistance is even more extensive, since a master's power of life and death over his slaves is deemed to be within the purview of his external rights.

Grotius concludes his description of rights over captives by noting that the law of nations has not always been accepted consistently, nor is it accepted among all nations.[82] Among Christians, in particular, the rules under consideration no longer exist: instead, with the establishment of the mercenary system, the practice of enslaving captives has been replaced generally by that of ransoming them.[83] A similar practice is found among Muslims.

(3) *Acquisition of the Governing Power of the State* (imperium civile) *over the Conquered*

In III. viii, Grotius discusses the acquisition of governing power as a result of war and its effects.[84] In doing so, he draws an analogy between acquiring *imperium* over an entire people and enslaving individual prisoners. It is not at all strange that one who can subject individuals to personal servitude is able to subject to himself an aggregation (*universitas*) of men—whether they formed a state (*civitas*) or part of a state—in a subjection which may be purely civil, or purely personal, or mixed.[85] This subjection may involve the state as a whole, its individual members, or both. In the first case, the victor will acquire governing power over the vanquished. When governing power originally belongs to a king or another ruler, the victor only succeeds to this power. When governing power belongs to the people, the victor acquires it in such a way that he may even alienate it.[86] In the second case, the governing power over a people as its master (*imperium herile*) may be acquired. In this case, a people previously constituted as a state may disintegrate and become annexed to the conqueror. The power vested in its master is not a power vested in a political authority which aims to ensure the welfare of a free people as its sovereign, but rather a power exercisable solely for the profit of the ruler. The

[82] III. vii. 8. [83] III. vii. 9.

[84] Grotius had already stated in I. iii, that as it is possible to acquire private ownership (*dominium privatum*) by means of just war, so it is possible to acquire public authority (*dominium civile*) or the right to govern (*jus regendi*) (I. iii. 8(6)). With regard to formal war, however, while acquisition of land is dealt with in III. iii, the concept of *dominium civile* as governing power is nowhere dealt with explicitly in comparison with *dominium privatum*. Acquisition of *imperium civile* by means of war is discussed by analogy to the enslavement of captives (III. vii). Moreover, slaves are regarded as property. From this viewpoint, it should be clear that the governing power of a master over his slaves excludes neither the concept of *dominium privatum* nor that of *dominium civile*.

[85] III. viii. I(I). [86] III. viii. I(2). Also see I. iii. II(I).

third case involves partly *imperium civile* and partly the power of a master over a slave, so that an element of servitude is mixed with a certain degree of personal liberty (*libertas personae*).[87]

(4) *Postliminy*

In III. ix Grotius discusses the question of postliminy (*postliminium*): how external changes in ownership based on the rights of acquiring booty and enslaving captives discussed in III. vi–viii can be restored to their original status. Tracing the term postliminy to its Latin origin, he defines it as 'a right which arises from a return to the threshold, that is, to the public boundaries'.[88] According to the agreement of nations (*consensus gentium*), postliminy occurs not only when a person, or a thing in regard to which postliminy is possible, has reached his own country, but also when he has reached his allied territory. The significance of postliminy is that the principle of the external effects of war is excluded. However, if a captive of a belligerent state is sold and taken to a third state, postliminy does not occur, and it would be necessary to pay a ransom to free the captive.[89]

Although postliminy may occur both in peace and in war, in peace it is severely limited, for third parties cannot safely determine whether a belligerent has a just cause for waging war. Thus it is advisable to let nations respect the facts that have emerged as a result of war as rights, by regarding prisoners of war as if they were captured on the basis of just causes of war.[90] On the other hand, postliminy in time of peace is recognized for those trapped on enemy territory when war broke out: although it would not be unjust to detain innocent persons to reduce the potential power of the enemy while the war is in progress, there is no longer any reason to do so if an agreement is reached on bringing the war to an end. With regard to slaves and property, postliminy cannot thereafter arise, since if it did, this would touch off a vicious circle of war begetting another war.[91] While a war is in progress, those captured who had the status of free men (*liberi homini*) may be returned to their own people, while slaves and certain other property may be recovered by their former masters or owners. Those who surrendered to the enemy have no right of postliminy.

[87] III. viii. 3. [88] III. ix. 2(1). [89] III. ix. 2(2).
[90] III. ix. 4(2). [91] III. ix. 4(3).

The principle of postliminy applies also to an entire people or nation (*populus*). Thus people who were free but were temporarily ruled by the enemy may regain their liberty if their allies extricate them from enemy rule. However, since the very nature of a people consists in its perpetual union, once a people dissolve that union and disperse under the rule of the enemy (as in the case of enslavement), the people in question are considered to have perished outright, and cannot keep its identity. Even if it has a chance to gather itself again, it cannot be considered the same people, nor can its liberty be restored by postliminy.[92]

Postliminy also applies to property.[93] Slaves, whether alienated to another or manumitted by the enemy, may be recovered by postliminy, because the former master is not bound to obey the law of the enemy. For a slave to be recovered, he must actually be held by his former master or be in a condition where he can be easily obtained. Therefore, unlike other property, it is not enough for a slave to be brought within the frontier: this fact must be made known to others. Territory and concomitant rights over territory are recovered when the enemy is driven out of the territory and can no longer trespass on it openly. By contrast, movables are not subject to postliminy. In cases where property has not yet been brought within a fort, it can be recovered without relying on postliminy even if it is in fact possessed by the enemy, because the effect of ownership under the law of nations has not yet been perfected. Municipal law may restrict or extend these effects of postliminy, but it cannot prevent foreigners from claiming rights recognized under the law of nations.

8.5. Demands for Internal Justice in an Unjust War

8.5.1. The Relativization of External Effects

The law of nations, which confers special effects on formal war, was introduced as a matter of human convenience and practicality to restrain the conduct of war, to bring about an early conclusion to wars, and to prevent their recurrence. Grotius could not have been unaware of the logical gap between the actual outcomes which the law of nations sanctions and his system of natural law defined

[92] Ibid. [93] III. ix. 9.

according to right reason. Thus, after discussing in detail the rules of the law of nations, Grotius in III. x takes great pains to adjust the effects sanctioned by the law of war on the level of the law of nations so as to bring them in line with the argument in Books I and II. He states: 'I must retrace my steps, and must deprive those who wage war of nearly all the privileges which I seemed to grant, yet did not grant to them.'[94]

As noted earlier, Grotius did not introduce the law of nations governing formal wars merely because it was difficult to distinguish between the just and unjust causes of wars between peoples or nations. His overriding concern was to bring wars to an early conclusion, rather than become embroiled in a debate over the justness of a war. However, if this concept of the law of nations were to prevail, there might be those with no substantive just cause for initiating a war who wilfully arranged to meet the formal requirements of war with the sole aim of attaining the external effects of formal war, a situation Grotius could never admit. Thus, Grotius seeks to revert to the position of 'right reason'. He maintains that men will continue to act rationally even after the outbreak of war. Even those who firmly believe in the justness of their war because of ignorance of law will strive to correct the injustice when they realize that they do not have a just cause. Such rationality should lead to a solution based not on outward appearances but on the truth. This reasoning shows Grotius's expectation and conviction of human goodness.

However, the level of argument to which he returns is not that of natural law itself. Instead, he resorts to 'internal justice (*interna justitia*)', a concept which, while sharing the same content as natural law, is not accompanied by any institutional means of enforcement.[95] Even with regard to formal war, 'what is done by reason of an unjust war is unjust from the viewpoint of internal justice'.[96] This reasoning tends to weaken the first general rule of natural law which confers extensive rights upon those waging a just war. This is because the content of the requirements of internal justice may be so extensive as to constitute the basis for modera-

[94] To compensate for the weakness of the concept of internal justice, Grotius goes so far as to state that those who commit injustice cannot be admitted to heaven without repentance: III. x. 1.

[95] On this point see also III. x. 3, and Haggenmacher 1983: 573.

[96] See the title of III. x. 3.

tion, *temperamenta*, and may thus have a wider application and be much more humane in its operation than natural law itself. It is at least theoretically possible to infer that even what is done in a just war for the sake of realizing justice may be unjust from the viewpoint of internal justice, a proposition which it would be difficult to admit within the framework of Grotius's just-war doctrine based on natural law.

What Grotius specifically mentions in III. x is that, despite external effects under the law of nations, those who wage an unjust war should make reparation for any injurious acts they commit and should also return to the original owner any booty captured during the course of war.[97] Those without rights under natural law remain so regardless of what human law may stipulate. Thus internal justice makes restitution and postliminy obligatory. Grotius draws an analogy with rights and obligations arising from an unequal agreement.[98] The law of nations regards them as lawful on the grounds that they are based on an agreement.[99] Since this does not alter the fact that this agreement is unfair under natural law, those acquiring such rights are obliged to return any excess value they have acquired unjustly. But this obligation is no more than a natural obligation, with its execution exclusively entrusted to those on whom the obligation in question falls. Similarly, the demand of internal justice with respect to the external effects of war is entrusted to those waging an unjust war.

8.5.2. Self-Evident Reason, External Effects, and Internal Justice

Grotius does not discuss the relation between this internal justice and natural law. He merely contrasts internal justice in a formalistic way with external effects under the law of nations. There are two reasons for this: (1) the desire to prevent the recurrence of war; (2) the desire to preserve the non-discriminatory nature of the regulations provided by the law of war. Internal justice demands that those who wage an unjust war should abandon of their own accord the external effects they receive under the law of nations and make reparation for damage done. This amounts to restoring the rightful condition, in which there is complete agreement with natural law. But to express this clearly as the demand of natural law would be

[97] III. x. 4–6. [98] III. x. 5(2). [99] II. xix. 6.

tantamount to recognizing the right of just claimants to assert their rights by force. This would mean a vicious circle of controversies over the justness of war. The law of nations exists precisely to avoid this. In short, Grotius seeks to prevent the invocation of internal justice as a substantive just cause of war, by distinguishing it from an obligation under natural law, and by treating it instead as a requirement entrusted to the spontaneous obedience of those waging an unjust war.

The concept of internal justice presupposes the distinction between a just war and an unjust war. This is directly opposed to the principle of non-discrimination under the law of nations, which is why Grotius introduced the contrast between 'internal' justice and 'external' effects. He seeks to weaken the element of discrimination inherent in internal justice by developing his statements on it as corresponding, chapter by chapter, to non-discriminatory external effects. This is why the *temperamenta* assume the form of revisions based on internal justice under strict correspondence with the rights of war, and ensured by the law of nations discussed from III. iv–ix. *Temperamenta*, discussed in III. xi, are grounded in internal justice, and as a result, Grotius was able to discuss it *as if temperamenta* were an appeal directed equally to both belligerents in a formal war. Although even the *temperamenta* explicitly only refer to acts committed in a just war, Grotius's notion of internal justice here is close to that of Cicero, whom he cites, and is contrasted with law as related to external judgements. It includes 'justice to all living creatures (*communis jus animatium*)'.[100] Thus internal justice is rather a deep-rooted sentiment of justice that exists at a stage logically prior even to natural law, which is established on the basis of self-evident 'reason'. In that sense, internal justice is a *sentiment* of justice on which the very reasoning about justice is founded.

[100] III. x. 1(3). Aristotle's 'absolute justice' is also referred to as relativizing the justness of slavery arising through war: III. x. 2(1).

9

Temperamenta (Moderation)

9.1. The Problem

In III. iii–ix, Grotius discusses what is 'permissible' under the law of nations in a formal war—killing and wounding enemies, devastating and pillaging, acquiring captured goods, enslaving prisoners of war, and acquiring supreme governing power—and examines the issue of postliminy. However, he then reverses his position and insists that he does not necessarily approve of these unrestrained liberties (*licentia*).

How does Grotius justify withdrawing the rights he had earlier granted, under the law of nations, equally to both parties waging a formal war? This is the most important question in assessing the significance of the chapters III. x–xvi (which include the chapters devoted to the admonition of *temperamenta*).[1] It also provides an important clue to understanding Grotius's fundamental aim of minimizing bloodshed, as revealed in his discussion of 'pardon' in relation to punishment, in his appeal to the renunciation of war, and in other similar arguments throughout *JBP*.

There is another question: whether the rights of war (*jus belli*)[2] under what Grotius calls the law of nations, or *temperamenta*, or both, can be traced genealogically to the so-called laws of war as formulated in positive international law in the period from the late eighteenth century to the Second World War. In other words, how is Grotius's inquiry into what is permissible in war related to the laws of war in the modern sense?[3] In this chapter, we point out the

[1] *Temperamenta* (the plural form, as used in each ch. heading, of *temperamentum*) may be trans. as either 'moderation' or 'pardon'. To avoid confusion with less technical terms, the Latin original will be used. In *JBP*, the terms *moderatio* and *modestia* also appear sporadically.

[2] *Jus belli* means both rights of war and laws of war. It is ultimately reduced to the question of what can justly be done in war. Killing and Injuring enemies often represent what are called rights of war (III. iv. 5(1)). For a discussion on the multiplicity of meanings of the term *jus*, see 2.2.

[3] Verzijl (1968: 441) says that in the area of methods of warfare, the classical

points of similarity or coincidence between Grotius's theses and the rules or principles of positive international law.[4] We also assess the significance of these similarities or coincidences, in order to identify the relation between the two.

9.2. Unjust War

At the beginning of III. x, Grotius states: 'I must retrace my steps, and must deprive those who wage war (*bellum gerentes*) of nearly all the privileges which I seemed to grant, yet did not grant to them.' Here his intention to restrict the acts of war permitted by the law of nations is clearly revealed. His argument may be paraphrased as follows: where actions are said to be 'permissible' under the law of nations this means that they may be done with impunity (*impunitas*),[5] that is, that they are protected in such a way that the courts would recognize their validity. But the actions themselves may either deviate from righteous rule (*recta regula*) (whether this has its basis in law strictly so-called, or in the admonitions of other ethical or religious codes) or may at least more righteously be omitted. It is noteworthy that various standards ranging from strict rules of law to simple praiseworthiness are already enumerated and contrasted to the external effects of actions.[6]

thought of international law, including that espoused by Grotius, exerted an influence on positive international law, but that the latter was undermined by the invention of even crueller methods of warfare. This may have been true in some cases, but the real problem is to verify the process.

[4] When we contrast the laws of war as a part of positive international law with Grotius's views, we refer mainly to positive international law prevailing in the period between the late 18th and early 20th cents.

[5] Grotius refers to impunity and ownership as external effects accompanying a formal war according to the law of nations (III. iv. 4; III. vi. 1–2). A similar argument is found in II. xx. 17(1). In disapproving of the effect of transfer of ownership in the course of an unjust war, Grotius contrasts this specifically with the internal obligation of restitution. In Roman law, it was not possible to pursue restitution and punishment simultaneously. In this sense there are many cases where the effect of impunity is understood as connoting also the effect of transfer of ownership. This is perhaps why in III. x, Grotius refers to impunity only. See Funada 1970: 375, 376 n. 4; Kaser 1979: 394 ff.; Harada 1982: 219 ff.

[6] Grotius cites works that refer to a sense of shame (*pudor*) as examples of such standards of value. Here again, either in the expressions of the original authors or in his comments on them, the sense of shame is linked to that which is equitable and good, to justice, and even to the law of nature. In addition, while citing Cicero, Grotius contrasts a sense of reverence (*verecundia*) with law understood in its external effects; citing Seneca, he contrasts piety (*pietas*), humanity (*humanitas*), generosity (*liberalitas*), justice (*justitia*), and good faith (*fides*) with law (III. x. 1).

This reasoning is mainly applied to actions permitted under the law of nations. Grotius cites the old custom of enslaving those captured in war (*servitus ex bello*) as an example of a practice that deviates from natural equity, and the injustice of which could be readily perceived according to the sense of law (*Rechtsbewußtsein*) shared by his contemporaries. He then proceeds to discuss unjust war on the basis of this general principle.[7] If the substantive cause of war, even of a formal war, is unjust, all acts which arise therefrom are unjust from the viewpoint of internal injustice (*interna injustitia*): he thus categorically denies the justness of all hostile acts committed in an unjust war, as well as the justness of their outcomes. Here the discussion seems to revert to the level of the law of nature. But as long as Grotius concedes that, according to the law of nations, acts in a formal war are not punishable, it is impossible to condemn them as unjust under that law. Grotius seeks to restrain these acts by arguing that those who engage in an unjust war, or participate in such a war, will neither reach the Kingdom of Heaven nor achieve salvation without repentance.[8]

In seventeenth-century Europe, the warning that salvation may not be achieved might have been convincing up to a point. But given the political realities of the process by which many European countries were developing into nation states through incessant war, such a warning could have only a limited value as a restraining principle.[9] Besides, to seek effective control on this level alone hardly corresponds with Grotius's methodological position of constructing a philosophy of law based on a secularized natural law.

It is true that not all the rules of natural law Grotius expounds are supported by institutional means of enforcement. In the Prolegomena he takes the precautionary measure of stating that a law does not become invalid even if it lacks external effects, and

[7] Since Grotius does not specifically distinguish just from unjust wars in the opening passage of III. x, Grewe concludes that III. x–xviii elaborate restrictions to be imposed equally on both belligerents (1984: 255). This overlooks the fact that, except in the opening passage, Grotius directs the entire argument of III. x only at the unjust party.

[8] III. x. 3.

[9] In a Europe acquainted with Machiavelli's thought and which had experienced the Reformation and the subsequent 'struggle of confessionalism', the appeal to salvation after death for good deeds done in the secular world was no longer very persuasive; this is why the secularization of natural law became the main current in jurisprudence (Fukuda 1971: 23–4, 33–4. See also Mizuta 1963: 97 ff.).

that justice is supported by a clear conscience, the approval of good men, and the protection of God.[10] Nevertheless, the rules of natural law that constitute the substantive just causes of war are assumed to be realized institutionally through the judgement of tribunals and accordingly through war, since there is an analogy between wars and lawsuits.[11] By contrast, once the external effects of war under the law of nations are conceded, the denial of the justness of acts in an unjust war can no longer be supported by human institutions. Any other view might precipitate the worst possible case of an incessant chain of wars, a consequence which Grotius did his best to avoid.

Grotius himself is not content with his appeal to restraint in the hope of salvation. In arguing that one cannot reach the Kingdom of Heaven without repentance, he deftly replaces 'repentance' with the internal obligation to make reparation for wrongs done. He thus seeks to reduce the issue to the level of the (secular) rule of law relating to restitution (*restitutio*).[12] This is not enough to make up for the lack of any institutional means of enforcement, but it is an attempt to develop the argument on the level of secular law as far as possible. However, rather than inquiring into this point more deeply, Grotius shifts his argument to the scope of the obligation of restitution.

According to Grotius, those who initiate a war on their own authority (*belli auctor potestatis jure*) or by conspiring with another (*consilio*) are liable to make restitution. This liability extends not only to the usual consequences of war but also to any unusual consequences if those responsible for them ordered or advised the acts which caused those consequences, or did not prevent them when they should have done. Thus a commander-in-chief (*dux*) must make reparation for everything done under his command. Soldiers who take part in a joint operation are collectively responsible for the total damage. Each soldier is responsible for the damage he himself has caused if he was acting individually. Grotius does not recognize any exception to this principle.[13]

If this line of argument were carried to its logical extreme, then

[10] Prol. 19–20. See also Prol. 11–13; I. i. 10(1)–(2).
[11] I. iii. 1–2; II. i. 2.
[12] This is also the aim of Midgley 1975: 165.
[13] III. x. 4–5(1).

after a war had ended, a party who believed its opponent had committed unjust acts and had not fulfilled its obligation to make restitution might feel they had a just cause to resume the war, or rather to resort to a new war. Grotius argues that the reason it is necessary to introduce the concept of external ownership (*dominium externum*), accompanied by the internal obligation (*obligatio interna*) to make restitution, is precisely to enable people at peace to avoid being involved in war against their will. That is, failure to comply with the internal obligation of restitution cannot constitute a just cause for initiating a war. It is thus distinguished from the rights and duties constituting the substantive just causes of war developed in Book II. In other words, the legality of killing and wounding enemies, changes in ownership, and the like effects resulting from a formal war are institutionally established and become irrevocable, as far as their legal effects are concerned, once the act in question has been completed. Even if injustice is left unrepaired, it cannot be corrected by war. The fulfilment of internal obligation can only be left to the conscience of those responsible,[14] although Grotius still calls for the fulfilment of the internal obligation of restitution.[15]

After expounding the obligation of those who engage in an unjust war to make restitution, Grotius introduces the notion of *temperamenta* by asserting that there is something morally unjust even in a just war. With regard to unjust wars, Grotius refers only to restitution (*restitutio*) as a moral obligation: it is not clear whether that term includes the idea of compensation for damages (*Schadenersatz*) as we think of it today. But considering that Grotius's concept of restitution is intended to restore natural equity, it is likely that some form of compensation should be made for killing and wounding enemies or for devastation carried out.[16]

[14] Midgley's 'dissatisfaction' (1975: 165–6) stems from his failure to consider this point. As an example of something that closely resembles an internal obligation of this sort, Grotius cites a contract that gives rise to inequality (*inaequalitas*) based on fraud: it is possible by the law of nations to compel one who has entered the contract to fulfil his promise, but *aequalitas* is demanded as the duty of a pious man. Incidentally, the cross-reference II. xi, indicated in the margin of III. x. 5(1), should be II. xii. 26. See also II. xix. 6.

[15] The obligation of restitution applies not only to him who inflicts the loss, but also to a third party who possesses a thing taken from another who wages an unjust war. See III. x. 6.

[16] Roman law does not contain a separate idea of compensation for damage: it

9.3. *Temperamenta*

After disapproving every act of those engaged in an unjust war, Grotius seeks to restrain the acts even of those who wage a just war,[17] acts which are not only justifiable according to the law of nature but are 'permitted' according to the law of nations under the title of rights of war. This restraint constitutes what Grotius calls *temperamenta*. Related to this notion is the contrast between external effects and internal justice (*interna justitia*), as well as the contrast between justice strictly so-called and humanity or love.

With one exception,[18] *temperamenta* are appeals directed, at least at first sight, to those waging a just war. Thus, if the discussions from III. i–x were enclosed within parentheses, *temperamenta* might be regarded as a variation of the discussion of the formal causes or just methods of warfare within the Scholastic just-war doctrine. But this was probably not Grotius's intention. Since he treats all matters relating to war comprehensively and on various levels of law throughout *JBP*, it is hard to believe that he would have been satisfied categorically to deny the justness of hostile acts committed by those waging an unjust war, or of the justness of their consequences, without giving a detailed explanation of the injustice of such acts. It is probably closer to Grotius's intention with regard to *temperamenta* to say that he maintained that certain acts are restricted from the viewpoint of internal justice, even in a just war, and *a fortiori* in an unjust war.[19] To this extent, Haggenmacher is correct in referring to the rights of war and *temperamenta* as two types of laws of war which are not mutually exclusive.[20]

seems that this idea was established only during the European medieval period. In Roman law the principle of restoration of the *status quo ante* (*restitutio in integrum*) is defined as payment in kind. But if the institution of compensation for damage was established in the laws of European medieval city-states, as Mitteis states, it is quite possible that Grotius was familiar with it. See Kaser 1977: 338–9; Mitteis = Lieberich 1981: 27, 92; Harada 1982: 219, 406.

[17] The word (un)lawful used in Kelsey's trans. of the sections which follow III. x. 6 is in the original *bellum (in)justum* (just war or unjust war).

[18] See 9.3.6.

[19] See 9.4.3.

[20] Haggenmacher 1983: 600–1. However, accepting at face value Grotius's disapproval of unjust wars, he regards *temperamenta* as appeals directed only to those waging a just war. This misunderstands Grotius's intention to limit the cruelties of war in as many ways as possible.

9.3.1. On the Right of Killing

(1) *General Rules*

Grotius first seeks to restrain the right to kill (*jus interficiendi*). Citing Cicero, he explains that certain duties must be performed even towards those from whom one has received an injury, and that there is a limit to vengeance and to punishment. Who then may be killed in a just war without violating internal justice? Grotius states that no one may justly be killed intentionally (*ex proposito*) except as a just punishment or by necessity, i.e. when there is no other way to protect one's life or property. However, the killing of a person in order to protect things of only transitory value is against the law of love (*lex caritatis*), even if it is not repugnant to justice strictly so-called (*justitia stricte dicta*).

In discussing killing as a form of punishment, Grotius categorizes the elements which merit punishment as wrongs (*injuriae*), faults (*culpae*), and misfortunes (*infortunia*). Misfortunes are cases where the outcome of an action could not have been foreseen and there is no evil intention. The actor in such cases neither merits punishment nor is liable to make reparation. Faults are cases where the outcome of an action could have been foreseen but there was no evil intention. The actor in such cases is liable to make reparation but does not deserve punishment, especially capital punishment. Wrongs are cases where the outcome of an action could have been foreseen and there is an evil intention. Those who commit wrongs deserve punishment and are also liable to make reparation.[21] In short, Grotius limits punishment only to those who purposely do wrong.[22]

Grotius next gives one reason after another for pardoning even those who purposely do wrong. First, he distinguishes between those under whose authority a war is waged (*auctor belli*)[23] and those who merely follow them. But he advocates pardon even for those who are themselves responsible for initiating and waging a war.

[21] In the theory of punishment, Grotius does not develop his concept of criminal responsibility in a similar way, though the distinction between misfortune and wrong is found in II. xxi. 5. Criminal responsibility discussed here differs from that found in Roman law. See nn. 5 and 6.

[22] III. xi. 3–4.

[23] The expression *actores belli* is used in III. xi. 5 because Grotius probably depended on quotations. It should be interpreted as having the same meaning as *auctores*.

He argues that it is sometimes in accordance with the spirit of moderation (*modestia*) and high-mindedness to exempt from punishment even enemies who deserve death. Those who wish to observe not only what human laws permit, but what their duty requires and what is just and pious (*quod fas et pium est*), should pardon their foes. And mercy, if not justice, demands that no innocent person be killed, even by accident.[24]

Thus Grotius restricts the right to kill at a number of levels: the level of substantive just causes (punishment, necessity), the level of the principle of responsibility (misfortune, fault, wrong), the level of the subject of responsibility (those who are directly responsible for war, their followers), and the level of the causes of individual acts. He then seeks pardon even for those who deserve death. Making these fine distinctions, carefully formulating a graduated system of granting pardon, is a procedure followed throughout the discussion of *temperamenta*. It is also one of the main characteristics of his thought. This is why his just-war doctrine is free from the extremes of achieving substantive justice at any cost and of accepting that a belligerent may shed the blood of his foe so long as his acts are just.

(2) *Women and Children*

Grotius specifies categories of people who may not be killed. These include children, women (unless they themselves have committed a crime or are fighting in place of men), old men, members of the clergy, men of letters, farmers, merchants, and artisans. These people should be spared because in principle they do not bear arms.[25] In explaining this, Grotius cites Livy's phrases 'laws of war, that is, natural laws' or '*jus belli* in harmony with nature'. Again we can assume that, while refraining from drawing conclusions in his own words, he hoped his readers would interpret his concept of *temperamenta* as akin to the requirements of natural law.

(3) *Prisoners of War and Those Who Surrender*

In certain cases even prisoners of war who have borne arms should not be killed. In addition to the argument that there is no longer any need to fear them, he invokes such considerations as honour and equity, the laws of war, and the nature of goodness and justice.

[24] III. xi. 5–8. [25] III. xi. 9–12.

Similarly, the surrender (*deditio*) of those who yield on the condition that their lives be spared should not be rejected. Here Grotius cites, rather exceptionally, the practice of his own age in addition to that of the Roman empire. Furthermore, those who surrender unconditionally or who beg for mercy should be spared.[26] In short, since prisoners of war and those who have surrendered no longer pose a threat, they cannot justly be executed unless they have committed a crime which deserves capital punishment. Grotius sometimes calls this assertion 'the dictate of equity and natural law (*aequitatis ac juris naturalis praeceptum*)',[27] an expression reminiscent of the mandatory law of nature discussed earlier,[28] and which might very well give rise to the misunderstanding that its violation constitutes a new just cause of war. He dares to choose such an expression to make his assertion as persuasive as possible.

(4) *Additional Rules or Requirements*

Finally, Grotius takes up certain miscellaneous instances where pardon should be granted. First, where the number of people to be killed is very large, Grotius recommends they be spared, even though the number of those to be killed is not directly related to justice in the strict sense. Grotius is evidently drawing a conclusion from the practical viewpoint. Secondly, it is a mistake to deem hostages to have consented to being killed if the obligation in respect of which they were taken as hostages is not fulfilled. The right (*dominium*) over life is reserved to God: no one by his own consent alone can transfer to another a right over his own life. Therefore it is not permissible to kill a hostage unless he himself breaks a pledge or commits a crime.

Grotius concludes III. xi with an all-inclusive appeal for restraint: since hostilities which do not contribute to bringing about justice or ending a war are compatible neither with the duty of Christians nor with humanity, rulers who bear arms in the name of God should strictly prohibit such hostilities.[29] Grotius's abhorrence of bloodshed[30] is manifest in these diverse, sometimes even inconsistent, arguments for restraint.

[26] III. xi. 13–16. See II. xxi. 5–6.
[27] III. xi. 16(1). [28] 2.3.1(1). [29] III. xi. 17–19.
[30] See Murphy 1982: 481. However, his expression 'vision of world order', shared by some modern scholars in the USA, might lead to a misunderstanding of Grotius's position.

9.3.2. On Devastating and Pillaging

Grotius's argument in expounding *temperamenta* in respect of devastation and pillaging in a just war is similar. The only causes for which another's property may be destroyed are necessity (*necessitas*), debt (*debitum*), and punishment. Moreover, destruction should not be resorted to unless it helps to reduce the strength of the enemy. Devastation for devastation's sake is absurd and should be avoided.[31] This principle has several corollaries. First, devastation will not be allowed if, as a result of its occupation, the land and its produce are effectively withheld from the enemy. Secondly, even where the occupation of territory is precarious, devastation will not be allowed if an early victory can be expected, the result of which will be the acquisition of both the land and its produce. The same holds true if the sea or other territories, from which the enemy can secure his means of subsistence, are open to him. Finally, since some things are intrinsically useless for waging war, reason dictates that they be spared. Common to these conclusions is the judgement whether or not devastation serves to weaken the enemy's ability to continue waging the war.[32]

Grotius also insists that one should refrain from destroying or pillaging works of art, particularly those devoted to sacred purposes. Such things may not be devastated or pillaged because they cannot be diverted to secular use.[33] Reverence for sacred objects (*rerum divinarum reverentia*) requires that sacred buildings and their furnishings be preserved. Those who believe in the same God, although they may disagree over doctrine or ritual, agree that the preservation of such objects is in accordance with the law of God.[34] Here, Grotius uses such harsh expressions as contempt of humanity, madness, impiety, and offence against God, in criticizing cases where sacred buildings have been destroyed. Doubtless he had in mind contemporary religious wars when he urged people to refrain from acts of destruction. The strong bond that unites Christians requires supreme rulers and commanders, who desire to be judged as true Christians by God and men, to prohibit the pillaging of cities: such devastation is incompatible with the innate goodness of Christians (*bonitas Christiana*) and with justice.[35]

Grotius also expounds the benefits derived from moderation:

[31] III. xii. 1. [32] III. xii. 2–5. [33] III. v. 2.
[34] III. xii. 6–7. [35] III. xii. 8(4).

here again his emphasis is on utility. He begins by saying that his primary aim is not to ask what is useful, but rather to restrict the licence of war (*bellandi licentia*) to what nature will permit, or to the more desirable among various permissible purposes. However, even in the light of virtue (*virtus*), underestimated in Grotius's age, one should be able to evaluate *temperamenta* from the viewpoint of utility. Thus, dissatisfied with merely enumerating the various virtues apart from law as principles with which to restrict violence, Grotius seeks to enhance the persuasiveness of his argument by invoking utility, which he originally professed to place outside his investigation.[36] The notion of utility invoked here amounts to the claim that to refrain from destroying or pillaging property increases the likelihood of victory by depriving the enemy of the great weapon of despair, and that clemency helps to reduce the enemy's enmity.[37] These considerations are often said to be the *raison d'être* of the laws and customs of war in modern international law. While Grotius's assertions should not be identified too readily with those later laws and customs, one can assume that his utility-oriented approach helped to make his *temperamenta* more acceptable.

9.3.3. On Captured Goods (*Res Captae*)

Grotius discusses the external effects of war under the law of nations under two headings, the effects of impunity and of ownership.[38] He seeks to restrict the effect of impunity in regard to killing, wounding, devastating, and pillaging, by contrasting external effects with internal obligation, and by appealing to the law of love, humanity, and other virtues. He uses the same technique to restrict the effect of ownership. The capture or acquisition of enemy property even in a just war is not always devoid of wrong (*peccatum*), or free from the obligation of restitution. It is not permissible to acquire property of greater value than the enemy's liability or debt (*debitum*).[39] A liability or debt may be owing as a result of inequitable or unconscionable conduct (*inaequalitas rerum*)

[36] It is true that Grotius categorically distinguishes justice from utility and regards the latter as an object of political science (Prol. 57). See Iltung 1983: 73–5. Despite this, he does not hesitate to invoke utilitarian arguments based on considerations of utility.

[37] III. xii. 8(1)–(3).

[38] III. iv. 4.

[39] III. xiii. 1(1). This rule does not extend to security (*securitas*) taken in relation to a debt or liability. However, since the obligation to make reparation arises after the danger has been removed, in the end there is no significant difference.

or by way of a punishment.[40] Enemy property may be acquired for either of these causes. The right to acquire such property may extend even to the property of enemy subjects if a liability or debt arises by virtue of inequitable or unconscionable conduct, but not so if it arises by way of a punishment. This difference is based on Grotius's belief that in the case of a liability or debt arising as a result of inequitable or unconscionable conduct, the creditor's right under the law of nations involves not only impunity or external recognition by the courts, but is a right admitted by common consent. Such a right has the same effect as a transaction by mutual consent, under which one party acquires not only an external but also an internal right (*internum jus*) to the other's property. Grotius explains that this rule of the law of nations was introduced not only to avoid a greater evil but also to secure the right of each person to his property.[41] In the case of punishment, it cannot be presumed that nations have reached an agreement that such a right extends to the property of subjects. Unless subjects are themselves guilty of a crime, their property cannot be acquired by the enemy as punishment for the crime of their superior.[42] Here again we can see Grotius's tendency to avoid punitive wars as far as possible and to call for restraint and forgiveness.[43]

Even with regard to a liability or debt that arises by virtue of

[40] For details on debt for amercement and actions therefor (*actiones poenales*) under Roman law, see the works by Harada, Funada, and Kaser cited in n. 5.

[41] III. xiii. 1(2). Here, in addition to the term *jus gentium*, the term *lex gentium* is used. While the latter appears only occasionally, there does not seem to be any significant difference between the two terms.

[42] III. xiii. 2. However, as indicated in the same section, magistrates who fail to punish crimes are included among those who have themselves done wrong. See II. xxi. 1–2, 7–12.

[43] II. xx. 22–4; II. xxiv. 2 and 7. The distinction here between liabilities arising from crimes and from unconscionable conduct is interesting also from the viewpoint of criminal responsibility. Subjects may be held collectively responsible for debts of the state or its ruler based on the principle of security under the law of nations (III. ii. 2–3; III. xiv. 2(1)). But Grotius is reluctant to see punishment inflicted on subjects for a crime of the state or its ruler, and insists that for subjects to be punished, they must at least have tacitly consented to the crime in question (II. xxi. 7 and 17–18). Grotius's endorsement of collective responsibility for state debts reflects the fact that his theory of the state scarcely treats the state as a body independent of its members, unlike the concept of the state as a moral person (*persona moralis*) advanced by Pufendorf (1934 ⟨1688⟩, I. i. 12–13; VII. ii. 13). In other respects Grotius seems to incline towards the modern principle of individual responsibility for offences. But his rejection of collective criminal responsibility is not consistently maintained, as shown by his view that one may be held responsible unless one expressly opposes crime committed by the state or its ruler (see also 9.3.4).

inequitable or unconscionable conduct, Grotius requires the creditor to exercise moderation. But since the latter's right also involves an internal right, it is not possible to argue on the basis of the distinction between external effects and internal justice. Instead, Grotius urges people not to exercise their rights to the fullest, on the grounds of humanity and the law of love. A merciless creditor does not conform to the dictates of humanity, even though he may not be at variance with law in the strict sense. In this context, the dictates of love or those of humanity are distinguished from the law of nature.

As indicated above, in the case of a liability or debt that arises by virtue of inequitable or unconscionable conduct, Grotius states that it is possible to acquire not only an external but also an internal right, as long as the property of enemy subjects is acquired by capture. The acquisition of the property of enemy subjects not only has an external effect, but there is no internal obligation to return the property concerned. The basis of this assertion is the rule of the law of nations which Grotius introduces in order to secure the right of each person to his property. In this respect it is important to distinguish the effect of ownership from that of impunity under the law of nations. As long as it is possible to characterize a war as one of recovery, the acquisition of ownership as a result of such a war frees the possessor of captured goods from the moral burden of returning them, and makes their possession or transfer to another morally proper.

9.3.4. On Rights over Prisoners of War

The principle of *temperamenta* concerning captured goods also applies to so-called slaves of war, because they are regarded as property according to the law of nations.[44] Grotius himself recognizes that, even in those places where the capture and enslavement of prisoners of war is customary, such usage should be restricted, in the same way as in the case of property, according to internal justice. This can be summarized as follows: in cases where a person in captivity has himself committed a wrong (*delictum*) meriting the loss of liberty, it is not contrary to justice to enslave him, whereas the acquisition (*acquisitio*) of such a person is permissible only when the loss of his liberty can be estimated as within the amount of his

[44] III. vii. 5(4).

original and derivative debt. When such conditions are met, rights over prisoners of war may be transferred to others.

Since Grotius's main concern is with moderating the harsh consequences of war under the law of nations, it is obvious that the conclusion that prisoners of war are property should be modified. It cannot be permissible to enslave all prisoners of war without exception. It is a requirement of fairness to draw distinctions from the viewpoint of internal justice, and thus to consider whether each person deserves the loss of liberty involved in enslavement.[45]

Basing himself on this principle, Grotius examines to what extent the right to own a slave[46] should be permitted according to internal justice. He maintains that the risk of loss of liberty when captured is a kind of surety (*fidejussio*)[47] on behalf of the state, and that a right to a person under such a surety should not be as extensive as the right of punishment against one who has committed a crime. A general right over those captured in a just war should be less rigorous than the specific right of masters over those who have sold themselves into slavery of their own accord due to extreme poverty. There is a great difference between that which may be done to a slave with impunity under the law of nations and that which is permitted by natural reason: since slaves are human beings rather than mere property, servitude constitutes merely a permanent obligation of service for permanent sustenance given by the master. In other words, Grotius assumes a kind of reciprocal agreement involving a mutual obligation between a slave and his master.[48]

It is significant here that Grotius compares the relationship between a master and his slave to that between God and man, or between a state and its subject.[49] These comparisons are intended to stress that slaves are no less human than others. But they also reflect his view of man and the state. He uses the expression 'the right, which is called the right of life and death over the slave, causes the master to have domestic jurisdiction (*jurisdictio*

[45] III. xiv. 1. [46] III. xiv. 2.

[47] According to Roman law, *fidejussio* means the dictate of faith, which has the widest range of application of all forms of personal security or surety: Harada 1982: 255–6. Here this term is used in the sense that subjects are held responsible for a debt of the state or that of the king.

[48] III. xiv. 2 and 6(1).

[49] III. xiv. 2(3)–3. In III. xiv. 2(3), Grotius quotes Seneca: 'Although against a slave all things are permissible, there are some things which the common law of living things forbids to be done against a human being.'

domestica), which, indeed, is to be exercised with the same care as in the case of public jurisdiction'.[50] Such comparisons testify to the pre-modern nature of Grotius's concept of a state's jurisdiction over its subjects, a jurisdiction which is essentially similar to the right of the head of a household (*paterfamilias*).

Specific rules on slavery can be summarized as follows. First, severe punishment is not allowed, and even light punishment must be exacted with equity and clemency. Nor is it permissible to require excessively hard work from slaves.[51] Even slaves have a kind of right to own property, such as that gained through work exceeding the measure of their duty as slaves.[52] A person who is captured by one waging a just war may not be allowed to escape. Such captives were enslaved because of a debt of their state or their king: in such cases, by the common consent of nations, they are obliged to serve as slaves on behalf of their own country, unless they have no choice other than escape because of intolerably cruel treatment by their master.[53] But under the law of nations, a person captured by one waging an unjust war may be permitted to escape.[54]

Thus a distinction is made on the basis of whether the substantive cause of war is just or unjust. There are many difficulties in drawing such a distinction on the level of the law of nations, even if one could find a good reason to do so with respect to *temperamenta*. The core of the law of nations, as discussed in III. iv–ix, is to place both sides in a formal war on an equal footing, regardless of whether their substantive causes are just. Relations between them in terms of legal rights should be established on the basis that both belligerents benefit from the external effects of hostile acts in war. At the level of the law of nations, it would be consistent for Grotius to maintain the logic of non-discrimination. Only at the level of internal justice could he argue that a person

[50] III. xiv. 3.

[51] III. xiv. 4–5. In this context, the head of a household is defined as 'one who rules the household justly'. For the significance of this concept in Grotius, see Tanaka 1984: 80–1.

[52] III. xiv. 6. [53] III. xiv. 7.

[54] III. vii. 6. If captives who were free men before being captured escape to their own country while the war is still being waged, they regain their freedom according to the right of postliminy. But if they escape to some other country while the war is continuing, or escape to their own country after peace is restored, they are not permitted to regain their freedom but must be restored to the master who claims them. This is a consequence of the principle of external effects.

captured by one waging a just war may not attempt to escape, but that a person captured in an unjust war may do so. He unconsciously reveals a contradiction in that he seeks to limit his discussion in the sphere of the law of nations to external effects, but cannot completely ignore the general framework of his just-war doctrine.

The position of children born of slaves depends on the category of slave. In cases where the parents became slaves because they had committed crimes meriting death, the children are bound to slavery, for they would not have been born had the parents been killed. The situation is different in cases where parents became slaves because of the liability of their state or king. Children already born are, like their parents, bound to slavery in such cases. Children not yet born at the time their parents were captured are bound to slavery perpetually if their parents give the master their express consent, but they have to be resigned to their slave status only until they have worked long enough to cancel all that has been expended for their maintenance: that is, they owe their master nothing more than mere sustenance.[55]

These arguments are also problematical. From the viewpoint of the law of nations under which slaves are regarded as property, it is a natural consequence that children of slaves should also be deemed property and accordingly bound to slavery. But Grotius clearly stated that slaves are human beings in the context of *temperamenta*. The argument that children of slaves should be treated as slaves contradicts the proposition that children should not be punished for their parent's crimes.[56] As far as those enslaved because of their crimes are concerned, Grotius fails to distinguish the logic of the law of nations from that of *temperamenta*. On the other hand, with regard to those enslaved because of a debt of the state, Grotius confers hypothetically a kind of personal right upon parents over their children, and uses this right as a medium for affirming the children's enslavement.

Grotius states that where the enslavement of prisoners of war ceases to be customary the best course is to exchange prisoners; the next best course is to release them for a price proportionate to the value of their freedom. The latter amounts to an uncritical acceptance of the realities of war waged by mercenaries: Grotius

[55] III. xiv. 8. [56] II. xxi. 13.

even referred to the market price of slaves. But to Grotius, who sought authority for his argument mainly in the writers of European antiquity, contemporary practice must have seemed far more tolerable than the custom of enslaving prisoners of war. It was not until the institution of mercenaries became obsolete that Grotius's position could be criticized.

9.3.5. On Acquiring Governing Power

On the acquisition of governing power, Grotius develops a very similar principle of *temperamenta*. Equitableness and humanity are sought even to a higher degree for peoples or for subgroups of peoples because both kindness (*beneficentia*) and injury become more significant when a large number of persons are involved. This is the same argument Grotius used in insisting that enemies should be spared if their number is large. He enumerates cases where the governing power of a ruler over a people (*jus imperantis in populum*) or of a people over itself may be acquired in a just war. Governing power may be acquired as punishment for a crime, as a means of collecting a debt, or in order to avoid imminent public danger.[57]

Grotius then indicates the specific contents of *temperamenta* in various stages. First, it is desirable that conquerors abstain from exercising any of their rights over the conquered. Secondly, they should incorporate the conquered in the conquering state on an equal footing. Thirdly, they should allow conquered kings or peoples to retain the governing power they previously held. These three stages amount to an appeal to the conqueror to refrain from depriving the vanquished of their governing power. The benefit of doing so would be freedom from the burden of keeping large provinces. Fourthly, when governing power is acquired for the sake of the conqueror's security, a portion of the power should be left to the conquered peoples and their kings. Fifthly, if governing power is completely taken away from the conquered, they should be allowed to have their own laws, customs, and subordinate rulers with respect both to private matters and to public matters of no real importance. Sixthly, even when such partial self-government is not allowed, the vanquished should not be deprived of their own religion except by persuasion. On the other hand, if the vanquished themselves enforce a false religion on others, the victor has the

[57] III. xv. 1.

right to protect the true faith from oppression. Seventhly, even when the most complete type of governing power, equivalent to that of a master over his slave (*imperium quasi herile*), is acquired,[58] the vanquished should be treated with compassion so that the interests of the victor may be eventually joined with those of the vanquished. The enumeration of these different levels attests to Grotius's commitment to lessening the cruelty of war by casting multifold nets of restriction upon the victor.

9.3.6. On Persons and Things Not Covered by the Right of Postliminy under the Law of Nations

Postliminy (*postliminium*) is the reversion of captured persons or property to their former status by returning them across the border. The right of postliminy can be invoked in cases where a person who once enjoyed the status of a free man, after being captured while waging war, escapes from his captor and returns to his own country or its ally, or where slaves or property, after being captured, are recaptured by those who belong to the country in which they were possessed before the war, or by an ally of theirs. But this right (with its Roman law origins)[59] is subject to special agreement between the parties concerned.

The *temperamenta* concerning persons and things that do not constitute an object of the right of postliminy are slightly different from the *temperamenta* noted so far. Even those waging a just war may not directly claim any right over persons or property once captured by it but subsequently liberated by postliminy. This may be regarded as an external effect, though it is a question more of acknowledging the actual state of affairs than of applying a rule of law. The argument here is not concerned with the belligerent parties themselves, but with a third party who has acquired, through transactions or other means, ownership and rights over persons from the party waging an unjust war. In this case, external effects are established according to the law of nations, and there is no room for postliminy.

However, from the viewpoint of *temperamenta* those who have

[58] II. xv. 2–12. There is no consistency in the Kelsey trans. of *imperium* in the chs. on *temperamenta*. Words used include empire, dominion, rule, domination, authority, and government, as well as sovereignty and sovereign power.

[59] Kaser 1979: 138.

acquired ownership and rights over persons from the party waging an unjust war are expected to return them to their original status. This is because the person who first captured them does not acquire internal ownership (*dominium internum*). While a third party acting in good faith may have external ownership, it is not morally just to enjoy the advantages which accompany it. In the light of this internal obligation, an unjust war is equivalent to theft and the third party who acquired the stolen goods has a moral obligation to return them to the original owner.[60] If peoples or subgroups of peoples come under the rule of one waging an unjust war, they should be returned to the ruler who originally had governing power over them, or to themselves if they were originally free people (*sui juris*). Thus the internal obligation of restitution is imposed on those who have acquired ownership and rights over persons from the side waging an unjust war.

9.4. The Law of Nations, Internal Justice, and the Law of Love

9.4.1. External Effects under the Law of Nations

Among things which are permissible, Grotius draws a distinction between 'that which is right (*rectus*) in the sense of being dutiful (*pius*) in every aspect, although at times there might be something else that could be done more honourably', and 'that which is not punishable among human beings, although sometimes it may deviate from piety (*pietas*) and duty'. He adds that the latter is widely recognized, despite being remote from the original meaning of the word 'permissible', and that sometimes that which is permissible may be contrasted with that which is just.[61] The external effects under the law of nations of formal wars fall in the latter category. Grotius's reluctant approval of the external effects of war shows that their only justification is to determine rights and duties between enemies by displacing moral judgements on killing, wounding, seizing, and other acts in a formal war.

On the other hand, the law of nations is based on the consent of nations and its existence can only be proved a posteriori.[62] The

[60] III. xvi. 1–3. [61] III. iv. 2. [62] See 2.3.1; 2.3.2.

general tendency manifested in the various sources and usages is understood to constitute the content of the law of nations. The substantive content of the law of nations as explained by Grotius—the killing of enemy subjects, regardless of age or sex, indiscriminate devastation, pillage, and capture of property, and the enslaving of captives—can almost be said to be a literal description of the realities of war from European antiquity onwards.[63] To approve them without qualification would have only increased the horrors of war which Grotius tried so painstakingly to reduce. In the context of the law of nations, Grotius repeatedly explains that permission, or external effect, is far from the proper meaning of the word 'permissible', and reserves the possibility that the conclusion would be different if considered in the light of some higher value. These reservations express Grotius's reluctance to approve many of the things permitted under the law of nations.

The main purpose of his discussion of external effects is to exclude the possibility of an incessant chain of war after war.[64] To accomplish this, it is desirable to admit the legality of hostile acts committed in a formal war as much as possible, and to admit their external effects. But Grotius is not committed to the moral content of the law of nations. The cruelty reflected there highlights in contrast the moral condemnation of hostile acts in an unjust war and the admonition of *temperamenta*. The order of the argument in Book III—after explaining the harsh contents of the law of nations, Grotius again calls for restraint, denies the justness of hostile acts in an unjust war, and finally calls for *temperamenta*—is an attempt to enhance the persuasiveness of his call for restraint.

[63] See Lawrence 1923: 33, 371–2.

[64] It may be possible to argue that the unlimited chain of wars bringing about new wars could be cut off once a peace treaty is concluded. But a difficult problem will arise if the content of the peace treaty is unjust. Observance of good faith is the basis of the obligation to abide by a peace treaty under the law of nature, but this cannot secure the justness of the treaty's content. If the external effects under the law of nations did not intervene, different types of obligation would be placed in opposition to each other on the same level of natural law: on one hand, the obligation under the law of nature to restore what has been acquired unjustly—the just cause for resort to a war of recovery if viewed from the standpoint of the other party—and on the other hand, the obligation to observe good faith under the law of nature. In order to avoid such a consequence and to give priority to the observation of peace treaties, it is necessary to give priority to external effects under the law of nations, despite the fact that it is legally subordinate to the law of nature.

9.4.2. The Logic of Disapproving of External Effects

(1) *External Effects versus Internal Justice*

Both in disapproving of belligerent acts in an unjust war, and in expounding *temperamenta*, Grotius advances the viewpoint of internal justice. The things which are permissible according to internal justice in a just war are limited to those which can be justified by one of three causes: (1) self-defence or necessity; (2) the enforcement of debt owed by the enemy, and (3) punishment.[65] There is no difference between these three causes and the substantive causes of war advanced in Book II.

Grotius also disapproves of all the acts performed in an unjust war and their consequences. He further maintains that it is necessary to restore to their rightful owner things which have been taken by those waging an unjust war, a rule which extends to people or property for which there is no postliminy.[66] In addition, Grotius speaks of the internal obligation to make reparation which is accompanied by external ownership,[67] internal right contrasted with external right,[68] and internal ownership contrasted with external ownership.[69] These terms involve restating internal justice in terms of specific rights and obligations, the content of which is naturally the same as the rights and obligations under the law of nature set forth in Book II. In this way, as far as content is concerned, it can be said that internal justice is virtually the same as the law of nature.

(2) *Justice in its Strict Sense versus the Law of Love*

Grotius then invokes the law of love in his effort to restrain even such acts as are free from condemnation according to internal justice. He refers to a range of related virtues: the rules of humanity, the duty of humanity, justness and piety, clemency, equitableness, the duty of a Christian, Christian goodness, and the like.[70] For Grotius, they are on the same level as the law of love, the purpose of which is to mitigate conclusions drawn from justice

[65] III. xi. 2; III. xii. 1(1); III. xiii. 1(2); III. xiv. 1; III. xv. 1. See also III. xiv. 6(4).
[66] III. x. 3; III. xvi. 1(1).
[67] III. x. 5(1); III. xvi. 5.
[68] III. xiii. 1(2); III. xiv. 8(1); III. xvi. 1(2) and 5.
[69] III. xvi. 1(1).
[70] III. xi. 2; III. xiii. 4.

in the strict sense.[71] These virtues are often connected with nature, the law of nature, or the law of God.[72] Consequently, there is no clear boundary between what should not be done because it deviates from internal justice and what should be avoided from the viewpoint of these other virtues. In calling for restraint in harming innocent people or their property, or for a balance between a crime or debt and harm or punishment inflicted as a means of collecting the debt, Grotius often uses expressions which closely resemble 'law', and appeals to the sense of equity (*aequitas*). On the other hand, clemency (*misericordia*, *clementia*) is mostly used in calling for pardon when a person deserves penalty or execution.

9.4.3. The Structure of Book III, and the Normative Levels of III. x and *Temperamenta*

It seems, then, that internal justice, as contrasted with external effects admitted under the law of nations, may, at least as to content, be equated with the law of nature. And it seems that the law of love and similar concepts which are contrasted with justice in the strict sense may be defined as higher virtues than the law of nature. But this understanding presents many difficulties.

(1) *The Framework of Natural Law*

In raising the question of what is permissible in war at the beginning of III. i, Grotius draws a distinction between that which is 'permissible in itself (*nude*)', and that which is 'permissible in relation to a previous promise'. The discussion of the latter is developed in chapters from III. xix, while the discussion in III. i–xviii is based on the former. The discussion of what is 'permissible in itself' is further divided into what is permissible according to natural law and what is permissible according to the law of nations, which is discussed in III. ii–ix. Thus, III. i and

[71] e.g. III. xi. 7–8 and 10(2); III. xiv. 4; III. xv. 1.

[72] Examples of quotations are found in III. xi. 1; III. xi. 13. Grotius's comments are found e.g. in III. xi. 13(2), where, regarding Sallust's 'law of war', he refers to 'the equitable justice and the usage of more civilized peoples' and in III. xi. 14, where, citing Cicero, he refers to 'what is equitable according to nature'. Examples of Grotius's own terms include 'the canon law, in accordance with natural equity (equitableness)' (III. xi. 10(2)); 'precepts (*praecepta*) of equity and the law of nature' (III. xi. 16(1)); 'the law of God' (III. xii. 8(4)), and 'agreement with the canon law' (III. xiii. 4(4)).

x–xviii should be understood as a discussion on the law of nature.[73] If so, the disapproval of hostile acts in an unjust war and the discussion of *temperamenta* should both be developed on the level of the law of nature.

However, it is difficult to treat the discussion in III. x–xviii as a development of the law of nature on the same level as III. i. Grotius explains the fundamental principle of natural law when he starts his inquiry into what is permissible in war as follows:

> with regard to moral matters (*morales materia*), a means to an end is provided with an intrinsic value (*aestimatio intrinsica*) by the end itself. Therefore, we possess rights over matters and means which are deemed necessary to attain our purpose of securing rights (*ad finem juris*). However, here a necessity should be understood not in a physical but in a moral sense.

If we take Grotius's just-war framework literally, this would mean that those waging a just war may justly resort to any means necessary to achieve its end, whether through defence, recovery, or punishment. Conversely, the means which those waging an unjust war employ to achieve its end should be unjust because their purpose is unjust. This led to the disapproval of every act of warfare in an unjust war, as discussed in III. x.[74] Thus it becomes possible to understand III. i and x within the framework of the just-war doctrine according to the law of nature. To that extent, the law of nations in III. ii–ix might be 'read as a grand insertion'[75] into his just-war doctrine.

But we should not too readily connect the principle of III. i with that of III. x. If one sought to maintain the consistency of the just-war principle formulated in III. i on the level of the law of nature, acts committed by the unjust side would be deprived of all justness. For example, killing or wounding an enemy would be nothing but a criminal act (murder or bodily injury). In consequence, as long as the effects of such an act continue, those on the just side should have the right to resort to a punitive war at any time. But Grotius cannot accept such a consequence. This is precisely why the law of nations intervenes to eliminate the legal possibility of one just war

[73] III. i. 1; III. xix. 1(1); III. ii. 1(1).

[74] Vlugt 1925: 436. However, Vlugt, perhaps regarding III. x as a natural conclusion of Grotius's theory of just war, makes no reference to it. This is why he is unable to place the concept of 'internal justice' in its proper perspective.

[75] See 8.1.2.

being caused by another. This is also why III. x can only be based on the viewpoint of internal justice and internal injustice.

Furthermore, the principle declared in III. i can hardly serve as a principle for restraining acts in a just war. Rather it is likely to contradict the requirements of internal justice. In order to accomplish substantive justice, which is the purpose of a just war, nothing would prevent those carrying on a just war from killing, wounding, or capturing persons, nor from destroying or seizing property that gets in the way.[76] It would not matter whether an individual person or the owner of the property is culpable or not.[77]

By contrast, the principles of *temperamenta* require that the justness of harming an enemy be judged according to the liability of each individual enemy. Harming the enemy can be said to satisfy the requirement of internal justice only when it is a matter of necessity (including defence), punishment, or debt. This is why one must refrain from killing or wounding innocent people. Consequently, it is difficult to define the justness of harming an enemy without contradiction. In order to determine whether harming an enemy is just, it might be inconsistent with *temperamenta* if one were to adhere to the principle outlined in III. i. If the 'necessity' of this principle were equated to the necessity referred to in *temperamenta*, that is, as one of the just causes of harming an individual enemy, harming the enemy would be just without qualification. But the internal restitution to make reparation would still remain if the enemy in question did not commit any wrong. If this were the case, in the final analysis the justness of a means to an end would turn out to be nothing but impunity.

In resolving this contradiction, the first possible interpretation is to regard the end referred to in the principle of natural law discussed in III. i as the realization of the substantive just causes of war, and the 'means' as the resort to war. This would be consistent with the thesis Grotius expounded in *De Jure Praedae Commentarius*.[78] However, we are unable to accept this interpretation, because here the discussion is limited to what is permissible in war. A second possibility would be to interpret the word 'moral', in the principle stated in III. i, in an extremely limited manner, as meaning not only the necessity of reaching a just goal but also

[76] This is why even killing an enemy by poison is permitted under the law of nature (but prohibited under the law of nations).

[77] III. i. 4(1). [78] See Grotius 1950 ⟨1604⟩, (Eng. 31).

including the inevitability of harming an individual enemy. Under this interpretation each individual harmed should not only belong to the unjust side but also be held directly responsible for some crime he has committed or some debt he has owed. Again, we cannot adopt this interpretation, for in *JBP* Grotius abandons the position of *De Jure Praedae Commentarius*,[79] of treating just methods of warfare as one of the just causes of war (*causae formales*), and instead affirms the external effects of war under the law of nations. While in *De Jure Praedae Commentarius* he treats the prohibition on harming women and children as a formal cause,[80] in *JBP*, after acknowledging that even killing or wounding them is permitted under the law of nations, Grotius admonishes that, as an application of *temperamenta*, they should not be killed or wounded. In actual warfare, it is unrealistic to expect those who wage a formal war with the conviction that they have the just cause to decide whether they may harm a person or goods belonging to an enemy only after examining individual culpability. It is thus almost inevitable that an inconsistency should arise between the principle of the law of nature which infers justness of means from the justness of the end itself and the logic of *temperamenta* according to which the justness of harming an enemy must be determined in the light of internal justice.

However, the practical significance of *temperamenta* is that they specify the categories of persons and things that should be spared. Those who do not take up arms in their proper capacity—women, children, clergymen, scholars, merchants, farmers, and artisans—or those who are put *hors de combat*—prisoners of war, those who surrender, etc.—are excluded from the categories of persons who may be killed. In addition, farmland, temples, etc., are excluded from the categories of things that may be destroyed. Limitations are also set on the right to capture people or property. As to *temperamenta* regarding things for which the right of postliminy is not recognized, Grotius stresses the obligation of third parties to restore to their original status things acquired from those who themselves acquired them in an unjust war. This is consistent with the argument of III. x, but its practical significance is the same as other kinds of *temperamenta*. Thus it matters little if Grotius's theory of *temperamenta* is criticized for its inconsistency. It is suf-

[79] See Ito 1965*a*: 10–11, 40–73; Haggenmacher 1983: 63–6.
[80] Grotius 1950 ⟨1604⟩, (Eng. 109–10).

ficient for Grotius that his readers clearly understand his practical intention of specifying the people and property that ought to be spared.

(2) *The Framework of Internal Justice*

If the structure of Book III is seen in terms of the just-war doctrine based on natural law in the strict sense, the concept of internal justice cannot be located in it without inconsistency. But we can restore consistency if we limit our inquiry to the discussion in III. x and subsequent chapters dealing with the concept of internal justice, and if we enclose within parentheses the principle of natural law that those waging a just war have the right to resort to all means necessary to achieve a just end.

First, should we draw a distinction between III. x and *temperamenta*? There is a distinction in that the former treats those who wage unjust wars, while the latter seems to be addressed to those who wage just wars.[81] In addition, whereas 'internal injustice (*injustitia interna*)' is used in III. x, 'internal justice (*justitia interna*)' appears in *temperamenta*. But the concept of the internal obligation to make restitution in *temperamenta* is also used in III. x. Internal injustice and internal justice are two sides of the same coin: their frame of reference is the same. It has already been noted that *temperamenta* are actually directed both to those waging a just war and those who are not. Thus we cannot categorically separate III. x from *temperamenta*. The viewpoint of internal justice is maintained in both.[82]

Secondly, as indicated earlier, the assertions made in the name of internal justice only summarize the law of nature as a source of substantive just causes of war. An unjust war is disapproved of because of the lack of a just cause, and the justness of individual acts of war committed in it is consequently denied. Even in a just war, according to these criteria, the argument that people are responsible only for their own acts and that it is not permissible for one side unjustifiably to enrich itself are maintained.[83] Thus the

[81] See the opening part of 9.3.

[82] Dumbauld 1969: 70–1, identifies III. x with *temperamenta* without sufficient analysis.

[83] II. x. 2(1); II. xii. 8. Also in contracts, though external effects are not approved from the viewpoint of justice, they are admitted under municipal law or under the law of nations for the sake of breaking the incessant chain of lawsuits (II. xii. 22 and 26).

concept of internal justice constitutes the frame of reference for III. x–xvi as a natural-law doctrine.

Thirdly, internal justice is a concept invoked when what is permissible in war is considered in itself, that is, apart from any previous promise, from municipal law, and so on. For example, in surrendering unconditionally to the enemy (conditional surrender implies an agreement),[84] the expression 'put oneself at the mercy of the enemy's good faith and clemency' is usually employed. Since the term good faith here means merely goodwill or pity, however severely the person accepting the surrender treats the vanquished, he is immune from condemnation. Nevertheless, from the viewpoint of justness, only those who deserve the death penalty should be killed. In this sense, internal justice may be regarded as a form of natural law guided by the inherent nature of war independent of previous promise, municipal law, etc.[85]

Fourthly, even if internal justice equates to the law of nature in terms of its content and also in the sense that it is distinguished from products of the human will, this law of nature is decisively different in one respect from that developed in Book II, in that it cannot be invoked as a new just cause of war. There is thus no guarantee that this internal justice will ever be realized institutionally. The fulfilment of such internal justice can only be entrusted to the conscience and initiative of those concerned, with the support of the ultimate assurance of spiritual salvation.

(3) *Appeals to the Law of Love and the Precepts of Humanity*

Since the law of love and the precepts of humanity are contrasted with justice in the strict sense, they should presumably also be distinguished from the law of nature. However, the range of ideas and values resembling them, and the frequent reference to the law of nature or to similar concepts, raise doubts as to whether the law of love and the precepts of humanity should be so clearly distinguished from the law of nature. In some cases they stand

[84] III. xx. 49–51.

[85] Midgley (1975: 165–6) categorically separates the law of nature from internal justice, finds 'an element of obscure defeatism in Grotius' attitude toward natural law regarding those points which may be in conflict with the evil practice of states', and criticizes him for turning some precepts of natural law into mere admonitions to refrain from acts which deviate from these precepts. This criticism reveals a complete lack of understanding of the pains Grotius took to base his argument, not on the law of nature in the strict sense, but on the concept of internal justice.

parallel to the law of nature without any explicit distinction.[86] It even seems that Grotius, who normally paid close attention to differences in concepts, especially legal concepts,[87] is here deliberately leaving the distinction unclear. However, the clearer this distinction becomes, the greater the impression that only those with especially high moral qualities need to obey the law of love, while ordinary people may ignore it if their conduct is compatible with justice. Should this happen, Grotius's effort to reduce the horrors of war would end in failure. He may have hoped that people would mistake these precepts for law and regulate their behaviour accordingly, with a resultant mitigation of the horrors of war.

Therefore, although the law of love and the precepts of humanity logically ought to be distinguished from internal justice, in reality they form an integrated whole, the demarcation lines among constituent parts of which are difficult to discern. By and large, they may be understood as a virtue higher than a law, or as a law of nature itself—albeit an imperfect one. As a result, the persuasiveness of the law of love is actually enhanced.

The frequent reference to utility in *temperamenta* is due to Grotius's desire to enhance the persuasiveness of the law of love and to make up for the imperfect character of internal justice. The way he takes utility into account may be summarized in the assertion that it would be useless to injure an enemy unless that served to weaken the enemy as a whole, and foolish to injure an enemy for injury's sake. In actual war, since the ultimate purpose of the belligerents is to gain victory, such an appeal would be more persuasive than an appeal to internal justice, the law of love, or the precepts of humanity. If the lack of institutional means for realizing these virtues were compensated for by considerations of utility, and the cruelty of war lessened as a result, Grotius's practical intentions would be realized.

To summarize, with regard to Book III, we can find a double framework: (1) a framework focusing upon the proposition that 'every means necessary for carrying out a just war is permissible' (III. i–x); and (2) a framework based on internal justice in III. x–xiv. However, since Grotius affirms the external effects of war under the law of nations, the natural-law doctrine flowing through (1) and (2) is on the point of breakdown. Without noting

[86] III, xviii. 2(1). [87] Prol. 39ff., esp. 40–1 and 56.

this inherent contradiction, Grotius stitches (1) and (2) together from the viewpoint of 'what is permissible in war itself apart from . . . promises'. He then incorporates (1) and (2) into the 'system' of just-war doctrine through the whole of *JBP*—with the law of nations also constituting its integral part in the sense of 'being just because it is permissible'.

9.5. Grotius and the Laws of War in Modern International Law

Wheaton once remarked that Grotius's more moderate and humanitarian principles concerning the laws of war, i.e. *temperamenta*, were supported by Vattel and unanimously adopted by international-law scholars in the nineteenth century.[88] Referring to *temperamenta*, Lawrence concluded that, since the publication of *JBP* many humanitarian maxims had come to be generally accepted by belligerents.[89] Although he traces the process by which the severity of war was mitigated, he does not identify any direct link with Grotius: he merely speaks of the correspondence or coincidence between Grotius's *temperamenta* and that process. With the exception of contraband, Wheaton does not even examine instances of correspondence.[90]

If the structure of Book III (discussed in 9.4) and the overall framework of the just-war doctrine based on natural law are disregarded, it is possible to identify cases where the rules Grotius discusses in the name of the law of nations and *temperamenta* correspond to the laws of war in modern international law, especially the laws of land warfare. The prohibition of the use of poison under the law of nations corresponds to Article 23(*a*) of the Hague Regulations on Land Warfare, and the prohibition of rape to Article 27 of Convention Relative to the Protection of Civilian Persons in Time of War of 12 August 1949. With regard to *temperamenta*, the call to pardon those who do not take up arms, such as women, children, and clergymen, corresponds to the provisions of Articles 50 and 51 of Protocol I. As regards treatment of prisoners of war, the 1949 Geneva Convention III contains numerous regulations that reflect Grotius's call for restraint.

But to attribute these instances of correspondence to Grotius is

[88] Wheaton 1836: 149.

[89] Lawrence 1923: 97.

[90] Ibid. 371, 377–8, 408–9, 534–5; Wheaton 1853: 471, 482 *et passim*.

not only to fail to understand his influence but to ignore the process through which the laws of war have developed. For example, it was not until 1929 that the protection provided by the Geneva Convention was expanded to include prisoners of war. Until then, prisoners of war were treated, at best, according to domestic instructions modelled after the Hague Regulations of Land Warfare. Before the institution of mercenaries was abolished in the eighteenth century, the most one could expect was to pay a ransom to free prisoners of war, something Grotius regarded as a second-best course of action.[91]

Despite this, it is not irrelevant to indicate points of correspondence. Of the various arguments made by Grotius, we can find what corresponds to the laws of war in modern international law more in *temperamenta* than in *jus belli* under the law of nations.[92] This suggests that the contents of the law of nations, which reflected the realities of war from European antiquity onwards, were not subsequently received as the laws of war.

Although there are few studies that fully examine the issue,[93] opinions are divided over whether Grotius's argument, especially his *temperamenta*, exerted any influence on positive international law beyond mere correspondence. On one hand, some claimed that *temperamenta* came to be regarded as part of international law.[94] The famous anecdote that the King of Sweden, Gustavus Adolphus, always carried a copy of *JBP* to the battlefield and at times put it into practice provided support for this view. On the other hand, some concluded that, at least in the eighteenth century, Grotius had practically no influence on positive international law.[95]

Cases where Grotius exerted some influence can be cited.[96] In

[91] According to Lawrence, the last ransom agreement was concluded between France and England in 1780 (1923: 378).

[92] Haggenmacher argues that, while Grotius did not anticipate it, his *temperamenta* constitute the bud from which international humanitarian law applicable to armed conflicts was to sprout (1983: 602–3). This might be correct if *temperamenta* are compared with the laws of war. But even this does not go beyond mere correspondence.

[93] There are still writers who try to apply Grotius's assertions directly to modern problems. These are mere arguments from authority, an authority usually taken out of context. A recent example is Willems 1981: 103 ff.

[94] See e.g. Nussbaum 1947: 107; Verzijl 1968: 438–41. For van Vollenhoven's assessment see Dumbauld 1969: 69 n. 67.

[95] See e.g. Vlugt 1925: 452.

[96] See Starke 1972: 172–5; Ruddy 1972: 178, 191–4.

1632 Gustavus Adolphus issued a domestic instruction to his forces which indicated the acceptance in principle of the idea of *temperamenta*. Vlugt cites his influence on the United States–Prussian Treaty of 1785.[97] *JBP* was read widely in intellectual circles in seventeenth- and eighteenth-century Europe and must have exerted some influence at least on the élites. On the other hand, brutalities repeatedly occurred, not only in the Thirty Years War, but also through the Napoleonic Wars. We can infer that hardly any attention was paid to *temperamenta* regarding the acquisition of supreme governing power, amid the ceaseless wars of conquest by Great Powers. Grotius's appeals were hardly persuasive in wars waged against a background of strong ideological or political opposition.

The most important point is that, even if the individual assertions made by Grotius were accepted in one form or another, his central theses were not accepted as a matter of positive international law. The positive international law of war came to be established only after the just-war doctrine based on natural law had lost most of its influence. In an international society where sovereign states coexist as equals, to demand that belligerent parties have a substantive just cause for the war would be practically of no significance: both sides would use the legitimate causes of war merely as an excuse for their own claims. War can never be regarded as a means of realizing substantive justice. It was on the basis of this 'realistic' awareness or resignation that the rules of positive international law were accumulated and 'positivism' as a reflection of this awareness developed. The laws of war were able to be incorporated into modern international law applicable to both belligerent parties only when war became accepted as an institution.

The basic principle underlying the normative 'system' for regulating war which Grotius strove to establish consists in limiting justifiable wars as much as possible, while rejecting resort to war on unjust or trivial grounds. The reason he accepted certain immoral or inhumane customs of war as part of the law of nations—despite the fact that many of them were a heterogeneous element in the just-war doctrine based on natural law—was that it was necessary to exclude the vicious circle of wars causing new wars, through

[97] Johnson 1983: 25. Johnson's claim that military discipline was better under the mercenary system is difficult to accept.

establishing a 'circuit-breaker' in the doctrine of external effects. As a result, internal justice, a concept which should have constituted an integral part of a just-war doctrine based on natural law, though devoid of any institutional means of realization, served as the criterion for prohibiting unjust wars and limiting the horrors of war. It was only after Grotius's efforts at *simultaneously* cataloguing the substantive just causes of war, excluding an endless chain of wars begetting new wars, and limiting the horrors of war had failed and was seen to have failed that rules corresponding to some extent to his *temperamenta* came to be established in positive international law.

In the aftermath of the First World War, with the progress towards the outlawry of war, the world was again reminded of the just-war doctrine.[98] The emergence of fascism, including militarism in Japan and Nazism in Germany, brought calls for a revival of natural law.[99] But modern attempts at the outlawry of war are based on an idea which is entirely foreign to just-war doctrine. Their aim in principle is the prohibition of the threat or use of force by individual states in their international relations, regardless of the substantive justice of their claims. In tandem with developments in the outlawry of war, writers stressed, often with facile references to Grotius, the obsolescence of the laws of war. More recently, the malfunctioning of the collective security system of the United Nations has brought about a re-examination of the laws of war.

What we can learn from Grotius is not necessarily the individual assertions or arguments he makes. The twentieth-century 'revival of natural law' was not a reversion to earlier natural-law doctrine, one of the crowning achievements of which was the work of Grotius. Grotius sought to construct a theory of the law of war and peace by confronting the contradictions (*aporia*) inherent in attaining substantial justice and simultaneously minimizing the horrors of violence.[100] Whatever the deficiencies in his arguments, it is precisely this effort which moves us beyond time and space, reminding us of a serious and perennial problem in the study of international law.

[98] See Kunz 1951: 528–34.
[99] Examples are found in Mitteis 1971: 6–7 ff.
[100] See Grewe 1984*a*: 258–9; Murphy 1982: 480–3.

10

Agreements between Nations: Treaties and Good Faith with Enemies

10.1. Introduction

This chapter examines II. xv and III. xix–xxv of *JBP*. Public agreements (*conventiones*), which Grotius discusses in II. xv, are agreements made on the basis of governing power. In addition to treaties concluded by supreme rulers, they include sponsions made by a subordinate ruler or military commander without any delegation from the supreme ruler. Peace treaties, which Grotius considers the most important kind of treaties, are discussed in Book III. III. xix–xxv deal with the general theory of good faith (*fides*) between enemies, as well as the problems of peace and cease-fire between enemies, and of good faith in relation to subordinate rulers and private persons. Since the discussion in Book III mainly focuses on what is permissible in war, particularly in formal war, the *fides* of private persons is discussed only in the context of laws governing the relation between nations. Correspondingly, this chapter examines Grotius's arguments about *fides* or agreement in the relations between nations. One important aim is to clarify the relationship between the theory of agreements in Book II and the theory of *fides* in Book III. In particular, we ask why Grotius uses the concept of *fides*, which he rarely mentions in Book II, as the core of his argument in III. xix–xxv.[1]

[1] See also ch. 6 and Kimura 1984: 11–18.

10.2. Treaties and Sponsions (Public Agreements)

10.2.1. Definition and Classification of Public Agreements

In II. xv, Grotius discusses agreements of a public nature. Citing Ulpian he states that public agreements (*conventiones publicae*) can be made only by those with governing power (*jus imperii*), though a difference may exist between governing powers at different levels. He distinguishes public agreements not only from contracts (*contractus*) of private persons, but also from contracts made by a king in relation to private matters.[2] A war may arise from a private contract, but the possibility of a public agreement being a cause of war is much greater. Thus, following the discussion of agreements in general, it is necessary to discuss this special class of agreements.[3]

Public agreements can be divided into treaties (*federa*), sponsions (*sponsiones*), and other pacts (*pacta*).[4] Treaties are agreements made by supreme rulers (*summa potestas*) or by persons authorized (*mandatum*) by supreme rulers to agree on their behalf. The people (*populus*) itself is ultimately liable for any violation of treaties. By contrast, sponsions are agreements by which persons not authorized by supreme rulers make a promise which might substantially affect the latter in its content.

10.2.2. Treaties

(1) *Classification of Treaties*

Treaties are divided into two categories: (1) those which restate rights which already exist under the law of nature,[5] and (2) those by which some additional rights are conferred. Treaties which

[2] Vitanyi (1980: 546) says that the so-called functional criterion of treaties (as public agreements between states) in modern theory is based on this definition.

[3] II. xv. 1. Lauterpacht notes, as part of the historical background against which Grotius stressed the strict observance of treaties, that 'the Pope claimed the right to release rulers from the binding obligation of oaths and treaties, by way of interpretation or express dispensation, and the view was widely adopted and acted upon that there is no binding force in treaties concluded not only between Christians and infidels but also those between Catholics and Protestants' (1975: 353).

[4] With regard to the distinction between *foedus* and *sponsio* under Roman law, see Taube 1930: 328–30.

[5] Whereas Grotius recognizes the usefulness of treaties that confirm rights based on natural law, Pufendorf criticizes such treaties as meaningless (1934 ⟨1688⟩, VIII. ix. 2).

recognize the rights of hospitality (*jura hospitii*) and commerce (*jura commercii*) on a reciprocal basis are included in the first category,[6] since the right of commerce is a right under natural law. Thus Grotius, like Vitoria,[7] admits the existence of the right of commerce and trade, in conformity with the demands of European nations of his time.

Treaties which confer rights beyond those granted under natural law may be classified as equal or unequal.[8] Equal treaties are those which have the same terms for both contracting parties and which can be called equal from the standpoint of both. They may be made for the purpose of peace or of alliance. Equal peace treaties (*aequalia federa pacis*), which are commonly arranged for the restoration of captives and captured property, or for guaranteeing security, are discussed in III. xix–xxiv in connection with the effects and consequences of war. Equal treaties of alliance (*aequalia federa societatis*) cover such matters as commerce and co-operation in war. Equal treaties concerned with commercial relations are made for various purposes.[9] Treaties of alliance and treaties for the purpose of war also take various forms, including offensive and defensive alliances. For example, such an agreement may take the form of not allowing fortresses to be built or not offering passage to enemies.[10]

Unequal treaties include both those which impair governing power (*imperium*) and those which do not.[11] The former category includes conditional surrender, but not unconditional surrender (*deditio pura*) which involves not an impairment but a complete transfer of the governing power. Unequal treaties which do not impair governing power are divided further into those which impose only temporary burdens and those which impose permanent ones.[12] Grotius does not limit unequal treaties to those between

[6] II. xv. 5.

[7] Vitoria 1917 ⟨1696⟩, III. 2. 3. See also Appendix.

[8] II. xv. 6.

[9] II. xv. 6(2).

[10] II. xv. 6(3).

[11] II. xv. 7. See Bozeman 1980: 118 (but the overall tone of this study is very biased).

[12] When Grotius talks of unequal treaties, he has in mind, among other things, treaties of alliance concluded during the period of the ancient Roman republic. As an example of an established form of treaty of alliance from that period, Meyer cites one which stipulated the duty of allied peoples to 'observe the supremacy of the Roman people willingly (*majestatem populi Romani comiter conservare*)' (1964: 229). In this regard, see also ch. 5.

victors and the defeated, but includes treaties concluded between a powerful and powerless nation, although they have not been engaged in war with each other. He admits the possibility of unequal treaties between supreme rulers to such an extent that the concept of *summum imperium* becomes a highly relative one.

(2) *Treaties with Non-Christians* (Federa cum His qui Alieni sunt a Vera Religione)

Grotius devotes a considerable amount of space in *JBP* to the question whether it is permissible to conclude a treaty with those who are foreign to 'true religion', i.e. with non-Christians. Natural law confers upon every man the right to make treaties, hence discrimination based on religion is clearly inadmissible.[13] But hitherto the binding force of treaties concluded with non-Christians had been recognized only to a limited extent. For example, the Roman Church prohibited Christians from entering into treaties with non-Christians, and denied their binding force.[14] Writers before Grotius who commented on this issue did not generally recognize the validity of such treaties. For example, Gentilis devoted a whole chapter to this issue, reaching a very negative conclusion.[15] After simply affirming the permissibility of treaties with non-Christians under natural law, Grotius deals with the question as a matter of divine law. Before the law of Moses, it was permissible for Hebrews to conclude a mutual non-aggression treaty with non-Hebrews, and this did not change under the law of Moses. It is true that that law commanded the Hebrews to do good to their own people, as stated in the commandment 'Love your neighbour',[16] and in many instances prohibited them from establishing close relations with other peoples. This, however, did not mean that they were not permitted to do good to strangers. The exclusivity of close-knit Jewish communities, conspicuous in Grotius's time, stemmed from a misunderstanding of that command by later leaders. Although some passages in the Old Testament prohibit

[13] II. xv. 8. Kelsey *et al.* trans. this as 'the right to enter into treaties', but only the word *jus* appears in the original Latin text. Whewell interprets this as *jus naturae* and renders it as '[Natural Law] is so far common to all men that it recognizes no distinction of Religion.' See Grotius = Whewell 1853: II. xv. 8. This seems the better interpretation.

[14] Taube 1930: 357–8. Also see Higgins 1965: 19–21.

[15] Gentilis 1933 ⟨1612⟩, III. xix. See Higgins 1965: 19–21.

[16] Lev. 19: 18.

Hebrews from making alliances with non-Hebrews for the purpose of war,[17] such a prohibition applied because of the special character or intention of the other party, and was not meant to be a general prohibition on making treaties.

Nor does the law of Christ prohibit Christians from making treaties with non-Christians. Indeed, it clearly allows them to make a treaty of assistance with non-Christians when they have a just cause.[18] It is not only praiseworthy to do good to others, but Christians are commanded to do so. Becoming friends with non-Christians is not prohibited: what is prohibited is to become excessively intimate with non-Christians or with apostates. Thus making treaties with non-Christians is not prohibited as such, but may be permitted, depending on the circumstances. In determining the legitimacy of such treaties it is necessary to avoid, for example, influencing the weak by becoming too intimate with non-Christians, or reinforcing the power of non-Christians by making alliances with them, unless there is very special need to do so.[19]

Thus Grotius's argument for the permissibility of treaties with non-Christians focuses on the problems of divine law, not on natural law. Consciousness of the obligations inherent in Christianity was still strong, and the interest in such problems could not be ignored.[20] In dealing with these problems, Grotius had not the slightest doubt about the validity of treaties with non-Christians under natural law: in the event, he affirmed that they were also permitted under divine law.

(3) *Other Related Problems*

Grotius discusses two miscellaneous problems involving treaties. The first is the problem of priority where one nation has concluded treaties of alliance with both belligerent parties: which party should be assisted?[21] He argues that no obligation arises to assist in an unjust war, even if a treaty of alliance has been concluded. This is a corollary of his just-war doctrine and of the proposition that any

[17] e.g. intercourse with Ammonites and Moabites is prohibited in Deut. 23: 3–6.

[18] Grotius cites the passage from Matt. 5: 45: 'For he makes his sun to shine on bad and good people alike, and gives rain to those who do good and to those who do evil', as well as works by Vitoria and others (II. XV. 10).

[19] II. XV. 11.

[20] See II. XV. 12, where Grotius discusses the obligation to form an alliance against enemies of Christianity.

[21] II. XV. 13; II. XXII. 3.

agreement contrary to natural law is invalid.[22] Thus the problem under discussion arises only where both parties have just causes. Such cases should be exceptional, according to his assumption of the self-evident nature of what is just according to natural law. Grotius simply states that, where this is the case, and if it is impossible to assist both parties, the party with whom the alliance was first made should have preference. But although the general rule (as in the case of two conflicting contracts in commercial dealings) is that an earlier promise is to have priority, a later treaty of alliance takes priority if it involves a high degree of subjection of one party to another, analogous to an assignment of ownership.

The second issue involves the termination of treaties. If one party violates a treaty, the other party may rescind it on the ground that each provision of the treaty has effect as a condition. To avoid rescission of treaties on account of trivial violations, Grotius recommends including in treaties a specific clause stating that *de minimis* violations are not to be a ground for rescission. This recommendation reflects his desire to secure the stability of treaties.

10.2.3. Sponsions

A sponsion, like a treaty, can cover a wide range of matters. It is different only in the authority needed to conclude it. Two questions normally arise with regard to sponsions. The first is what kind of liability is to be borne by the signatories if their sponsion was not approved by the king (*rex*) or the state (*civitas*) of which they are a part. When the sponsion is not approved, neither the supreme ruler nor the people itself is bound by it. However, the signatories are bound to pay damages, under Roman civil law, to restore the original state of affairs in accordance with equity, and to surrender themselves to the other party in accordance with customary law. Grotius considers the liability of the signatories to be so strict that they are bound to pledge themselves to be slaves if they fail to tender a security sufficient to cover any damages suffered by the other party.[23]

The second question is whether a supreme ruler is bound to abide by the sponsion if he knew of its existence but kept silent. The answer depends on whether the sponsion was made uncondi-

[22] II. xi. 9.
[23] II. xv. 16. With regard to sponsions, see also II. xxii; III. xxiv.

tionally, or on the condition that it be confirmed by the supreme ruler. In the latter case, the sponsion is void if this condition is not satisfied.[24] Even in other cases, silence itself cannot constitute sufficient grounds for presuming the existence of a clear intention to endorse a sponsion. However, this is not true if there is an additional and unequivocal act, similar to that which is required where ownership is presumed to have been abandoned.[25]

10.2.4. Grotius's Theory of Treaties

In *JBP*, a treaty is not as such part of the law of nations. In Grotius's time, treaties did not have the status of an independent source of law. In this sense, it is misleading to regard Grotius's arguments on treaties as an exposition of agreements from which the law of nations originates.[26] Lauterpacht's view of Grotius's concept of treaties is also problematic. He regards *pacta sunt servanda* as constituting, for Grotius, the basis of municipal law and civil society, as well as of international law.[27] This view treats 'pacts' as the basis of the association of nations, and thus over-emphasizes the element of human will. For Grotius, treaties are specific legal acts, and not the basis, or even a separate source, of international law.[28]

Natural law, which governs agreements in general, applies to public agreements as one category of agreements. Why, then, does Grotius single out public agreements for discussion? The first reason is that public agreements are often a cause of war.

Secondly, if the binding force of agreements were paramount, it would be necessary to allow wars to be waged on the ground of their violation. This would frequently lead to war, which is not desirable. Thus Grotius draws a sharp distinction between the binding force of public agreements, on the one hand, and promises and contracts concerning the private affairs of kings, on the other.[29]

[24] II. xv. 17. In this case, neither the supreme ruler nor the signatories themselves will be bound.

[25] See II. iv. 5(3).

[26] See e.g. Vitanyi 1980: 546. Vitanyi himself sees in Vattel the origin of the idea that treaties have the status of a source of *Le droit des gens* (ibid. 553).

[27] Lauterpacht 1975*b*: 353.

[28] Diesselhorst points out that, while Grotius argues in *JBP* that the law of nations is ultimately based on agreement, he barely touches on the mechanism by which the law of nations in general is formed by treaties (1959: 35–7).

[29] II. xiv. 1; II. xv. 1.

As long as public agreements are based on governing power, both subjects and successors are bound by them. But they are not necessarily bound by an agreement personally entered into by a king. Subjects are thus innocent with regard to wars fought on the ground that a personal agreement of the king has been violated. This has important consequences for the avoidance of war and for *temperamenta*.

Thirdly, although Grotius does not regard treaties as an independent source of international law, he may be aware that they are more than mere agreements. He admits that a mixed form of contract and law can exist, and gives an agreement with a neighbouring king as an example.[30] To show that the right of legation is part of the law of nations, he points out that it is provided for in many treaties.[31] Starke notes that the historical background against which Grotius wrote *JBP* precluded him from fully discussing treaties.[32] Had he witnessed the Peace of Westphalia, one of the first treaties to have major constituent significance in international law, he might have regarded treaties as an independent source of law, or at least made a more detailed analysis of them.

10.3. *Fides* between Enemies

10.3.1. Introduction

The title of III. xix is 'On Good Faith between Enemies (*De Fide inter Hostes*)'. In the first eighteen chapters of Book III, Grotius examines what is permissible in war with reference to what is permissible in itself (*nude*). In III. xix–xxiv, he discusses what are permissible acts where a previous promise has been made, i.e. the question of good faith between enemies.[33] Cicero and other publicists are cited to show that good faith should be observed even between enemies. Grotius argues that 'men do not cease to be human beings even if they are enemies. Anyone who is capable of exercising reason may enjoy the right derived from a promise.'[34] The binding force of a promise derives from a combination of

[30] II. xiv. 9. [31] II. xviii. 1.

[32] Starke 1972: 173, 175. See also Eysinga 1980: 10.

[33] III. xix. 1(1). See 8.1.2 for discussion of the significance of the domain of what is permissible in itself.

[34] III. xix. 1(2).

reason and speech. The statement in III. i,[35] that lying to an enemy is sometimes permissible, does not apply to pledged faith, for while the obligation to speak the truth arises from a cause which was valid before the war, a promise confers a new right.[36]

According to Grotius, although agreements with tyrants or pirates do not give rise to that special community of legal obligations which the law of nations produces between enemies engaged in a formal war, their validity under natural law should none the less be recognized.[37] Although he emphatically distinguishes in III. iii[38] between a state as the author of public war and a gang of robbers or pirates as bodies organized for the purpose of doing wrong, he makes no such distinction so far as the validity of *fides* is concerned. This reflects his strong emphasis on the value of *fides*.

Grotius had earlier argued that anyone may inflict punishment on atrocious criminals according to natural law, and that criminals who deserve capital punishment should also be deprived of their property and rights. Logically, rights created by promises should be included, so that there would be no need to keep faith with criminals. But Grotius agrees with this only if the promisor was unaware that the person to whom the promise was made was such a criminal. This is an application of the principle of interpretation that an act should be construed in favour of its validity.[39] Again Grotius is concerned to ensure the stability of existing relations created by agreements.

Fides should be observed even with subjects who have rebelled. Grotius argues in I. iv, that subjects, in principle, are not allowed to take up arms against their rulers.[40] Nevertheless he concludes that, even if they do so, punishment cannot be inflicted contrary to a subsequent promise.[41]

A problem which arises in this connection concerns the relationship between the promise of a supreme ruler to his subjects and the former's lawmaking power and right of eminent domain. If it can be assumed that the latter extend to all property and claims of subjects, the rights created by a promise made to subordinates during a war would be included within their scope. If so, such a

[35] III. i. 8–20. See 8.2.2 for the argument about lying to an enemy.
[36] III. xix. 1(3). See also III. i. 18.
[37] III. xix. 2. [38] III. iii. 2. See also 8.3.2.
[39] This principle is presented in II. xvi. 6.
[40] I. iv. Also see 3.3.2. [41] III. xix. 6.

promise would be meaningless, and it would be extremely difficult to terminate the war by such a promise. Grotius argues that the exercise of right of eminent domain is not permissible in all cases, but only if it is exercised in the general interest of the state. When a ruler and rebels conclude an agreement to bring their war to an end, to keep such an agreement would indeed be in the general interest.[42] By admitting the binding force of agreements Grotius encourages the termination of civil war at an early stage, since protracted civil wars can cause as much damage as public wars. The discussion of wars with subjects in III. xix demonstrates that Grotius does not necessarily limit himself to public wars, let alone to formal wars, when he discusses wars in III. xix–xxv.

Finally, Grotius argues that no promise made in the course of a formal war or made for the purpose of terminating the war can be nullified on grounds of duress. Many acts which would otherwise vitiate agreements are regarded as lawful under the law of nations, and intimidation committed by each side in a war is a typical example.[43] Indeed, it would be impossible to terminate a war if this principle were not applied.[44] Thus, peace treaties are valid, although they may have been imposed under strong pressure on the vanquished by the victors.

Are there, then, circumstances where it would be unnecessary to abide by *fides*? Grotius singles out changes of circumstances as an example:[45] when the other party fails to carry out his obligations as agreed, or when some compensatory act has already been performed in place of those obligations. However, where an agreement is reached by the parties to a pending lawsuit, the acts which gave rise to the litigation and the costs of the litigation cannot be offset. Similarly, while a war continues, compensation is not available for what originally caused the war, nor for what are customarily accepted as belligerent rights under the law of nations. This is because agreements reached during the course of a war are presumed to have been made without taking into consideration the dispute which originally gave rise to the war. Matters that can

[42] III. xix. 7.

[43] Here the Kelsey trans. is unclear.

[44] III. xix. 11(1). The external effects of the law of nations naturally do not extend to acts prohibited by it (III. xix. 12).

[45] III. xix. 14. Also see II. xvi. 25(2). For a discussion on Grotius's attitude towards *clausula rebus sic stantibus*, see 6.3.5; 6.4.3. See also Diesselhorst 1959: 135–40.

be offset against what is promised, while a war lasts, include the obligations of the other party arising from another agreement entered into during the war, damage caused during a truce, violation of the inviolability of ambassadors, or anything else which the law of nations condemns between enemies. Grotius also insists that *fides* should be kept even after a violation is committed, for to keep faith is the sign of a noble spirit.[46]

10.3.2. Classification

Book III. xx–xxiv, develop the subject of *fides* between enemies. These chapters elaborate in more detail the principles relating to promises and agreements explained in Book II and relating to *fides* between enemies in III. xix.[47] Grotius offers a classification of agreements with enemies: these may be express or implied, public or private. *Fides publica* attributable to the supreme ruler can be distinguished from *fides* attributable to inferior powers (*potestates inferiores*). The former is subdivided into peace treaties (III. xx) and agreements which are effective only while war is in progress (III. xxi).

10.3.3. *Fides* Relating to the Termination of War

(1) *Peace Treaties*

The king (in the case of a kingdom) or a majority of those with decision-making power (in the case of an aristocracy or democracy) has the right to make a peace treaty. In the latter case, those who oppose a peace treaty made by the majority are none the less bound by the treaty.[48] Grotius then takes up the question of the proper objects of such an agreement, and whether governing power may be alienated in whole or in part in order to establish peace. In his

[46] III. xix. 19.

[47] Augé points out the dichotomy between 'promise' and 'contract' in Book II, as well as the coexistence of the principles of agreement and of contract (1968: 109–12). A discrepancy does exist between 'promise' in II. xi and 'contract' in II. xii. From this point of view, we may be able to say that, of the matters discussed in Book III, while treaties may be related to the principle of contract, faith between enemies is in many cases based only on the principle of promise. But in *JBP* the concepts of promise, agreement, and contract are not clearly distinguished. Moreover, it is doubtful how important such a distinction is, as far as natural law and the law of nations are concerned. See 6.3.5(1).

[48] III. xx. 4.

time, most kings had royal power in the sense of usufruct but no longer had full patrimonial powers. Hence they were required to obtain the consent of the entire people in alienating governing power to another kingdom or people.[49] The people and any successor to the king were bound by his promise only when he had sufficient authority to bind them. The scope of obligation imposed upon the people is to be judged according to reason.

(i) Interpretation of Peace Treaties So far as the interpretation of peace treaties is concerned, Grotius first states that an ambiguous clause should be interpreted in such a way that the party which had the just cause in the war may attain its aims and recover its loss and expenses. This implies that whether a party to a war had a just cause is capable of influencing the interpretation of the resulting peace treaty. However, only under natural law can this conclusion be drawn. Grotius states realistically that 'it is rare for parties in a war to admit their own wrongs and arrive at peace', and concludes that both parties should be treated equally in the interpretation of the treaty, irrespective of the justice of the war. Thus he supports, in doubtful cases, the principle that property relations thrown into doubt during a war should be adjusted in accordance with the state of ownership at the time the war ended,[50] on the basis that the fact of possession is sufficient evidence of ownership.[51] Here again he is guided by the practical desire to avoid a situation where the restoration of peace is prevented by disputes over ownership. Thus, in terminating a war, priority is to be given to the restoration and maintenance of peace, a priority which is achieved by means of the concept of 'the external right of ownership accompanied by the internal duty of restitution'.[52]

(ii) Breach of Peace Treaties Grotius distinguishes the violation of a peace treaty from an act that would constitute just cause for a new war, both in terms of the punishment which may be inflicted upon the offender and of the effects each has in releasing the other party from the obligation of good faith in other respects. Violations of peace treaties are of three kinds: (1) violation of fundamental conditions inherent in the treaty, (2) violation of specific provisions of

[49] III. XX. 5. Also see 4.3.3(2). [50] III. XX. 11.
[51] III. XX. 12. [52] See 9.2.

the treaty, and (3) violation of terms implied from the nature of the treaty.[53]

An attack without any just cause falls within the first category.[54] But when a party to a peace treaty attacks an ally of the other party, this is not as such a breach of the treaty. When an attack is carried out by private persons, it is necessary to determine whether or not the act was officially authorized or publicly approved. As stated in II. xxi. 2–6, it will be regarded as publicly approved if there was official acquiescence in it, or if the capacity to punish was accompanied by no attempt to do so. The existence of such a capacity will be presumed unless proved otherwise, and the non-execution of punishment will be regarded as following from the fact that punishment was not inflicted within a reasonable period of time.[55] Since peace is made so as to secure the safety of all subjects, an attack on a subject, even if not on the state itself, should be regarded as a violation of a peace treaty.[56]

The second category involves the violation of a peace treaty by an act contrary to one of its specific provisions.[57] Grotius denies that any distinction can be drawn on the basis of the importance of the particular article that has been violated, since all articles contained in a treaty of peace must be observed. However, for the purpose of stabilizing a treaty he advises the negotiators to stipulate that breach of less important provisions of the treaty is not to be construed as a breach of the treaty itself, or that there should be a resort to arbitration before any resort to force. Even after *fides* is broken, the aggrieved party has the right to affirm the treaty, if that is in its interests.

The third category involves a violation of a peace treaty where what is violated is an implication from the specific nature of the treaty.[58] For example, a treaty of friendship (*fedus amicitiae*) should be regarded as violated by an act which is contrary to friendship. This is because the respect which friendship demands is required

[53] III. XX. 27. [54] III. XX. 28–33. [55] III. XX. 30.

[56] II. XX. 32. In case a new cause emerges, even in time of peace subjects are allowed to protect their own persons and property by force. But it is not permissible to punish or to recover stolen property by force, unless the judgement of a competent court has been denied.

[57] III. XX. 34–8.

[58] III. XX. 39. It is likely that Grotius has in mind the treaties between ancient Rome and foreign countries which included not only *foedus*, but also *hospitium* and *amicitia*. For these treaties, see Yuge 1977: 174.

under such a treaty as an implied obligation. Thus a treaty of friendship can be violated by an injury or a contempt, inflicted without violence. The existence of malice, however, should not be presumed even in such cases. Where a wrong is directed against those who have close relations with a contracting party to a peace treaty, or against the latter's subjects, it should not be understood as directed against the party himself unless the intention to do so is clear. Here again Grotius strives to limit as much as possible situations which may be construed as violations of a peace treaty.

According to Grotius's argument in Book II, particularly in II. xv, a peace treaty is a form of agreement which generates substantive rights.[59] From this viewpoint, a violation of a peace treaty should certainly be a just cause for a new war of recovery. However, Grotius explains in III. xx. 27 that it is necessary to distinguish a violation of a peace treaty from an act which gives a just cause for a new war. How can this apparent contradiction be resolved?

A peace treaty is an agreement concluded as a result of a war, and hence there is no guarantee that the justice required by natural law will always be realized, or that both parties will be satisfied with the settlement of the dispute which brought about the war. If the force of an agreement which has barely managed to keep the peace disappears as a result of a violation by one of the parties, it is highly likely that the original dispute will be revived and a new war will start. In this sense, a peace treaty is an agreement made against a background generated by war—in most cases, shelving the issue of substantive justice. Consequently, peace which is guaranteed only under a treaty is much more vulnerable than a real peace, maintained by fully abiding by natural law. However, even such a vulnerable peace can approximate to real peace, if the peace continues for a long time and the dispute that originally caused the war is, in the course of time, resolved. It is precisely because of this possibility that the observance of *fides* based on a peace treaty is a necessary condition for achieving real peace.

(2) *Lots or Duels*

Grotius illustrates two further principal methods of terminating a war: drawing lots or engaging in a duel. Drawing lots means

[59] II. xv. 6(2).

entrusting the fate of a state to chance. Only the supreme ruler can decide on this method of ending a war. Even when the supreme ruler has a just cause, it would be permissible to resort to this method if the other party has such overwhelming military advantage that there is no hope of victory. Similarly, duels may serve the state only if otherwise the unjust party is likely to win the war and a large number of innocent subjects to be killed.[60] This, however, is merely an argument which assumes that one of the belligerent parties has the just cause. Grotius admits that in many cases both sides claim to have the just cause and therefore does not altogether deny the usefulness of duels between rulers to avoid war.[61] His pragmatic approach to avoiding bloodshed underlies this argument on lots and duels.

(3) *Arbitration*

Arbitration is a method of ending a war by entrusting the determination of the content of the peace settlement to someone other than the belligerents. Grotius enumerates two forms of arbitration: what we would today call mediation (as contrasted to arbitration), and arbitration properly so-called, which requires obedience to the award. The arbitration he actually refers to here, as one of the ways to avoid war, is of the second kind. Unlike arbitration under domestic law, arbitration between kings or nations is final and conclusive. No appeal is allowed. Even if an award is unjust, the obligations of the contracting parties are not affected, though the arbitrator might be criticized for failure to fulfil his trust. The reason is that an arbitration is binding because of the agreement between the contracting parties to entrust a third party with the determination of the basis for peace, and the binding force of the agreement between the contracting parties to obey the arbitration is not impaired, regardless of the manner in which the arbitration is determined.[62]

Grotius proceeds to discuss the duty and authority of an arbitrator. Is he expected to play the role of a judge, or to be accorded even greater power than a judge? Seneca and Aristotle state that a judge passes judgement based on law only, whereas an arbitrator may give an award according to a wider range of standards. This

[60] III. xx. 42. See also II. xxiii. 9.
[61] III. xx. 43. See also II. xxiii. 10.
[62] III. xx. 46.

form of arbitration is not only more usual in municipal practice but was recommended to Christians by the Apostle Paul (1 Corinthians 6). Grotius argues, however, that in case of doubt the authority of an arbitrator should be limited to that of a judge, since no judge has jurisdiction over supreme rulers and arbitration should be the equivalent of a trial, just as a war is.[63]

(4) *Surrender*

Surrender may be unconditional or conditional (II. XV. 7). In III. XX, Grotius treats unconditional surrender. To entrust oneself to an enemy by surrendering to him is similar to arbitration, where one entrusts the solution of a problem to the decision of another.[64] But there is an important difference between the two. In the case of unconditional surrender one becomes a subject of the person to whom one has surrendered, conferring on him governing power over oneself. The term *fides* used by Roman historians in the expression 'to surrender oneself to the faith (and clemency) (*tradere in fidem* (*ac clementiam*))' of an enemy refers to nothing other than the victor's probity (*probitas*).[65] Those who surrendered were at the victor's mercy. This *tradere in fidem* should be construed as the victor's expression of favour to the vanquished,[66] and thus an unconditional surrender is not to be regarded as an agreement.[67]

Grotius classifies what the defeated should endure into three categories: (1) that which can be done lawfully; (2) that which is consistent with the fulfilment of duty; and (3) that which is most proper or appropriate. (A similar division occurs in his discussion of *temperamenta*.) The first category corresponds to the laws of war

[63] III. XX. 47. As noted above, the parties to the arbitration are bound by the award even if the arbitrator gave an award not according to law, but on meta-juridical considerations. Nevertheless, Grotius develops this argument, because he hopes to realize justice based on natural law by, on one hand, requiring the belligerent parties to end their war according to the decision reached through arbitration, and on the other, making certain that the said decision is handed down as much as possible according to law.

[64] The very word *arbitrium* has the meaning of free decision.

[65] III. XX. 50(3). See also Meyer 1964: 255, 256.

[66] III. XX. 50(4).

[67] Conditional surrenders are different in that they either secure the interests of those who surrender by agreement, so that their lives, liberty, or certain property are preserved, or establish conditions related to an entire people (III. XX. 51). Grotius also discusses hostages and pledges as accessories to treaties (III. 52–9). In Book II he cites conditional surrender as an example of an unequal treaty that impairs supreme governing power (II. XV. 7(2)).

(the law of nations); the second to natural law; the third to the law of love.[68] More precisely, natural law here corresponds to internal justice as discussed in *temperamenta*, in that its force is limited by the principle of external effects under the law of nations. From the viewpoint of the first category, the vanquished becomes a subject (*subditus*) by virtue of the surrender. As a matter of external right (*jus belli externum*) under the law of nations, the vanquished places himself in a position where he may be stripped of everything—life, personal liberty, and property. And this principle applies in the case of public war to the property not only of the state but also of private persons.[69] But from the viewpoint of natural law (the second category), if the victor wants to avoid injustice he should be sure to kill no one other than prisoners who deserve this fate because of their own acts, and to take nothing from anyone except as a lawful penalty.[70] From the viewpoint of the third category, so far as one's own safety permits, it is not only praiseworthy (*honestas*) to exercise clemency and generosity, but in some circumstances such a course may even be required by custom (*ex morum regula necessarium*). Thus Grotius concludes by saying that wars are best ended by pardons.[71]

10.3.4. *FIDES* DURING WAR

(1) Fides *between Supreme Rulers*

Grotius states in II. xxi that supreme rulers extend to each other certain rights even in war, citing as examples truce, safe conduct, and ransom of prisoners.

A truce is an agreement (*conventio*) to stop the actual fighting for a certain period: 'a truce is not peace, for war continues though fighting ceases'. What is agreed to be effective during a war should also be effective during a truce, unless the agreement in question specifically stipulates that it is to be strictly applied only to acts of war. Conversely, an agreement applicable in time of peace is, in general, not applicable to a truce.[72] Since war is not terminated by

[68] See esp. 9.4.3(2). [69] III. xx. 49.

[70] III. xx. 50(1). [71] Ibid. See also III. xv. 12.

[72] Grotius admits that a truce may last for 100 years (III. xxi. 1(3)). This implies that a truce may actually have the same effect as peace achieved by agreement. It should not be concluded, however, that Grotius intended to secure peace merely by prolonging and consolidating truces. He is fully aware that even peace realized through a peace treaty concluded after a war is ended cannot be identified with

a truce, but is only dormant, if the truce ends the war resumes forthwith, without the need for a new declaration of war.

A truce becomes effective immediately after it is concluded, so far as the contracting parties are concerned. In order to bind the subjects and soldiers of each contracting party, however, it must take the form of a law duly promulgated and published.[73] If a subject violates the truce before it is promulgated and published, he should not be punished, although the contracting party is liable to pay compensation for any loss caused.[74] If one of the contracting parties violates the faith of a truce (*fides induciarum*), the injured party will be free to take up arms again without declaring war. However, that justification will be lost if a penalty (*poena*) is demanded and is paid by the party which violated the truce.[75] Finally, private acts in themselves do not violate a truce unless they have been ordered or authorized by the supreme ruler.[76] The rejection of the view that public responsibility arises as a direct result of a private act is consistent with Grotius's earlier explanation of violations of the peace by private persons.

(2) Fides *between Subordinate Rulers and Private Persons*

(i) Fides *between Subordinate Powers* A supreme ruler may be bound by the action of a subordinate ruler or military commander in two ways: (1) when there are probable grounds to believe that the action was within the scope of the authority vested in the subordinate ruler or military commander and his accompanying duty (*officium*), or (2) even outside this scope of authority and duty, when there was a special responsibility known to the public or to those with an interest in the matter.[77] In addition, consent may be the basis of the obligation assumed by a supreme ruler. Consent may be given expressly or through tacit ratification (e.g. the tacit approval of sponsions discussed in II. xv. 17).[78] The actions of a commander (*praepositus*)[79] contrary to secret orders none the less

peace in the true sense, but he rests his hope for true peace in the perpetual maintenance of a cease-fire based on a peace treaty. For a slightly different view, see 10.3.3(1).

[73] Kelsey *et al.* trans. *exterior publicatio* as publication abroad, but *exterior* here means merely outside. See Grotius = Whewell 1853: III. xxi. 5.

[74] III. xxi. 5. [75] III. xxi. 6–12. [76] III. xxi. 13.

[77] III. xxii. 2. [78] III. xxii. 3. See also II. ix. 5.

[79] Kelsey *et al.* trans. *praepositus* as agent, but it is likely that the word means commander (III. xxii. 4). See also II. xi. 12–18.

bind the high command, provided the commander acted within the limits of his public authority. By contrast, if a subordinate ruler is unable to carry out a promise given outside the limits of his actual authority, he is as a rule personally liable for any loss he may cause.

Since making peace is a function of supreme rulers, the power to enter into negotiations concerning the causes of a war or its consequences is not included among powers normally vested in commanders.[80] Terminating a war is an act distinct from waging it. Even a commander who has been given full powers (*maxima potestas*) is only authorized to conduct the war.[81] In contrast, not only commanders but also officers of lower rank are authorized to make a truce effective among those fighting under the commanders in question. The powers regarding booty normally vested in commanders do not derive from their inherent authority but from the customary practice of nations.[82] Specifically, commanders are not authorized to distribute slaves, goods, or territories already captured in the course of war. A decision regarding one who has surrendered unconditionally to a particular commander is a matter either for the victorious people or king,[83] not for the commander.

(ii) Fides *between Private Persons* Citing Cicero,[84] Grotius argues that anyone, whether combatant or civilian, is equally bound to keep faith. Captives would be utterly unprotected and unable to gain their freedom unless this principle was accepted.[85] Thus the rule of public faith, i.e. the rule of natural law[86] that not only promises given to an enemy recognized by the law of nations but also those given to a robber or a pirate must be kept, is also applied to private persons. According to the rules on duress discussed in II. xi. 7, if a promise is made out of fear unjustly inspired by the other party the promisor should be able to escape from his contractual obligation. But according to the law of nations, this rule does not apply in the case of a fear arising from a formal war,[87] since private persons, like public powers, are bound not only by natural law but also by the principle of external effects under the law of nations.

[80] Here the power of a ruler (*magistratus*) over a townsman (*oppidanus*) is discussed as an equivalent to that over a subordinate.

[81] III. xxii. 7. [82] III. vi. 15. [83] III. xxii. 11.

[84] See Cicero 1913: I. xiii. 39. [85] III. xxiii. 1. [86] III. xix. 2.

[87] The original Latin text is *ex bello publico* (III. xxiii. 2). Kelsey *et al.* trans. it as 'public war'. Judging from the context, it should be 'formal war'.

Grotius also recognizes the binding force of a promise made by a captive to return to prison, or not to return to a certain place, as well as of a promise not to escape. He rejects the view that such promises are not binding because they are contrary to the duty which a person owes his state, arguing that what is contrary to duty is not necessarily void, and that it is not contrary to duty to secure one's liberty by promising what the enemy could in any event compel.[88] He argues that private persons should be compelled by their ruler to fulfil their promises in a formal war, because of the rule of the law of nations by which the belligerents are bound to render justice to each other even with respect to the acts of private persons.[89] Thus, although the law of nations applies to promises made by private persons with foreigners, supreme rulers are liable to secure compliance with such promises only in the event of a formal war. In other cases, although it is perfectly permissible to exercise the right under natural law to compel private persons who have broken their promises to make restitution, rulers are not liable for their citizens' broken promises.

Why was it necessary for Grotius to develop such a detailed argument about *fides* between subordinate rulers and private persons? The direct answer is that Grotius constructed a multi-layered normative structure to regulate and restrain war. Underlying this approach is a broad, all-inclusive notion of war which includes not only public wars but also private wars.[90] This position was adopted against the background of the realities of contemporary war: even public wars were often fought between armed forces comprised of nobles, various classes of warriors, and mercenaries. Agreements relating to war were also entered at a variety of levels, not limited to supreme rulers. It would have been impossible to expect wars to be effectively terminated, or acts of war to be mitigated, merely by emphasizing *fides* between states in the abstract or between supreme rulers. It was not unusual for a private person actually taken prisoner to make certain promises in exchange for money to secure his or her own life. Whether those promises were binding or not was indeed a matter of life and death. In order to regulate and restrain violence in a comprehensive

[88] III. xxiii. 6–8. As Kelsey *et al.* note, the numbering of the sections after xxiii. 6, in their English trans. differs from that of the Latin original. In the present ch. we use the former.

[89] III. xxiii. 10. [90] See 3.3.4.

manner, Grotius had to provide rules applicable to subordinate rulers and private persons as well.

10.3.5. Implied Faith (*Fides Tacita*)

An agreement (*conventio*) may be public, private, or mixed, and express or tacit. Examples of tacit agreement include a guarantee of the safety of those who take part in a cease-fire parley, and symbols customarily accepted as a sign of surrender. Grotius also discusses what acts on the part of the supreme ruler can be regarded as a tacit approval of a sponsion concluded by a commander.[91] A right, in whatever form it may be expressed, may be transferred to another by consent (*consensus*). In III. i, Grotius had declared that even tacit promises ought to be kept, and that this was the case even with enemies. He develops this point in III. i. 18, giving examples of forms of consent other than written or spoken language, and of specific promises and agreements. These examples include the presumption of abandonment of ownership, and the tacit declaration of intent on the basis of which customs are established.[92] Thus, Grotius did not confine his discussion of *fides* to actual agreements. *Fides* includes the obligation to abide by the expression of one's intent. Indeed, *fides* is the basis not only of actual agreements but also of the state and of the association of nations, which are not necessarily based on agreements.[93]

10.4. Admonitions to Preserve Faith and Peace

At the beginning of the last chapter (III. xxv) of *JBP*, Grotius states that he ends not because he has said all that should be said but because he has said enough to lay the basic foundations on which, he hopes, others may construct a more complete and imposing system.[94] What is important here is the significance of *fides* as a foundation of peace. *Fides* should be preserved so as not to discourage the hope of peace. Not only each state but also 'that great society of nations (*major illa gentium societas*)' is sustained by *fides*.[95] Grotius reaffirms Aristotle's assertion that 'all intercourse

[91] III. xxiv. 3–6.
[92] II. iv. 5. [93] III. xxv. 1.
[94] III. xxv. 1. Kelsey *et al.* trans. the title, *Monita ad fidem servandam*, as 'Admonitions to preserve peace'. This should be 'Admonitions to keep good faith'.
[95] See Cicero 1913: II. xxiv, p. 84.

among men will cease to exist'[96] if *fides* is lost, stressing in particular that faith should be maintained by supreme rulers. According to Grotius, justice (*justitia*) certainly contains elements of obscurity, but the bond of *fides* is self-evident. It is, then, all the more the duty of kings to cherish *fides* scrupulously, for conscience's sake, and also for the sake of the reputation by which the authority of the royal power is supported.[97]

Violence, a characteristic of wild beasts, is manifested most conspicuously in war. Human beings will degenerate to the level of beasts unless they exert the greatest effort to temper war with humanity. As Augustine said, war is waged that peace may be secured. If peace can be maintained by condoning offences, it will be right to condone them. Relying on Paul,[98] Grotius emphasizes the significance of peace, particularly for good Christians.[99]

Finally, after stating that the argument based on the self-evident nature of *fides* and on Christian ethics *ought* to be sufficient, he resorts to his ultimate weapon, the notion of *utilitas*. Making peace is advantageous to the weaker, because a long contest with a stronger opponent is dangerous, and a greater misfortune must be avoided at some loss. It is advantageous even to the stronger, because peace is bounteous and creditable to those who grant it while their affairs prosper: it must be kept in mind that 'Mars is on both sides'. Peace is advantageous also for those who seem to be equal to each other, for the best time to treat of peace is when each has confidence in himself.[100] This peace must be preserved by reason of the sacred principle of *fides*.[101]

Grotius thus utilizes his three major weapons, 'self-evident' natural law, Christian ethics, and the notion of *utilitas*, to make his final appeal to his readers. Characteristically he relies most on the third weapon, emphasizing the paramount value of peace, rather than the realization of justice, as is manifest in the expression 'peace, *whatever the terms on which it is made*, ought to be preserved absolutely'.[102] Nothing could more vividly reveal his aim in writing *JBP*.

[96] Aristotle 1968: 92.

[97] III. xxv. 1.

[98] 'Do everything possible on your part to live in peace with everybody' (Romans 12: 18).

[99] III. xxv. 3.

[100] III. xxv. 4–6.

[101] III. xxv. 7 (emphasis added).

[102] Ibid.

10.5. Conclusion

Why did Grotius use the notion of *fides* as his core concept in Book III? He indicates in the Prolegomena and in Book III that *fides* signifies keeping promises or agreements, that it is a requirement of justice, and thus a matter within the domain of natural law.[103] But, despite its importance as a basis of the theory of agreement in Book II, the term *fides* is hardly used there.[104] One reason has to do with the long-standing dispute over the binding force of a bare agreement (*nudum pactum*). Grotius argues that agreements in general, whether they are bare agreements or not, are binding.[105] He emphasizes that promises and agreements are binding under natural law, even if they are not binding under municipal law.[106] In Book III, he does not have to discuss agreements under municipal law. Thus, respect for *fides* in the sense of keeping promises is strongly affirmed. Secondly, the scope of the concept *fides* in Book III is less certain than that of agreement as a specific act in the law in Book II. Since Grotius argues, in Book II, that violations of agreements are a just cause of war, the concept of agreement has to be strictly delimited. In contrast, since Grotius discusses agreement in Book III mainly as something that moderates the severity of wars, effects truces, and even terminates wars, it is desirable that their scope be widened.

Thirdly, the term *fides* has a historical significance. In ancient Rome it was considered important as the basis of the bond between people.[107] The process through which the legally binding force of agreements was expanded was in one respect an effort to substantiate the concept of *fides* as a legal principle, and to place it within the framework of law.[108] Cicero's views on *fides*, often cited

[103] Prol. 8 and 15. Also see III. xix. 1(1) and (3).

[104] Ahsmann comments that Grotius had already placed *fides* at the foundation of international law in 'De fide et perfidia' (a ch. from the 3rd vol. of *Parallelon rerum publicarum*, 'his "oldest known book" on law'), and that his emphasis on *fides* between enemies in Book III of *JBP* is 'an enlargement of an idea already set out in "*De fide et perfidia*"' (1983: 37–8, 41).

[105] III. xi. For further detail, see 6.3.

[106] He rejects the identification of the *jus gentium* of Roman law with natural law: the former is merely an example of human volitional law.

[107] Meyer 1964: 31, 255.

[108] For a discussion on the basis of agreements under the *jus gentium* in Roman law, see Kaser 1979: 49.

in *JBP*, are related to this development in Roman law, and particularly in the *jus gentium*.

By contrast, theologians such as Augustine and Thomas Aquinas used *fides* primarily in a religious sense. This did not weaken its power to bind, but rather strengthened it. It was believed that *fides* sustained the binding force of a feudal contract, supported by oath before God. Belief as a form of *fides* in God complemented good faith as a form of *fides* between men.

In this way, *fides* had great salience in the European tradition.[109] But its significance was rather as a religious and ethical than as a legal norm: breach of faith was not regarded as a violation of law in the strict sense. Apart from secular law, religious and ethical sanctions were themselves important. But *fides* based on religious and ethical views could not regulate the conduct of those who did not belong to the same religion, as shown by the religious wars between Christians and non-Christians, between Catholics and Protestants, and even between different Protestant denominations.

That Grotius treated the principle of *fides* as based on natural law was accordingly very significant. If *fides* was understood as a principle of natural law common to all people, then differences in religion or civilization would not pose an obstacle to compliance. Grotius also made full use of the ambiguity of *fides* as a legal, ethical, and religious concept to enhance the persuasiveness of his argument, as well as stressing the utilitarian argument that one could not hope to terminate or mitigate a war without *fides*.

In presenting the theory of agreements in Book II, Grotius focuses his attention on agreements which if violated give rise to the right to resort to war. By contrast, in the theory of *fides* between enemies advanced in Book III Grotius emphasizes that *fides* must be kept even in war. A party with a just cause for war is bound by the same rules as those imposed on the other side by the law of nations. A peace treaty brings a war to an end, whether or not it has achieved a just goal. After the conclusion of a peace treaty, obligations based on it prevail over any rights derived from the original just cause.[110] This is because Grotius is concerned to prolong the peace as much as possible once a war has come to an end.

[109] For a discussion on the origin of the concept of *fides* in ancient and medieval Europe, see 6.2 and Taube 1930.

[110] See 10.3.3(1).

Grotius derives the binding force of agreements directly from natural law, quoting a passage of the Digest: '[t]he man who according to *jus gentium* ought to pay, and on whose good faith (*fides*) we have relied is indebted by natural law.'[111] In his theory of interpretation in II. xvi, he also stresses *fides* on the grounds that it is the dictate of natural reason that one to whom a promise has been made has the right to compel the promisor to do what the right interpretation suggests.[112] Consistently with this goal he approves of treaties concluded with non-Christians, and does not categorically deny the validity even of promises made to robbers or under duress.[113]

Although Grotius emphasizes the principles of *fides*, he does not encourage one who has suffered from a breach of good faith to take revenge on the wrongdoer. He remonstrates against breaches of *fides* that may lead to war, but urges forgiveness of such breaches as far as possible. In the final chapter of *JBP*, Grotius states that 'faith should be preserved, not only for other reasons, but also in order that the hope of peace may not be done away with'. This does not mean that the observance of *fides* is of paramount significance. Rather, *fides* is significant because it serves to mitigate the cruelty of war, to bring it to an end, and to maintain peace after the war. This is the basic justification of *fides*, to which Grotius again and again resorts to vindicate his ideal.

[111] D. 50. 17. 84. 1 (II. xi. 1).

[112] II. xvi. 1. For Grotius's theory of *fides* in the interpretation of treaties, see Ehrlich 1928: 15–21.

[113] II. xv. 8–12.

11

Conclusion: Law Dancing to the Accompaniment of Love and Calculation

11.1. *JBP*: A Book with a Practical Aim

This study presents a comprehensive view of *JBP* based closely on the text. However, since it is not an annotated commentary, some questions discussed by Grotius are not covered (e.g. rights of burial). Conversely, although repetition has as far as possible been avoided, it was necessary for some questions to be discussed from different perspectives in different chapters (e.g. Grotius's view of the state). This chapter summarizes the conclusions reached in this volume as a whole.

JBP was designed to achieve the practical aim of regulating and restraining war, both interstate and private, by means of a multi-layered normative structure which Grotius himself called 'jurisprudentia'. To avoid misunderstandings based on modern associations of the term 'war', it may be more appropriate to say that *JBP*'s aim was to minimize bloodshed and violence. This aim is clearly expressed in the famous passage in Prol. 28. Grotius's letter to a friend also expresses his intention.[1] But we should not take his words at face value,[2] or sanctify him as the sage of Delft who devoted his life to the cause of peace by establishing the rule of law in international society. Considerations of practicality and utility play a much more important role in *JBP* than has generally been thought.

The view that *JBP* is a treatise designed to serve the practical aim of regulating and restraining violence is not only based on

[1] Letter from Hugo Grotius to Johann Crellius, 10 May 1631, in Meulenbroek 1964: 392–3 (English trans. in *Biblioteca Visseriana*, 7 (1928), 208).

[2] See Fruin 1925: 7; Gellinek 1983: 114; Roelofsen 1990: 98, 122–3.

Grotius's own statements in Prol. 28 and his letter. That conclusion emerges, ineluctably, from the whole structure and argumentation of *JBP*, which cannot be understood as a coherent and consistent treatise unless it is read in this way. The basic premisses maintained throughout *JBP* include (1) the consistent attempt to avert the outbreak of war, the killing and wounding of enemies, and the devastation or pillaging of enemy property, an attempt often made at the expense of systematic consistency; (2) the method of argument by which rights to kill or wound enemies and to devastate or pillage enemy property, accorded in earlier sections, are for various reasons retracted in later sections; and (3) the comprehensive discussion, to the point sometimes of being laboured, of almost any problem capable of causing war and violence. The treatment of each problem and the development of each point of argument in *JBP* is to be explained by Grotius's paramount aim of minimizing bloodshed.[3]

11.2. The Realities of War in *JBP*

The war Grotius sought to regulate and restrain was not just some particular war of the seventeenth century. His target was war in general, as is evident from the statements in Prol. 1–3, 25–31, 38, as well as from his consistent attempt to formulate propositions of universal validity. And yet the concept of war actually employed in formulating these 'universal' propositions to a large extent reflected the contemporary realities of war in Europe.

The concept of war in *JBP* is a comprehensive one that includes not only wars between states but also wars between private persons.

[3] This is indicated, *inter alia*, in the following sections: I. iv, where, while prohibiting the execution of orders given by a tyrant that deviate from the law of nature and divine law, Grotius urges people to seek a resolution not by rebellion but by submission and endurance; II. i, where, while demonstrating the lawfulness of war, he advises escape or non-resistance according to the law of the Gospel and other higher precepts; II. xx, where, while recognizing the lawfulness of a punitive war, he seeks to limit the scope of punishment, those entitled to exact it, and the exercise of the right to exact it by appealing to the doctrine of rehabilitation, the law of the Gospel, and the principle of pardon; II. xxiii, where he urges avoidance of war when the cause of war is doubtful; II. xxiv, where he advocates avoidance of war even when one possesses a just cause; the relation between III. iv–ix and III. x–xvi, where, while ostensibly approving the laws and customs of war in Europe since antiquity, he ultimately disapproves or limits the right of war under the law of nations for those waging an unjust war; and III. xxv, where he ends by an appeal to the observance of good faith and peace.

This is a crucial point in understanding *JBP*. The all-inclusiveness of Grotius's concept of war must be understood in terms of (1) its relation to the dominant views or theories which preceded Grotius; (2) his concept of legitimate authority over the use of force, and (3) the historical conditions in the distribution of power prevailing in his time. As to the first, previous studies on Grotius and on the just-war doctrine are generally reliable. The question of war was repeatedly treated in European intellectual history as an issue of how a Christian could legitimately take up arms to fight his enemy without contradicting the teachings of Christianity. In the Scholastic just-war doctrine, the questions of substantive just causes, the just authors, the just methods, and the just objectives or intentions of war were all discussed from the viewpoint of one of the belligerent parties. On the other hand, Ayala and Gentilis, who directly preceded Grotius, paved the way for the development of a formal just-war doctrine, limiting the concept of war to wars between states. Grotius's comprehensive concept of war was an attempt to overcome the narrowness of the concepts of war common to these two theories.

This much is well understood. But as to the second and third points, previous studies on Grotius and on the history of international law in general have been beset by the serious weakness of projecting modern concepts onto the past.[4] A typical example is the assumption that the relation between a state (*civitas*) and a private person (*privatus*) as understood by Grotius is the same as or closely analogous to that which exists today between a state and an individual. Other examples of distinct historical concepts in *JBP* with no clear modern equivalents include Grotius's incomplete

[4] For a similar view, see Haggenmacher 1983: 11, 621. Oudendijk 1980 severely criticized van Vollenhoven for distorting Grotius in pursuit of his own project. Kooijmans, while accepting that this criticism was to a large extent correct, defended van Vollenhoven by analogy, on the basis that a later musician must be free to interpret the music of an earlier time in a way which might be different from its composer (1983: 85, 87). One can accept Kooijmans's conclusion, to the extent that what Falk terms the Grotian quest should not be confused with the Grotian solution. But his analogy is somewhat misleading. Later scholars inevitably interpret a classical work against the background of their own time and place and under the influence of dominant ideas and institutions. However, there is a difference between interpretative freedom and licence, in music as in scholarship. To interpret classical works on the assumption that their terminology, argumentation, and ways of thought are the same as those of the interpreter can be quite simply misleading and wrong. It is this tacit assumption that Oudendijk regarded as inexcusable.

separation of *causa* in the sense of the law of causality and *causa* in the sense of ethical cause; the hazy and undeveloped distinction between private and public; the complex relationship between rights over persons and rights over things in his treatment of *imperium* and *dominium*; and the transitory or equivocal character of *jus gentium* as between *jus gentium* in Roman law, law common to various peoples, and international law.

Hitherto in Europe, independent powers on various levels had existed within a lattice-like feudalistic relationship of rule, submission, and alliance. A head of a household (*paterfamilias*) had power and authority over his family which were not, in principle, distinguished from the power and authority of rulers. The supreme governing power vested in a king, the head of the state, was at base the same as the patriarchic power vested in the head of a household. Subjective rights of private persons, guaranteed by the principle of self-help, constituted an inseparable part of the objective legal order. By the early seventeenth century this typically medieval concept of a decentralized regime of power and authority had already become obsolete as a result of the centralization of power in the hands of absolute monarchs. But this centralization of power itself was defined and restricted by the medieval principle of social status. As long as absolute monarchical states were established on the basis of that principle, they could not wholly overcome their decentralized character.

In *JBP* private wars within a state (*bellum privatum*, war between 'private persons' (*privati*)) are prohibited after the establishment of the state, and the rights of war are recognized without discrimination to all states involved in a formal war, including states waging an unjust war. To this extent there is a clear distinction in legal status between the state (a public entity) and a private person. But the essential feature of Grotius's theory of war lies in the fact that he treats wars between private persons, between private persons and states, and between states, as on the same plane, and seeks to regulate them within the monistic framework of a just-war doctrine based on natural law. Whereas the modern concept of the individual assumes individuals stripped of both the authority to rule others and the legitimate means of violence, the term *privatus* as used by Grotius assumes a head of a household or independent power (*sui juris*) vested with both.[5]

[5] This concept of a head of a household was influenced by Grotius's admiration

This has an important bearing on Grotius's view of the state. While it is possible to discern in *JBP* a 'contractual' basis for the state, the free men who are the constituent units of the state are not morally indifferent individuals divested of all the trappings of social and political institutions. Rather, they are heads of households with power and authority over their family and slaves. Nor is there any idea of the state of nature as a methodological concept for establishing the state as an artificial entity. The shift from the state of nature to the state as an institution is not a change in principle but a natural process of development, based on the existing social order. The notion of a contract or agreement is invoked not to construct the state itself but as a basis for the citizens' submission to municipal law. The theory of social contract in the strict sense of the term is not adopted in *JBP*.

The existence of independent powers at various levels, sharing the right and means to resort to force, also characterizes Grotius's view of 'international society' and of the 'subjects of (international) law'. Whether Grotius viewed international society as comprised of states or as a community of individuals has often been debated.[6] It has also been asserted that Grotius recognizes the essential identity of states and individuals, and rejects the existence of a double standard as between them.[7] But it is wrong to read *JBP* on the assumption of a dualistic scheme of state and individual. In *JBP* injuries against citizens constitute for their country a just cause for war, but this war is fought for the sake of *others*. An armed rebellion by subjects against their ruler is treated as a war (*bellum*) identical to that between states (such a war is rarely legitimate, but its legitimacy is as much the proper subject of inquiry as in the case of interstate wars). Such a society has little in common with an international society composed of sovereign, independent states. On the other hand, the constituent members of that society are not individuals. They are multi-layered independent powers with their own subjects, and states are only the most powerful of those

for European antiquity, and was somewhat anachronistic even in his time (see 3.1 n. 13). But it remained relevant in that the distance between private persons and states in terms of the mechanism for using force was much closer then than today, and the enforcement mechanism of the state was dependent of enforcement mechanisms largely based on decentralized independent powers. See 3.3.4.

[6] See e.g. Basdevant 1904: 254; Reeves 1924: 22, 27; Bourquin 1926: 96; Sukiennicki 1927: 119–20; Tabata 1958: 51–7.

[7] Lauterpacht 1975*b*: 336–40.

powers. States in the modern sense did not become established until legitimate authority over others and a monopoly of the means of enforcement came to be held by states to the exclusion of various independent powers. Nor did people become individuals in the modern sense until this stage. To assume the dualistic scheme of state and individual merely projects modern concepts on to the past.

11.3. Grotius's Normative Approach

Under the historical conditions outlined above, and living in exile without position or power, Grotius sought to construct a general theory of law (*jurisprudentia*) relating to war (and to peace, its antithesis), as the only method of achieving his practical aim. While admitting that the true motive of war is usually the desire for profit, he rejects in principle a discussion of the problem of war and peace from the viewpoint of utility (*utilitas*). What he claims to rely on is a *jurisprudentia* based on a deductive, even mathematical logic. However, he has to revise and modify this attitude throughout *JBP*, because his ultimate aim of regulating and restraining war cannot be achieved merely through the abstract logic of law. Instead, he has to interpret law itself in a practical and utilitarian way, even at the risk of equivocation. He appeals to religious and moral norms on the periphery of law, including the law or rules of love (*lex caritatis*, *lex dilectionis*, *caritatis regula*), the precepts of humanity (*regula humanitatis*), the duty of Christians (*officium Christianum hominum*), and the rules of prudence (*regula prudentiae*). Thus what is actually expounded in *JBP* is not a coherent and distinct jurisprudence but rather a comprehensive normative approach, reinforced by appeals to the spirit of love and utility.

A 'secularized' natural law is a key to Grotius's normative approach. According to him, even God cannot alter natural law as the dictate of right reason. As a universal higher norm that regulates human relations everywhere and under all circumstances, it occupies the highest position in his system of law. And precisely because it occupies such a pivotal position, it had to be separated from the rampant religious disputes of the time. A system of natural law captured by one of the disputing religious parties could not have the authority to regulate those disputes. This is a major reason why he dared to assert the seemingly impious and therefore dangerous hypothesis, 'even if we should concede . . . that there is no God' (Prol. 11).

On the other hand, his European contemporaries were still heavily influenced and directed by societal norms based on Christianity. Whether one was perceived to be a good Christian still had an important bearing at the level of *realpolitik*, including the politics of war and peace. A convincing view of natural law had to incorporate many of the precepts of Christianity if it was to achieve the practical goal of restraining war. Thus natural law, which had supposedly been secularized, came to embrace many aspects of Christian ethics transformed into societal norms. In this way Grotius's concept of natural law was substantiated not only by rules of law but also by moral, ethical, and religious values shared by contemporary Europeans.

Merely applying natural law, however, was not enough to regulate the spectrum of relations ranging from those between private persons to those between states. By definition natural law is an inflexible law, universal and immutable, and with a content limited to self-evident rules, as determined by the judgement of rational beings. Thus it is necessary to posit a permissive domain of natural law which neither belongs to natural law properly so-called nor contradicts it. Within this domain, human relations are regulated by divine and human volitional law. This permissive domain gave Grotius a virtually free hand in assessing and incorporating into his system existing legal, political, and social institutions, the practices of various nations, and religious and moral norms. Its benefits were twofold.

First, within the permissive domain of natural law, the 'inherent nature (*natura*)' of man-made institutions is protected by natural law. Even though human institutions themselves are not based on nature but are the products of man's design, it is not permissible under natural law to violate institutions that have come into existence without deviating from natural law. On this ground, Grotius can choose and justify particular existing institutions as he wishes. Actually, the existing order of governance as a whole is justified in II. ii–xix, where he discusses substantive rights as just causes of war.

Secondly, within the permissive domain of natural law are included those man-made institutions or practices which are not punishable because they are not prohibited under (mandatory) natural law, but of which it is difficult to approve from the viewpoint of minimizing the cruelties and casualties of war. The rules and customs of war in Europe (especially those of antiquity), which allowed belligerent parties to commit a wide range of cruel and destructive acts, are examples. To sanctify even these rules and practices in the name of natural law would be contrary to the basic aim of *JBP*. Thus, by introducing norms embodying higher virtues such as internal justice, the law of love, and the rules of humanity, Grotius ultimately restricts, qualifies, or disapproves of these rules and practices. III. i–xviii, which first approve the right to injure others or to capture property under the law of nations, then disapprove most of these rights on grounds of internal justice and other higher virtues, form a typical example of this retractive method of argument.

11.4. A Multi-Layered Normative Structure

11.4.1. Functions of Multi-Layered Norms

Thus in *JBP* Grotius gives himself a wide discretion in passing judgement on existing rules, institutions, and practices, accepting some and disapproving others. The multi-layered structure of law, or rather of norms, is a conceptual device through which he makes these judgements. Various norms with different standards and of different dimensions, including moral and religious as well as legal norms, are woven into this structure, as can be seen from Fig. 11.1. How these multi-layered norms function as a framework for judgement as well as a means of minimizing bloodshed is typically shown in the argument on the lawfulness of war in I. ii–iii and II. i. The general lawfulness of war is examined and in principle acknowledged, according first to the law of nature, secondly to the law of nations, thirdly to divine law centred on the Old Testament, and finally to the law of the Gospel. However, the law of the Gospel does not approve of killing or wounding a third party in order to save one's life, body, or property, or of disproportionate counter-attack, such as retaliating against injury by killing the enemy. Indeed, choosing to be killed rather than to kill is considered praiseworthy, especially for Christians. Thus, in the final analysis the right to resort to war approved by natural law and other laws is significantly restricted by the law of the Gospel and other religious and ethical norms.[8]

The same pattern can be observed in the theory of punishment in II. xx. Punishment is 'an evil of pains which is inflicted because of an evil of action' (II. xx. 1(1)). By his crime, a criminal subordinates himself to everyone who has not committed the same category of crime, and is therefore deemed to have consented to allowing anyone to exercise, as a superior, the right to exact punishment on him. Under this theory of the fictitious superior, a large number of people would have the right of punishment, and could therefore wage punitive war. This would be contrary to Grotius's aim of minimizing bloodshed. He is thus driven to limit the execution of punishment (the occurrence of punitive wars), first by limiting the number of people who may under the law of nature exact punishment, on the ground that punishment must have distinct purposes, then by mitigating and imposing limits on the right of punishment according to the law of the Gospel, and finally by appealing to pardon.

In the general case of wars and in the special case of punitive war we thus have a clear picture of Grotius's regulatory system. Multilayered legal, religious, and ethical norms function both as standards of judgement and as a means of restraining the outbreak of war.

11.4.2. The Multi-layered Normative Structure in the Relations between the Laws of War and *Temperamenta*

(1) *The Laws of War*

Whereas the earlier argument concerning the general lawfulness of war and punishment is designed to regulate and restrain war by arranging a multitude of norms at the same level, the argument

[8] However, the argument in I. ii–iii and II. i is aimed at demonstrating the lawfulness of certain categories of war as a basic premise of the just-war doctrine. The negative assessment of war is mentioned merely as a qualification to the general lawfulness of war. What is important here is the fact that Grotius dared to add such a qualification to the proposition of the general lawfulness of war. Had Grotius not had the practical aim of minimizing violence, he would not have added such a qualification, for this would have been unnecessary, or even undesirable, from the viewpoint of the smooth or coherent development of his argument.

LEGAL NORMS

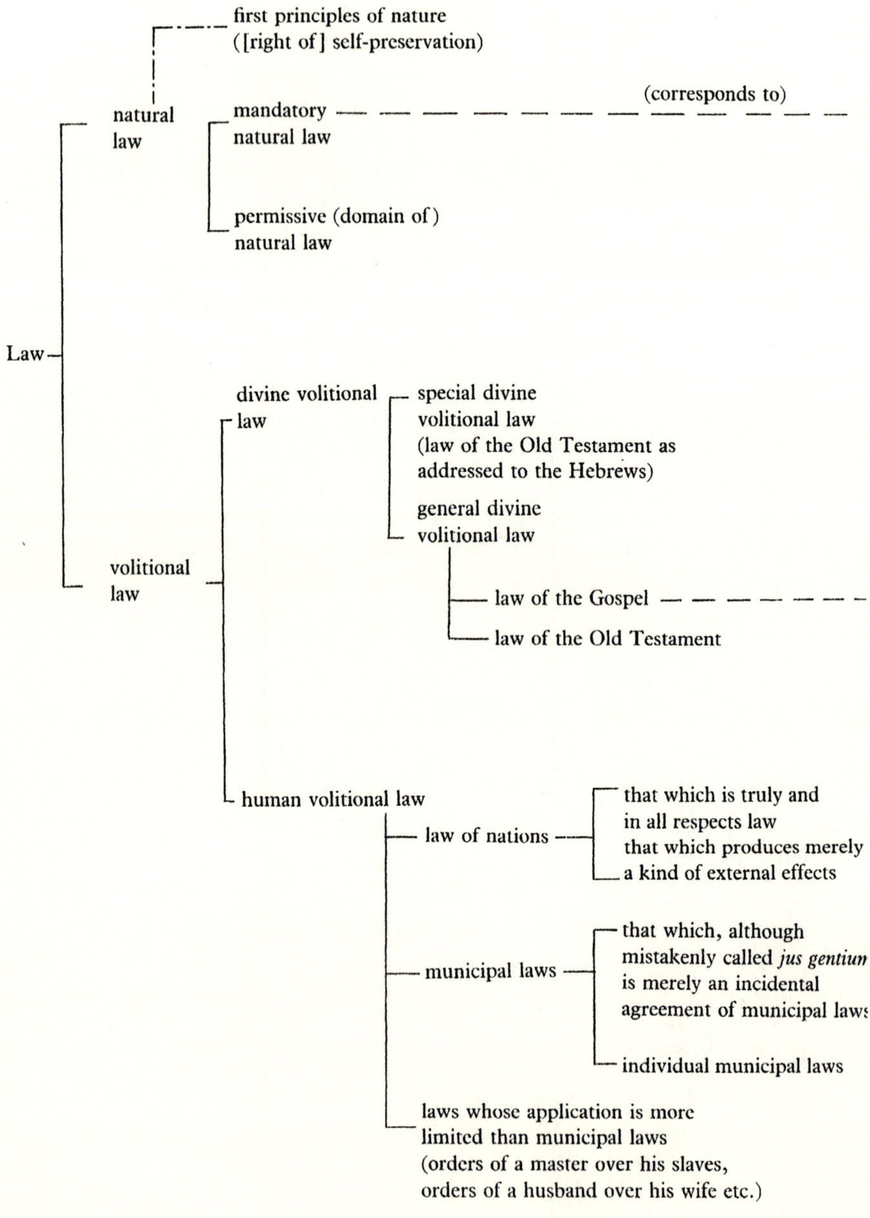

FIG. 11.1. Various norms in

ETHICAL OR RELIGIOUS NORMS

— — — — — — — — — internal justice

(corresponds to)

— — — — — — — — — —
- law of love
- rules of love
- rules of humanity
- duty of Christians
- norms demanding piety and honesty
- other religious or ethical norms

De Jure Belli ac Pacis

concerning the laws of war and *temperamenta* is designed to minimize bloodshed by making the multi-layered norms function at different levels and in different ways. In Books I and II, Grotius provides a comprehensive catalogue of substantive rights as just causes of war, in order to prevent 'men from taking up arms for slight cause, or no cause at all' (Prol. 28). This catalogue naturally serves to provide a frame of reference for determining which party is just in a particular war. But its role is not limited to it. Since man is a rational being, he should refrain from resorting to war if his claim is not included among the just causes of war. This catalogue ought to be, of itself, the basic scheme for restraining the outbreak of war.[9]

On the other hand, Grotius constructed his just-war doctrine by abandoning the Scholastic concept that just wars should be fought in a just manner, and defining just wars solely from the viewpoint of substantive just causes. The general proposition in III. i. 2, that '[i]n war things which are necessary to attain the end in view are permissible', is a corollary of this doctrine. It provides no basis for regulating the conduct of war waged by those with a just cause. Conversely, the acts of those who wage an unjust war should be merely an accumulation of unlawfulness. But this does not mean that there are no customs or rules limiting the conduct of war. Although Grotius characterized wars fought in Europe in his time as those 'even barbarous nations would be ashamed of' (Prol. 28), there were rules and customs which could be conceived of as laws of war. They were for the most part applied to both belligerents in a non-discriminatory way: otherwise they could hardly have been effective in the actual conduct of hostilities. Since his aim was to construct a practical theory capable of effectively regulating and restraining wars, those laws of war could not be ignored.

In Book III Grotius devotes eight chapters (III. ii–ix) to incorporating the rules and customs of war into his law of nations. However, this part of the law of nations cannot coexist with other norms at the same level. Whereas the substantive just-war doctrine discriminates between belligerent parties, the law of nations applicable in time of war is based on a non-discriminatory principle. Had they operated at the same level, there would have been an apparent contradiction. In addition, these 'positive' laws of

[9] See 3.2.1; Kasai 1984: 43–5.

warfare, reflecting the realities of war in Europe, allowed stringent rights of inflicting injury and destroying or capturing enemy property, not only in relation to belligerents but also to non-belligerents.[10] For Grotius, whose paramount concern is to minimize bloodshed, these harsh laws had to be modified.

Accordingly, he retracts the rights of war he earlier granted under the law of nations to those who wage war, just or unjust. But in doing so, it is imperative that the restriction or negation of the effects of the laws of war should not become itself a cause of new wars. Hence the need for the different aspects of his normative structure to function at different levels. For these reasons Grotius adopts the concept of the law of nations as a 'law that generates only certain types of external effect'.[11] Since the law of nations which regulates the conduct of war in a non-discriminatory way does not conform to the substantive just-war doctrine, it is necessary to argue that the former does not have all the attributes of law. This is why the laws of war have only *external* effects.[12]

(2) *Restriction and Modification of the Rights of War*

The term 'external effects' implies the existence of distinct or even opposing norms involving the internal or inherent nature of things. Indeed, immediately after the argument concerning the external effect of the laws of war, Grotius introduces the notion of 'internal justice (*interna justitia*)', which is used to regulate and modify the harsh rights of inflicting injury and capturing enemy property under the laws of war. He states: 'I must retrace my steps, and must deprive those who wage war of nearly all the privileges which I seemed to grant, yet did not grant to them.'[13] Many things permissible under the law of nations '. . . either deviate from the righteous rule (whether this has its basis in law strictly so called, or in the admonitions of other virtues)', or 'at any rate may be omitted on higher grounds and with greater praise among good men'.[14]

[10] Whether the 'positive' laws of warfare Grotius describes in III. ii–ix faithfully reflected the contemporary laws of war is another question, which cannot be discussed here. Since he relies heavily on the practice of European antiquity, when the treatment of enemies and their property tended to be harsh, it may well be that the laws of war as described in III. ii–ix were harsher than they were in his time. Grotius himself admits this with regard to the status and treatment of prisoners of war (III. vii. 9). See also Roelofsen 1990: 124.

[11] Prol. 41 (*effectum quendam externum*).

[12] See 8.5; 9.4.

[13] III. x. 1(1).

[14] Ibid.

Grotius first restricts the rights of war of those who wage a formal war for an unjust cause. He who wages an unjust war cannot reach the kingdom of heaven without repentance, even if the war is a formal one. The principal form of repentance is to carry out the internal obligation (*interna obligatio*) of making restitution for injuries inflicted in the course of waging the war.[15]

Next, in III. xi–xvi, he restricts even the rights of war which in III. iv–ix he had granted to those who wage a formal war for a just cause. In urging or soliciting them not to exercise their rights of war, but to pardon unjust enemies, he resorts not only to the notion of internal justice, but also to various quasi-legal, religious, and ethical norms.[16] According to internal justice, one who wages a formal war for a just cause is permitted to engage only in acts of war based on the substantive causes developed in Books I and II. In other words, the rights of belligerency expanded by the law of nations are not endorsed. However, failure to fulfil the obligation of internal justice does *not* constitute a just cause for initiating a war. If a violation of that obligation were to be a ground for waging a just war, the aim of breaking the incessant chain of wars through the device of external effects would be defeated.[17]

But had this obligation had any real chance of being fulfilled without coercion, Grotius would have had no need to write *JBP*. Thus he is compelled to appeal to a set of moral and religious norms, including the law of love, as well as the duty and innate goodness of Christians. On one hand, these norms restrain, by the threatened sanction of denying salvation, acts which cannot be suppressed by the notion of internal justice. On the other hand, they reinforce and substantiate the notion of internal justice. Underlying this restraining function is the reality that being labelled an impious Christian was a stigma that led to serious secular and political disadvantages.[18] Thus internal justice overlaps not only with the law of nature but also with moral and religious norms. In this way, Grotius performs the intricate task, fraught with contradictions, of introducing the concept of internal justice, at once synonymous and not synonymous with the law of nature, to help ensure that belligerents fulfil their 'obligation' to refrain from their rights of war, under the condition that their failure to meet this obligation is not to be construed by the other party as a just cause for waging another war.

[15] III. x. 3–6. [16] III. xi–xvi. [17] Kasai 1984: 58. [18] See 3.1.4.

(3) *The Significance of the Appeal to Utility in* Temperamenta

Grotius uses the threat that a king, a nobleman, or other political and military leaders will suffer from being *reputed* an impious Christian, a reputation detrimental to them as a matter of *realpolitik*. Although he ostensibly dismissed from the field covered in *JBP* the investigation of things in terms of utility (matters within the purview of political science), upon the conviction that legal, moral, and religious norms in themselves had some power to regulate and restrain war,[19] he was nevertheless aware that he could not afford to ignore the tendency of men to act for motives of expediency. This is confirmed by such remarks as 'there are also other causes which influence men through regard for what is expedient and differ from those that influence men through regard for what is right', or '[i]n most cases those who go to war have persuasive causes with or without just causes'.[20] Even stronger evidence is his method of argument. Whenever he encounters a critical issue, he almost always seeks to persuade his readers by appealing to considerations of utility and practicality. Refraining from waging punitive wars, the binding force of agreement and mitigation of the exercise of rights of war are all examples.

Thus considerations of utility and practicality underlie the whole structure of *JBP*, either in making the contents of laws consistent with reality or as a frame of reference for determining the lawfulness or permissibility of existing institutions and usages.[21] In the *temperamenta* set forth in III. xi–xvi, the appeal to utility plays a critical role. For example, Grotius argues that moderation in war can deprive the enemy of the 'great weapon' of despair which may inspire desperate resistance.[22] This is because *temperamenta* are appeals to those waging a just war to refrain from exercising rights which, properly speaking, they are fully justified in exercising as a means of realizing justice.

According to Grotius, one who wages war for an unjust cause, and is therefore deprived of the rights of war in III. x, is, properly speaking, an unjust person. The only reasons Grotius conferred, in III. iv–ix, certain rights of war even on such an unjust belligerent are passive ones: (1) avoiding the even greater disadvantage of an incessant chain of wars; and (2) incorporating into his just-war doctrine the contemporary laws of warfare applied to both

[19] Prol. 18–20, 57.
[20] II. i. 1(1); II. xxii. 3(1).
[21] See 3.1.3; 11.5.3.
[22] III. xii. 8.

belligerents in a non-discriminatory way. Since they are merely external effects cut off from internal justice, Grotius has no difficulty taking back the rights he earlier granted to such passive holders of rights. This is why he needs only a small part of III. x (i.e. III. x. 3–6), to retract the rights of war from those who wage formal war for an unjust cause.[23]

One who wages a just war is in a very different case. Such a belligerent is properly speaking a bearer of justice. The lengthy argument in Books I–II deals precisely with the requisites for such a bearer of justice, and with the legal effects of his acts. He who wages a just war is either a defender of his own rights which have been violated, or a defender of justice who assists those waging a just war or wages a war of intervention to rescue the subjects of another country suffering from tyranny (II. xxv. 8). In other words, among those waging a just war there are those who are protecting common interests or values as altruists. It is difficult to appeal to such defenders of justice to refrain from exercising rights which they may properly exercise. Since Grotius breaks from the Scholastic just-war tradition of waging a just war in a just manner, and defines the concept of just war solely from the viewpoint of substantive cause, the difficulty is fundamental. Thus, while he devotes only two pages to retracting the rights of war from those waging an unjust war, he devotes as many as forty pages to withdrawing the rights of war from those waging a just war. Whereas in III. x he uses the term *monita* (caution) for those waging an unjust war, he uses the terms *temperamenta* or similar terms, such as *moderatio* and *modestia*, for those waging a just war. Furthermore, after examining in III. xi–xvi one right of war after another approved in III. iv–ix, Grotius frequently employs moral and religious norms, including the law of love, and, above all, repeatedly appeals to considerations of utility. These all exhibit Grotius's efforts to overcome his fundamental difficulty.

[23] III. x is entitled 'Cautions in Regard to Things which are Done in an Unlawful War (*in bello injusto*)'. But there is an obvious difference between the descriptions in III. x. 1–2 and those in III. x. 3–6. In III. x. 1 Grotius states: 'I must deprive *those who wage war* of nearly all the privileges I seemed to grant' (emphasis added) and not 'those who wage unjust war.' This suggests that III. x. 1–2 are addressed to those who wage formal war in general (the term used in III. x. 1 is 'those who wage war (*bellum gerentibus*)', but because they are vested with rights of war under the law of nations, it should be 'authors of formal war'), and that cautions directed to those who wage unjust war are to be found in III. x. 3–6.

Scholars have disagreed on the reasons for this disparity between *monita* and *temperamenta*.[24] Why are most of the arguments for *temperamenta* directed not to those who wage *formal* wars but to those who wage *just* wars? Kasai stresses the significance of the framework of the just-war doctrine throughout *JBP*, but makes the following intriguing observation. It might be said that Grotius places *temperamenta* after III. iv–ix, where he admits the rights of war under the law of nations to *both* parties to a formal war, because he expects this passage, whose constituent parts correspond to the respective rights of war, to be read—or rather misread—as an appeal to *both* parties in a formal war. It might even be said that the *temperamenta* was inherited by later generations *because* it was misread in this manner.[25]

Whether or not Grotius actually intended his *temperamenta* to be so misread, it must be granted that such a misreading is quite possible. But even if *temperamenta* was accepted as an appeal addressed only to those waging a just war, its effect may not have been very different. The basic premiss of Grotius's just-war doctrine is that it is *inconceivable* that man would knowingly wage an unjust war. This is partly based on his somewhat optimistic view of human nature as inherently rational and social. But it is also based on his view that as a matter of *realpolitik* it would be difficult for an avowedly unjust author of war to find anyone to fight under his command or as his ally. It is true that a just cause for a war may be nothing more than an ideology that hides motives of expediency. Nevertheless, not only legitimacy but real power derives from the perception that one has a just cause, since this strengthens the appeal to third parties (monarch, feudal lord, etc.), who are free to side with either party, to enter into an alliance with the party perceived to be just. If, as Grotius assumes, a man would not knowingly wage an unjust war, in most cases those who resort to war should be not obviously unjust, may believe that they have justice on their side, or at least claim that they have a just cause.[26] It was thus natural to appeal for self-restraint in the exercise of the rights of war by briefly cautioning those waging an unjust war (for such cases should be exceptional), and by urging, at length and

[24] See Edwards 1981: 128–9; Grewe 1984*a*: 255; 9.4.3.

[25] Kasai 1984: 42–51, 54–5.

[26] In the later middle ages in Europe, virtually every prince, in practice, claimed that a war he had avowed was just (Keen 1965: 68–70).

in detail, that even those who wage a just war should exercise moderation.

The cautions Grotius gives in III. x. 3–6 to those waging an unjust war are simple indeed. He discusses only their internal obligation of restitution, and fails to express their obligation to refrain from the rights of killing or wounding enemies or destroying enemy property. As far as Grotius's actual intention is concerned, this obligation has already been indirectly asserted in III. x. 3: 'What is done by reason of an unjust war is unjust from the viewpoint of internal injustice (*interna injustitia*)'. Since even those waging a just war should refrain from exercising their rights of war according to *temperamenta*, it should be apparent that those waging an unjust war should all the more refrain from exercising those rights.[27]

To summarize, in III. iv–ix, Grotius uses a different kind of argument (that of external effects under the law of nations) from the argument used in developing his just-war doctrine, thereby introducing the non-discriminatory principle by which the laws of war are applied in a formal war. Then in III. x–xvi, he disapproves of those external effects mainly by resorting to the notions of internal justice, the law of love, and other moral or religious norms. The multi-layered norms, which functioned in Books I and II on the same plane as a framework for judging and restraining specific actions or institutions, here function on different levels. In the just-war doctrine discussed in I and II, Grotius demonstrated the lawfulness of war, both generally and in his theory of punishment, but always qualified this by his insistence that killing and wounding are not desirable. This pattern is maintained to a degree even in III.

[27] Bull comments that 'although he admits the idea of laws for the conduct of war that do not discriminate among the belligerents with regard to the causes they pursue, Grotius weakens its force by stating alongside it the contrary doctrine he derives from natural law . . . It is clearly not the view of Grotius that those who are fighting an unjust cause thereby place themselves *outside* international society' (1966: 59–60). It is certainly not Grotius's view that those waging an unjust war are expelled from international society. The interpretation in the text avoids this mistake, but allows us to interpret *temperamenta* as addressed to those waging a just war. According to our interpretation, the laws of war are not stated *alongside* the contrary doctrine, a just-war doctrine based on natural law. They are located within the just-war doctrine, with their unique force of *effectum externum*. That the force of the laws of war is limited is a deliberate choice of Grotius, who sought to achieve mutually contradictory goals described in the text. In the light of his paramount aim, they are not contradictory, for they all serve to minimize bloodshed.

iv–ix, where harsh rights of war are approved. The same pattern can be observed in the relationship between III. iv–ix and III. x–xvi. The precept 'Thou shalt not shed blood' underlies it all. Grotius's theory is not based on the simple dualistic division whereby restraining the outbreak of war involves natural law, while regulating the conduct of war falls within the purview of the law of nations.[28] The law of nations as well as the moral and religious norms discussed in III must be located within the monistic just-war doctrine. On the other hand, it is evident that Grotius does *not* seek to establish a just-war doctrine for the sake of the doctrine itself. His just-war doctrine is the most important means of fulfilling his paramount goal of minimizing bloodshed.

II.5. 'Systematic' Presentation of Just Causes of War

To catalogue the substantive rights constituting the just causes of war not only establishes a framework for judging whether a specific war is just, but should also, through its publicity and attendant moral persuasion, itself have a deterrent effect on war. This important task of cataloguing the substantive rights requires three things: (1) all-inclusiveness of subject-matter and materials, so that any problem that may constitute a just cause of war is covered; (2) a systematic conceptual framework within which these materials may be selected and arranged in the proper order; and (3) relevance to reality, so that the argument will have persuasive power in the real world. While all three features are found in *JBP*, the way they are related to each other is rather problematic.

II.5.1. All-Inclusiveness of Subject-Matter and Materials

The most immediately impressive feature of *JBP* is the all-inclusiveness of its subject-matter and of the materials cited. The starting-point for Grotius is the general proposition: 'Where there is a violation of rights, there is a judicial solution; where there is no judicial solution, there is war'. He then examines a comprehensive range of rights, from what we would today call private rights (including real rights, incorporeal rights, and rights related to contract and inheritance) to governing powers on various levels,

[28] Kasai 1984: 55–60.

and even rights relating to legation and burial. He discusses bearers or subjects of rights of every kind, from minors to heads of households, subordinate rulers, various types of kings, and entire peoples. He considers a panoply of acts, ranging from acts affected by fraud, error, or coercion, occupation, and prescription, to criminal acts, punishment, and pardon, and further to the public acts of kings and peoples. Everything that could possibly constitute a cause or ground for resorting to war is taken up, examined, and assessed. He also discusses comprehensively the various acts committed in the course of war.

This all-inclusiveness of subject-matter is reflected and expressed in the all-inclusiveness of the materials referred to. Although Grotius ostensibly adopts a deductive method of proof based on self-evident propositions, he actually relies on inductive methods, making full use of what Huizinga described as an 'inexhaustible' diversity of materials. In terms of methodology, he stresses the teachings of the Scholastic school, but in his detailed descriptions of substantive rights in Book II he mobilizes a vast knowledge of Roman law. Other theories and authorities acceptable and persuasive to the ruling class and intellectuals of his time are cited and relied on, including the Old and New Testament, patristic theology, authors of European antiquity, and Aristotelian philosophy. Some of these sources have only an indirect relevance, others hardly any relevance at all. Such a cumbersome, comprehensive method of citation was, to a degree, adopted by all humanistic writers of the time,[29] but even in such company the sheer range of material Grotius cites is overwhelming. It should be noted that this all-inclusiveness was not meant to cover every field of 'international law' but only so far as it was relevant to the restraint and regulation of war. To this extent we agree with Haggenmacher, who stresses that *JBP* is a book on the just-war doctrine rather than on international law in the modern sense.[30] On the other hand, it cannot be denied that this all-inclusiveness of subject-matter and materials tends to verbosity and undermines the systematic consistency of *JBP*.

[29] See Roelofsen 1983*b*: 74.

[30] Haggenmacher 1983: 8 *et passim*. See also Bourquin 1926: 110. However, we cannot agree with Haggenmacher's statement that the humanization of the conduct of war is not Grotius's principal purpose, only a possible result (1983: 600–1 n. 921). '[F]ixer les *droits* en la matière', which Haggenmacher claims to be Grotius's aim, itself serves to minimize bloodshed.

11.5.2. Conceptual Frameworks of Various Norms

Three conceptual frameworks contribute to Grotius's attempt to build a 'system' of substantive rights as just causes: (1) the permissive domain of natural law; (2) differences in degree as to what is permissible within the permissive domain of natural law; and (3) the reformulation of the relations between the law of nations properly so-called, the law of nature, and municipal laws, based on the correction of widespread misconceptions about them. The law of nature properly so-called (mandatory natural law) is the dictate of right reason, which either dictates man to take or prohibits him from taking specific actions. But there is an intermediate and extensive domain where acts are neither enjoined nor prohibited under this (mandatory) natural law. This permissive domain of natural law may be regulated by volitional law. There is a significant difference in the degrees of moral desirability, from conduct which, though praiseworthy, is too high-minded to be regarded as obligatory under natural law, to that which, though morally undesirable, is so expedient or useful to man's livelihood that it may be done with impunity. Grotius justifies both those institutions and practices which are highly desirable and those which, while not necessarily moral, should be maintained for practical reasons, on the basis that, though the institutions and practices concerned themselves fall under volitional law, it is the dictate of natural law that human beings should abide by the nature (*natura*) of these man-made institutions and existing practices. This argument is of particular significance in structuring and sanctifying the 'system' of substantive rights developed in Book II. Conversely, as to institutions or practices which Grotius considers undesirable, having regard to his ultimate aim of minimizing bloodshed, he at first recognizes their permissibility, but ultimately seeks to deny their legitimacy on the grounds of the law of God or of higher moral and religious norms.

In presenting a 'system' of substantive rights as just causes, Grotius tends to adopt the legal institutions and ideas prevailing in contemporary Europe, many of which derived from Roman law, interpreting them in accordance with his enlightened conception of law. But he also denies the universality of certain prevalent or traditional institutions or ideas, and presents opposing ideas as 'natural'. Even when he relies on ideas found in traditional Roman law, he often modifies or recasts them to suit his purpose. Rules on prescription, occupation of ownerless things, discovery of buried property, acquisition of fruits, and the binding force of bare agreements, are examples of deviations from the traditional ideas or institutions of Roman law. The distinction between original and derivative acquisition and the classification of contracts are examples of modification or recasting.

Grotius's denial of the universality of Roman law and other prevalent ideas and institutions, and his assertion of the 'naturalness' of alternate ideas, is often simply based on transcendental prepositions ('according to nature', 'naturally (*naturaliter*)'). Ultimately, the argument develops by an appeal to common sense, but at the formal legal level he bases his argument on differences between the law of nations properly so-called and municipal law: (1) *jus gentium* in Roman law is an institution based on Roman law, not the law of nations (*jus gentium*) based on mutual consent between all or a great many nations;[31] (2) even if a number of states should happen to be in agreement, this should not be regarded as involving the law of nations in the true sense, unless the agreement has in view the common interest of the 'mutual society of nations' or 'that greater society of nations'.[32] In these contexts, Grotius simply states that some dominant ideas and institutions are not part of the law of nations. He makes no particular mention of their not being part of the law of nature. And yet he asserts alternative ideas and institutions, using such expressions as 'According to (the law of) nature . . .' or 'If one follows natural reason . . .'. For Grotius it is probably self-evident that what is not part of the law of nations cannot possibly be part of the law of nature: there is thus no need to mention the latter.

Institutions or norms of Roman law, of municipal law, and of the law of nations are thus selected, with some being approved and sanctified, others not. But these are not the only institutions and norms which are subject to scrutiny. As long as existing institutions or norms are in some way related to war, they are taken up, discussed, and assessed. For example, while the power of a master over his slaves is regarded not as a product of nature but as a man-made institution, this does not mean that it was instituted by municipal law. Rather, state institutions are supposed to have

[31] e.g. II. viii. 1. [32] Prol. 17; II. viii. 1(2) and 26.

developed from the power of the master. Thus Grotius discusses in detail the power of a master over his slaves. Institutions or norms of divine volitional law are also subject to his selection and scrutiny. Depending on whether or not they possess a 'universal' quality, various rules contained in the Old Testament are regarded either as general divine volitional law applied to all peoples (the law of Moses basically belongs to this category) or as special divine volitional law (e.g. Hebrew law as it applies only to the Hebrew people).

II.5.3. Common Sense: The Ultimate Ground of Persuasiveness in *JBP*

The norms thus adopted in *JBP* are composed of the law of nature, divine volitional law, the law of nations, municipal law, human volitional law which is narrower in scope than municipal law, and various moral and religious norms. Different roles are assigned to each according to its source, effectiveness, and range of application. These norms are supposed to constitute a 'system' under which the catalogue of substantive rights is presented as the just causes of war. However, this 'system' contains many defects from the viewpoint of consistency. There is a lack of logical consistency even in the arguments about resort to force, the most basic problem for Grotius. The argument that '[n]o other just cause for undertaking war can there be excepting injury received'[33] should clearly be based on natural law properly so-called: those who have not received an injury ought to be prohibited, by mandatory natural law, from undertaking war. But the right of war, to kill and to wound enemies under the law of nations, is justified as falling within the permissible domain of natural law, as in the expression 'something is said to be *permissible* . . . because among men it is not liable to punishment'.[34]

The framework of common sense, based on considerations of practicality and utility, enables Grotius to make up for these defects and thereby to maximize the persuasiveness of *JBP*. While freeing law from religion as a matter of principle, in terms of content he incorporates religious norms so as to take advantage of their actual influence on the behaviour of his contemporaries in Europe. While

[33] II. i. 1(4). [34] III. iv. 2(2) (emphasis added).

drawing conceptual distinctions between law and morality, as well as between law and religion, he achieves flexibility by placing these normative systems on a continuum, unifying them from a practical viewpoint. The importance attached in *JBP* to practical considerations deviates from the statement in Prol. 57, and perhaps for that reason has been virtually ignored in past studies. Here we would stress four points.

First, without taking into account Grotius's practical and utility-oriented approach, *JBP* cannot be read as a coherent study. For example, the argument that there is no conflict between the lawfulness of war and biblical precepts, the ultimate basis for the binding force of agreement, his approval of wars of punishment while urging restraint with respect to them, his approval of rights of war under the law of nations while calling for moderation—all these are made plausible only through his appeal to common sense, especially to considerations of utility. *JBP*'s fundamental premiss, that cataloguing just causes of war in a clear and comprehensive manner will serve as a deterrent to war, is not only based on his expectation that man as a rational being obeys moral and legal precepts. It is also based on his view that man will calculate that allies and subordinates may refuse to fight if he disregards the just causes of war. Grotius's model of 'rational man' is the common-sense image of a man basing his acts not only on legal and ethical requirements, but on considerations of practicality and utility.

Secondly, Grotius was by no means purely a speculative scholar. He spent most of his life in literary pursuits while grappling with the realities of politics. An outstanding jurist, he was active as the right-hand man of Oldenbarnevelt, one of the principal political leaders of the Netherlands of his time. After he fled his country, he spent most of his lifetime as a Swedish ambassador to France. Some observers have claimed that he was neither a competent statesman nor an able diplomat.[35] But even if he was not always successful in the world of diplomacy (at a time when bribery and other means were not considered disgraceful), or in the politics of the Netherlands, this does not mean that he ignored the importance of actual motives for conduct when he wrote his books. We are apt to be dazzled by Grotius's genius as a speculative thinker, but we should not overlook his political experience and aspirations, which

[35] See e.g. Vreeland 1917: 198–207.

persisted throughout his life.[36] *JBP* clearly reflects this aspect of his character, no matter how earnest his assertions to the contrary in the Prolegomena.

Thirdly, this emphasis on his practical viewpoint is not inconsistent with the fact that he was a pious Christian who continued to hope for the reunification of the church and made every effort towards that goal. In Furukawa's words, Grotius played in *JBP* a 'duet between love and calculation'. Deeply involved in the political strife unfolding in the Netherlands, and as a result of his political and diplomatic experience, Grotius knew that war could not be regulated by appeals to 'love' or piety alone. He had to introduce the element of 'calculation'.

Fourthly, Grotius sought a general theory to regulate and restrain wars in general. But the war he had to deal with was the prevalent religious war, where religion was manipulated as an excuse for violence. It may be that, in *JBP* as in his later writings, he hoped to help bring about a true reunification of Christianity by seeking to prevent religious antagonism from developing into armed conflict. His devotion in later life to the cause of the reunification of the church supports this view. But regulating and restraining wars, especially religious wars, was *the* goal in *JBP*, and religious considerations had to be subordinated if this goal was to be achieved. Thus 'law', independent of religion as a matter of principle, came to perform at centre stage, with an accompaniment of 'love and calculation', without which the audience would not have been convinced, playing behind the curtain.

11.6. The Position of *JBP* in the History of International Law

How should *JBP* be assessed in the history of international law? A complete answer to this question would require thorough analysis not only of *JBP* but of the work of other major scholars of international law and of the international usages, judgements of courts, and principal treaties of various periods. This is not the place for such an analysis. But underlying the appraisal of *JBP* by the contributors to this book is a common view of the history of international law as a whole which does need to be articulated, if only in a schematic and general way.

[36] For a similar view, see Roelofsen 1990: 97–8, 122–5.

11.6.1. Past Studies

JBP is the most famous work in the field of international law, and it was a commonplace to regard Grotius as the 'father of international law'. For example, in Lauterpacht-Oppenheim's *International Law*, generally regarded as the representative textbook of international law in this century, the account of the development of international law is divided into 'before Grotius' and 'after Grotius'. According to Lauterpacht and Oppenheim, Grotius 'bears by right the title of "Father of the Law of Nations"'.[37] Most earlier scholars shared this view.

However, this view has often been challenged and has been modified or qualified in various respects. When Grotius is called the 'father of international law' the reference is to modern international law. But was his thought so modern? This criticism has been made for almost a century by jurists, many of whom have a strong leaning towards the Scholastic or Thomist doctrine.[38] They cast doubt on traditional appraisals of Grotius as the 'father of modern natural law', many of which took literally the phrase 'even if we should concede that there is no God' in Prol. 11 and overestimated his 'modernity' based on the 'secularization of natural law'. The influence of the late Scholastic school on Grotius is now much better understood.[39] As a result, simplistic views of Grotius, whether as an advocate of modern natural law or a theorist in modern international law, are no longer held, at least by experts. Most of the treatises and articles published around the quadricentennial of Grotius's birth in 1983 either rejected this simplistic understanding altogether or severely qualified it.

The best recent study, by Haggenmacher, also emphasizes Grotius's pre-modernity. By rigorously analysing the original text and preceding theories, Haggenmacher demonstrates that Grotius's interest to the end was with the tradition of the just-war doctrine, and that *JBP* is not a book on modern international law.[40] In many respects we share Haggenmacher's view. None the less, to under-

[37] Oppenheim and Lauterpacht 1955: 91.

[38] See Nys 1882; Nys 1894; Kohler 1918; Vanderpol 1919; Sauter 1932; Rommen 1947; Ottenwälder 1950.

[39] In addition to those cited in n. 38, many of the studies on Grotius published in recent years (e.g. Edwards 1981; Ago 1983) agree in rejecting the idea of Grotius as a modernist who paved the way for a new era, emphasizing instead his continuity with the late Scholastics.

[40] Haggenmacher 1983.

stand Grotius solely within the framework of the late Scholastic school, or to over-emphasize his 'pre-modernity', is in turn to lose sight of the historical significance of his assertion of the independence of law (jurisprudence) from religion (theology) as a matter of principle. While conforming in its content to Christian precepts, natural law as conceived by Grotius is not *grounded* in them.[41] Moreover, Haggenmacher's view is open to question on two further counts. First, he tends to overestimate the continuity between *De Jure Praedae Commentarius* and *JBP*, and to underestimate the different positions from which Grotius wrote the two works. The former was written from the standpoint of a lawyer defending one of the parties to a dispute, the latter from that of one constructing an objective, all-inclusive science of law with a view to regulating and restraining war.[42] Secondly, while Haggenmacher is correct in saying that *JBP* was concerned with just-war doctrine and not with international law in the modern sense, he does not tell us why *JBP* came to be *read* as the latter. These two questions are closely connected, and have in common one important matter: how later generations read and understand a particular thinker's work. In order to answer the two questions, we must re-examine later generations' understanding of Grotius, as well as other major figures of international law, and clarify problematic features of such 'understandings'.

Who have been seen as the alternatives to Grotius as the principal 'founder' of international law? One option has been to substitute the Spanish school of Vitoria or Suárez: in particular James Brown Scott was most energetic in asserting this view.[43] However, as Nussbaum rightly points out,[44] Scott fails to analyse or understand key concepts in Vitoria and Suárez such as *jus gentium*, *civitas*, and *gens*. He merely takes certain statements made by the two theologians out of context and identifies in them the origins of the various principles and rules of modern international law. Scott's view of the origin of international law is thus unacceptable.[45] We

[41] 3.1.2(1). See also Ago 1983: 386, who states that 'Ce n'est qu'indirectement qu'on pourrait le rapporter à la volonté divine'.

[42] For a similar view see Oudendijk 1980: 7.

[43] See e.g. Scott 1934; 1944. The best concise description of the process of elevating Vitoria in place of Grotius is given in Haggenmacher 1988: 33–5.

[44] Nussbaum 1954: 296–304.

[45] Scott's voluminous, repetitive assertions apparently exerted a certain degree of influence in the early 20th cent., but there is little support for them today. Although

do not deny that Vitoria played a critical role in the history of international law. However, as will be discussed in the Appendix, this assessment is based on the view of Vitoria's thought as a prototype of modern Eurocentric international law, which justified European dominance over other civilizations. It is not concerned with sanctifying Vitoria, as Scott and others tended to do.

Alternatively Vattel has often been nominated as the 'father of international law'. It has been said that modern international law is to be defined as a law of an atomistic international society, based on the equality of independent states bound not to interfere in each other's domestic affairs. This concept was introduced, not by Grotius, but by proponents of a more rationalistic law of nature, including Pufendorf, Wolff, and Vattel. Of the three scholars, Vattel has had the greatest influence on later generations and must be considered the most important, as Tabata Shigejiro has convincingly argued.[46]

It is true that Grotius has no clear concept of a free and independent state as a distinct entity, bound to refrain from interfering in the domestic affairs of other states. Nor did he fully develop the idea of an atomistic international society composed of sovereign states. We can see in Pufendorf and Wolff a much clearer concept of an atomistic international society consisting of free and independent nations. On this view, interstate relations are nothing other than relations between free persons living in the state of nature.[47] On the other hand, the question of a law peculiar to interstate relations is treated only partially in Book VIII of Pufendorf's principal work, *De Jure Naturae et Gentium libri octo*. His overriding concern was to establish a general science of law, and his treatment of international law as a law regulating the relations between states patently lacks the independence, self-sufficiency, and comprehensiveness, all of which are required for a discipline of international law.

Compared with Pufendorf, Wolff's system of international law is much more autonomous, self-sufficient, and comprehensive.[48] However, his principal work in the field of international law, *Jus*

Truyol Serra seems somewhat dissatisfied with Nussbaum's criticism of Scott (e.g. Truyol Serra 1983: 438, 449 n. 14), he tacitly admits that Scott was careless in his reading of Grotius (ibid. 438). See also Haggenmacher 1988: 38–63.

[46] Tabata 1956; 1958; 1966: 49, 53–60.

[47] Pufendorf 1934 ⟨1688⟩, II. ii. 4; Wolff 1934 ⟨1764⟩, *praefatio*, p. I.

[48] For discussion of Wolff see Yanagihara 1981; 1989*a*, *b*; and 1991*a*, *b*.

Gentium Methodo Scientifica Pertractum, was not as successful in terms of popularity among his contemporaries and in its influence on later ages. By contrast, although Vattel was inferior to Wolff as a thinker and a disciplined scholar, his *Droit des gens* acquired far greater fame and influence. This is one of the major reasons why Vattel rather than Wolff is referred to in discussions of the origin of modern international law, and is usually referred to alongside Grotius in that context.[49]

Vattel emphasized the importance of the equality and independence of states, thereby affirming the decentralized and horizontal nature of international legal order. If one accepts the definition of international law in terms of horizontal norms among equal and independent states, and stresses the importance of 'influence on later ages', the view that Vattel is the founder of modern international law may be persuasive. However, the problem lies precisely in these two respects. First of all, does this definition cover all or at least the essential aspects of modern international law? It is true that modern international law has constituted a horizontal order in the formal sense of the term, for the international society lacks a monopoly of authority and power. But it is also true that international law has, in its basic features, been influenced by the maxim 'Might is right'. The validity of unequal treaties, the lawfulness of conquest as a territorial title, and the tacit approval of colonial rule (at least until 1919): all these features indicate the firmly established vertical structure of international law.[50]

Secondly, it is certainly true that one should take into consideration the influence of a work of some thinker on later ages in evaluating that work. However, when one refers to the 'influence' of some work or thinker, one has to ask what this influence means. In assessing Grotius in comparison with other authors, including Vattel, it is helpful to consider Lauterpacht's famous 'Grotian tradition' as a clue to the question of influence on and acceptance by later generations.

In an article which he himself regarded as his most important,

[49] See Sukiennicki 1927: 122–7; La Pradelle 1950: 123–66; Tabata 1955: 48–9, 52–3.

[50] Although the international legal order has a horizontal structure in the sense that power and authority are not monopolized by some unified institution, it does have a *functional* vertical structure in that its efficacy is to a large extent dependent upon the will and power of leading states to realize specific rules. This functional equivalent of the vertical structure of domestic legal orders is indispensable if international law is to exist as a legal order.

Lauterpacht enumerated eleven principles as constituting the 'Grotian tradition' in international law.[51] Among these, some principles are clearly inappropriate in understanding Grotius, such as the essential identity of states and individuals, and the fundamental rights and freedoms of the individual. Indeed many of these principles of the Grotian 'tradition' were hardly accepted in international law until very recently.[52] However, Lauterpacht is right when he states:

> What Grotius did was to endow international law with unprecedented dignity and authority by making it part not only of a general system of jurisprudence but also of a universal moral code . . . [A]t that time—as, indeed, at any time—it was important that the relations of states should be conceived and taught as part of ethics as well as part of law. Grotius' great merit is that he performed both tasks in one work.[53]

JBP played a paramount role in establishing the *raison d'être* of international law, and exerted great influence, in the sense that it asserted a normative framework for bodies politic lacking a common superior authority, a normative framework associated with the name of Grotius, and which has been established in the normative consciousness of peoples in general. In this essential contribution to human history, *JBP* occupies a far more important position than any other works, including Vattel's *Le Droit des gens*, in the field of international law.

11.6.2. The Succession to and Distortion of *JBP*: Ideological Function and Normative Significance

The historical significance of *JBP* has to be examined in four respects: its significance in the history of the theory of international law; its significance in the history of ideas; the problematic features of the 'inheritance' to Grotius by later scholars and thinkers; and the question of the 'acceptance' of Grotius in state practice.

(1) *Significance in the History of the Theory of International Law*

What influence did Grotius exert as a scholar of international law on his contemporaries and in subsequent ages? Oppenheim-

51 Lauterpacht 1975*b*: 327–63.
52 As Lauterpacht himself acknowledges: ibid. 363.
53 Ibid. 363–4.

Lauterpacht classified seventeenth- and eighteenth-century scholars of international law into three groups: the naturalists (Pufendorf, Thomasius, Hutcheson, Rutherforth, Barbeyrac, and Burlamaqui); the positivists (Rachel, Textor, Bynkershoek, Moser, and Martens); and the Grotians (Wolff, Vattel, and many others). Oppenheim = Lauterpacht argued that Grotius's influence had been so enormous that the majority of the authors of the seventeenth and eighteenth century were Grotians.[54] To place Grotius and his disciples between the two contrasting schools of naturalists and positivists may seem reasonable, considering Grotius's eclectic method. But further analysis at least qualifies this view. For example, it is highly doubtful to what extent Pufendorf, who is regarded as a leading naturalist, actually differed from the 'Grotians' who are said to recognize the rule of both natural law and positive law in international relations.

Pufendorf, following Hobbes, defined (positive) law as the dictate of a superior[55] and the relations between states as a natural condition where there was no superior.[56] Consequently, there was no room for positive international law, and the bulk of the law of nations in Grotius was regarded either as natural law, or as mere custom or temporary agreement falling within the realm of history. However, despite this apparently clear denial, Pufendorf actually incorporates Grotius's law of nations into his theoretical system by making full use of the latter's 'hypothetical' notion of natural law (*hypothetica praecepta juris naturalis*).[57] In addition, he devotes only 50 of the 928 pages in *De Jure Naturae et Gentium libri octo* to the relations between states, and deals with a very limited number of issues, such as the laws of war and peace treaties. His claim that only natural law exists between states[58] (Pufendorf as a typical 'naturalist') must be understood against this background. It is highly doubtful that he could have maintained his position had he discussed the actual rules regulating the relations between states in a comprehensive and detailed manner.

Grotius, no less than Pufendorf, emphasizes the importance of natural law as a source of rules regulating the relations between states as between private persons. Even realms regulated by human volitional law, i.e. by positive law, are ultimately under natural law

54 Oppenheim = Lauterpacht 1955: 98. See also Tabata 1966: 29–30.

55 Pufendorf 1934 ⟨1688⟩, I. vi. 4.

56 Ibid. II. iii. 24 (Lat. 158).

57 Ibid. II. ii. 4.

58 Ibid. II. iii. 23.

in its permissive domain.[59] Thus it is at least misleading to draw a rigid distinction between Pufendorf and Grotius, and to characterize the former simply as a 'naturalist'. Pufendorf is also known for his effort to integrate Grotius and Hobbes, and his works are strongly influenced by both. He was the first incumbent of the new chair of the Law of Nature and of Nations created at Heidelberg by the Elector of the Palatinate, and in advancing this budding discipline he repeatedly stressed the importance of Grotius. Pufendorf was himself famous as a natural-law scholar, and for a scholar of his calibre to stress the significance of Grotius no doubt contributed to the latter's renown. Many of the interpretations of Grotius that gained currency in later ages, including his reputation as the 'father' of international law, are largely based on Pufendorf.[60]

(2) *Significance in the History of Ideas*

However, it is primarily the appeal of *JBP* itself that enabled it to have such an enormous impact, not only on the history of international-law theory but also on the history of ideas in general. *JBP* was the most comprehensive among the writings dealing with war and peace, published at the very time when they were needed, in the midst of the Thirty Years War. With its combination of theoretical independence from yet practical absorption of religious norms, and its practical approach, it related both to existing ideas and institutions and to emerging ideas and institutions represented by the 'secularization' of law, respect for the right of ownership, and the sanctity of contract. Above all, Grotius tackled the problem of restraining war, state violence, the most difficult problem mankind has faced, taking up all matters deemed necessary to solve this problem, from the most fundamental to the most trivial.

By the middle of the twentieth century, more than 86 impres-

[59] 3.1.2(3). Although Ago's statement that, for Grotius, general international law existed only in the form of *jus naturale*, not *jus gentium* (1983: 387, 396–7 n. 37) is not correct, he is right to emphasize the significance of *jus naturale* as pivotal in *JBP*. See Onuma 1987: 406–11.

[60] See Pufendorf 1934 ⟨1688⟩, *V–VII et passim*, and the literature cited in nn. 38–9 for criticisms of this view. Together with Pufendorf, Barbeyrac's French trans. (which ran into 6 edns.—1724, 1729, 1746, 1759, and 2 edns. in 1768) played a significant role in spreading Grotius's reputation. Barbeyrac's annotated trans. is a daring one, including the translator's characteristic, sometimes even high-handed interpretations. Although Barbeyrac's 1720 edn., together with his notes, is praised by Tuck (1979: 73 n. 31), we agree with Haggenmacher that Barbeyrac's version was too intrusive to be an authentic trans. (1983: 4 n. 4).

sions of *JBP* had been published, including 52 editions of the Latin original, 9 French translations, 10 English, 6 Dutch, 6 Spanish, 1 Chinese, and 1 Japanese.[61] It is true that its influence cannot be assessed simply on the basis of the number of editions. Moreover, the number of new impressions of the Latin original with detailed explanatory notes fell off sharply after the Lausanne edition of 1751. Thereafter, it has been said, *JBP* was replaced by Vattel's *Droit des gens* (first published in 1758) as the most influential international-law treatise.[62] Vattel was cited far more frequently than Grotius in American cases involving international law decided in the eighteenth and nineteenth centuries.[63] This was a period when positivism dominated all fields of learning, including jurisprudence. Given this general historical background, it is not surprising that Grotius, as a representative advocate of natural law, should lose the high esteem he had earlier enjoyed.

However, it is simplistic to assert that Grotius was replaced by Vattel. It is more accurate to say that *JBP* was read more as a classic involving justice, natural law, international law, jurisprudence, history, Roman law, etc. than as a textbook dealing with international law on an 'up-to-date' basis. Had *JBP* been written merely as a textbook of international law, it might well have been revised by subsequent editors in order that its content would be relevant to each subsequent period. But *JBP* was not written as such a textbook, and apart from the addition of comments and explanatory notes, the text itself remained essentially unrevised. Vattel's book, written in French, was more comprehensive than *JBP* as a textbook on international law and better adapted to the eighteenth-century world. It is hardly surprising that it should have been read widely by eighteenth- and nineteenth-century diplomats and international lawyers, have been again and again reprinted and edited, and have been often cited by courts.[64] But this does not mean that Vattel commanded more authority than Grotius. Even in the nineteenth century, an age dominated by legal positivism,

[61] Based on the year 1950, when the Japanese trans. and the new German trans. were published, this count includes reprinted edns. and abridgements. Apparently there were partial trans. into Italian and Russian (Ter Meulen *et al.* 1950: nos. 670–4), as well as a Swedish trans. (Nussbaum 1954: 113).

[62] Reeves 1925*b*: 257; Starke 1972: 163–4.

[63] Dickinson 1932: 259 n. 132.

[64] Even on this point it is doubtful whether Vattel surpassed Grotius in judicial precedents and publications, except in the USA. See Nussbaum 1954: 162–3.

many textbooks on international law cited Grotius as the primary authority.[65] For good or ill, he was, and continues to be, regarded as something more than mere international lawyer.

That *JBP* is more than an international-law textbook is evident also from the attitudes towards it taken by Locke, Rousseau, Saint-Pierre, Adam Smith, and other major figures in the history of ideas. Whether approving or criticizing, these thinkers confronted *JBP* as a treatise on philosophy and method applied beyond the limits of a single discipline. It is this quality that made *JBP* survive as a classic, even in the late nineteenth century when Vattel's work was no longer much referred to. And *JBP* was revived as part of the revival of the natural-law and just-war doctrine in the twentieth century. Although there are many problems in equating Grotius's theory with modern theories of natural law and just war, the fact remains that *JBP* has been read in such a way.

(3) *Problems in the 'Acceptance' of* JBP*: Normativity and Ideology*

But in the way *JBP* was read and passed down there lies a vital problem. In many cases *JBP* was read or 'inherited' in a way which was contrary to Grotius's own intentions. This 'inheritance', however cruel it might be to Grotius himself, sometimes paradoxically revealed the logical consequences of *JBP*. Typical examples include: (1) that the war-as-status concept within the framework of a monistic just-war doctrine came to be identified with the war-as-status concept within the dualistic framework of international law, which regards war as a metajuridical phenomenon, a completely different assumption from Grotius's; (2) that the rationalist theory of agreement guided by considerations of practicality came to be understood solely within the context of voluntarism, represented by the maxim *pacta sunt servanda*; and, (3) that the multi-layered normative structure, Grotius's most important device for regulating and restraining war, was dismantled, as law came increasingly to be regarded as independent of religion and morality, with the result that the substantive just-war doctrine and the 'laws of war' (including *temperamenta*) were regarded as independent categories, although both were thought of as 'inherited' from Grotius.

[65] Grotius was highly praised in representative 19th-cent. textbooks on international law, including Klüber 1847: 15; Phillimore 1985 ⟨1854⟩, pp. viii–ix; Wheaton 1863: 1–2; Martens 1883: 202–3; Holzendorf 1885: 395–414.

It is certainly true that many of these later misinterpretations and misunderstandings of *JBP* resulted from a lack of historical perspective, or from a tendency to wrench Grotius's words out of context in order to lend authority to later scholars' own views. It is always necessary to reinterpret the past, to try to reconstruct major works in a way which is as faithful as possible to their intent and original context. Naïve projections of modern ideas or concepts on to *JBP* must be avoided, as this study has repeatedly stressed. However, that misreadings and misinterpretations take a certain persistent form itself tells us something important. They cannot, and should not, simply be dismissed as mistaken. Grotius himself has to take at least part of the blame. In order to achieve his paramount aim of restraining war, Grotius often had to sacrifice logical consistency and systematic clarity. The reader of *JBP* is often left with a maze of ambiguities and contradictory interpretations. Given these internal tensions, it was virtually inevitable that in later ages scholars should differ in their reading of *JBP* and in emphasizing its various aspects.[66]

Shortcomings are often the obverse of strengths—and this is the case here. The ambiguity of *JBP*, which bewildered later scholars, is a choice that Grotius, living in a period of transition when Europe was shifting from a 'religious' to a 'secular' age, or the age of feudalism to the age of nation states, had to make if he was to realize his aim. This ambiguity itself reflects the fertility and productiveness of Grotius's thought. It is because of this quality that Grotius has been handed down and developed over the years. This process has been a complex one, defined by conditions prevailing in each age. It may be that it expressed Grotius's ideas in a way significantly different from the original, but this does not necessarily signify a 'betrayal' of original intent. As Kasai points out with respect to the relationship between *temperamenta* and the laws of war in the later period, the original intention of Grotius 'may be correctly inherited by being misread'.[67]

It is in this complex sense that we can find features of the 'Grotian tradition' in many areas of international law. Despite our criticism of Lauterpacht's version of the 'Grotian tradition', we can accept ideas which are fundamental to the structure of the discipline: for example, the subjection of the totality of international

[66] See Roelofsen 1983*a*: 16–17; 1990: 125. [67] Kasai 1984: 55.

relations to the rule of law, the rejection of *raison d'état*,[68] the binding force of promises, and the idea of peace as the 'normal condition' of states. It can also be argued that the acceptance of natural law as a source of international law is recognized, for example in the form of arbitration *ex aequo et bono*, in the assumed universality underlying general principles of law, and in the comparatively greater role of individual scholars in the creation and development of international law. Many other rules and principles of international law can be thought of as associated with Grotius. They include the principle of the freedom of the seas, the *culpa* doctrine in the theory of state responsibility, the right of legation based on the notion of quasi-extraterritoriality, the distinction between belligerents and civilians, even the just-war doctrine itself, which is said to have been revived in the present century.[69]

Is this identification of so many rules and principles of international law with the name of Grotius a mark of success, even of grandeur? Considering the realities of international law on one hand, and Grotius's passionate desire and the great pains he went to in writing *JBP* on the other, one cannot help feeling a kind of 'emptiness' in the outcome. Is not Grotius's fame after all a pyrrhic victory? What would his reaction be to the modern world and its system of international law, which is held to derive ultimately from his ideas? One thing is certain. His thought has been influential because it conformed to the conditions of later ages. This implies that his thought was brought into conformity with the dominant ideas and the power structure of a particular age through a process of struggle and compromise. In other words, to the extent that Grotius's thought was accepted, it also functioned as an ideology in support of the dominant institutions of the age concerned, whether in the international or domestic arena.

This discussion has an important bearing on the problem of the acceptance of Grotius in state practice. The 'inheritance' of Grotius's ideas by scholars, whether or not it deviated from the original intent, did not generally involve deliberate distortion. When a state adopts Grotius's theory, the case is different. How-

[68] However, one can argue that since the dualistic scheme 'reason of individuals' versus 'reason of state' is not to be found in Grotius, it is not surprising that *raison d'état* was rejected. Even to inquire whether *raison d'état* was approved or rejected, in a sense, involves projecting modern notions on to the past.

[69] See also Kingsbury and Roberts 1990: 5–6, 15–16, 51–64.

ever strongly Grotius may reject *raison d'état*, the state accepts (or rather *uses*) Grotius on the basis of what is beneficial to it—whether in the long or short term. That a particular theory is accepted in state practice means that both intentional and unintentional distortions, as well as one-sided emphases and misunderstandings, are also accepted. Such 'acceptance' cannot be expressed merely as the triumph of the theory.

Consider, for example, how Grotius's paramount concern of restraining war has been 'accepted' by states. Grotius is often referred to when particular rules or principles which correspond to *temperamenta* or his just-war doctrine are asserted by states, or are alleged to be accepted in later state practice. It is certainly true that many rules and basic ideas of the laws of war established in the late nineteenth and early twentieth centuries, such as the prohibition of devastation and pillage, correspond to *temperamenta*. Nor is it surprising that Grotius was relied on as an authority when the 'outlawry of war' was emphasized in the twentieth century, because the persistent view of the liberty of all states to go to war (the non-discriminatory view of war of the nineteenth and early twentieth centuries) had to be overcome. However, while Grotius's ideas in *temperamenta* were 'accepted' as part of the positive law of war, they were completely cut off from his substantive just-war doctrine. His paramount aim of restraining *both* the outbreak of war and the conduct of war was thus flatly denied in the very process of 'acceptance'. Similarly his just-war doctrine was often used by states to justify acts whose lawfulness was doubtful according to positive international law: for example, the military assistance given by the 'neutral' United States to Great Britain in 1939–41, the legal foundation of the Nuremberg and Tokyo War Crimes Trials.[70] These and other cases show the distortions involved in the 'acceptance' of *JBP* by states.

For ideas or theories to have any real meaning in the domain of state power, they will usually have to go through such a process. But there is no cause for despair. In many cases a doctrine or idea first seemingly adopted as an ideology by a particular power later came to restrain the latter's conduct. For example, the notion of outlawry of war, once utilized as an ideology justifying the assistance given to Britain by the United States, later oriented the

[70] See Onuma 1975: 121–57.

conduct of the United States, giving rise to the notion of 'crimes against peace',[71] and being used against the United States itself by the anti-war movement in the Vietnam War. The notion of the 'sacred trust of civilization', an ideology used to justify colonial domination, was taken over by the League of Nations' mandate system, and has been used to criticize not only South Africa's rule over Namibia but the activities of the United States in Micronesia, and of Australia, New Zealand, and the United Kingdom in Nauru. In the final analysis, what scholars can do is to strive, through professional detachment and scholarly technique, to minimize doctrinal distortions—to eliminate them is impossible—and to assume, in full awareness of the political realities, responsibility for those (perhaps limited) realms where doctrine may have some effect.

Seeing the tragedy of the Thirty Years War, Grotius shut his eyes to the structural violence of 'peace' and focused his efforts on reducing overt violence. Against this background, it is interesting to ask what would be the equivalent work in today's world. Would it warn against a nuclear war that could annihilate the human race? Or call for the relief of minorities, refugees, or political prisoners, or the numberless victims of continuing religious, ethnic, and political persecutions? Or denounce the stark contrast between the poverty of the Third World and the gluttony of the advanced industrial nations? Or would it accept the logic of deterrence, based on the 'practical wisdom' that the lesser evil of local war and tyranny is to be preferred to the risk of total war?

No doubt these questions are beyond the realm of scholarly inquiry. But ultimately no learning can be vivid and creative unless backed by imagination and intellectual curiosity. Without these there will no longer be learning, only the skeleton of learning. Certainly *JBP* is a book worth researching in its own right. But considering how seminal a work it has been, *JBP* the more keenly recalls Basho's maxim: 'Seek not what the sages taught, but what the sages sought.'[72]

[71] See ibid. 362–70, 374–84.

[72] Falk's emphasis on the 'Grotian quest' rather than the 'Grotian solution' (1981*b*: pp. xiii–xxi) calls to mind this saying by a distinguished 18th-cent. Japanese poet—an example, perhaps, of the universality of truth, overcoming barriers of nationality and time.

Appendix

Eurocentrism in the History of International Law

The reappraisal of Grotius's place in the history of international law cannot be discussed separately from the reappraisal of the history of international law itself. Modern international law is a result of the globalization of the European interstate order, which was one of many regional interstate orders which existed at some time or other. In writing *JBP*, Grotius assumed that his standpoint, terminology, framework, and theory had a universal validity. However, this universality was actually confined within the European world of his time. It was only after European powers subjugated non-European nations and forced them to accept European international law as regulating interstate relations all over the world that Grotius's 'universality' became truly universal. Thus it is not the quality of the theory alone, but the theory in combination with an actual superiority of power, that turned European international law into global international law.

As is demonstrated in the preceding chapters, Grotius's theory is certainly universal in the sense that its key concept, *jus naturale*, is independent of Christianity and can be validly applied as a neutral norm to non-Christians as well. However, theoretical universality and neutrality are not peculiar to Grotius. They can be found in other writers such as Vitoria (although their kind of universality and neutrality is somewhat different from in Grotius). Moreover, these ideas had distinct implications for the process by which the superiority of European powers, in terms of military strength, came to be reflected in the globalization of the European interstate order, a process which took its first manifest step in the Spanish conquest of America. Thus it is necessary to reconsider the dominant view of Grotius as the 'father of international law' from a viewpoint critical of Eurocentrism. This leads us to reconsider the significance of Francisco de Vitoria, not for the purpose of deifying him in place of Grotius, but because he embodied the 'universal' or 'neutral' theory in the context of the military superiority of Europe, a prototype of the structure of modern international law.

1. The 'Partitioning of the World' by Spain and Portugal

Before the fifteenth century, the world was characterized by the existence of independent regional civilizations—Europe, China, Ottoman, etc.—separated by oceans, mountain ranges, and other natural barriers. Although the constituent members and the geographical scope of these civilizations changed from one period to another with the rise and decline of particular civilizations, they consisted basically of bodies politic in subordinate positions, and an empire or central powers that enjoyed military, economic, and cultural superiority. In other words, they formed loose systems of states or bodies politic based on a hierarchy of power. Since those spheres of civilization were aggregates of bodies politic sharing a common culture and normative concepts and possessing a certain degree of permanence, they can be described as coexisting regional interstate orders, or at least interstate systems. Relations between these regions were usually limited, although they were not wholly cut off from each other, as evidenced by the trickle of trade and the occasional dispatching of missions.[1] In some cases an empire within a certain sphere of civilization possessing enormous military strength would invade another sphere of civilization and bring the latter under its rule, for example, the expeditions of Alexander the Great or Genghis Khan. None of these extended rules, however, lasted very long.

These conditions, which had prevailed since ancient times, did not change much before the late fifteenth century. However, the age of 'geographical exploration' and the 'partitioning of the world' by Spain and Portugal marked the first step in the development of European civilization into a global civilization, a process extending over the next four centuries. One may argue that we are still preoccupied by Eurocentrism if we define the late fifteenth century as marking the first step of the globalization of European civilization. If one compares contemporary civilizations, Europe was not at that time the leading or even the most remarkable one. In the world of Islam, the Ottoman empire, having already overthrown the Eastern Roman empire in 1453, enjoyed its golden age under Suleiman I the Magnificent. In East Asia there existed a Sinocentric tributary system composed of China under the Ming dynasty and its peripheral nations. Although the Ming dynasty's golden age was already over by the late fifteenth century, still Ming society was probably far more prosperous and civilized than the contemporary European societies.[2]

[1] In the case of peripheral bodies politic or nations, where the military, economic, and cultural relations with the central power or powers were limited, contact with bodies politic belonging to other spheres of civilization was sometimes substantial. In such a case, the very sense of belonging to or affiliation with a particular civilization or central power was tenuous.

[2] Various assessments have been made of the Ming dynasty, but scholars are

None the less, the fact remains that it was neither Muslims nor Chinese who came to dominate the world. It was the European states which established the global colonial system. It was European international law, not the Sinocentric tributary system, which came to regulate interstate relations on a global scale. Accepting these as undeniable facts, we must explore the structure of this global domination. It is only through the acceptance and understanding of this history, not through an arbitrary adoption of a 'non-Eurocentric' viewpoint, or through an overestimation of the non-European 'origin' of, 'influence' upon, or 'contribution' to the ideas and institutions of international law, that we can truly liberate ourselves from Eurocentrism. Thus, we must treat the late fifteenth and early sixteenth centuries as marking the first step of the globalization of European civilization, one of the regional civilizations of the time.

By this time Portugal had already actively begun exploring the coastal regions of north-west Africa. Spain had also commenced its world exploration. These two powers engaged in a fierce competition of exploration, expedition, and colonial acquisition. Columbus's arrival in America in 1492 and Vasco da Gama's 'discovery' of the seaway to India in 1498 were epoch-making events, inaugurating a period of Western 'discovery' and colonial acquisition. There followed a series of invasions and conquests—including the establishment of footholds in Goa, Malacca, and Amboina by Alberquerque (the Portuguese viceroy in India), the conquest of Mexico by Cortés, and of Peru by Pizarro and others. Thus, from the late fifteenth century, Portugal and Spain established their respective spheres of influence, the former in Asia and Africa, the latter in the Americas. The pope issued a number of bulls sanctifying and justifying the 'partitioning of the world' between Portugal and Spain,[3] although the two powers sometimes modified these bulls, varying the line of demarcations of their respective spheres of influence by bilateral agreements.[4] They carried out their expeditions and colonial acquisitions mainly under the pretext of spreading Christianity, which was naturally the major theme of the papal bulls.

This 'partitioning of the world' by the Iberian nations involved little more than control over certain strategic points. In the case of the Americas, where the Inca and Aztec empires rapidly collapsed, the Spanish rule did involve a degree of territorial control. But considering the scarcity of the

agreed that the Sinocentric interstate order based on the tributary system was conspicuous during the Ming dynasty. See e.g. Mote 1988*a*: 2.

[3] The following bulls were issued: *Inter caetera*, 3 May 1493; *Eximiao devotionis*, 3 May 1493; *Inter caetera*, 4 May 1493; *Dudum siqudem*, 26 Sept. 1493 (Davenport 1917: 56–83).

[4] e.g. treaty between Spain and Portugal concluded at Tordesillas, 7 June 1493 (ibid. 84–100).

Spanish population in the vast areas of America, it was very different from the image that the term territorial control connotes today. In the case of the Portuguese 'commercial empire', the reality of its control was even more tenuous. The empires that existed in Asia (e.g. the Ming dynasty in China) were far more powerful than Portugal and boasted a far superior culture. Even the nations in south-east Asia were not so weak as to allow a small European state like Portugal to impose territorial rule over them. What Portugal was capable of achieving, and what it actually did achieve, was to establish a foothold in the major ports of the Asian continent and islands, largely on the strength of its superiority in firearms, and to enter the commercial network that already existed from East Asia to Arabia, thereby acquiring a certain degree of power over commercial trade.[5]

Furthermore, any overall view of power relations between Europe and other regional powers reveals that the image of a lively, active, expanding Europe is very one-sided. It was precisely during the period of 'European expansion' that Suleiman the Magnificent steadily extended Ottoman control over European territories and menaced the Habsburg empire by the siege of Vienna. The whole Christian world was gripped by the nightmare of being overridden by the Muslim Turks.

The situation with regard to the recognition of the legitimacy of the 'partitioning of the world' was basically the same. Even in Europe, England and the other Protestant powers did not recognize it. Not even Catholic France gave it clear approval. To the nations and peoples belonging to regions other than Europe, the 'partitioning of the world' meant literally nothing. To China the 'partitioning' must have appeared nothing more than a joke conjured up by barbarians. It is not until the late-nineteenth century that the Chinese empire was forced to recognize the bankruptcy of its Sinocentrism.

Despite this, the historical significance of the 'partitioning of the world' between Spain and Portugal cannot be denied. Its significance lies in the fact that for the first time in history, permanent human relations came to be established on a global scale as intercontinental relations—although Oceania was not incorporated into these relations for another two-and-a-half centuries. Commercial intercourse between Europe, Asia, and Africa was vitalized by the 'discovery of the New World' and the exploration of the silver mines there. Due to the tremendous flow of silver from America to Europe, a standing trade network was established between Europe, Asia, Africa, and America. In the sixteenth century, the intercontinental trade between Asia and central America was also established. In this way, for the first time in world history, a standing global system of human activities arose, under the hegemony of European powers.[6]

[5] Kawakita 1970: 123–7. [6] See Otsuka 1969: 37–73.

The claims of these European powers to dominance were justified in various ways. Some relied on the authority of the pope, resorting to the theory of *dominium mundi*. Others emphasized the power and authority of the Roman empire. Still others resorted to the title of discovery. Of all these arguments, Francisco de Vitoria's theory is most remarkable, for it exhibits a prototype of normative justification of international law which remained basically the same for the next four centuries, a period during which the European powers (and later also the United States) exercised hegemony over the world.

2. International Law as an Ideology of Modern European Civilization

Through history, various empires asserted their universality and regarded their own interstate order, with their own nation at its centre, as the world itself. But none of these empires actually amounted to anything more than a regional interstate order. By contrast, the European interstate order as it expanded overcame the other regional powers and their regional interstate orders, actually achieving the status of an international order covering the globe.[7]

This was a result of a series of dazzling successes achieved in the 'modern age of Europe': the stimulation of commercial activities brought about as a result of the 'geographical exploration'; the Renaissance and the Reformation, which freed men's energy from the fetters of religion; and the Industrial Revolution that was prepared by the Scientific Revolution and flowered in the eighteenth and nineteenth centuries. These developments conferred upon European nations overwhelming economic and military strength. Furthermore, with the expansion of such economic penetration and political or territorial rule (the colonization and semi-colonization of the various regions of the world by the European powers), even in the field of intellectual activity such as learning, education, and the arts, not to mention science and technology, European achievements overwhelmed those of non-European peoples and came to dominate, as if European culture was self-evidently the most advanced culture in the world.

For example, in the eighteenth century, the early European visitors to China, the 'southern barbarians', were forced to negotiate within the Sinocentric tributary system. But in the Opium War of 1840, the Europeans appeared with military strength unmatched by China and eventually forced

[7] It was not a single empire but an interstate system under the hegemony of several Western powers that covered the entire world. Whether we should call this an interstate order, an interstate system, or a world capitalist system is, to a large extent, a matter of semantics. See Wallerstein 1974: 15 ff.; Wight 1977: ch. 1; Bull 1977.

the Ching dynasty to surrender. Of course in Chinese history the 'Middle Kingdom' had often been brought under military control by 'barbarians'. The Yuan dynasty was a case in point, and the very dynasty that surrendered to Great Britain in the Opium War was one established by the Manchus, a nomadic Mongolian people native to Manchuria. However, the Chinese culture was sufficiently strong to assimilate even such powerful 'barbarians', which is why China was thought of as the 'Middle Kingdom'.

This did not happen in the case of the European powers which forced China to surrender in the nineteenth century. Not only did they deny the superiority of Chinese culture, but in most cases they looked upon themselves as *the* bearers of civilization. Meanwhile, China was forced to recognize not only the military superiority of the 'barbarians', but also their cultural superiority. This meant that the 'barbarians' were no longer barbarians, and that China was no longer the Middle Kingdom. China had no choice but to follow the humiliating path of assimilating itself into modern European civilization.[8]

The interior regions of Africa were not incorporated into the Eurocentric international order until the late nineteenth century, but they too succumbed to colonial rule at the turn of the century. Japan escaped being colonized, and struggled with all its might to catch up with the Western powers. From the middle of the nineteenth century, it sought to assimilate European ideas and technology in order to make the nation richer and more powerful, and to be recognized as a 'civilized nation' in the Eurocentric international society.[9] Central and South American nations separated themselves from European colonial rule during the nineteenth century, but remained under European dominance in terms of, among other things, language, religion, and the tendency to equate modernization with Westernization.

It was this background that produced the way of thinking which assumes European ideas, notions, standards and institutions as taken for granted or as having universal validity; the modern age in Europe as the modern age in world history; the Christian calendar as the common calendar of the world; English and French as the common languages of the world; the terminology which refers to Syria and Lebanon as the 'Near East', Iran and Iraq as the 'Middle East', and China and Japan as the 'Far East'. In

[8] For details, see Sato 1977. Because Sinocentrism was, from the Chinese perspective, so self-evident and had endured so long, it took a considerable time even after the defeat in the Opium War to adopt the European concept of an international society composed of sovereign states on an equal footing, and to abandon the traditional concept of universe with the Chinese emperor at its centre. Thus it was only after the defeat of the Sino-Japanese War (1894–5) and the loss of suzerainty over Korea that China finally adhered to the European concept of international society.

[9] See Onuma 1986: 23–47, esp. 27–31, 40–1.

other words, there has been a tendency for a Eurocentric way of thinking to dominate intellectual life throughout the world.[10]

We have time and again pointed out that a major characteristic of Grotius's theory of law is its claim to universality, centred on his concept of natural law, and that it has an all-inclusive basis which to some extent justifies his claim. This claim to universality has so far been accepted without question. But underlying it is the fact that the world has been dominated by a Eurocentric way of thinking. The law of nature in *JBP* is theoretically independent of the Christian God, and to that extent goes beyond Christian 'universality'. However, the existence and universality of natural law, which according to Grotius should be self-evident, is verified inductively and empirically on the basis of a vast array of material covering the period from European antiquity to medieval Europe. This array of material comes almost entirely from the framework of European civilization.[11] While Christ is cited, Buddha is not; Aristotle and Cicero are quoted as authority, Confucius is not.

True, there is a distinction between the universality of ideas and the universality of the authorities cited as giving expression to those ideas. But it is obvious that the natural law which Grotius insists is the universal law of mankind would not have been recognized as such, for example, in China or in India at the same period. Moreover, Grotius did not insist that the law of nations must be always common to all nations, but was satisfied if it was accepted by a great many nations, 'European nations', or 'nations having the same higher civilization as that of Europe'.[12] Tacitly assumed here is the practice of states within the sphere of European civilization, a civilization going back to the age of the Greek city-states and located in a particular part of the world.

Alexandrowicz once criticized the nineteenth-century positivist school for abandoning the universality maintained by the natural-law school.[13] It is true that many international lawyers in the nineteenth century argued that positive international law was valid only for European nations. But we should not overlook the fact that the very 'universality' claimed by the natural-law school was also basically limited to Europe.[14]

Of course, it is not fair to point out only the limitations or problematic features of European thought. Non-European thought was often no more universal. At least modern European thought contained normative elements that were more universal and open than those found in the dominant concepts of other regional interstate orders. Concepts of fundamental

[10] Onuma 1984: 1–5; 1988: 55–7, 95–101.

[11] See the interesting discussion of Wight 1977: 121–2, 125–8.

[12] Prol. 17; I. I. 14(1); III. iv. 15(1) and 16(1).

[13] Alexandrowicz 1967.

[14] Onuma 1987: 438–43. For a similar view, see Wight 1977: 119.

human rights, the doctrine of popular sovereignty, the principle of separation of powers, and the concept of equality of states are examples. To some extent non-European peoples may have been forced to accept these ideas, but they also willingly accepted them. It was not naked power alone, but the combination of physical and economic power and the power of ideas, that consolidated European dominance.

Moreover, modern international law, as elaborated in Europe, is probably more desirable, certainly more suited, to the era of nation states, than any of the regional alternatives. This is because, *inter alia*, modern international law recognizes the equality of states as its fundamental principle. Interstate normative ideas in other regions, whether in Eastern Asia or in the Islamic world, were more or less characterized by their hierarchical nature, involving a tributary system or suzerain relations. Such a system might work in a regional interstate order where a single empire can subordinate other nations, but cannot work in a global interstate order where no single state has the capacity and resources to subordinate all others.[15]

But one should not over-emphasize the egalitarian aspects of modern international law. It is the concept of formal equality that has prevailed as a principle of international law.[16] Although there has been no single empire subjugating all other nations, there has always existed a group of empires, or Great Powers, ready to enforce their political will upon weaker nations. The efficacy of international law has been dependent upon the collective will of these major powers. Even within Europe, the rights of smaller nations were often restricted, neglected, or even violated under the pretext of the balance of power (which was once regarded by some as a principle of international law). The validity of unequal treaties imposed upon weak or small nations has been recognized. The most conspicuous example of this concealed hierarchical aspect of modern international law can be seen in the relations between European and non-European nations.

In the process of codifying rules concerning state responsibility, Padilla Nervo, a member of the International Law Commission, commented that:

> The vast majority of new States had taken no part in the creation of the many institutions of international law which were consolidated and systematised in the nineteenth century . . . With state responsibility, however, international rules were established, not merely without reference to small states but against them, and were based almost entirely on the inequality between Great Powers and small States. (ILC 1957: 155.)

[15] There is a major problem of cost and efficiency in maintaining a great empire. A truly world empire probably cannot exist because it would cost too much to maintain its order in the form of a state. See Wallerstein 1974: 15–17.

[16] Onuma 1989: 145–6. For a slightly different view, see Tabata 1958: 5–42, 108–56.

Fitzmaurice rejected this criticism, citing the fact that the rules relating to the denial of justice had existed between states of equal status 300 years prior to Grotius:

> The reason why the rules had been evolved was that the treatment of foreigners in most European countries had, in those days, been such as to give rise to numerous altercations and disputes. It was . . . perfectly natural that centuries later, where foreigners were treated in that way, the European countries should have *applied* the same rules that had enabled them to settle such problems satisfactorily among themselves.(Ibid. 163; emphasis added.)

This argument arose out of the Commission's discussion of individual rules concerning state responsibility, and Padilla Nervo was directing his criticism at the nineteenth-century positivist school of international law.[17] But the issue can be understood at a more general level. As Fitzmaurice states, it was certainly 'entirely natural' for European nations to 'apply' to non-European nations the rules which had proved appropriate for them. But he ignores the essential point that it was not only European countries that had rules applicable to interstate relations; non-European nations had their own rules and institutions. The real question was: which was to prevail?

When two nations or groups of nations which have different interstate rules enter into and regulate their relations on the basis of a shared normative system, they must adopt either one or the other of their systems, or a third (perhaps hybrid) system that both can accept. Thus it is entirely possible for European and non-European nations to adopt as shared rules the norms that were valid for European nations. This did occur in the pre-modern period, just as the converse also occurred (e.g. Europeans had to obey Sinocentric rituals and other rules when they wanted to have trade relations with China).[18]

[17] Rules relating to state responsibility, together with the protection of aliens and the legitimacy of intervention in certain cases were, as Padilla Nervo claimed, established in the 19th cent., in the interest of the Great Powers. Great Britain, then the most influential nation in the field of international law and relations, rapidly increased its investments abroad during the early 19th cent., organizing the world economy by reason of her vast capacity to produce and invest. The safety of investment became more and more crucial to her economic dominance. In 1848, Palmerston made it clear that, although the British government had been reluctant to collect debts from debtor nations, it was now ready to do so. Later events revealed Great Britain intervening forcibly in the affairs of debtor nations to secure the debts of its nationals. The latter half of the 19th cent. witnessed a considerable development in the law of state responsibility and the protection of aliens. The growth of these two fields was a reflection of the growing economic dominance of the North Atlantic powers over Latin America.

[18] According to the Chinese notion of interstate relations (a part of cosmology), the emperor was emperor of the universe. His task was to enlighten all people under heaven. Trade with foreign nations or peoples was construed, in theory, as accepting

The problem is that, in the case of modern international law, many rules advocated by European nations were not applied by agreement based on the free will of non-European nations on an equal footing with European nations. For non-European nations, the application of those rules in their relations with European nations was tantamount to an imposition. They were more or less *forced* on them because of the superior military and economic strength of the European powers. For example, when China and Japan became members of the Eurocentric international order in the nineteenth century, they were effectively compelled to abandon the Confucian norms which had traditionally governed their foreign relations, and instead to abide by the rules of European international law. What Fitzmaurice called 'application' was little more than coercion.

Furthermore, many of the non-European peoples were first ruled as European colonies, and incorporated, as it were from within, into the Eurocentric international order. From the beginning these colonies and their people were not recognized as subjects of international law. Colonies were within the 'domestic' jurisdiction of the colonial rulers: 'domestic matters' were an area of non-intervention in international law. Moreover, in modern international law, the lawfulness of colonial acquisitions by European nations was never repudiated (although the principle of self-determination was used to reverse the effects of colonial acquisition, to a considerable extent, in the process of post-war decolonization).

It has been sometimes argued that Vattel's *Droit des gens* is 'international law based on the principles of 1789', and that whereas Grotius wrote the international law of absolutism, Vattel wrote the international law of political liberty.[19] Vattel did indeed stress the principle of non-intervention, arguing for a system of international law based on the concept of equality among states. But this assessment of Vattel is one-sided. Viewed in the context of the European colonization of the Americas, his theory has other aspects.

Vattel's theory was strongly influenced by Locke, who sanctified ownership as an absolute concept by way of the idea that ownership of property is a product of investing human labour in land. This was an important theoretical device for overcoming Hobbes's view, which on the basis of scarcity of resources and the behavioural principle of man's desire for self-preservation, concluded that the human condition is a 'war of all against all (*bellum omnium contra omnes*)'.[20] However, when Locke's theory was 'applied' to the relations between the colonists or conquerors who arrived

tribute from them and granting donations in return. Because those foreign people engaged in trade were deemed to have recognized the authority of the emperor by their 'tributes', they were expected to abide by various rules based on Confucianism, which regulated the relations between the emperor and foreign peoples.

[19] La Pradelle 1916: pp. xxviii–xxx, lv.

[20] See Fukuda 1971: 283–6.

in the 'New World' from Europe and the original inhabitants of America and Oceania, it served to justify the former in taking away the latter's land. Locke's theory enabled European colonists to regard the land on which the original inhabitants lived according to their own concept of labour, under a condition of scarce population, as being empty land to which labour had not been added, and over which ownership had accordingly not been established.[21]

Thus, the differences in life-style in different cultural settings was construed as a matter of laziness or lack of industriousness. The whole process of forceful colonization by Europeans could thus be justified and sanctified through the labour-investment doctrine. It is to be noted that this era of wholesale colonization of the American continent by Europeans was considered to be the era of Enlightenment. The term 'civilization' was also born during this period.[22] The idea of progress took shape, first in Turgot (1750), and most evidently in Condorcet (1775). The belief in the ever-conquering power of enlightenment based on modern science dominated the era.

Vattel's theory was widely accepted in the United States. This was partly because it was critical of absolutism and even recognized secession from despotic regimes. At the same time, it should be remembered that his theory of colonial acquisition conveniently justified the expulsion of the original Amerindian inhabitants by the European colonists.

Rules regulating state responsibility, the validity of unequal treaties, and Vattel's theory relating to colonization are only examples of the hierarchical structure and justificatory function of modern international law. Modern international law was formed and developed as a closed system of law, primarily to regulate the relations between independent bodies politic in Europe. It involved non-European peoples through the process in which they were either colonized by European powers or, if their independent status was recognized, brought under European spheres of influence. People living in non-European areas were basically no more than objects, alienated from international law. In this way, modern international law served as an ideology justifying the relationship between the dominating European powers and subordinated non-European people. Most significant in this respect is the fact that this justification was carried out by the combination of modern notions such as equality and universality, liberated from any particular religious belief, and the superiority of physical power on the part of Europeans. And one can see this combination already in the relationship between Spain and the Amerindians in the early sixteenth century.

[21] Locke frequently referred to the situation in America when he expounded his theory on property (1960: ii. 36, 41, 43, 46, 48, 49).

[22] The *OED* dates the first use of the word at 1704, and its first use as meaning 'civilized condition or state' at 1772.

3. Francisco de Victoria and *De Indis*

As noted earlier, the modern European international order started with the formation of permanent international relations on a global scale under the hegemony of Spain and Portugal. This formative process was accompanied by a series of heated debates dealing with the legitimacy of Spanish colonization of America. Such famous figures as Columbus, Pope Alexander VI, Queen Isabel of Castile, King Ferdinand of Aragon, King Charles V of the Habsburg dynasty, Cortés, Pizarro, Las Casas, Sepulveda, and Francisco de Vitoria were involved, directly or indirectly, in this issue.

The Spanish *Conquista* of America in the age of 'geographical exploration' was a natural extension of *Reconquista*. That Columbus's 'discovery' of America occurred in the year of the *Reconquista* of the Iberian peninsula is symbolic. By the same token, Alexander VI's bulls sanctioning the 'partitioning of the world' were based on the claim of the pope found in earlier bulls issued to the Portuguese: the claim to the ownership of unknown lands (*terrae incognitae*).[23] The bull *Inter caetera*, issued on 4 May 1493, states:

> And in order that you may enter upon so great an undertaking with great readiness and heartiness endowed with the benefit of our apostolic favour, we . . . give, grant, and assign to you, kings of Casille and Leon, together with all their dominations, . . . all rights, jurisdictions, and appurtenances all islands and mainlands found and to be found, discovered and to be discovered towards the west and south, by drawing and establishing a line from the Arctic pole, namely the north, and to the Antarctic pole, namely the south . . . (Davenport 1917: 77.)

The wording of the sentences granting the 'discovered' lands to Spain in the earlier bull *Inter caetera* (3 May 1493)[24] was basically the same (ibid. 62). The rulers of Spain relied, at least in the early stages, on these bulls in justifying their rule over the American continent, although they carefully added 'other just titles' as a basis of their claims. Thus the declaration of the acquisition of the New Continent by the King of Castile stated: 'By the Papal grant and other just and legitimate titles, we [Queen Isabel of Castile and King Ferdinando of Aragon] are the rulers (*Señor*) of the West Indies and all the Islands and mainlands found and to be found in the Atlantic Ocean. These lands, moreover, have been annexed to the Castilian Crown (*Real Corona*).'[25]

Although the Alexandrine bulls and the declaration of the Castilian king

[23] The bulls *Romanus Pontifex* issued by Nicholas V in 1455 and *Inter caetera* issued by Calixtus III in 1456 'granted' to the Portuguese various kinds of rights, jurisdiction, and profits of the coasts of Africa, especially in Guinea. Likewise, the bull *Aeterni Regis* issued by Sixtus IV sanctioned the Treaty of Alcacovas of 1479 and recognized Castile's possession of the Canaries. See Rubin 1990: 11–12.

[24] Davenport 1917: 62.

[25] *Recopilación* 1943 ⟨1680⟩, Ley la., Tit. I, Lib. III (523).

are significant as authoritative statements of the European powers of the time—secular as well as religious—which justified the colonization of America, the rationales invoked for that purpose could not long survive. Spain itself later abandoned the idea of papal grant. In contrast, Vitoria's argument in *De Indis*, although it was not so conspicuous at the time, is most significant in that it implies a prototype of a logical and normative structure justifying the European domination of the world, a structure which was assumed by subsequent international law.

De Indis was presented in 1539 as part of a series of special lectures in theology. In it Vitoria addressed the question of the legitimacy of the contemporary Spanish colonization of America and brutal conquest of the Amerindians. Cortés conquered Mexico in 1521, and Pizarro conquered Peru in 1533. The accompanying tragedies were being reported in Spain by indignant missionaries such as Las Casas.

Vitoria begins his argument by rejecting seven titles which were widely claimed and accepted in Spain to justify its colonization. They are imperial claims to world supremacy, papal grant, discovery, propagation of Christianity by force, sin on the part of the Indians, agreement based on 'free will', and special divine gift. According to Vitoria, the Amerindians have the right to own lands and to choose their own rulers. They should not be forced to convert to Christianity.[26] Considering the ideological conditions prevailing in Spain, this shows how surprisingly egalitarian Vitoria was.[27]

But Vitoria's claims did not end here. He cited eight titles as just causes which could legitimize Spanish rule over the Amerindians.[28] Among these, the title of sociality and intercourse (*titulus naturalis societatis et communicationis*) and the title of propagating Christianity (*causa religionis Christianae propagandae*) are most important. The other five just titles are the protection of those Indians who have converted to Christianity, papal appointment of a ruler to govern the Indians who have converted to Christianity, intervention against tyranny, truly spontaneous agreement, and aid to allies. Under the title of sociality and intercourse, the Spaniards were entitled to travel peacefully to America, to sojourn there, and to carry on trade among the native Indians. If the Indians prevented the Spaniards from enjoying any of these rights, the Spaniards could resort to war to defend them, and ultimately could depose the native rulers and install new ones. Under the title of propagating Christianity, Vitoria argues that it is

[26] Vitoria 1917 ⟨1696⟩, sec. II (Eng. 129–49); Ito 1965*b*: 224–66. For the English trans., the Simon edn. is used. Ito's trans. is based on the Lyons edn.

[27] From this Scott created an exaggerated image of Vitoria as an advocate of modern principles of equality and humanism. See Nussbaum 1954: 296–304 for criticism of Scott's view.

[28] Vitoria's attitude towards the 8th title—lack of capacity for self-government—is ambiguous (See Ito 1965*b*: 269–91.)

not only the right but also the duty of Christians to preach and declare the Gospel in 'barbarian' lands. The Indians are not only in sin, but outside the pale of salvation. The Spaniards may preach the Gospel despite the unwillingness of the Indians and are ultimately allowed to remove a pagan ruler by resorting to war and appointing a new ruler in his place.[29]

Two points should be kept in mind in assessing Vitoria's arguments. First, he made these claims when the Spaniards were already in America, when no Amerindian was in Europe, and when the Spaniards had already conquered the Amerindians or were in the process of doing so. As was noted earlier, Vitoria's attitude towards the issue is extremely egalitarian in theory. His argument for the right of intercourse is also based on this egalitarianism. Together with his flat denial of papal authority on the issue, this is the basis for claims of his modernity.[30] Even Las Casas, who was much more radical in practice, theoretically remained within the world of medieval Christendom, for the only just title he recognized for Spanish rule over Amerindians was papal donation.[31]

However, Vitoria expounded this 'modern' theory in the midst of Spanish colonization, where the Spaniards were actually in America engaged in opening silver mines and conquering the Amerindians, and the possibility of the converse situation was nil. In such an asymmetrical context, Vitoria's egalitarianism functioned as an ideology justifying the Spanish conquest of America. As a result of the combination of the military and technological superiority of the Spaniards and Vitoria's egalitarianism, that is, as a result of the manifestation of these two elements as *a totality of European civilization*, the Spaniards achieved their domination over peoples belonging to non-European civilizations.

Sepulveda, Vitoria's contemporary, is well known for having asserted that Amerindians are by nature apt to be slaves, an application of the Aristotelian idea. Although Las Casas failed in his attempt to persuade Charles V to ban this theory, Sepulveda's idea did not have much influence. In fact, European domination over non-Europeans, starting with the Spanish colonization of America, did not need such blatantly discriminatory

[29] Ito 1965*b*: 269–83.

[30] It has also been asserted that Vitoria's concept of *jus gentium* is modern because he defined it as 'quod naturalis ratio inter omnes gentes' instead of its traditional definition 'quod naturalis ratio inter omnes homines' given by Gaius. By replacing *homines* by *gentes*, it has been argued, Vitoria defined *jus gentium* as law between nations in the modern sense, rather than law common to all peoples. But as Ito and Haggenmacher have demonstrated (Ito 1965*b*: 62–76; Haggenmacher 1988: 38–63), it cannot be believed that the replacement of *homines* was intended to have any special significance, let alone producing such a basic change in theory. Reference to Vitoria's modernity extends only so far as the text describes. See also Kennedy 1986, esp. 13–40, although I believe that his classification of scholars into primitive (pre-1648), traditional (1648–1900), and modern (1900–80) is somewhat artificial.

[31] See Carro 1971: 271–3; Martínez 1971: 338–9.

concepts as those of Sepulveda. The combination of formal equality and factual superiority was enough. In regulating the relations between various peoples, modern international law has always regarded this formal equality as a fundamental principle. In this sense, the combination of Spanish power over the Amerindians and Vitoria's ideas reveals the same structure as the subsequent combination of the European nations' power over non-Europeans and the theory of modern international law.

Secondly, despite Vitoria's egalitarianism, his ideas are based fundamentally on a principle that discriminates against Amerindians, namely, the notion of Christianity's superiority over other religions. Underlying Vitoria's theory is his firm conviction that Christianity is the sole truth: not only does it bring happiness to man, but it is the only faith that can save his soul after death. In order to be released from the condition where man cannot avoid committing sin and to find salvation after death, man *must* accept the Christian faith. Since their pitiful ignorance is the cause of the Indians' refusal to accept Christianity, it is the duty of Christians to proselytize among them. Thus, in the all-important area of faith, Vitoria's ideas, which seem egalitarian at first, are decisively limited by the discriminatory principle that Christianity is superior to all other religions.[32]

It goes without saying that as Europe became 'secularized', from the seventeenth century, these ideas were not followed in their original form by the theorists of international law. However, the idea of international law as basically a law of Christian nations was maintained until the early nineteenth century, and traces of it lingered until much later. In particular, the concept of civilization, which had been generally accepted in Europe from the late eighteenth century, remained predominant until the mid-twentieth century as a fundamental standard in international law. This concept of civilization was, in a sense, a secularized form of the idea of Christian supremacy. In late nineteenth-century Europe, there was no concept of the coexistence of various civilizations. Western civilization was deemed ultimately to be the only civilization. Peoples in Africa and Asia were to be guided from primitive stages to more advanced stages of development. In this way, European powers convinced themselves that they were fulfilling a sacred mission, rather than engaging in ruthless exploitation on a global scale. This ideological structure was parallel to that of Spaniards convincing themselves that they were carrying out the sacred mission of proselytizing Christianity to drive salvation to the 'barbarians'.

The definition of international law as the 'law of civilized nations' prevailing in the period from the nineteenth century to the first half of the twentieth century is a striking manifestation of this concept of 'civilization'. Its traces are still to be found in the expression 'the general principles

[32] For an important insight on this point, see Schmitt 1950: 71–85.

of law recognized by civilized nations.'[33] Thus, while changing its content from 'Christianity' to 'civilization'—connoting modern European civilization—the discriminatory principle contained in Vitoria's assertion that Christianity is superior to all other religion has often been adopted, more or less in disguise, in subsequent theories of international law.

In pointing out the significance of Vitoria's theory in modern international law, we do not intend to set Vitoria up as 'father of international law' in place of Grotius. Nor do we intend to criticize Vitoria merely because his theory had the effect of justifying the Spanish colonization of America. The illusion of universality is not limited to European civilization. Indeed, modern European civilization is less flawed in that it has developed the notion of equality, applicable not only to individuals but to nations as well.

The major reason why Vitoria's theory played an ideological role in justifying Spanish domination over Amerindians, and the reason why we stress this aspect, is simply that European powers did dominate the world. Had China dominated the world, had Islamic civilization subjugated other civilizations, it would have been necessary to criticize the hierarchical and discriminatory structure of the Chinese interstate notion based on Confucianism, or the proselytizing and zealous nature of the Islamic theory of interstate relations, with the idea of *jihad* at its core. As is shown in Chapter 11, any theory which comes to be associated with a dominant power cannot escape an ideological role. Thus it is both the grandeur and misery of Europe that are chiefly responsible for the condition of the modern world, a world in which we live with mingled hope and despair. Modern international law constitutes an integral part of this grand and miserable modernity.

[33] ICJ Statute, art. 38(1)(*c*).

Select Bibliography

Reprinted editions are cited as, for example, A. Gentilis 1933 ⟨1612⟩. This citation indicates that the contributor used the 1933 reprint of the 1612 edition. Divisions, such as I. i. 1 (Eng. (or) Lat. 1), indicated after the year of publication ((⟨1612⟩), follow the same divisions as in *JBP*.

Contributors utilized various versions, editions, and translations of works by various scholars: e.g. Otto von Gierke (1902/1968/1981), *Johannes Althusius und die Entwicklung der naturrechtlichen Staatstheorien: Zugleich ein Beitrag zur Geschichte der Rechtssystematik* (2 Aufl., Breslau, 1902; 6 Aufl., ed. by J. von Gierke, Aalen, 1968; 7 Aufl., ed. by J. von Gierke, Aalen, 1981). In the text, footnotes provide author, year, and page information. In the Bibliography, we designate each version or edition by the year of publication; e.g. in the case of Otto von Gierke above, the first year listed (1902) corresponds to the first listing (2 Aufl., Breslau, 1902) and the second year (1968) corresponds to the second listing (6 Aufl., ed. by J. von Gierke, Aalen, 1968), and so on.

Although contributors primarily utilized original-language editions of scholarly works, some contributors were obliged to use translated works. In the footnotes, when a translation is used, the name of the original author, the year of publication of the translated edition, and a page number citation to the translated work are provided. In the Bibliography, however, full citation data is provided in the following order: name of the original author, the year of publication of the original language edition and the year of publication of the translation, the full title, the place and year of original publication, the name of the translator, and the place and year of the publication of the translation: e.g. Hazard, P. (1961/1973), *La Crise de la conscience européenne 1680–1715* (Paris, 1961; trans. by K. Nozawa, Tokyo, 1973).

I. Grotius's Writings

De Imperio Summarum Potestatum Circa Sacra (Frankfurt-am-Main, 1690; repr. Aalen, 1970).

De Jure Belli ac Pacis libri tres (Amsterdam, 1646), Latin texts and trans. by Francis W. Kelsey, A. E. R. Boak, H. A. Sanders, J. S. Reeves, and H. F. Wright, *The Classics of International Law*, I–II (Oxford, 1925).

De Jure Belli ac Pacis libri tres (Amsterdam, 1650).

De Jure Belli ac Pacis libri tres (Amsterdam, 1712).

De Jure Praedae Commentarius (original MS., 1604), Latin texts and trans.

by G. L. Williams, *The Classics of International Law*, I–II (Oxford, 1950; repr. of English trans., New York, 1964).
Mare Liberum (Leiden, 1618, repr. Osnabrück, 1978).
Mare Liberum: The Freedom of the Seas (trans. with a revision of the Latin text of 1633 by R. V. D. Magoffin, London, 1916).
H. Grotius = J. Barbeyrac (1724), *Le Droit de la guerre, et de la paix*, trans. by J. Barbeyrac, I–II (Amsterdam).
H. Grotius = J. Barbeyrac (1746), *Le Droit de la guerre, et de la paix*, trans. by J. Barbeyrac, I (Basle).
H. Grotius = R. Lee (1926), *The Jurisprudence of Holland by Hugo Grotius*, I (Oxford).
H. Grotius = M. Pradier-Fodéré (1867), *Le Droit de la guerre et de la paix* trans. by M. P. Pradier-Fodéré, I–III (Paris).
H. Grotius = W. Whewell (1853), *De Jure Belli ac Pacis libri tres*, accompanied by abridged trans. by William Whewell, I–III (Cambridge).

II. Other Works

Ago, R. (1983), 'Le Droit international dans la conception de Grotius', *Recueil des Cours*, 1983-IV: 375–98.
Ahsmann, M. (1983), 'Grotius as a Jurist', *Hugo Grotius: A Great European 1583–1645* (Delft): 37–50.
Alexandrowicz, C. H. (1960), 'Freitas versus Grotius', *British Year Book of International Law*, 35: 162–82.
—— (1967), *An Introduction to the History of the Law of Nations in the East Indies, 16th, 17th and 18th Centuries* (Oxford).
—— (1972), ed., *Grotian Society Papers 1972: Studies in the History of the Law of Nations* (The Hague).
—— (1973), *The European-African Confrontation: A Study in Treaty Making* (Leiden).
Anand, R. P. (1972*a*), *Asian States and the Development of Universal International Law* (Delhi).
—— (1972*b*), *New States and International Law* (Delhi).
Andrews, K. R. (1964), *Elizabethan Privateering 1585–1603* (Cambridge).
Aomi, J., Ito, M., and Murakami, J. (1976), *Hogaku shi* (Tokyo).
Aristotle (1926/1934), *Nichomachean Ethics* (trans. by H. Rackham, Loeb Classical Library, Cambridge, 1926; rev. edn., London, 1934).
—— (1936), *Magna Moralia* (trans. by G. C. Armstrong, Loeb Classical Library, Amsterdam).
—— (1926/1968), *'Art' of Rhetoric* (trans. by J. H. Freese, Loeb Classical Library, London, 1926; trans. by M. Yamamoto, Tokyo, 1968).
—— (1984), *Politics* (trans. by Lord Carnes, Chicago).

Arnaud, A. (1969), *Les Origines doctrinales du code civil français* (Paris).

Atiyah, P. S. (1979), *The Rise and Fall of Freedom of Contract* (Oxford).

Augé, G. (1968), 'Le Contrat et l'évolution du consensualisme chez Grotius', *Archives de philosophie du droit*, 13: 99–114.

Austin, J. (1885), *Lectures on Jurisprudence*, I (5th edn. by R. Campbell, London).

Ayala, B. (1912 ⟨1582⟩), *De Jure et Officiis Bellicis et Disciplina Militari libri tres* (Duaci, 1582), Latin texts and trans. by J. P. Bate, *The Classics of International Law*, I–II (Washington, DC, 1912).

Baelde, M. (1976), 'De pacificatie van Gent in 1576', *Bijdragen en Mededelingen betreffende de Geschiedenis der Nederlanden*, 91: 369–93.

Balogh, E. (1929), 'The Traditional Element in Grotius' Conception of International Law', *New York University Law Quarterly Review*, 7: 261–92.

Barschak, L. (1925–6), 'Die Staatsanschauung des Hugo Grotius', *Bijdragen voor Vaterlandsche Geschiedenis en Oudheidkunde*, 3/6: 193–232.

—— (1926), 'Die Staatsanschauung des Hugo Grotius', *Bijdragen voor Vaterlandsche Geschiedenis en Oudheidkunde*, 6 de reeks IV: 9–28.

Basdevant, J. (1904), 'Hugo Grotius', in Pillet 1904: 125–267.

Bärmann, J. (1961), 'Pacta sunt servanda: Considérations sur l'histoire du contrat consensuel', *Revue internationale de droit comparé*, 13: 18–53.

Beccaria, C. (1822), *Des délits et des peines* (trans. with comm. by Voltaire, Paris).

Behnen, M. (1986), 'Der gerechte und der notwendige Krieg: "Necessitas" und "Utilitas reipublicae" in der Kriegstheorie des 16. und 17. Jahrhunderts', in Kunisch 1986: 43–106.

Bell, J. (1975), 'Hugo Grotius: Historian' (Ph.D. diss., Ann Arbor, Mich.).

Bendix, R. (1977), *Nation Building and Citizenship* (New enlarged edn., Berkeley, Calif.).

Benöhr, H.-P. (1965), *Das sogennante Synallagma in den Konsensualkontrakten des römisches Rechts* (Hamburg).

Bergfeld, C. (1968), *Franciscus Connanus (1508–1551): Ein Systematiker des römischen Rechts* (Cologne).

Berki, R. N. (1977), *The History of Political Thought* (London).

Bodin, J. (1577/1583/1977 ⟨1583⟩), *Les Six Livres de la République* (Paris, 1577; Paris, 1583; repr. of 1583 edn., Paris, 1977).

Borkenau, F. (1934/1965), *Der Übergang vom feudalen zum bürgerlichen Weltbild: Studien zur Geschichte der Philosophie der Manufakturperiode* (Paris, 1934; trans. by H. Mizuta, Tokyo, 1965).

Bourquin, M. (1926), 'Grotius et les tendances actuelles du droit international', *Revue de droit international et de législation comparée*, 3rd ser. 7: 86–125.

Bozeman, A. B. (1980), 'On the Relevance of Hugo Grotius and De Jure

Belli ac Pacis for Our Times', *Grotiana*, NS I: 65–124.

Brandt, R. (1974), *Eigentumstheorien von Grotius bis Kant* (Stuttgart).

Brierly, J. L. = Waldock, H. (1963), *The Law of Nations: An Introduction to the International Law of Peace* (6th edn. by H. Waldock, Oxford).

Brimo, A. (1978), *Les Grands Courants de la philosophie du droit et de l'état* (New edn., Paris).

Brownlie, I. (1979), *Principles of Public International Law* (3rd edn., Oxford).

Brunner, O. (1965), *Land und Herrschaft: Grundfragen der territorialen Verfassunsgeschichte Österreichs im Mittelalter* (Vienna).

—— (1968/1974), *Neue Wege der Verfassungs- und Sozialgeschichte* (Göttingen, 1968; trans. by S. Ishii, Tokyo, 1974).

——, Conze, W., and Koselleck, R. (1975), eds., *Geschichtliche Grundbegriffe: Historisches Lexikon zur politisch-sozialen Sprache in Deutschland*, II (Stuttgart).

——, Conze, W., and Koselleck, R. (1982), eds., *Geschichtliche Grundbegriffe: Historisches Lexikon zur politisch-sozialen Sprache in Deutschland*, III (Stuttgart).

Bull, H. (1966), 'The Grotian Conception of International Society', in Bull, Butterfield, and Wight 1966: 51–73.

—— (1977), *The Anarchical Society: A Study of Order in World Politics* (New York).

——, Butterfield, H., and Wight, M. (1966), eds., *Diplomatic Investigations: Essays in the Theory of International Politics* (London).

——, Kingsbury, B., and Roberts, A. (1990), eds., *Hugo Grotius and International Relations* (Oxford).

Carro, V. D. (1971), 'The Spanish Theological-Juridical Renaissance and the Ideology of Bartolomé de Las Casas', in Friede and Keen 1971: 237–78.

Cassirer, Erich (1919, 1963 ⟨1919⟩), *Natur- und Völkerrecht im Lichte der Geschichte und der systematischen Philosophie* (Berlin, 1919; repr. Aalen, 1963).

Cassirer, Ernst (1932/1962), *Die Philosophie der Aufklärung* (2nd edn., Tübingen, 1932; trans. by Y. Nakano, Tokyo, 1962).

—— (1946/1960), *The Myth of the State* (New Haven, Conn., 1946; trans. by M. Miyata, Tokyo, 1960).

Chailley, P. (1932), *La Nature juridique des traités internationaux selon le droit contemporain* (Paris).

Chauveau, M. E. (1891), *Le Droit des gens, ou droit international public* (Paris).

Chévrier, G. (1929), *Essai sur l'histoire de la cause dans les obligations* (Paris).

Cicero, M. (1913/1965), *De officiis* (trans. by W. Miller, London, 1965;

1965 Latin edn., A. Mondadori, 1913).
Cocceji, H. von (1744), *Grotius Illustratus seu Commentarii ad Hugonis Grotii de Jure Belli et Pacis libros tres*, I (Breslau).
—— (1746), *Grotius Illustratus seu Commentarii ad Hugonis Grotii de Jure Belli ac Pacis libros tres*, II (Breslau).
Cohen, M. (1933), 'The Basis of Contract', *Harvard Law Review*, 46: 553–92.
Coing, H. (1982*a*), *Gesammelte Aufsätze zu Rechtsgeschichte, Rechtsphilosophie und Zivilrecht 1947–1975*, I (Frankfurt-am-Main).
—— (1982*b*), 'Zur Geschichte des Begriffs "subjectives Recht"', in Coing 1982*a*: 241–62.
Cooper, J. P. (1970), ed., *The New Cambridge Modern History*, IV (Cambridge).
Corpus Juris Canonici (1695), *Corpus Juris Canonici Gregorii XIII* (Paris).
Corpus Juris Canonici (1834), *Das Corpus Juris Canonici*, I–II (trans. by B. Schilling, Leipzig).
Corpus Juris Civilis (1973), *Corpus Juris Civilis*, I. *Institutiones et Digesta* (22nd edn. by P. Krüger and T. Mommsen, Dublin).
Corvisier, A. (1976), *Armée et sociétés en Europe de 1494 à 1789* (Paris).
Davenport, F. G. (1917), ed., *European Treaties Bearing on the History of the United States and its Dependencies to 1648* (Washington, DC).
Del Vecchio, G. (1962), 'Grotius and the Foundation of International Law', *New York University Law Review*, 37: 260–6.
D'Entrèves, A. P. (1939), *The Medieval Contribution to Political Thought* (Oxford).
—— (1970), *Natural Law* (2nd edn., London).
Denzer, H. (1972), *Moralphilosophie und Naturrecht bei Samuel Pufendorf: Eine geistes- und wissenschaftsgeschichtliche Untersuchung zur Geburt des Naturrechts aus der Praktischen Philosophie* (Munich).
Despotopoulos, C. (1968), 'La Notion de synallagma chez Aristote', *Archives de philosophie du droit*, 13: 115–27.
Dickinson, E. D. (1920), *The Equality of States in International Law* (Cambridge, Mass.).
—— (1932), 'Changing Concepts and Doctrines of Incorporation', *American Journal of International Law*, 26: 239–60.
Diesselhorst, M. (1959), *Die Lehre des Hugo Grotius vom Versprechen* (Cologne).
—— (1976), *Zum Vermögensrechtssystem Samuel Pufendorfs* (Göttingen).
Dilcher, G. (1984), 'Ehescheidung und Säkularisation', in Dilcher and Staff 1984: 304–59.
——, and Staff, I. (1984), *Christentum und modernes Recht: Beiträge zum Problem der Säkularisation* (Frankfurt-am-Main).
Dilthey, W. (1957), *Gesammelte Schriften*, II (Stuttgart).

Diósdi, G. (1981), *Contract in Roman Law: From the Twelve Tables to the Glossators* (Budapest).

Draper, G. I. A. D. (1990), 'Grotius' Place in the Development of Legal Ideas about War', in Bull, Kingsbury, and Roberts 1990: 177–207.

Drathé, R. (1970/1986), *Jean-Jacques Rousseau et la science politique de son temps* (Paris, 1970; trans. by N. Nishjima, Tokyo, 1986).

Dreier, R. (1987), 'Eigentum in rechtsphilosophischer Sicht', *Archiv für Rechts- und Sozialphilosophie*, 73: 159–78.

Dufour, A. (1972), *Le Mariage dans l'école allemande du droit naturel moderne au XVIIIe siècle: Les Sources philosophiques de la Scolastique aux Lumières—La Doctrine* (Paris).

—— (1980), 'L'Influence de la méthodologie des sciences physiques et mathématiques sur les fondateurs de l'École du Droit naturel moderne (Grotius, Hobbes, Pufendorf)', *Grotiana*, NS 1: 33–52.

——, Haggenmacher, P., and Toman, J. (1985*a*), eds., *Grotius et l'ordre juridique international: Travaux du colloque Hugo Grotius Genève, 10–11 Novembre 1983* (Lausanne).

——, ——, —— (1985*b*), 'Grotius: Homme de loi, homme de foi, homme de lettres', in Dufour, Haggenmacher, and Toman 1985*a*: 9–32.

Dumbould, E. (1969), *The Life and Legal Writings of Hugo Grotius* (Norman).

Edwards, C. S. (1981), *Hugo Grotius, the Miracle of Holland: A Study of Political and Legal Thought* (Chicago).

Ehrlich, L. (1928), 'L'Interprétation des traités', *Recueil des Cours*, 1928-IV: 1–145.

Eikema Hommes, H. J. van (1979), *Major Trends in the History of Legal Philosophy* (Amsterdam).

—— (1983), 'Grotius on Natural and International Law', *Netherlands International Law Review*, 30: 61–71.

Elders, J. L. M. *et al.* (1984), *Hugo Grotius: 1583–1983. Maastricht Hugo Grotius Colloquium March 31, 1983* (Assen).

Eppstein, J. (1935), *The Catholic Tradition of the Law of Nations* (London).

Eyffinger, A. (1983), 'The Dutch Period in the Life of Hugo Grotius', in *Hugo Grotius: A Great European 1583–1645* (Delft): 5–23.

Eysinga, W. J. M. von (1952), *Hugo Grotius: Eine biographische Skizze* (Basle).

—— (1958), *Sparsa Collecta: Een aantal der verspreide geschriften van Jhr. Mr. W. J. M. van Eysinga* (Leiden).

—— (1980), 'Grotius Resurgens', *Grotiana*, NS 1: 5–15.

Falk, R. (1981*a*), *Human Rights and State Sovereignty* (New York).

—— (1981*b*), 'Preface' of Edwards 1981: pp. viii–xxi.

—— (1983), *The End of World Order: Essays on Normative International Relations* (New York).

Faucci, D. (1980), 'L'estimazione del giusto' selon Grotius et selon Vico', *Grotiana*, NS 1: 125–37.

Feenstra, R. (1973), 'L'Influence de la scolastique espagnole sur Grotius en droit privé: Quelques expériences dans des questions de fond et de forme, concernant notamment les doctrines de l'erreur et de l'enrichissement sans cause', in Grossi 1973: 377–402.

—— (1978), 'Eigentumsbegriff bei Hugo Grotius im Licht einiger mittelalterlichen und spätscholastischen Quellen', *Festschrift für F. Wieacker zum 70. Geburtstag* (Göttingen): 209–34.

—— (1983*a*), 'L'Influence de la pensée juridique', *XVII*[e] *Siècle*: 487–98.

—— (1983*b*), 'Grotius et le droit privé européen', *Recueil des Cours*, 1983-IV: 453–69.

Fehr, H. (1952), *Deutsche Rechtsgeschichte* (5th edn., Berlin).

Fenwick, C. G. (1965), *International Law* (4th edn., New York).

Fernández-Santamaria, J. A. (1977), *The State, War and Peace: Spanish Political Thought in the Renaissance, 1516–1559* (Cambridge).

Feuerbach, P. J. A. (1966 ⟨1799⟩), *Revision der Grundsätze und Grundbegriffe des positiven peinlichen Rechts*, 1 (Erfurt, 1799, repr. Aalen, 1966).

Figgis, J. N. (1916), *Studies of Political Thought from Gerson to Grotius 1414–1625* (2nd edn., London).

Finnis, J. (1980), *Natural Law and Natural Right* (Oxford).

Fisch, J. (1984), *Die europäische Expansion und das Völkerrecht: Die Auseinandersetzungen um den Status der überseeischen Gebiete vom 15. Jahrhundert bis zur Gegenwart* (Stuttgart).

Fischer, H. F. W. D. (1962), ed., *Hugonis Grotii Institutiones Juris Hollandici* (Haarlem).

Frank, A. G. (1967), *Capitalism and Underdevelopment in Latin America* (New York).

—— (1978), *Dependent Accumulation and Underdevelopment* (London).

Fried, C. (1980), 'Book Review (The Rise and Fall of Freedom of Contract by P. S. Atiyah)', *Harvard Law Review*, 93: 1858–68.

—— (1981), *Contract as Promise: A Theory of Contractual Obligation* (Cambridge, Mass.).

Friede, J., and Keen, B. (1971), *Bartolomé de Las Casas in History* (De Kalb).

Friedrich, C. J. (1963), *The Philosophy of Law in Historical Perspective* (2nd edn., Chicago).

Fruin, R. (1925), 'An Unpublished Work of Hugo Grotius', *Biblioteca Visseriana*, 5: 3–74.

Fukuda, K. (1971), *Kindai seiji genri seiritsushi josetsu* (Tokyo).

Fulton, T. W. (1911), *The Sovereignty of the Sea: A Historical Account of the Claims of England to the Dominion of the British Seas, and of the Evolution of the Territorial Waters: with Special Reference to the Rights of Fishing and the Naval Salute* (Edinburgh).

Funada, K. (1970), *Romaho* (Tokyo).

Fuwa, T. (1950), *Keijiho jo no shomondai* (Tokyo).

Garçon, E. (1922), *Le Droit pénal: Origines-évolution-état actuel* (Paris).

Gardot, A. (1934), 'Jean Bodin: Sa place parmi des fondateurs du droit international', *Recueil des Cours*, 1934-IV. 549–747.

Gellinek, C. (1983), *Hugo Grotius* (Boston).

Gentilis, A. (1933 ⟨1612⟩), *De Jure Belli libri tres* (Hanover, 1612), Latin texts and trans. by J. C. Rolfe, *The Classics of International Law*, I–II (Oxford, 1933).

Gesellschaft für Seerecht der Deutschen Demokratischen Republik (1983), ed., *Hugo Grotius 1583–1645* (Rostock).

Gierke, O. von (1881), *Das deutsche Genossenschaftsrecht*, III. *Die Staats- und Korporationslehre des Alterthums und des Mittelalters und ihre Aufnahme in Deutschland* (Berlin).

—— (1902/1968/1981), *Johannes Althusius und die Entwicklung der naturrechtlichen Staatstheorien: Zugleich ein Beitrag zur Geschichte der Rechtssystematik* (2 Aufl., Breslau, 1902; 6 Aufl., ed. by J. von Gierke, Aalen, 1968; 7 Aufl., ed. by J. von Gierke, Aalen, 1981).

—— (1913/1954 ⟨1913⟩), *Das deutsche Genossenschaftsrecht*, IV. *Staats- und Korporationslehre der Neuzeit* (Berlin, 1913; repr. Graz, 1954).

—— (1950 ⟨1934⟩), *Natural Law and the Theory of Society, 1500 to 1800*, I–II (trans. by E. Barker, Cambridge, 1934, repr. Cambridge, 1950).

Goez, W. (1958), *Translatio Imperii: Ein Beitrag zur Geschichte des Geschichtsdenkens und der politischen Theorien im Mittelalter und in der frühen Neuzeit* (Tübingen).

Goubert, P. (1973), *L'Ancien Régime*, II. *Les Pouvoirs* (Paris).

Gough, J. W. (1936), *The Social Contract: A Critical Study of Its Development* (Oxford).

Grewe, W. G. (1984*a*), *Epochen der Völkerrechtsgeschichte* (Baden-Baden).

—— (1984*b*), 'Grotius-Vater des Völkerrechts?' *Staat*, 23: 161–78.

Grossi, P. (1973), ed., *La Seconde Scolastica nella formazione del diritto privato moderno: Incontro di studio Firenze, 16–19 ottobre 1972, Atti* (Milan).

Günther, H., Hilger, D., Iltung, K. H., Koselleck, R., and Moraw, P. (1982), 'Herrschaft', in Brunner, Conze, and Koselleck 1982: 1–102.

Guggenheim, P. (1958), 'Contribution à l'histoire des sources du droit des gens', *Recueil des Cours*, 1958-II: 3–84.

—— (1961), 'Droit international général et droit public européen', *Annuaire suisse de droit international*, 18: 9–28.

Hägerström, A. (1943), 'Über den Grund der bindenden Kraft des Konsensualkontraktes nach römischer Rechtsanschauung', *Zeitschrift der*

Savigny-Stiftung für Rechtsgeschichte, Romanistische Abteilung, 63: 268–300.

Haggenmacher, P. (1983), *Grotius et la doctrine de la guerre juste* (Paris).

—— (1985), 'Grotius et le droit international: Le texte et la légende', in Dufour 1985*a*: 115–43.

—— (1988), 'La place de Francisco de Vitoria parmi les fondateurs du droit international', in Truyol y Serra *et al.* 1988: 27–80.

—— (1990), 'Grotius and Gentili: A Reassessment of Thomas E. Holland's Inaugural Lecture', in Bull, Kingsbury, and Roberts 1990: 133–76.

Hanga, V. (1981), 'Les Problèmes de l'État dans le "De Jure Belli ac Pacis" de H. Grotius', *Grotiana*, NS 2: 30–43.

Hanke, L. (1949), *The Spanish Struggle for Justice in the Conquest of America* (Philadelphia).

—— (1974), *All Mankind is One: A Study of the Disputation between Bartolomé de Las Casas and Juan Ginés de Sépulveda in 1550 on the Intellectual and Religious Capacity of the American Indians* (De Kalb).

Harada, K. (1975/1982), *Romaho* (Tokyo, 16th edn., 1975; 18th edn., 1982).

Hart, H. L. A. (1961), *The Concept of Law* (Oxford).

Hartung, F. (1949/1982), 'L'État c'est moi', *Historische Zeitschrift*, 169 (1949), 1–30; trans. by O. Naruse, in Naruse 1982: 285–323.

—— (1950/1980), *Deutsche Verfassungsgeschichte vom 15 Jahrhundert bis Gegenwart* (9 Aufl., Stuttgart 1950; trans. by O. Naruse and E. Sakai, Tokyo, 1980).

Havinghurst, H. C. (1961), *The Nature of Private Contract* (Evanson, Ill.).

Hazard, P. (1961/1973), *La Crise de la conscience européenne 1680–1715* (Paris, 1961; trans. by K. Nozawa, Tokyo, 1973).

Hervada, J. (1983), 'The Old and the New in the Hypothesis "Etiamsi Daremus" of Grotius', *Grotiana*, NS 4: 3–20.

Higgins, R. (1965), *Conflict of Interest* (London).

Hinsley, F. (1986), *Sovereignty* (2nd edn., Cambridge).

Hirata, K. (1969), *Shimin shakai to shakaishugi* (Tokyo).

—— (1971), *Keizaigaku to rekishi ninshiki* (Tokyo).

Hironaka, T. (1964), *Keiyakuho no kenkyu* (Tokyo).

—— (1974), *Keiyaku to sono hoteki hogo* (Tokyo).

Hobbes, T. (1839/1958/1966 ⟨1839⟩), *Leviathan, or the Matter, Form and Power of a Commonwealth Ecclesiastical and Civil, Parts I and II* (ed. by W. M. Bart, London, 1839; ed. by H. W. Schneider, New York, 1958; repr. of 1839 edn., Aalen, 1966).

Höbel, E. (1954/1984), *The Law of Primitive Man* (Cambridge, Mass., 1954; trans. by M. Chiba and F. Nakamura, Tokyo, 1984).

Hobsbawm, E. (1962), *The Age of Revolution: Europe 1789–1848* (London).

Hoffmann-Loerzer, G. (1971), *Studien zu Hugo Grotius* (Munich).
Hofmann, H. (1977), 'Hugo Grotius', in Stolleis 1977.
—— (1984), 'Von den Ursprüngen deutschen Rechtsstaatsdenkens in der nachchristlichen Sozialphilosophie: Eine Erinnerung an Hugo Grotius (1583–1645) und Samuel von Pufendorf (1632–1694)', *Juristische Schulung*, 24: 9–14.
Holk, L. E. von, and Roelofsen, C. G. (1983), eds., *Grotius Reader: A Reader for Students of International Law and Legal History* (The Hague).
Holzendorf, F. von (1885), *Handbuch des Völkerrechts*, I (Berlin).
Horwitz, M. (1977), *The Transformation of American Law 1780–1860* (Cambridge, Mass.).
Hoshino, E. (1972), *Minpo ronshu*, III (Tokyo).
—— (1983), 'Keiyaku shiso, keiyakuho no rekishi to hikakuho', *Kihon hogaku IV, Keiyaku* (Tokyo): 3–79.
Howard, M. (1976), *War in European History* (Oxford).
Hrabar, V. E. (1925), 'Le Rôle de Grotius dans le développement scientifique du droit international', *Revue de droit international et de législation comparée*, 3rd ser. 6: 537–55.
Huber, E. R. (1942), 'Reich, Volk und Staat in der Rechtswissenschaft des 17. und 18. Jahrhunderts', *Zeitschrift für die gesamte Staatswissenschaft*, 102: 593–627.
Huizinga, J. (1941/1968), *Nederland's beschaving in de zeventiende eeuw, een schets* (Haarlem, 1941; trans. by F. Kurihara, Tokyo, 1968).
—— (1952/1965), *Erasmus of Rotterdam* (London, 1952; trans. by N. Miyazaki, Tokyo, 1965).
Idman (1913), *Le Traité de garantie en droit international.*
ILC (1957), *Yearbook of International Law Commission*, 1957-I: 155–63.
Iltung, K.-H. (1983), *Naturrecht und Sittlichkeit* (Stuttgart).
Inoue, T. (1984), 'Shakai keiyaku setsu no rironteki kachi ni kansuru ichi hansei', *Ho Tetsugaku Nenpo*, 1983: *Shakai keiyakuron* (1984), 73–103.
Institute for the Study of Western History, Kyoto University, Faculty of Literature (1955), *Yohei seido no rekishiteki kenkyu* (Kyoto).
Ishimoto, Y. (1958*a*), *Churitu seido no shiteki kenkyu* (Tokyo).
—— (1958*b*), 'Iwayuru "jijitsu jo no senso" ni tsuite,' *Yokota sensei kanreki shukuga: Gendai kokusaiho no kadai* (ed. by Y. Takano, Tokyo, 1958).
Israel, J. I. (1982), *The Dutch Republic and the Hispanic World 1601–1661* (Oxford).
Ito, F. (1957*a*), 'Aruberikus Gentirisu no senso no gainen', *Hosei Kenkyu*, 24/1: 21–40.
—— (1957*b*), *Suaresu no kokusaiho riron* (Tokyo).
—— (1963), 'Hokakuhoron ni okeru Gurotiusu no kokusaiho (banminho) no kihon kannen—kokusaiho gakusetsu shi no kadai', in Maehara

Mitsuo kyoju kanreki kinen ronbunshu, *Kokusaihogaku no shomondai* (Tokyo): 179–219.

—— (1965*a*), 'Hokakuhoron ni okeru Gurotiusu no seito sensoron—kokusaiho gakusetsu shi no kenkyu, (1)', *Kokusaiho Gaiko Zasshi*, 63: 393–431.

—— (1965*b*), *Bitoria no kokusaiho riron* (Tokyo).

—— (1973), 'Gurotiusu no Jiyukairon no bunseki', *Hosei Kenkyu*, 39/2–4: 201–48.

—— (1977), 'Defense of Hugo Grotius for his Mare Liberum', *The Japanese Annual of International Law*, 20: 1–16.

—— (1984), *Gurotiusu no jiyukairon* (Tokyo).

Iwasaki, M. (1982), *Herenizumu no shisoka* (*Jinrui no chiteki isan*, 10, Tokyo).

Jellinek, G. (1960 ⟨1913⟩/1976 ⟨1913⟩), *Allgemeine Staatslehre* (3. Aufl., 1913, unter Verwertung des handschriftlichen Nachlasses durchgesehen und ergänzt von W. Jellinek, Bad Homburg von der Höhe, 1960; repr. Kronberg, 1976).

Jessup, P. C., and Deák, F. (1976 ⟨1935⟩), *Neutrality: Its History, Economics and Law* (New York, 1935, repr. 1976).

Johnson, J. T. (1975), *Ideology, Reason, and the Limitation of War* (Princeton, NJ).

—— (1983), 'Grotius' Use of History and Charity in the Modern Transformation of the Just War Idea', *Grotiana*, NS 4: 21–34.

Jomparto, J. (1987), 'Vitoria kokusaiho riron no kindaiteki igi', *Jochi Hogaku Ronshu*, 30/2–3: 265–92.

—— and Kuwabara, T. (1985), *Jinmin shuken shiso no genten to sono tenkai: Suaresu no keiyaku ron o chushin to shite* (Tokyo).

Jonge, H. J. de (1983), 'Grotius as an Interpreter of the Bible, Particularly the New Testament', in *Hugo Grotius: A Great European 1583–1645* (Delft): 59–65.

Jordan, W. K. (1965), *The Development of Religious Toleration in England (1603–1640)* (Gloucester).

Kägi, W. (1961), 'Pacta sunt servanda', in Strupp and Schlochauer 1961: 710–16.

Kalshoven, F. (1985), 'Grotius' Jus in bello with Special Reference to Ruses of War and Perfidy', in Dufour 1985*a*: 89–100.

Kaltenborn, C. von (1848/1965 ⟨1848⟩), *Die Vorläufer des Hugo Grotius auf dem Gebiete des ius naturae et gentium* (Leipzig, 1848, repr. Frankfurt-am-Main, 1965).

Kant, I. (1922), *Metaphysik der Sitten*, I. *Metaphysische Anfangsgründe der Rechtslehre*, *Immanuel Kants Werke*, VII (Berlin).

Kasai, N. (1984), 'Gurotiusu ni okeru senso to shokokumin no ho: Seitosei to gohosei no kosaku', *Kokusaiho Gaiko Zasshi*, 83/1: 31–63.

Kaser, M. (1977/1979/1983/1986), *Römisches Privatrecht: Ein Studienbuch* (Munich, 10. Aufl. 1977; 11. Aufl. 1979; 13. Aufl. 1983; 14. Aufl. 1986).

Kato, S. (1979), *Kindai seiji tetsugaku to shukyo: Junana seiki shakai keiyaku setsu ni okeru shukyo hihan no tenkai* (Tokyo).

Kawakita, M. (1970), 'Yoroppa no shogyoteki shinshutsu', *Iwanami koza sekai rekishi*, XVI (Tokyo): 117–85.

Keen, B. (1971), 'Introduction: Approaches to Las Casas, 1535–1970', in Friede and Keen 1971: 3–65.

Keen, M. H. (1965), *The Law of War in the Late Middle Ages* (London).

Kelsen, H. (1928), *Die philosophischen Grundlagen der Naturrechtslehre und des Rechtspositivismus* (Berlin).

—— (1957), *What is Justice? Collected Essays by Hans Kelsen* (Berkeley, Calif.).

—— = Tucker, W. (1966), *Principles of International Law* (2nd edn., rev. and ed. by W. Tucker, New York).

Kennedy, D. (1986), 'Primitive Legal Scholarship', *Harvard International Law Journal*, 27: 1–98.

Kennedy, P. (1987), *The Rise and Fall of the Great Powers* (London).

Kern, F. (1956/1968), *Law and Constitution in the Middle Ages* (Oxford, 1956; trans. by T. Sera, Tokyo, 1968).

Kikumori, H. (1977), *Ruta to doitsu seishin shi* (Tokyo).

Kimura, K. (1966), 'Keimo shiso to kindai keiho', in *Taikei keiho jiten* (Tokyo): 10–13.

Kimura, M. (1984), 'Gurotiusu senso to heiwa no ho ni okeru goiron', *Kokusaiho Gaiko Zasshi*, 83/1: 1–30.

Kingsbury, B., and Roberts, A. (1990), 'Introduction: Grotian Thought in International Relations', in Bull, Kingsbury, and Roberts 1990: 1–64.

Kinoshita, T. (1985), *Eibei keiyakuho no riron* (2nd edn., Tokyo).

Kirchmann, J. H. von (1869), *Des Hugo Grotius Leben und Schriften*, *Philosophische Bibliothek*, 15 (Berlin).

Kitamura, I. (1976), 'Keiyaku no kaishaku ni taisuru Furansu Hakiin no kontororu (1)', *Hogaku Kyokai Zasshi*, 93/12: 1737–1800.

—— (1983), 'Shihojo no keiyaku to ishi jiritsu no genri', *Kihon hogaku*, IV. *Keiyaku* (Tokyo): 165–208.

Klüber, J. L. (1847), *Europäisches Völkerrecht* (2. Aufl. by C. E. Morstadt, Heidelberg).

Knight, W. S. M. (1925), *The Life and Works of Hugo Grotius* (London).

Kohler, J. (1918), *Grundlagen des Völkerrechts: Vergangenheit, Gegenwart, Zukunft* (Stuttgart).

Kooijmans, P. (1983), 'How to Handle the Grotian Heritage: Grotius and Van Vollenhoven', *Netherlands International Law Review*, 30: 81–92.

Kossman, E.H., and Mellink, A. F. (1974), *Texts Concerning the Revolt of the Netherlands* (London).

Kosters, J. (1925), 'Les Fondements du droit des gens: Contribution à la théorie générale du droit des gens', *Bibliotheca Visseriana*, 4: 1–273.

Krause, O. W. (1982), *Naturrechtslehre des sechzehnten Jahrhunderts: Ihre Bedeutung für die Entwicklung eines natürlichen Privatrechts* (Frankfurt-am-Main).

Kubo, M., *et al.* (1977), *Zakusenshupigeru rantoho* (Tokyo).

Kunisch, J. (1986), ed., *Staatsverfassung und Heeresverfassung in der europäischen Geschichte der frühen Neuzeit* (Berlin).

Kunz, J. L. (1945), 'The Meaning and the Range of the Norm Pacta sunt servanda', *American Journal of International Law*, 39: 180–97.

—— (1951), 'Bellum Justum and Bellum Legale', *American Journal of International Law*, 45: 528–34.

Kurihara, F. (1969), 'Nederuranto kyowakoku', *Iwanami koza sekai rekishi*, XV (Tokyo): 79–139.

Kuwabara, T. (1968), ed., *Ruso kenkyu* (2nd edn., Tokyo).

Lachs, M. (1982), *The Teacher in International Law: Teachings and Teaching* (The Hague).

—— (1984), 'Pacta sunt servanda', *Encyclopedia of Public International Law*, VII (Amsterdam): 364–71.

Lademacher, H. (1983), *Geschichte der Niederlande* (Darmstadt).

Landsberg, E. (1898), *Geschichte der deutschen Rechtswissenschaft*, III/I (Munich).

La Pradelle, A. de (1916), 'Introduction', in Vattel 1916: pp. iii–lv.

—— (1950), *Maîtres et doctrines du droit des gens* (2nd edn., Paris).

Las Casas, Bartolomé de (1552/1987), *Brevíssima relación de la destruyción de las Indias: Colegida por el Obispo don fray Bartolomé de las Casas/o Casaus de la orden de Sancto Domingo* (Seville, 1552; trans. by Y. Ishihara, Tokyo, 1987).

Laun, R. (1950/1974), 'Naturrecht und Völkerrecht', *Jahrbuch für Internationales Recht*, 3 (1950; trans. by H. Kobayashi, Tokyo, 1974).

Lauterpacht, H. (1927), *Private Law Sources and Analogies of International Law: With Special Reference to International Arbitration* (London).

—— (1933), *The Function of Law in International Arbitration* (Oxford).

—— (1975*a*), *International Law: Being the Collected Papers of Hersch Lauterpacht*, II (ed. by E. Lauterpacht, London).

—— (1975*b*), 'Grotian Tradition in International Law', in Lauterpacht 1975*a*: 307–65.

Lawrence, T. J. = Winfield, P. H. (1923), *The Principles of International Law* (7th edn., rev. by P. H. Winfield, Boston, Mass.).

Le Fur, L. (1927), 'La Théorie du droit naturel dupuis le XVIIe siècle et la doctrine moderne', *Recueil des Cours*, 1927-III. 259–442.

Lee, R. (1930), 'The Introduction to the Jurisprudence of Holland of Hugo Grotius', *Transactions of the Grotius Society*, 16: 29–40.

Link, C. (1979), *Herrschaftsordnung und bürgerliche Freiheit: Grenzen der Staatsgewalt in der älteren deutschen Staatslehre* (Vienna).

—— (1973/1982), '"Jus divinum" im deutschen Staatsdenken der Neuzeit', in *Festschrift für U.Scheuner* (Berlin, 1973; trans. by J. Murakami, Tokyo, 1982).

—— (1983), *Hugo Grotius als Staatsdenker* (*Recht und Staat in Geschichte und Gegenwart*, 512, Tübingen).

Liszt, F. von (1905*a*), *Strafrechtliche Aufsätze und Vorträge*, I (Berlin).

—— (1905*b*) 'Der Zweckgedanke in Strafrecht', in Liszt 1905*a*: 126–79.

Locke, J. (1960), *Two Treatises on Government* (Critical edn. with an introduction and apparatus criticus by P. Laslett, Cambridge).

Losada, A. (1971), 'The Controversy between Sépulveda and Las Casas in the Junta of Valladolid', in Friede and Keen 1971: 279–308.

Lossen, M. (1894), *Die Lehre vom Tyrannenmord in der christlichen Zeit: Festrede gehalten in der öffentlichen Sitzung der königlichen bayerischen Akademie der Wissenschaften zu München zur Feier ihres 135. Stiftungstages am 28. März 1894* (Munich).

MacCormick, N., and Bankowski, Z. (1989), eds., *Enlightenment, Rights and Revolution* (Aberdeen).

McCoubrey, H. (1987), *The Development of Naturalist Legal Theory* (New York).

McNair, A. D. (1925), 'The Legal Meaning of War and the Relations of War to Reprisals', *Transactions of the Grotius Society*, 11: 29–51.

McNeil, J. T. (1967), *The History and Character of Calvinism* (New York).

Maine, H. A. (1870), *Ancient Law: Its Connection with the Early History of Society and its Relation to Modern Ideas* (4th edn., London).

Marcus Aurelius (1952/1959 ⟨1952⟩), in *Great Books of the Western World*, ed. R. M. Hutchins, XII. *Lucretius, Epictetus, Marx Aurelius* (Chicago, 1952; repr. 1959).

Martens, F. de (1883), *Traité de droit international*, I (trans. by A. Léo, Paris, 1883).

Martínez, M. M. (1971), 'Las Casas on the Conquest of America', in Friede and Keen 1971: 309–51.

Matsukuma, K. (1985), *Gurotyusu to sono jidai—seitan 400 nen o kinen site* (Hakata).

Matsuo, Y. (1983), 'Supein ni yoru Indiasu shihai to Barutorome de Rasu Kasasu', *Ajia Hogaku*, 17/2: 69–97.

Matsushita, K. (1959), *Shimin seiji riron no keisei* (Tokyo).

Meinecke, F. (1924/1957 ⟨1924⟩), *Die Idee der Staatsräson in der neueren Geschichte* (Munich, 1924; repr. 1957).

Merzbacher, F. (1967/1982), 'Staat und Jus publicum im deutschen Absolutismus', in *Gedächtnisschrift H. Peters* (Berlin, 1967; trans. by S. Ishii, Tokyo, 1982).

Meulenbroek, M. (1964), ed., *Briefwisseling van Hugo Grotius*, IV, *1629–1630–1631* (The Hague).

Meyer, E. (1964/1978), *Römischer Staat und Staatsgedanke* (3. Aufl. Zürich, 1964; trans. by I. Suzuki, Tokyo, 1978).

Midgley, E. B. F. (1975), *The Natural Law Tradition and the Theory of International Relations* (London).

Mikazuki, A. (1946*a*), 'Keiyakuho ni okeru keishiki shugi to sono hokai no shiteki kenkyu, (1)', *Hogaku Kyokai Zasshi*, 64/2: 117–28.

—— (1946*b*), 'Keiyakuho ni okeru keishiki shugi to sono hokai no shiteki kenkyu, (2)', *Hogaku Kyokai Zasshi*, 64/5: 318–28.

—— (1946*c*), 'Keiyakuho ni okeru keishiki shugi to sono hokai no shiteki kenkyu, (3)', *Hogaku Kyokai Zasshi*, 64/6: 378–92.

Mishima, Y. (1980), *Ho shiso shi* (Tokyo).

Mitteis, H. (1948/1971), *Über das Naturrecht* (Berlin, 1948; trans. by T. Hayashi, Tokyo, 1971).

—— = Lieberich, L. (1981), *Deutsche Rechtsgeschichte* (16. Aufl., Munich).

Miyata, M. (1978), *Heiwa no shishoshiteki kenkyu* (Tokyo).

Mizuta, H. (1963), *Kindai jin no keisei: Kindai shakai kan seiritsu shi* (Tokyo).

Montesquieu, C. L. de (1949), *Œuvres complètes*, I (Paris).

Mote, F. (1988*a*), 'Introduction', in Mote and Twitchett 1988: 1–10.

—— (1988*b*), 'The Rise of the Ming Dynasty, 1330–1367', in Mote and Twitchett 1988: 11–57.

——, and Twitchett, D. (1988), eds., *Cambridge History of China* (Cambridge).

Murakami, J. (1979), *Kindaiho no keisei* (Tokyo).

Murphy, C. F., jun. (1982). 'The Grotian Vision of World Order', *American Journal of International Law*, 76: 477–98.

Nardin, T. (1983), *Law, Morality and the Relations of States* (Princeton, NJ).

Naruse, O. (1970), 'Juhasseiki no kokusai seiji', *Iwanami koza sekai rekishi*, XVII (Tokyo): 79–136.

—— (1979), '"Kindai kokka" keisei o meguru shomondai', in Yoshioka and Naruse 1979: 3–60.

—— (1982), ed., *Dento shakai to kindai kokka* (Tokyo).

—— (1984), *Kindai shimin shakai no seiritu: Shakai shisoshiteki kosatsu* (Tokyo).

—— (1988), *Zettaishugi kokka to mibunsei shakai* (Tokyo).

Nellen, H. J. M. (1983), 'Grotius' Exile', in *Hugo Grotius: A Great European 1583–1645* (Delft): 25–36.

Nerseshantz, B. (1986), *Istoriá politicheskikh i pravovykh uchenii* (Leningrad, 1983, trans. by Y. Kojima, Tokyo, 1986).

Ninomiya, H. (1979), 'Furansu zettai osei no tochi kozo', in Yoshioka and Naruse 1979: 183–233.

Nufer, G. (1969), *Über die Restitutionslehre der spanischen Spätscholastiker und ihre Ausstrahlung auf die Folgezeit* (Diss. jur., Barden).

Nussbaum, A. (1947/1954), *A Concise History of the Law of Nations* (1st edn., New York, 1947; 2nd edn., 1954).

Nys, E. (1882), *Le Droit de la guerre et les précurseurs de Grotius* (Leipzig).

—— (1889), 'Les Publications espagnoles du XVIe siècle et les droits des Indiens', *Revue de droit international et de législation comparée*, 21: 532–60.

—— (1894), *Les Origines du droit international* (Brussels).

Oestreich, G. (1969), 'Strukturprobleme des europäischen Absolutismus', *Vierteljahrschrift für Sozial- und Wirtschaftsgeschichte*, 55.

Ogasawara, H. (1979), *Shoki Ruso no seiji shiso* (Tokyo).

Ogawa, K. (1985), 'F. Konan no keiyaku riron, (1)' *Hokudai Hogaku Ronshu*, 35/6: 775–847.

Olivecrona, K. (1971), *Law as Fact* (2nd edn., London).

Onuma, Y. (1975), *Senso sekininron josetsu* (Tokyo).

—— (1983), 'Goi (1) (Senso to heiwa no ho no kenkyu),' *Horitsu Jiho*, 55/9: 86–95.

—— (1984), 'Pitfalls of Internationalization', *IHJ Bulletin*, 4/4: 1–5.

—— (1986), '"Japanese International Law" in the Prewar Period: Perspectives on the Teaching and Research of International Law in Prewar Japan', *The Japanese Annual of International Law*, 29: 23–47.

—— (1987), 'Hugo Gurotiusu ni okeru "ippan kokusaiho" no kannen', *Kokka Gakkai Hyakunen Kinen: Kokka to Shimin*, II. 393–443.

—— (1988), *Wakoku to kyokuto no aida: Rekishi to bunmei no naka no 'kokusaika'* (Tokyo).

—— (1989), 'Between Natural Rights of Man and Fundamental Rights of States', in MacCormick and Bankowski 1989: 135–54.

Oppenheim, L. = Lauterpacht, H. (1952), *International Law: A Treatise*, II. *Disputes, War and Neutrality* (7th edn., London).

—— (1955), *International Law: A Treatise*, I. *Peace* (8th edn., London).

Otsuka, H. (1969), 'Kindai oshu keizaishi josetsu', *Otsuka Hisao chosakushu*, II (Tokyo): 5–364.

Otte, G. (1964), *Das Privatrecht bei Francisco de Vitoria* (Cologne).

Ottenwälder, P. (1950), *Zur Naturrechtslehre des Hugo Grotius* (Tübingen).

Oudendijk, J. K. (1970), *Status and Extent of Adjacent Waters: A Historical Orientation* (Leiden).

—— (1980), 'Van Vollenhoven's "The Three Stages in the Evolution of the Law of Nations"', *Tijdshrift voor Rechtsgeschiedenis Tijdshrift voor Rechtsgeschiedenis*, 47: 3–27.

Ourliac, P., and Malafosse, J. de (1969), *Histoire du droit privé*, I. *Les Obligations* (2nd edn., Paris).

—— (1971), *Histoire du droit privé*, II. *Les Biens* (2nd edn., Paris).

Parker, G. (1976), 'The Dutch Revolt and the Polarization of International Politics', *Bijdragen en Mededelingen betreffende de Geschiedenis der Nederlanden*, 91.

—— (1977), *The Dutch Revolt* (New York).

Pasquier, E. (1966*a*), *Écrits politiques* (ed. D. Thickett, Geneva).

—— (1966*b*), 'Exhortation aux Princes et Seigneurs du Conseil Privé du Roy, Pour obvier aux seditions qui semblent nous menacer pour le fait de la Religion', in Pasquier 1966*a*: 35–90.

Pauw, F. de (1965), *Grotius and the Law of the Sea* (trans. by P. J. Arthern, Brussels).

Phillimore, R. (1854/1985 ⟨1854⟩), *Commentaries upon International Law*, I (Philadelphia, 1854; repr. Littleton, Colo., 1985).

Phillipson, C. (1979 ⟨1911⟩), *The International Law and Custom of Ancient Greece and Rome* (London, 1911, repr. New York, 1979).

—— (1933), 'Introduction', in Gentilis 1933: I. 9*a*–51*a*.

Pillet, A. (1904), ed., *Les Fondateurs du droit international: Leurs œuvres, leurs doctrines* (Paris).

Planitz, H. (1971), *Deutsche Rechtsgeschichte* (3 Aufl., bearb. von K. A. Eckhardt, Graz, 1971).

Plato (1976), *Politica* (trans. by N. Fujisawa, Tokyo).

Plucknett, T. (1956), *A Concise History of the Common Law* (5th edn., London).

Poelhekke, J. (1983), 'Hugo Grotius as a Frustrated Dutch Statesman', in *Hugo Grotius: A Great European 1583–1645* (Delft): 67–77.

Pollock, F. (1876), *Principles of Contract at Law and in Equity* (London).

Poole, S. (1974), ed., *In Defense of the Indians: The Defense of the Most Reverend Lord, Don Frey Bartolomé de Las Casas, of the Order of Preachers, Late Bishop of Chiapa, against the Persecutors and Slanderers of the Peoples of the New World Discovered across the Seas* (De Kalb).

Posthumus Meyjes, G. H. M. (1981), 'Jean Hotman and Hugo Grotius', *Grotiana*, NS 2: 3–29.

—— (1983), 'Grotius as a Theologian', in *Hugo Grotius: A Great European 1583–1645* (Delft): 51–8.

Pothier, P. J. (1861), *Œuvres de Pothier*, II (2nd edn. by M. Bugnet, Paris).

Pound, R. (1909), 'Liberty of Contract', *Yale Law Journal*, 18: 454–87.

—— (1922/1961 ⟨1922⟩), *An Introduction to the Philosophy of Law* (New Haven, Conn. 1922; repr. 1961).

—— (1923), 'Philosophical Theory and International Law', *Bibliotheca Visseriana*, I: 71–90.

Pound, R. (1925), 'Grotius in the Science of Law', *American Journal of International Law*, 19: 685–88.

—— (1959), 'Promise or Bargain?' *Tulane Law Review*, 33: 455–72.

Preiser, W. (1984), 'Basic Questions and Principles', *Encyclopedia of Public International Law*, VII (Amsterdam): 126–32.

Pufendorf, S. (1934 ⟨1688⟩), *De Jure Naturae et Gentium libri octo* (Amsterdam, 1688), Latin texts and trans. by C. H. and W. A. Oldfather, The Classics of International Law (Oxford, 1934).

Randelzhofer, A. (1967), *Völkerrechtliche Aspekte des Heiligen Römischen Reiches nach 1648* (Berlin).

Ranouil, V. (1980), *L'Autonomie de la volonté: Naissance et l'évolution d'un concept* (Paris).

Recopilación (1943 ⟨1680⟩), *Recopilación de Leyes de los Reynos de las Indias* (Madrid, 1680, repr. Madrid, 1943).

Reeves, J. S. (1924), 'La Communauté internationale', *Recueil des Cours*, 1924-II: 5–94.

—— (1925*a*), 'The First Edition of Grotius' De jure belli ac pacis, 1625', *American Journal of International Law*, 19: 12–22.

—— (1925*b*), 'Grotius, De jure belli ac pacis: A Bibliographical Account', *American Journal of International Law*, 19: 251–62.

Reibstein, E. (1958), *Völkerrecht: Eine Geschichte seiner Ideen in Lehre und Praxis*, I (Freiburg).

—— (1963), *Völkerrecht: Eine Geschichte seiner Ideen in Lehre und Praxis*, II (Freiburg).

Remec, P. P. (1960), *The Position of the Individual in International Law According to Grotius and Vattel* (The Hague).

Riedel, M. (1975*a*), 'Gesellschaft, bürgerliche', in Brunner, Conze, and Koselleck 1975: 719–800.

—— (1975*b*), *Metaphysik und Metapolitik: Studien zu Aristoteles und zur politischen Sprache der neuzeitlichen Philosophie* (Frankfurt-am-Main).

Rieg, A. (1957), 'Le Rôle de la volonté dans la formation de l'acte juridique d'après les doctrines allemandes du XIXe siècle', *Archives de philosophie du droit*, 2: 125–33.

—— (1968), 'Le Contrat dans les doctrines allemandes du XIXe siècle', *Archives de philosophie du droit*, 13: 31–49.

Röd, W. (1970), *Geometrischer Geist und Naturrecht: Methodengeschichtliche Untersuchungen zur Staatsphilosophie im 17. und 18. Jahrhundert* (Munich).

Roelofsen, C. G. (1983*a*), 'Grotius and International Law: An Introduction to Some Themes in the Field of the Grotian Studies', in Holk and Roelofsen 1983: 3–21.

—— (1983*b*), 'Some Remarks on the "Sources" of the Grotian System of International Law', *Netherlands International Law Review*, 30: 73–9.

—— (1990), 'Grotius and the International Politics of the Seventeenth Century', in Bull, Kingsbury, and Roberts 1990: 95–132.

Rommen, H. (1947/1956), *Die ewige Wiederherr des Naturrechts* (Munich, 1947; trans. by S. Anan, Tokyo, 1956).

Ropp, T. (1959), *War in the Modern World* (Durham).

Rousseau, J. J. (1915 ⟨1762⟩), *Du contrat social* (Paris, 1762), in C. E. Vaughan, ed., *The Political Writings of J.-J. Rousseau*, II (Cambridge, 1915), 21–134.

—— (1964), *Œuvres complètes*, III (Paris).

—— (1969), *Œuvres complètes*, IV (Paris).

Rubin, A. P. (1990), 'International Law in the Age of Columbus', *Netherlands International Law Review*, 39: 5–35.

Ruddy, F. S. (1972), 'The Acceptance of Vattel', in Alexandrowicz 1972: 177–96.

Russell, B. (1955/1969), *History of Western Philosophy and its Connection with Political and Social Circumstances from the Earliest Times to the Present Day* (London, 1955; trans. by S. Ichii, Tokyo, 1969).

Sabine, G. (1951/1953/1963), *A History of Political Theory* (London, 1951; trans. by T. Maruyama, Tokyo, 1953; 3rd edn., London, 1963).

Said, E. W. (1979), *Orientalism* (New York).

Saiki, S. (1938), 'Keimo jidai to hanzai ruikei', *Hogaku Ronso*, 39/3: 369–419.

St. Leger, J. (1962), *The 'Etiamsi daremus' of Hugo Grotius: A Study in the Origins of International Law* (Rome).

Sandifer, D. (1940), 'Rereading Grotius in the Year 1940', *American Journal of International Law*, 34: 459–72.

Sasaki, T. (1973), *Shuken, teikouken, kan-yo: Jan Bodan no seiji shiso* (Tokyo).

Sasaki, Y. (1976), 'Chusei Roma hogaku', in Aomi 1976: 75–116.

——, Chiba, N., Tsuji, Y., Nishimura, T., Fuchi, N., Yanagihara, M., and Yamauchi, S. (1985), '"Senso to heiwa no ho, Puroregomena" (De jure belli ac pacis, Prolegomena, trans. by Y. Sasaki *et al.*, Society for the Study of Grotius)', *Nihon Hogaku*, 51/1: 119–45; 2: 163–89; 3: 94–112.

Sato, S. (1977), 'Bunmei to bankoku koho: Kindai Chugoku ni okeru kokusaiho juyo no ichi sokumen', in Sogawa 1977: 181–300.

Sauter, J. (1932/1966 ⟨1932⟩), *Die philosophischen Grundlagen des Naturrechts* (Vienna, 1932; repr. 1966).

Savigny, F. K. von (1828), *Vom Beruf unserer Zeit für Gesetzgebung und Rechtswissenschaft* (2nd edn., Heidelberg).

Scharp, M. P. (1941), 'Pacta sunt Servanda', *Columbia Law Review*, 41: 783–98.

Scheltens, D. F. (1983), 'Grotius' Doctrine of the Social Contract', *Netherlands International Law Review*, 30: 43–60.

Schiedermair, H. (1983), 'The Influence of Grotius' Thought on the *Jus Naturale* School', *Recueil des Cours*, 1983-IV: 399–416.

Schildenberger, J. (1970), 'Covenant', *Bauer Encyclopedia of Biblical Theology* (London), 140–6.

Schindler, D. (1967), 'Aspects contemporains de la neutralité', *Recueil des Cours*, 1967-II: 221–321.

Schmitt, C. (1970 ⟨1928⟩), *Verfassungslehre* (Berlin, 1928, repr. 1970).

—— (1934), *Politische Theologie* (Munich).

—— (1950), *Der Nomos der Erde im Völkerrecht des Jus Publicum Europaeum* (Köln).

Schuchmann, P. (1962), 'Aristotle's Conception of Contract', *Journal of the History of Ideas*, 23: 257–64.

Schwab, D. (1975), 'Eigentum', in Brunner, Conze, and Koselleck 1975: 65–115.

Schwarzenberger, G. (1943), 'Jus pacis ac belli? Prolegomena to a Sociology of International Law', *American Journal of International Law*, 37: 460–79.

—— (1962), *The Frontiers of International Law* (London).

—— (1968), *International Law as Applied by International Courts and Tribunals*, II (London).

Scott, J. B. (1934), *The Spanish Origin of International Law*, I. *Francisco de Vitoria and His Law of Nations* (Oxford).

—— (1944), 'Introduction', in F. Suárez 1944 ⟨1612⟩: 3*a*–38*a*.

Seelmann, K. (1979), *Die Lehre des Fernando Vazquez de Menchaca vom dominium* (Cologne).

Seidl (1932), 'Σ υ ν α λ λ α γ μ α', in Pauly and Wissowa, *Real-Encyclopädie der classischen Alterhumswissenschaften*, II. Reihe, 8. Halbd. (Stuttgart, 1932), cols. 1322–4.

Seneca, L. A. (1970), *De Dementio: Überdie Güte* (ed. by *K. Büchner, Stüttgart*).

Seuffert, L. (1881), *Zur Geschichte der obligatorischen Verträge* (Nördlingen).

Shibata, M. (1976), 'Roma hogaku' in Aomi, Ito, and Murakami 1976: 23–74.

Shoji, K. (1954), 'Kindai keiho no gensho keitai', *Keiho Zasshi*, 5/2: 159–90.

—— (1972), 'Keibatsu seido no kiso riron', in Shoji, Otsuka, and Hiramatsu 1972: 3–30.

—— (1983), *Kindai keiho shiso shi josetsu* (Tokyo).

——, Otsuka, H., and Hiramatsu, Y. (1972), eds., *Keibatsu no riron to genjitsu* (Tokyo).

Sibert, M. (1956), 'Le Principe "Pacta sunt servanda" à partir du moyen âge jusqu'aux débuts des temps modernes', *Indian Year Book of International Affairs*, 5: 38–45.

Simpson, A. (1975), *A History of the Common Law of Contract: The Rise of the Action of Assumpsit* (Oxford).

Smidt, J. T. de (1984), 'The Expansion of Dutch Private Law outside Europe in the Seventeenth and Eighteenth Centuries', *World of Grotius*, 1984: 179–93.

Smith, A. (1963 ⟨1811–12⟩), *The Theory of Moral Sentiments*, in *The Works of Adam Smith* (Aalen, 1811–12, repr. 1963).

—— (1978), *Lectures on Jurisprudence* (ed. by R. L. Meek *et al.*, Oxford).

Sogawa, T. (1977), ed., *Kokusai seiji shiso to taigai ishiki* (Tokyo).

Söllner, A. (1960), 'Die causa im Kondiktionen und Vertragsrecht des Mittelalters bei den Glossatoren, Kommentatoren und Kanonisten', *Zeitschrift der Savigny-Stiftung für Rechtsgeschichte, Romanistische Abteilung*, 77: 182–269.

Someren, L. von (1965), *Umpire to the Nations: Hugo Grotius* (London).

Spies, F. (1928), *De l'observation des simples conventions en droit canonique* (Paris).

SR (1983), *Staat und Recht: Zum 400. Geburtstag von Hugo Grotius*, 32: 419–43.

Starke, J. G. (1972), 'The Influence of Grotius upon the Development of International Law in the Eighteenth Century', in Alexandrowicz 1972: 162–76.

Stolleis, M. (1977/1987), ed., *Staatsdenker im 17. und 18. Jahrhundert: Reichspublizistik—Politik—Naturrecht* (Frankfurt-am-Main, 1977; 2. Aufl., 1987).

Stone, J. (1954), *Legal Control of International Conflict: A Treatise on the Dynamics of Disputes—and War—Law* (London).

—— (1965), *Human Law and Human Justice* (London).

Stone, L. (1965), *The Crisis of the Aristocracy, 1558–1641* (Oxford).

Strauss, L. (1953), *Natural Right and History* (Chicago).

Strömholm, S. (1985), *A Short History of Legal Thinking in the West* (Stockholm).

Strupp, K., and Schlochauer, H. (1961), eds., *Wörterbuch des Völkerrechts*, II (2nd edn., Berlin).

Suárez, F. (1944 ⟨1612⟩), *De Legibus, ac Deo Legislatore* (Conimbricae, 1612) in *Selections from Three Works of Francisco Suárez, S.J.*, Latin texts and trans. by G. L. Williams, A. Brown, and J. Waldron, *The Classics of International Law*, I–II (Oxford, 1944).

—— (1944 ⟨1613⟩), *Defensio Fidei Catholicae, et Apostolicae Adversus Anglicanae Sectae Errores* (Conimbricae, 1613) in *Selections from Three Works of Francisco Suárez, S.J.*, Latin texts and trans. by G. L. Williams, A. Brown, and J. Waldron, *The Classics of International Law*, I–II (Oxford, 1944).

—— (1944 ⟨1621⟩), *De Triplici Virtute Theologica, Fide, Spe, et Charitate*

(Conimbricae, 1621) in *Selections from Three Works of Francisco Suárez, S.J.*, Latin texts and trans. by G. L. Williams, A. Brown, and J. Waldron, *The Classics of International Law*, I–II (Oxford, 1944).

Sukiennicki, W. (1927), *La Souveraineté des états en droit international moderne* (Paris).

Tabata, S. (1938), 'Shijin koi ni yoru kokka no kokusai sekinin', *Hogaku Ronso*, 39/5: 745–76.

—— (1955), *Kokusaiho ni okeru shonin no riron* (Tokyo).

—— (1956), 'Kindai kokusaiho shiso no seiritsu', *Ho teshugaku koza*, III (Tokyo): 145–69.

—— (1958), *Kokka byodo shiso no shiteki keifu* (Kyoto).

—— (1966), *Kokusaiho* (2nd edn., Tokyo).

—— (1973), *Kokusaiho*, I (Tokyo).

Taijudo, K. (1955), 'Kokusaiho jo no sensen ni tsuite: Sono rekishiteki kenkyu', *Hogaku Ronso*, 61/2: 36–99.

Takashima, Z., Mizuta, H., and Hirata, K. (1962), *Shakai shiso shi gairon* (Tokyo).

Takigawa, Y. (1948), *Keiho shi no danmen* (Kyoto).

Tanaka, T. (1984), 'Gurotiusu no imperium oyobi dominium gainen ni kansuru iti shiron', *Kokusaiho Gaiko Zasshi*, 83/1: 64–93.

—— (1986), '(Shokai) F. Ito, Gurotiusu no jiyukairon', *Kokusaiho Gaiko Zasshi*, 85/1: 76–81.

Taube, M. de (1930), 'L'Inviolabilité des traités', *Recueil des Cours*, 1930-II: 291–389.

Ter Meulen, J., and Diermanse, P. J. J. (1950), *Bibliographie des écrits imprimés de Hugo Grotius* (The Hague).

Tex, J. de (1973), *Oldenvarnevelt* (trans. by R. B. Powell, Cambridge).

Thieme, H. (1954), *Das Naturrecht und die europäische Privatrechtsgeschichte* (Basle).

—— (1971/1978), *Geschichte und Idee des Europäischen Rechts* (Tokyo, 1971; trans. by M. Kubo, Tokyo, 1978).

T. M. C. Asser Institut (1985), ed., *International Law and the Grotian Heritage* (The Hague).

Tochikawa, I. (1984), *Seio hoken shakai no hikakuteki kenkyu* (2nd edn., Tokyo).

Tooke, J. D. (1965), *The Just War in Aquinas and Grotius* (London).

Treumann, R. (1895/1976), *Die Monarchomachen* (Leipzig, 1895; trans. by T. Kobayashi and T. Sasaki, Tokyo, 1976).

Trevor-Roper, R. (1970), 'Spain and Europe 1598–1621', in Cooper 1970: 260–82.

Triepel, H. (1899), *Völkerrecht und Landesrecht* (Leipzig).

Troeltsch, E. (1913/1959), 'Renaissance und Reformation', *Historische Zeitschrift*, 110 (1913); trans. by Y. Uchida (Tokyo, 1959).

—— (1925*a*), *Gesammelte Schriften*, I (Tübingen).

—— (1925*b*), '*Die Aufklärung*', in Troeltsch 1925*a*: 338–74.

—— (1925*c*/1965 ⟨1925*c*⟩): *Die Soziallehren der christlichen Kirchen und Gruppen, Gesammelte Schriften*, I (Tübingen, 1925; repr. Aalen, 1965): 338–74.

Truyol y Serra, A. (1971), 'The Discovery of the New World and International Law', *Toledo Law Review*: 305–25.

—— (1983), 'Grotius dans ses rapports avec les classiques espagnols du droit des gens', *Recueil des Cours*, 1983-IV: 431–51.

——, Mechoulan, H., Haggenmacher, P., Ortiz-Arce, A., Marino, P., and Verhoeven, J. (1988), eds., *Actualité de la pensée juridique de Francisco de Vitoria* (Brussels).

Tsuneto, T. (1968), 'Ruso no shakai keiyaku setsu to ippan ishi no riron', in Kuwabara 1968: 127–57.

—— (1977), *Ho shiso shi* (Tokyo).

Tuck, C. R. (1979), *Natural Rights Theories: Their Origin and Development* (Cambridge).

—— (1983), 'Grotius, Carneades and Hobbes', *Grotiana*, NS 4: 43–62.

—— (1986), 'Book Review—Peter Haggenmacher: *Grotius et la Doctrine de la Guerre Juste* (1983)', *Grotiana*, NS 7: 87–92.

Tucker, R. W. (1977), *The Inequality of Nations* (New York).

Vanderpol, A. (1919), *La Doctrine scolastique du droit de guerre* (Paris).

Vansomeren, L. (1965), *Umpire to the Nations: Hugo Grotius* (London).

Vattel, E. de (1916), *Le Droit des gens, ou principes de la loi naturelle, appliqués à la conduite et aux affaires des nations et des souverains* (London), French texts and trans. by C. G. Fenwick, *The Classics of International Law*, I (Washington, DC).

Vera Lex (1983–4), *Vera Lex; Special Issue: Hugo Grotius 1583–1983 (400 Years)*, 4/1–2: 1–37.

Verdross, A. (1958), *Abendländische Rechtsphilosophie* (Vienna).

Verlinden, C. (1961), 'Le "Requerimiento" et la "paix coloniale" dans l'empire Espagnol d'Amérique', *Recueils de la Société Jean Bodin pour l'Histoire Comparative des Institutions*, 15. *La Paix, 2e partie*.

Vermeulen, B. (1983), 'Simon Stevin and the Geometrical Method in De Jure Praedae', *Grotiana*, NS 4: 63–6.

Verzijl, J. H. W. (1968), *International Law in Historical Perspective*, I (Leiden).

Villey, M. (1962), *Leçons d'histoire de la philosophie du droit* (New edn., Paris).

—— (1968), 'Préface historique à l'étude des notions de contrat', *Archives de philosophie du droit*, 13: 1–11.

—— (1975), *La Formation de la pensée juridique moderne* (New edn., Paris).

—— (1976), *Critique de la pensée juridique moderne (douze autre essais)* (Paris).

Vinogradoff, P. (1923), 'Historical Types of International Law', *Bibliotheca Visseriana*, 1: 3–70.

Vitanyi, B. (1980), 'L'Interprétation des traités dans la théorie du droit naturel', *Revue générale de droit international public*, 84: 535–86.

Vitoria, F. de (1917 ⟨1696⟩), *De Indis et de Jure Belli Relectiones* (Coloniae, 1696), Latin texts and trans. by J. P. Bate, *The Classics of International Law* (Washington, DC, 1917).

Vlugt, W. van der (1925), 'L'Œuvre de Grotius et son influence sur le développement du droit international', *Recueil des Cours*, 1925-II: 397–509.

Vollenhoven, C. van (1919), *The Three Stages in the Evolution of the Law of Nations* (The Hague).

—— (1925), 'Grotius and the Study of Law', *American Journal of International Law*, 19: 1–11.

—— (1926*a*), 'Grotius and Geneva', *Bibliotheca Visseriana*, 6: 1–81.

—— (1926*b*), 'The Growth of Grotius' De Jure Belli ac Pacis as it Appears from Contemporary Correspondence', *Bibliotheca Visseriana*, 6: 131–77.

—— (1929), 'The Growth of Grotius' De Jure Belli ac Pacis as it Appears from Contemporary Correspondence', *Bibliotheca Visseriana*, 8: 103–70.

—— (1931), *The Framework of Grotius' Book De Jure ac Pacis* (Amsterdam).

—— (1934), *Verspreide Geschriften*, 1 (Haarlem), 221–86, 349–602.

Voltaire, F. M. A. de (1970), *Traité sur la tolérance* (Geneva, 1763, trans. by M. Nakagawa, Tokyo, 1970).

Vorländer, K. (1978), *Von Machiavelli bis Lenin* (Leipzig, 1926, trans. by M. Miyata, Tokyo, 1978).

Vreeland, H. (1917), *Hugo Grotius, the Father of the Modern Science of International Law* (New York).

Wachetelle, N. (1971/1984), *La Vision des vaincus* (Paris, 1971; trans. by Y. Koike, Tokyo, 1984).

Wagner, H. (1938), *Das geteilte Eigentum im Naturrecht und Positivismus* (Breslau).

Walker, T. A. (1899), *A History of the Law of Nations* (Cambridge).

Wallerstein, I. (1974), *The Modern World System* (New York).

—— (1979), *The Capitalist World-Economy* (Cambridge).

Weber, M. (1925), *Grundriß der Sozialökonomik*, III. *Abteilung*, *Wirtschaft und Gesellschaft* (2nd edn., Tübingen).

—— (1923), *Wirtschaftsgeschichte* (Munich).

—— (1960), *Rechtssoziologie: Aus dem Manuskript Herausgegeben und Eingeleitet von Johannes Winckelmann* (Neuwied).

Wehberg, H. (1959), 'Pacta sunt Servanda', *American Journal of International Law*, 53: 775–86.

Welzel, H. (1962/1980 ⟨1962⟩), *Naturrecht und materiale Gerechtigkeit* (4. Aufl., Göttingen, 1962; repr. Göttingen, 1980).

Westerkamp, J. B. (1890), *Das Bundesrecht der Republik der Vereinigten Niederlande (1579–1795)* (Marburg).

—— (1968 ⟨1892⟩), *Staatenbund und Bundesstaat: Untersuchungen über die Praxis und das Recht der modernen Bünde* (Marburg, 1892, repr. Aalen, 1968).

Wheaton, H. (1836/1863), *Elements of International Law with a Sketch of the History of the Science* (Philadelphia, 1836; 2nd edn. by W. B. Lawrence, London, 1863).

—— (1853), *Histoire des progrès du droit des gens*, I (Leipzig).

Whitton, J. B. (1934), 'La Règle "Pacta sunt Servanda"', *Recueil des Cours*, 1934-III: 147–276.

Wieacker, F. (1952/1961/1967), *Privatrechtsgeschichte der Neuzeit unter besonderer Berücksichtigung der deutschen Entwicklung* (1. Aufl., Göttingen, 1952; trans. by R. Suzuki, Tokyo, 1961; 2. Aufl., Göttingen, 1967).

Wiegand, W. (1976), 'Zur theoretischen Begründung der Bodenmobilisierung in der Rechtswissenschaft', *Wissenschaft und Kodifikation des Privatrechts im 19. Jahrhundert*, III (Frankfurt-am-Main): 118–55.

Wight, M. (1977), *Systems of States* (ed. with an introduction by H. Bull, Leicester).

Wijn, J. W. (1970), 'Military Forces and Warfare 1610–48', in Cooper 1970: 202–25.

Willems, J. C. M. (1981), 'Grotius and the Atomic Weapon: The Nuclear-Weapon Discussion in the Light of the Theory of "Just War" with Hugo de Groot', *Grotiana*, NS 2: 103–14.

Willoweit, D. (1974), 'Dominium und proprietas: Zur Entwicklung des Eigentumsbegriffs in der mittelalterlichen und neuzeitlichen Rechtswissenschaft', *Historisches Jahrbuch der Görres-Gesellschaft*: 131–56.

Wilson, C. (1968), *The Dutch Republic* (London).

Wolf, E. (1927), *Grotius, Pufendorf, Thomasius* (Tübingen).

—— (1963), *Grosse Rechtsdenker der deutschen Geistesgeschichte* (4. Aufl., Tübingen).

—— (1982), *Studien zur Geschichte des Rechtsdenkens, Ausgewählte Schriften*, III (Frankfurt-am-Main).

Wolff, C. (1972 ⟨1749⟩/1934 ⟨1764⟩), *Jus Gentium Methodo Scientifica Pertractatum* (*Gesamte Werke*, 2nd edn., 25 (Halle, 1749, repr. Hildesheim, 1972); (Frankfurt/Leipzig, 1764), Latin texts and trans. by J. H. Drake, *The Classics of International Law*, I–II (Oxford/London, 1934).

Wolzendorff, K. (1916), *Staatsrecht und Naturrecht in der Lehre vom*

Widerstandsrecht des Volkes gegen rechtswidrige Ausübung der Staatsgewalt (Breslau).

World of Grotius (1984), *The World of Hugo Grotius: Proceedings of International Colloquium held at Rotterdam, April 6–9, 1983* (Amsterdam).

Wright, H. F. (1928), 'Some Less Known Works of Hugo Grotius', *Bibliotheca Visseriana*, 7: 131–238.

Wright, Q. (1965), *A Study of War* (2nd edn., Chicago).

Yamamoto, M. (1977), *Arisutoteresu: shizen gaku, seiji gaku* (Tokyo).

Yamamoto, S. (1982), *Kokusaiho ni okeru kiken sekinin shugi* (Tokyo).

Yamashita, T., and Maruyama, S. (1977), 'Monarukomaki kenkyu josetsu: Juroku seiki no kokka riron, tokuni Vindiciae Contra Tyrannos o megutte', *Saitama Daigaku Kiyo (Shakai Kagaku Hen)*, 25: 1–70.

Yamauchi, S. (1982), 'Shoki kindai yoroppa ni okeru ryakudatsu to sono hori, (1)', *Seijo Hogaku*, 24: 95–137.

—— (1983), 'Shoki kindai yoroppa ni okeru ryakudatsu to sono hori, (2)', *Seijo Hogaku*, 28: 87–171.

Yanagihara, M. (1981), 'Kindai kokusaihō genri no kozo to tenkai: Voruhu, Vatteru no ishi kokusaiho gainen o megutte' (Ph.D. thesis, Tokyo Univ.).

—— (1989*a*), 'Voruhu no kokusaiho riron, (1)', *Hosei Kenkyu*, 56/1: 1–34.

—— (1989*b*), 'Voruhu no kokusaiho riron, (2)', *Hosei Kenkyu*, 56/2: 47–86.

—— (1991*a*), 'Voruhu no kokusaiho riron, (3)', *Hosei Kenkyu*, 58/1: 39–69.

—— (1991*b*), 'Voruhu no kokusaiho riron, (4)', *Hosei Kenkyu*, 58/2: 1–37.

Yokoyama, K. (1968), 'Zaikei hotei shugi no saikosei', in *Saiki kanreki kinen: Hanzai to keibatsu*, 1 (Tokyo): 81–102.

Yoshioka, A., and Naruse, O. (1979), ed., *Kindai kokka keisei no shomondai* (Tokyo).

Yuge, T. (1977), *Chichukai sekai to Roma teikoku* (Tokyo).

Subject Index

Name Index

Index of Latin Terms

Printed in the United States
28168LVS00001B/4

9 780198 257097